Anthropologists at home in North America
Methods and issues in the study of one's own society

Anthropologists at home in North America

Methods and issues in the study of one's own society

DONALD A. MESSERSCHMIDT, EDITOR
Washington State University
Pullman, Washington

CAMBRIDGE UNIVERSITY PRESS

Cambridge
London   New York   New Rochelle
Melbourne   Sydney

Published by the Press Syndicate of the University of Cambridge
The Pitt Building, Trumpington Street, Cambridge CB2 1RP
32 East 57th Street, New York, NY 10022, USA
296 Beaconsfield Parade, Middle Park, Melbourne 3206, Australia

First published 1981

Printed in the United States of America

Library of Congress Cataloging in Publication Data
Main entry under title:
Anthropologists at home in North America.
Bibliography: p.
Includes index.
1. Anthropological research–United States–
Addresses, essays, lectures.   2. United States–
Social conditions–1960–   –Research–Addresses,
essays, lectures.   I. Messerschmidt, Donald A., 1940–
GN43.A57   301'.072073   81-3873
ISBN 0 521 24067 0 hard covers
ISBN 0 521 28419 8 paperback

For Kareen, Liesl, and Hans

Contents

Preface

This book deals with the very contemporary issue of doing anthropology at home in one's own society. All seventeen chapters are new and fresh, and not published elsewhere. They deal with methods and styles, theories and issues of doing research in contemporary North America. The authors, anthropologists from the United States and Canada, describe and define theoretical insights, methodological strategies, substantive data, and experiences that are current and important. They raise and examine issues at the forefront of American anthropology today.

Traditionally, the research domains of anthropologists have been societies and cultures other than North America. The relatively scant accounts of research methods and issues that exist in the literature tend to document and reinforce doing anthropology abroad, among the poor and the oppressed, in predominantly tribal and peasant societies, well away from home (see examples in Jongmans and Gutkind 1967; Frelich 1970; Spindler 1970; Foster et al. 1978). Lately however, there has been a surge of interest in research at or close to home – in the social milieu of the North American anthropologists.

The literature about the constraints and contingencies of doing research in one's own society is rapidly expanding (see the Bibliography at the end of this volume). But these studies are widely scattered, and, taken together, they lack unified focus or attention to such details as analytical style, strategy and research method, or new or recyclable tools of the profession. This book is intended to rectify the lack of focus in the growing field of anthropological inquiry at home.

Two reasons exist for publishing this collection of studies: (1) it is designed for use as a source book in the training of graduate and undergraduate students in the social sciences, and (2) it serves as a guide and reference (and perhaps as an inspiration) for professional social scientists who are considering or are presently engaged in anthropology at home and who are concerned with both practical (applied) and abstract (theoretical) issues and with the conjunction of these two parts of the discipline.

This work was first conceived as a collection of articles about method, but it became obvious that, as Gillin said in a critique of the anthropological study of modern society, "methods cannot be meaningfully discussed without reference to theory" (1949:393). Similarly when pursuing anthropology at home, method and theory cannot be meaningfully discussed without reference to the social issues that attract attention.

Taken together, the contributors to this volume confront the theoretical problems of what to study, the practical questions of why to study it, the professional (and sometimes personal) concerns for the entrée and rapport, the best methods with which to approach the data and their analyses, and the social issues and political constraints encountered in accomplishing goals. Here you will find rich and sometimes quite candid descriptions of the research techniques and orienting paradigms employed to order the data. They make this book a unique contribution to the literature – a discussion of strategies, concepts, and issues that, to paraphrase John Honigman (1976:2), have clearly shaped our experience and guided our perceptions and have aided us in discriminating between types of events central to the subject studied.

I want to thank my colleagues and students who gave help and suggestions and participated in dialogue during the lengthy period in which this book was conceived and developed. Kathryn Golitko-White and Robert H. McDaniel were important to this effort. I owe them, and the faculty and staff of the Department of Anthropology at Washington State University, my gratitude. I am also grateful to the final contributors (and to many others who expressed their interest along the way) for their patience and perseverance, as well as for their many insights into the topic. Finally, I thank several anonymous reviewers for their critical assessments of the manuscript, their suggestions for improvement, and their welcome encouragement to complete the task.

D.M.
Pullman, Washington
June, 1981

PART I Introduction

Change continually confronts anthropologists. We study it, we teach it, and we accommodate to it in our lives. Recent change in the environment of research and employment has forced us to create appropriate responses. One contemporary response is the pursuit of a vigorous anthropology at home.

The causes and challenges of change in modern anthropology are reviewed in Chapter 1. Two major questions are identified there that have guided the development of this book and are at the forefront of modern anthropology in North America: What are the methods? and What are the issues? Questions of why we do it and what we are doing are also asked. Many answers emerge, but in the long run those endeavors that are pragmatic and efficacious will clearly stand out above the others.

Anthropology at home is not a fad; neither is it a stopgap for unemployed Ph.D.s. It is, instead, a well-established branch of anthropology that has deep roots and a strong heritage. It links theory and action, past experience and present needs into a strong and vital aspect of the profession. It is contemporary and issue oriented, and it is here to stay.

Chapter 2 epitomizes part of the innovative quality of this anthropology at home. John Aguilar addresses the ongoing debate about the relative objectivity of insiders who study their own society. His method of exegesis is ethnographic. He examines both sides of the argument, its context and its manifestations, and he demonstrates keen insight and objectivity in his role as both an anthropologist and an insider-researcher.

In a telling point addressed to those who favor as well as those who disfavor doing anthropology at home, Aguilar notes that ethnocentrism exists both inside and out. The emic and the etic perspectives each have their faults. Ultimately, just as the insider must somehow seek distance to obtain objectivity, so the outsider must seek intimacy in order to understand. The argument does not stop there, but will doubtless continue indefinitely. Meanwhile, we strive to pursue our craft at home, as insiders to one degree or another.

1 On anthropology "at home"

DONALD A. MESSERSCHMIDT

In the past, it was considered a requisite and proper rite of passage for fledgling anthropologists – or "baby anthropologists" as Margaret Mead once disparagingly put it (Maday 1975:41) – to leave the comfortable nest of our own social upbringing and brave the trials and tribulations of study in other lands, or at least among people other than our own. Research elsewhere, preferably abroad, was the norm, the custom, an established tradition of the profession. As Cassell has noted, this was the "anthropological ideal," which in addition to establishing certain barriers to the entry of our profession, set up a "classic relationship" by which we created and perpetuated "a gulf, a social chasm between those who study and those who are studied" (1977:412).

Today, few members of our profession any longer believe that becoming proficient in anthropology requires the classic, exotic, other-cultural experience, although few would seriously question its efficacy. Wolcott (Chapter 17) suggests, for example, that whereas cross-cultural research experience is still recommended for the individual anthropologist, "ethnographic research carried out in one's *own* society may be the sine qua non for anthropology itself" (emphasis added).[1]

Some may wonder, however, if we can be anthropologists in the traditional sense of the term if we study only our own society. Are we not somehow grossly distorting the standard definition of anthropology? Some also wonder how we can do anthropology adequately in the context of modern and familiar environs at home. Do we possess the requisite objectivity, they ask, and are we not limited by methods and theories derived, in the main, from the study of essentially premodern peoples elsewhere?

If our basic concern is with archaic or primitive society, as Diamond (1974), Lévi-Strauss (1963:101 ff.), and others suggest, then pursuing anthropology at home in North America seems to be a contradiction of terms. But if anthropology is the study of human and social conditions broadly conceived – in modern as well as archaic society – then we have a definite role to play here and now.

Our subject has always been people, culture, social structure, and community in the widest variety of places, times, conditions, and expressions. Our methods have always

3

been both innovative and eclectic, borrowing from the past and from allied sciences and humanities to meet the demands of the present. Our goal has always been to enhance understanding of the human condition. Certainly, then, issues of life in contemporary, industrial societies in North America are as important and as revealing of human nature as those of the past and of so-called primitive societies elsewhere in the world.

To understand and appreciate better the substance and the tremendous potential of contemporary anthropological research such as ours, and in an attempt to formulate a framework for the study and practice of this variety of anthropology, certain questions about anthropology at home in North America need to be discussed. What are its issues? What are its methods? What is it we do, and why? Is it good? What is it called? And why write about it? Each of these issues is examined in the following pages of this chapter and throughout the book.

An anthropology of issues

On several occasions in recent years, I have heard elder anthropologists allude to a so-called golden age of anthropology, when researchers had a wide range of choice for study and employment. It is widely believed today that the golden age is gone, particularly as we find ourselves closed out of foreign societies and as we see many newly minted Ph.D.s going jobless in the academic world for which they have been groomed. On the other hand, however, many anthropologists – academic and nonacademic alike – find themselves practicing anthropology quite comfortably outside of the confines of academia in areas of planning and evaluation, in government and industry, and in schools and communes under conditions with which many of us would never have dreamed of becoming involved as recently as a decade or two ago. Anthropologists are becoming attuned more than ever before to nontraditional research and work opportunities, and the directions some of our more innovative and aggressive colleagues and students are now taking reflect important new directions for the profession. It is a change that relies on our time-honored and traditional methods and perspectives as a discipline but that is forcing us to focus on exciting, new, and different sorts of issues.

If coming home is the process, then coming to grips with social issues at home is the substance of the exciting changes we are pursuing. Many of us are turning directly to the issues that confront our own people. Urban-born anthropologists now attend to urban social concerns in business, industry, housing, education, and government. American Indian anthropologists are working on reservations and with urban Indian problems. Chicano anthropologists are helping to mitigate the social and economic plight of many Hispanics. Feminist anthropologists are engaged in women's political movements and in problems of sexism and social action. More than ever before we are staying home, where we study communal living, neighboring and cooperation, health and healing, old age and alienation, bureaucracy and political process, social relations and economics, ecology and social environments, local–federal relations, school–community issues, and much more. We are contracted for the short term or hired for long-term studies. We do needs assessment. We plan, design, implement, evaluate, report, and advise. What we do are the analogs of the traditional anthropologists' studies of kinship and community; alliance, economics, and exchange; political process and sociocultural change, as they find expression in today's technobureaucratic world.

We are witnessing and participating in the efflorescence of a new sort of anthropology – an anthropology of issues. This anthropology of issues is more than applied anthropology (usually and sometimes inaccurately defined only in terms of intervention and directed change), and it is more than theoretical (or pure, or abstract) anthropology. Rather, it implies a unique and indivisible link between them. More and more these days, anthropologists are combining pure and applied approaches in their professional and research endeavors. It now appears that we have arrived at a point well beyond the usual theory–practice dichotomy that has so long divided our discipline. For too long we have pitted an older, general anthropology against the study and practice of social-action anthropology. What seems to be emerging now is what Bastide (1973) calls "applied anthropology as a theoretical science of practice." He defines it as "a branch of anthropology" not simply oriented toward the rather standard approaches of planned acculturation or toward any reforming or revolutionary action (in the Marxist sense of *praxis*), but an anthropology that implies cooperation between action and planning. Looking back, Bronislaw Malinowski said as much in his well-known article on practical anthropology over half a century ago (Malinowski 1929). It is an anthropology that analyzes action and planning much as traditional anthropology analyzed the major topics that fill every introductory cultural textbook: kinship and descent, marriage and family, ecologic and economic systems, power and politics, religions and world view (see Bastide 1973:180–181, Angrosino 1976, Chambers 1979).

The opportunities and challenges of this form of anthropology beckon us home to apply our skills and our perspectives to the issues of our own society. It focuses our attention on the methods and theories of our profession as well as on the pressing problems around us, on their nature and on actions to deal with them. There are new lessons to be learned from the anthropology of issues, new insights to be gained into the human condition, about survival and improvement of the species. It should be stressed that this impetus is not singularly American: It has worldwide manifestations and implications as our profession comes of age by coming to grips with some of the signal issues of our time.

All the contributors to this book are engaged, in one way or another, in the anthropology of issues, and it is fast becoming a major force in the profession. It is a fully professional position that is concerned with more than the application of anthropological knowledge and skill and with more than the mere generation of social theory. It is a joining of theory and practice in a way that "does not prevent [us] from making a basic contribution to general anthropology on the one hand, [nor] to social practice on the other" (Bastide 1973:181).

The range of issues for study and the kinds of opportunities for employment in our modern society are very large, and we have only begun to scratch their surface. In turning homeward, we are abandoning neither our methodological heritage nor our holistic perspective. Rather, we are building on them with confidence and innovation. In this, we may be witnessing our profession's revitalization movement; we may be on the verge of a new "golden age" in anthropology.

Methods for anthropology at home

Roger Bastide has stated that the new anthropology uses "exactly the same techniques of approach" as the old (1973:181). Not everyone agrees. One of the overriding questions that unites the contributors to this volume is that of which methods, strategies, styles, and techniques can be used in the application of anthropology to the study of modern society. Each author was asked to consider whether or not, for instance, our profession's many traditions, developed in the study of less complex tribal and peasant societies, have utility and relevance in studying today's complex and highly industrialized society. This question has been the focus for debate for as long as anthropologists have been returning from, or turning away from, doing research in traditional, exotic, "primitive" or "other" cultures elsewhere; that is, for as long as we have been doing research among our own kind.

On the one hand, some social scientists are skeptical about the ability or success of anthropology's attempts to devise theory or method sufficient to the task of studying complex contemporary society. Gillin, for example, expressed concern over twenty years ago that as anthropologists "we still lack an adequate theoretical analysis of the modern national system from the cultural, as distinguished from the sociological point of view" (1957:27). Yehudi Cohen echoes Gillin's concern, arguing that "the concepts, paradigms, and methods developed in the study of tribal and peasant groups are inadequate, if not misleading, for the study of industrial societies" (Cohen 1977:389; see also Kushner 1969:80, Spicer 1974:11).

In an essay, "The Concept of Archaism in Anthropology," Lévi-Strauss is outspokenly critical of our attempts:

It is striking to note that, in losing awareness of its particular subject matter [the primitive],[2] American anthropology is permitting a disintegration of the method – too narrowly empirical, but precise and scrupulous – with which it was endowed by its founders, in favor of a social metaphysics which is often simplistic and which uses dubious techniques of investigation. [Lévi-Strauss 1963:102]

On the other hand, some anthropologists maintain and have demonstrated quite adequately that many of our methodological and theoretical traditions are directly applicable to modern and complex research settings (Despres 1968).[3] Proponents of this viewpoint say that "anthropology does not have to perish and be made over anew in order to study complex society" (Weaver and White 1972:124).

It is significant that not one of the authors in this book advocates a complete break with the theoretical roots and methodological traditions of our profession.[4] Rather, some of them demonstrate that our heritage is sufficiently rich and varied to find application in entirely new settings and in the face of challenging new issues. They maintain that many of our standard approaches to research are capable of being used effectively to address some unique research situations and contemporary social issues. In this volume, for example, Aamodt and Molgaard and Byerly use ethnoscience techniques in their studies of community health and healing practices. Graham demonstrates the continuing utility of network analysis in her study of social interaction in two mining towns. Bennett and Kohl rely on the precepts of cultural ecology to guide their research. And all of the contributors demonstrate the importance of maintaining the traditions of the participant-observer method, albeit in some novel ways, as in Zimmer's combination of participation and consultation in his study of urban food cooperatives.

Some contributors demonstrate, equally convincingly, that old ways can be successfully combined with new and different methods, some of which may be borrowed directly from other social sciences. For example, as Bennett and Kohl developed their longitudinal study in rural Canada, their anthropological theory and method "adopted and adapted a variety of analytical and theoretical tools from a variety of fields: agricultural economics, resource management and conservation, climatology, demography, rural sociology, agronomy, hydraulic engineering . . . " (Chapter 7).

Some authors write primarily of the related issues of research style and role, place and time, and of opportunities and responsibilities for research at home. Gwaltney portrays his entry and his rapport with fellow blacks in an urban ghetto with a measure of perception and sensitivity available only to indigenes. Wolcott, contrasting research Here (at home) and There (abroad), notes relatively more flexibility in choice of subject and in the availability of time for research in the familiar setting of home. His 1977 study of a complex suburban education system is a superb example of how to adapt traditional methods (observation and interview) and hypothesis (about moiety structure) to contemporary research problems. Serber, Feldman, and I all stress serious restrictions that may be felt in situations wherein a power differential exists between researchers and the bureaucrats they study or with whom they work. Sieber shows us the diverse strategies necessary for entry, rapport building, and data collection in three different urban school settings.

Not surprisingly, team research and multi- or interdisciplinary approaches are used to solve some of the problems created by the complexity of research in contemporary settings. That complexity and a need for a strategy of cooperation with which to address the problems of research inherent in modern society have long been recognized (for example, in Gillin 1949, Lévi-Strauss 1963, Sirjamaki 1971). In this volume the problems and solution to problems posed by working in teams and by employing multiple disciplinary perspectives are exemplified by Bennett and Kohl, Bohannan, Light and Kleiber, Molgaard and Byerly, and, indirectly, by Hennigh, Houghton, Feldman, and me in government research (see also Beals 1976, Belshaw 1976). Missing from all these discussions is any thorough discussion of the relationship between anthropology and sociology, but perhaps that is because we are still too busy trying to get our own act together in this genre to confront openly the thorny issue of how we differ from our sister discipline at home.

In most instances, the contributors discuss research at home with rich and insightful examples based on their own personal and professional experiences. They demonstrate the successful use of old as well as new concepts, paradigms, and methods in the pursuit of the craft of anthropology of issues. Perhaps the most important aspect of developing a methodology for anthropology at home is that it is often highly inventive in the sense that Barnett (1953) expounded a quarter century ago: We bring with us experiences and certain knowledge from the past, and, when confronted by the stimuli of present needs, we innovate. Innovation is defined as "any thought, behavior, or thing that is new because it is qualitatively different from existing forms" (Barnett 1953:7). It is innovation that gives our profession its strength and character. Innovations are the building blocks of the paradigm shifts by which scientists respond creatively to new demands made upon their science, and by which they maintain its resiliency and its relevance (Kuhn 1967).

A new native anthropology

In the pursuit of anthropology at home, the contributors to this book and many others (see the Bibliography) have demonstrated considerable sensitivity and imagination in choice of topics. Much of the anthropology at home has attracted us to the study of our own kind – kinfolk, neighbors, and associates in social and professional life. Anthropologists at home do not have to consider whether or not to make a commitment to "go native" in the research setting, for in many instances each of us is already one among the natives under study. According to Freilich's definition of "natives," our "speech, dress, eating and sleeping habits, interactions, social relations, and personal identification all . . . approximate community norms" (1970: 2). But no longer do we have to try hard to become like the natives. For many of us, the communities and the groups we study are intimately familiar; quite clearly, we are the natives. (Note, however, that Molgaard and Byerly, in Chapter 11, question this assumption.) Many of the people we study are those with whom we most closely identify: people of our ethnic group or subculture; people with our same social class, history, and traditions; our own language, color, and sex; as well as people within the institutional and bureaucratic centers of power with which we are all familiar and with which we cope daily.

In this volume the extent of relative "insidedness" and "identity" between researcher and subjects is best conceived of as a continuum from virtual oneness to a marginal nearness. Four of the contributors are closely identified with their subjects: Gwaltney as an urban black among his own folk, Aamodt as a Norwegian-American woman among her Wisconsin kinspeople, and Light and Kleiber as women studying a Canadian feminist health collective.

At the other end of the continuum are those contributors who are in most cases the relative equals of their subjects in social background and minority or majority identity but who are nonetheless unable to breach professional, philosophical, or subtle class boundaries to identify closely with their subjects. Molgaard and Byerly, describing research with a philosophically distinct counterculture commune, and Serber, working in the bureaucratic environment of two state insurance commissions, demonstrate this problem.

Somewhere in between these two points on the continuum fall most of the rest of the contributors. Hennigh identifies himself as a key informant in his rural Oregon community study. Graham, the anthropologist-spouse of a mine company employee, studies company towns in Arizona. Bohannan and his fellow researchers are urban Americans studying the elderly in San Diego. In my own three-year study of a Wyoming frontier school district, I describe my initial identification as a kindred soul, a fellow frontiersman. Sieber is an urban Brownstoner among fellow brownstone dwellers in one of the three urban schools he studied. Zimmer describes and analyzes San Francisco food cooperatives, with which he worked as a consultant.

Other contributors identify to one degree or another with the various subjects of their research, but their contributions tend to focus on issues somewhat removed from their personal or social identities. Feldman discusses problems of contract research in Alaska. Houghton describes the critical issue of how to communicate with the staff of a federal agency in rural Nevada. Wolcott compares personal styles of conducting research at home in the United States and away from home in Africa and Asia. Aguilar, in the book's major think piece, discusses the pros and cons of insider research.

How much we can claim to be true insiders in this sort of research venture at home is highly questionable. As Aguilar points out, the anthropologist's social identity as a professional, itself a class distinction, may make it impossible to identify fully with the subjects of our research. (Bailey [1977], however, has even accomplished this, as an academician studying fellow academicians.)

How native and how strange is the social scientist in the typical at-home research situation? Constraints on research in one's own society may vary considerably from what is normally experienced by the privileged stranger in societies other than his or her own. We often glibly assume that as anthropologists in foreign tribal or peasant societies, perceived as strangers, we can be excused for all sorts of misunderstandings, improprieties and insensitivities to local codes of etiquette. But do these excuses still hold for anthropologists at home? I think not.

Sayles (1978:211) cautions anthropologists that "personality differences and diverse cultural values demand an openness that is often more difficult to achieve in one's own culture than in another." Perhaps the most reasonable approach for determining what it is like to be inside a particular culture – be it a culture of power or of the oppressed, our own or someone else's – is to let the native informants speak as much for themselves as possible, as demonstrated in the contributions of Zimmer, Gwaltney, Light and Kleiber, and Bennett and Kohl.

The rationale

Recent commentators tend to agree that there are many intertwined reasons for the current upsurge in anthropological activity at home. Five reasons emerge from the summary insights of Aguilar (Chapter 2) and Hayano (1979) on this question. Four of them – funding, exclusion, competition, and specialization – reflect a concern for employment. The fifth reason, efficacy, is far more important in the long run.

Funding is presently a serious issue for all scientific research endeavors. Money for research at home and abroad has dwindled significantly in recent years. Just as the cost of everything has increased and budget priorities have changed, so the cost for scientific research, including the social sciences, has been critically reexamined and drastically cut by our parliamentarians and funding agencies. Employment opportunities have suffered accordingly.

Exclusion is a second problem many of us confront. Some newly independent countries, former colonies, simply do not want us and have devised exclusory policies to keep us at bay, or far away. As Hayano (1979) notes, we no longer have the protection of the colonial authorities to assist us. And those many new nation states that have not opted to exclude us have nonetheless put restrictions and qualifications on our work that make it less than attractive except to the very dedicated, the very favored, the very concerned, or, as noted below, their very own (see Nash and Wintrob 1972).

Competition on the home front is a third problem. North American anthropology is now witnessing an infusion of well-trained minority and foreign-born social science professionals, working in areas that were formerly the research monopoly of predominantly white, male Euro-American anthropologists. That monopoly is fast disappearing, and a healthy spirit of competition is being felt in its place. Women, ethnics, and non-Euro-Americans are entering the profession in increasing numbers. As Aguilar points out, the rise of ethnic study programs in North American colleges and universities has greatly encouraged interest among ethnic anthropologists to study their own kind. Many anthropologists place a high priority today on studying their own (Rosaldo and Lamphere 1974, Fahim 1977, Hayano 1979, Fahim et al. 1980). Gwaltney (Chapter 4), for example, speaks directly to the responsibility he feels as a black anthropologist "to augment the current minimal body of native anthropology" and to help incorporate "traditionally ignored perspectives into theory building." Other observers have noted the biases of traditional anthropology and have called for a new approach, a "reorientation of anthropology so that it studies *humankind*" (Reiter 1975:16, original emphasis) instead of some types of people to the exclusion of others.

Specialization in anthropological inquiry is a fourth concern. Specialization in such areas as urban studies, medical anthropology, aging, education, women's and ethnic studies, law and social impact assessment and analysis has emerged, and the students of these subdisciplines have begun looking for (and have been sought out for) research on problems closer to home. This has led "many graduate students to do at least some predoctoral fieldwork in their own backyards" (Hayano 1979:99), and many have opted to stay there and make a career of it. Even some long-established professionals who began on traditional research abroad are turning to the anthropology of issues at home.

In this volume, some contributors have narrowed the scope of research and others have joined two or more special interests, or methodologies, together. Aamodt, for example, is a nurse-anthropologist who has concentrated on neighboring behavior among her own kinspeople. Bohannan describes a project in urban aging. Light and Kleiber combine women's studies, urban anthropology, and a study of a health-delivery system. Graham applies a network methodology to the community-study genre.

Each of these concerns has had its effect on employment (or survival as some see it). The sociocultural setting in North America has changed dramatically in the past two decades, and that change has drastically affected our discipline's self-image. The crisis-ridden social and economic concerns of the 1960s and 1970s – racial injustice, war, poverty, energy, the environment, runaway inflation, and worldwide expression of anti-American sentiment – are reflected in new American social policies and new value orientations and in a demand for a clearer definition and explanation of who we are, where we have come from, and where we are headed as the unique plurality of peoples that we are. All of this change has radically altered the role of the academician in general and of the social scientist in particular.

Goldschmidt calls the change in anthropology a "crisis of jobs" and the change in American society that it reflects a "crisis of culture," both of which reflect a "crisis of values" (1977:300; see also Lévi-Strauss 1963:102). Herein is the case material for a more pragmatic anthropology. "Because it is a crisis in culture, it particularly needs anthropological examination," Goldschmidt concludes (1977:300). The society, the government, and the anthropologists have all responded. New opportunities are opening up in which to apply anthropology and to probe and help solve some of our social and economic ills and issues. The opportunities are legion, but they require aggressive and insightful recycling of old tools and research techniques; in some instances they suggest the need for a major overhaul of our discipline's approach.

The concern with jobs and joblessness in anthropology is widespread. Our professional editorialists are continually discussing and bemoaning the problem, as recent commentary and correspondence in the *Anthropology Newsletter* attest (Nelson 1977, Kay 1977, Thompson 1977, Angrosino et al. 1977, Hicks 1978). Even the general public has been apprised of our problems through the medium of the popular press. *Time* magazine's article, "Studying the American Tribe," for example, provides a candid assessment of the challenges and the reality of the anthropological dilemma:

When two well-dressed strangers turned up at a sleek apartment building on Chicago's Gold Coast, the doorman called the cops. The men explained they were anthropologists from the University of Chicago, anxious to study rich families. "The policeman couldn't believe it," said one of the men. "He looked first for my *Encyclopaedia Britannica*, then for my vacuum cleaner and then asked me what was the gimmick."

The gimmick is that anthropologists, after decades of following Margaret Mead to Samoa and Bronislaw Malinowski to the Trobriand Islands, have staked out new territory – the nonexotic cities and rural byways of the U.S. . . . .

The golden age of anthropology, as many older scholars wistfully call it, is now over. Increased concern with domestic social problems is part of the reason for the turn away from glamorous globetrotting. So is the growing shortage of primitive peoples, many of them now part of politically touchy developing nations which have set severe restrictions on visiting anthropologists. These days a candidate had better have outstanding credentials, the ability to prove he is not with the CIA, eagerness to share his findings with the host country and a total absence of subtle colonial attitudes. [*Time*, Dec. 23, 1974:54]*

In a direct reference to the employment problem (subtitled "No Jobs"), the *Time* article goes on to say:

Just at a time when foreign opportunities are decreasing, the profession is turning out Ph.D.s at a record rate . . . Traditionally, 90% of anthropologists return to the campus, but now colleges are expected to be able to employ only 25% of American anthropologists by 1990 . . . In an interview . . . [Margaret] Mead charged that anthropologists are producing "academic versions of themselves and aren't oriented to things that need to be done in this world. They have spent too much time discussing how many cross-cousins could dance on the head of a pin."

Said former A.A.A. [American Anthropological Association] President George Foster: "Unless we are able to train people to do new kinds of research and break down our false pride, we will wither on the vine." [*Time*, Dec. 23, 1974:54–55]

* Reprinted by permission from *Time*, The Weekly Newsmagazine; Copyright Time Inc. 1974.

This strong concern for unemployment and changing opportunities encourages me to paraphrase a recent observation by Paul Bohannan about epigenetic catastrophe (1980:512, after Waddington 1977). Epigenesis is the appearance of secondary or auxiliary symptoms in an organism or system, particularly as it is affected by a changing environment. It is a sort of metamorphosis.

Our discipline is going through such a metamorphosis, reflecting changes in the social, political, and academic environments in which we thrive. Not all of us can expect to continue to follow our mentors' traditional and time-honored paths of research and employment. The professional landscape has been altered and we are being forced to change with it. The adjustment can be painful, beautiful, revolutionary, enlightening, and rewarding all at once.

Efficacy is the fifth and the last issue which anthropologists at home must address, and it is potentially the most important. Efficacy is the power to produce intended effects or results. We are confronted with a variety of rationalizations for staying home, based on problems of funding, exclusion, competition, and specialization, all of which lead to immediate and practical considerations of employment. In the end, however, the most important results of anthropology at home may be its pragmatism, and its contribution to theory, combined. Goldschmidt (1977) raises the issue of our much-needed pragmatism, criticizing the relative insignificance of much of what we have traditionally defined and defended as anthropological problems. Aguilar devotes part of his chapter (Chapter 2) to the potential for theory generation that this new genre holds.

The efficacy and the challenges of anthropology at home were recognized several decades ago in America (see Taylor 1945, Gillin 1949, 1957, Eddy and Partridge 1978). But it may still be too early to document adequately any truly startling theoretical breakthroughs, although some lower level paradigm shifts have been suggested in contributions to this book.

The study of the so-called American Tribe is not new. Many of our mentors, such as Conrad Arensberg, Solon Kimball, Ruth Benedict, Margaret Mead, Walter Goldschmidt, John Gillin, and John Bennett were pursuing or writing about research in American society well before the present younger generation of anthropologists was born. Lévi-Strauss noted as early as 1958 that

the last twenty-five years in the United States have witnessed tremendous progress in social science research – progress which clearly expresses a crisis of values of contemporary American society (whose boundless self-confidence has begun to wane and which seeks a measure of self-understanding through examination by detached professional observers). [Lévi-Strauss 1963:102]

His words have never been truer. A count of the numerous references to research at home dating prior to 1960 in the Bibliography at the end of this volume will bear out his claim.[5]

Much of the anthropology conducted at home before the current employment crunch had great significance, relevance, utility, and efficacy. It was innovative and productive. It worked well and paid off with insightful new knowledge about the human condition. It had importance in its own right then, and it remains important today. It meets a need in modern society by viewing issues objectively and holistically – in terms of the total social phenomenon – that few other disciplines can claim. We recognized long ago the importance of addressing social issues for their own sake. Long after the current employment crisis is forgotten, the rationale of doing anthropology at home because it is needed and is efficacious will, I trust, remain uppermost.

In the long run

The chapters in this book and the works listed in the Bibliography are only some examples of research in North American society. How these studies rate in comparison with more traditional research elsewhere, not at home, can only be measured by the test of time. I am confident that they will meet the challenge.

If innovation is a virtue, then clearly our work on the methods and issues of research at home is virtuous. If goodness is measured by ethical standards, than what we see here is certainly honest and upright. We are clearly concerned for the subjects of our research, although some of us admit to an initial naivety about relationships between the powerful and the weak in North American society. Specific issues, such as research response to situations of power, do not however guarantee success or goodness. Other measures will tell us which works are the most valuable, the most useful, and the best. Our readers, the practitioners, teachers, and students of anthropology, will ultimately identify the classics of this genre.

A plethora of names

There are many ways to label anthropology at home. In this book and elsewhere in the literature you will encounter the terms *insider research* and *autoethnography* (Chapter 2; see also Goldschmidt 1977, Hayano 1979), *indigenous anthropology* (Fahim 1977, Fahim et al. 1980, Messerschmidt 1981), *native research* (Chapter 4; see also D. Jones 1970, Sordinas 1978), and *introspective research* (Chapter 9). There are still other descriptive terms, such as *endogenous research* and *incultural research* (Maruyama 1969), *peer-group research* (Cassell 1977), and *research competence by blood* (Aceves 1978). Hennigh (Chapter 9) uses the term *key informant* when referring to himself as a research tool, and he speaks of the *anthropologist-as-measuring-device* (see also Devereaux 1967, Cassell 1977). Maquet (1964) writes of the *perspectivist approach,* and some researchers talk of the *anthropology of origin cultures* (D'Addario 1978). Although anthropological research at home is by no means new, it is perhaps indicative of its phenomenal growth in recent years that so many terms exist. Among them I see a slight tendency for North American anthropologists at home to favor the term *insider anthropology,* whereas that subset of ethnic and minority anthropologists who study their own people tend to call what they do *native anthropology.*

Among anthropologists at home in the Third World, there is an inclination toward using the term *indigenous anthropology.* It should be noted, however, that some observers closely involved with this movement see no merit in inventing a special nomenclature to distinguish what they do from what anthropologists the world around claim as their ultimate aim: "the study of others" (Fahim et al. 1980:645). Elizabeth Colsen has openly attacked the whole notion: " 'Indigenous' is a misnomer, for all of us are indigenous somewhere and the majority of anthropologists at some time deal with their own communities" (in Fahim et al. 1980:650).

Embarrassing as it may be . . .

Why dwell on one's own research? What is the point of professional and sometimes personal introspection of the sort found in this book?

Writing about the hows, the whys, and the whats of anthropological research of any sort, at home or away, archaic or modern, requires care and probably reflects concern and self-consciousness as well (Nash and Wintrob 1972). But perhaps most of all, describing our methods, styles, and strategies in the conduct of research among close associates, friends, neighbors, and relatives requires something more akin to grace and humility.

In preparing this book for publication, in soliciting and editing the many contributions, I have been continually reminded of the sage words of one of the social sciences' most renowned international scholars, a pioneer of research in one's own society, Professor M. N. Srinivas. Years ago, when he wrote "Some Thoughts on the Study of One's Own Society" at home in his native India, Srinivas described anthropology at home as an encounter with the self. At the same time, however, he saw it as an essential step toward improving our abilities and sharpening our insights in the continual improvement of this most powerful of the social sciences. And ultimately he saw it as a necessary step toward a better understanding of our own rapidly changing human community. His is perhaps the best answer to why we dwell on what we do at home (or anywhere else) as social scientists:

I shall now consider briefly some methodological issues which stem out of the study of one's own society . . . In order to do this I shall have to refer to myself and my work, and embarrassing as this is I hope that the exercise will clarify for me, and perhaps for others also, certain problems which anyone engaged in the study of his own society has to face. It may also induce some of my colleagues to make a similar effort, so that the net result might be greater objectivity in the work we are engaged in. [Srinivas 1966:147]

2 Insider research: an ethnography of a debate

JOHN L. AGUILAR

The topic of this paper is the long-standing debate engaged in by some social scientists over the issue of insider research, the study of one's own society. The practice is not new – Firth and Gluckman, for example, began their careers with studies of their respective homelands, New Zealand and South Africa – but its incidence is on the rise. Among the reasons for this, I believe, are the scarcity of funds for study abroad, the exclusory policies of some newly independent nations, the formation of ethnic studies programs in North American colleges and universities, and perhaps an awareness on the part of some anthropologists of theoretical and methodological advantages in doing research at home.

But this trend has occurred against a background of polemics concerning epistemological, practical, and normative issues. For example, some advocates of insider research argue that because outsiders lack member knowledge – existential participation in a society's covert culture of implicit rules and ineffable sentiments and orientations – their research results are necessarily superficial. Critics of insider research, on the other hand, have characterized such knowledge as mere subjective involvement, a deterrent to objective perception and analysis. Indeed, it is widely held among anthropologists that, because of the outsider's greater ability to stand back perceptually and cognitively, he or she can more readily abstract from behavioral data a society's unconscious cultural grammar as well as record its conscious vocabulary. According to Foster (1972:60), this is how he arrived at his model of Tzintzuntzeños' covert Image of Limited Good, "inferred from behavior but not derived from the peasants' statements about their world view."

I once posed to an advocate of insider research the problem of the extent to which covert (or unconscious) culture is retrievable and therefore available for analysis. He responded simply that it need not be retrieved, that its proper role is to influence analysis on its own terms – implicitly. The insider researcher, he continued, should conduct his research as an insider because his or her covert orientation to field experiences enables ethnographic interpretations to stand not only as statements about the culture but also as expressions of the culture. He added that because cultures are normally interpreted in terms of the covert dispositions of foreigners, it is legitimate and desirable that the bias also slant in the

15

direction of the indigenous perspective. Another advocate of insider research, while conceding that unconscious materials might serve to reduce objectivity, also insisted that the covert culture of the insider has the heuristic value of lending psychological reality (or cultural validity) to ethnographic analyses. In effect, both insiders argued that their unconscious input is relevant to their research but that that of the outsider is not. Such is the nature of some of the epistemological issues involved in this debate.

In what follows I present something of a montage of arguments extracted in part from the literature but mainly from conversations over the years. In effect, it is an ethnography of this debate. Because most of the personally communicated opinions were expressed informally, I will cite sources only for published statements. In my conclusion I will argue that most of the discussion, both pro and con, rests upon erroneous assumptions about the structure of insider research. These assumptions, I contend, perpetuate, like the mortician's art, the appearance of life of a bogus issue.

The debate: claims and counterclaims

In their zeal for intercultural investigation some anthropologists assert that Western social science is too culture bound because its research is too close to home. This, they say, results in a number of epistemological restrictions. For one, the conduct of research at home often inhibits the perception of structures and patterns of social and cultural life. Paradoxically, too much is too familiar to be noticed or to arouse the curiosity essential to research. Intercultural or outsider research, on the other hand, involves a comparative orientation in which contrast promotes both perception and curiosity. The researcher undergoes a kind of heuristic culture shock that operates through curiosity as an impetus to understanding. As one advocate of this position put it, "when we return from vacations or other trips, the events we remember and relate to our friends or relatives are the out of the ordinary. Our curiosities and those of our listeners are not stimulated enough by the ordinary for us to even remember them." This argument rests on a sound principle. T. Schwartz (1968:16), although not necessarily arguing against insider research, has noted that "our consciousness of culture [itself] depends upon the prevalence of . . . deviations from our own emic structures and still more radically, depends upon our experience of whole alternative frameworks from those of our own emic systems." This applies, I believe, not only to the discovery of culture in the phylogenetic development of social science but also to the ontogenetic development of each social scientist who must achieve a sense of its meaning and (dare I say it?) reality before attempting to do a mature study of cultural phenomona.

Insider research has also been characterized as inherently biased. In this regard much criticism has been aimed at ethnic studies programs. Critics contend that since the primary function of such programs is to foster ethnic pride, there is in the research and teaching of ethnic studies scholars a strong propensity to select and interpret information in ways favorable to this goal. It is further argued that because the principal research goal of these scholars is the promotion of group interests rather than the disinterested search for truth, they function as advocates rather than scientists.

By contrast, the relative noninvolvement attributed to the outsider is said to be more conducive to disinterested scientific behavior. The outsider enjoys what Beattie (1964:87) has called "stranger value." Simmel (quoted in Merton 1972:32) described "the stranger" (or outsider) as free of commitments to the study group and therefore more able to adopt the role of relatively objective inquirer. According to Simmel, the stranger "surveys conditions with less prejudice: his criteria for them are more general and more objective ideals; he is not tied down in his action by habit, piety, and precedent." Merton adds to this that "it is the stranger... who finds what is familiar to the group significantly unfamiliar and so is prompted to raise questions for inquiry less apt to be raised at all by Insiders" (Merton 1972:33).

One anthropologist said to me that given certain elementary skills in interpersonal relations, the outsider is more readily made privy to secret information and opinions, because he is a noninterested party who can be trusted not to use the information against the informant – because he has no incentive to do so. This must have the ring of truth for most ethnographers. One common experience I have in highland Chiapas (where I do outsider research) must be the experience of many: Informants repeatedly say to me that what they tell me they cannot tell their fellow townsmen. I believe that in some cases this confidence results from the fact that these people see me as having no axe to grind. Because I am not a member of the community, I am not a competitor for its resources and not involved in the town's gossip network. But this is not complete. There are some individuals who for various reasons will not confide in me. In some cases I believe it is because they see me as socially too close to individuals with whom they are in a state of enmity. Therefore, I am potentially untrustworthy, a possible participant in the gossip network. In such cases, I am handicapped by the fact that I am not perceived as being enough of an outsider; I am a social insider with respect to the wrong people. This problem took another form in the days when I first began research in the area. Given my Spanish surname and non-Indian appearance, some Indians kept their distance from me, assuming that I was a Latino (the dominant ethnic group in the region) from another area. It became my task to convince these people that I was not a member of the local outgroup but a true insider, a North American. This was accomplished with relative ease. But some time later, at the time of the assassination of Allende in Chile, my North American status became a problem – one Latino accused me of being an agent of the CIA, an understandable opinion for the time.

Advocates of insider research make a number of counterclaims. Regarding their lack of culture shock, they point out that culture shock is in fact a research obstacle from which they are free. This is supported by Dennison Nash's observation that

the term "culture shock" has been coined to refer to the negative effects on the individual of his experience as a stranger... the condition of anomie inherent in the stranger's role is unlikely to permit [the unbiased objectivity claimed for it]. Rather, in such an anxiety-provoking situation one would expect an average citizen to develop and maintain strong, inflexible, "black and white" views and to display "perceptual sensitivity" and "perceptual defense" in keeping with them. [Nash 1963: 153–154]

In other words, culture shock may cause the individual to recoil from the alien situation rather than to pursue it under the impetus of curiosity. It has also been suggested that the metaphor of shock is inappropriate because the experience is in fact often a relatively chronic disorientation rather than a condition that appears and disappears abruptly.

Possibly the advantage most often claimed by ethnic insider researchers is that, because of their ability to blend into situations, they are less likely to alter social settings. Also, because they can more effectively meet the social behavioral requirements and expectations of the research community, and because of shared frames of reference and consensual meanings, interaction is more natural and they attain a more thorough rapport with informants. For these reasons, they say, they can engage in participant-observational research to a far greater extent than can the outsider. Some also claim to be able to participate in a wider range of indigenous activities and situations. For example, one individual pointed out that in formally exclusive in-group activities (such as ethnic political meetings), he can invoke his ethnic credentials, which normally provide him the moral right to admittance. Insiders also point out that because of their greater linguistic competence they can phrase questions in a manner more comfortable and meaningful to informants. Another claim is greater ability to read nonverbal indications of such subjective states as suspicion, confidence, and embarrassment. This enables the insider researcher to adapt his own behavior more effectively to facilitate the flow of information. This ability to read behavioral cues, according to one individual, permits him to gauge more accurately the trustworthiness of informants' verbal responses and accounts.

Some insider researchers argue that, because they are defined as members of research communities, subjects are less inclined to conceal their behavior and views, because whatever the researcher writes about them is also true of the researcher. For the same reason rapport is enhanced, because, in addition to the sharing of cultural characteristics, the ethnic-insider researcher is seen as being in the same sociopolitical boat as the subjects: Because the larger society classifies the researcher with them – as members of the same social category – this conduces to the greater confidence that connects social equals. Conversely, it is claimed that no matter how much the outsider researcher is outwardly accepted by the research community, he or she is always to some extent cast into the role of impersonal inquisitor, an alien who remains excluded from many aspects of social life and meanings.

Much of this is echoed by the African anthropologist Nukunya in his discussion of his research among his people, the Anlo Ewe:

Because I was one of them and not a "foreign intruder," the fear and suspicion which always lurk in the minds of subjects and informants during social research in general were almost absent. They had confidence in me because they knew I could not "sell them." Many a time informants were met who admitted "this is a thing we normally don't divulge to outsiders, but since it is you we shall give you all the necessary help." [Nukunya 1969:19]

Clearly these claims contradict those made by critics of insider research. If such discrepancies reflect more than perceptual distortion it might be that differences in communities' attitudes toward insiders and outsiders have to do largely with the state of both intracommunity relations (whether they are characterized by trust or mistrust) and the community's history of relations with outsiders.

Ethnic scholars are particularly emphatic about another dimension of this debate over the relative merits of insider and outsider research. They argue that, as insiders, they are far less inclined to construct opaque stereotypes of the people they study than outsiders would be. Instead, they are more accepting (and cognizant) of complexity and variation than is the outsider, who is more likely to form simplistic caricatures (see Romano 1968). Related to this is the claim that insiders are better equipped to get past the ideal side of social behavior and opinion and into the area of real life. One individual candidly qualified this with the observation that although he was generally able to penetrate into "the real life" of his community, he still had to cope with the ideal fronts put up by individuals against himself and other members of the community. F. G. Bailey has stated in the introduction to his insider study of political behavior in his own professional community that

it is singularly difficult to penetrate to the unprincipled side [the backstage area where ideals are set aside in favor of pragmatic considerations], when working in a political culture other than one's own. Not only do people have a proper reticence about letting a stranger, no matter how well disposed, behind the scenes, but also the back stage of politics is played out in a language of great subtlety which is often beyond the reach of those who are not native speakers. Admittedly, one loses something of the fresh perceptive eye when looking at the familiar, but in this instance I thought the price worth paying and the "natives" in this ethnography are my colleagues. [Bailey 1977:2]

Another insider claim is that insider research is more economical; insiders already have a tremendous amount of background information about the particular problem of study. Nukunya (1969:18–19) describes his own inside research in similar terms: "My prior knowledge of the area gave me certain advantages which made my work in the field much easier than would have been the case if I were a foreign investigator . . . Ewe is my mother-tongue, and, as I had already spent a large part of my life in the area, I had no problem of familiarization to local conditions."

The critic's claim that the insider's familiarity with events of everyday life precludes the curiosity resulting from novelty would seem true. While contrast with what is expected may promote perception – we notice the unfamiliar and unexpected more readily than the familiar and expected – this is a problem with which the foreign researcher must also contend. Graduate students about to embark on their first field trip in an alien culture are often advised to record their impressions during the early months of research, before events and situations, so striking in the beginning, fade into familiarity. Whyte validated this advice in the appendix to his own first field study:

I began as a nonparticipating observer. As I became accepted into the community, I found myself becoming almost a nonobserving participant. I got the feel of life in Cornerville, but that meant that I got to take for granted the same things that my Cornerville friends took for granted. I was immersed in it, but I could as yet make little sense out of it. I had a feeling that I was doing something important, but I had yet to explain to myself what it was. [Whyte 1943:321]

One could argue that the relative rapidity with which Whyte became "immersed" in Cornerville life was due to the fact that he was not so much an outsider as it would seem: The Italian-American youths of his study were bicultural, fluent speakers of (their brand of) English, and they lived not far from Whyte's university.

It should be noted, however, that the curiosity-arousing event is not necessarily a scientifically interesting one. Ultimately, theoretical considerations define what is interesting, not personal curiosity. In terms of the goals of science, the difference between the existentially familiar and unfamiliar is of little significance; hence, exoticism has no place in scientific ethnology. It may be said, furthermore, that the "scientific perspective" differs from the ordinary view of life in that scientists, like philosophers, marvel at the familiar, or the theoretical implications of normal events. Scientific inquiry seeks an understanding of events at a level deeper than that which is the object of idle curiosity.

Uchendu argues:

> The "native" point of view presented by a sympathetic foreign ethnologist who "knows" his natives is not the same view presented by a native. Both views are legitimate, but the native's point of view is yet to enrich our discipline . . . Many anthropologists acquire a cross-cultural perspective through reading and participating in foreign cultures, that is, knowing more than one culture at firsthand. The latter should not be confused with "living" more than one culture. Very few people are in a position to do this. Not even the celebrated ethnographer Malinowski could be credited with this: his stay of two years and seven months in the Trobriand Islands was not enough to produce a Trobriander. To "live" a culture demands more than a knowledge of its events' system and institutions; it requires growing up with these events and being emotionally involved with cultural values and biases. [Uchendu 1965:9]

A similar view was presented to me by an ethnic scholar who claimed that because he had grown up in a plural society (the United States), he is bicultural in the sense of living two cultures. As such, he claimed for himself the advantage of an epistemological amphibian, able to stereoscopically evaluate and understand events and meanings of the larger and minority cultures, each against the background of the other. This was, I suppose, a claim for a kind of objectivity – intrapsychic intersubjectivity. The outsider, on the other hand, has only one culture. Consequently, in attempting to grasp the point of view of people of another culture, he or she succeeds only in projecting onto them his or her own perspective, which is, finally, an outside view. Responding to this claim, an anthropologist pointed out to me that amphibians are also noted for their inability either to walk or swim very well – the physical properties permitting walking limit swimming ability, and vice versa. His point was, I believe, that unless the bicultural individual can effectively compartmentalize each of the two insider perspectives, each will function to block the other. In that case, the appropriate metaphor would be double vision rather than stereoscopy.

We might concede, however, that the individual who has lived in more than one social-class circumstances – for example, the individual who was raised in a lower-class family and later, in adulthood, acquired a middle-class status and life style – would be particularly well suited to study the social class of his or her youth. At least the individual would have a view of what each class looks like to the other. In such a case, however, the two perspectives would not be simultaneous: One would be current and the other retrospective.

This argument for living a culture was recently expressed in a televised interview of minority students in an ethnic studies department. At one point in the interview a student expressed dissatisfaction with his school's policy regarding the execution of courses in his department. He said that he was taking a course in the sociology and history of his ethnic group from a professor not of his own ethnic status and culture. He said that although the professor was academically qualified regarding the intellectual content of the course, he was nevertheless unqualified for the position because of his incapacity to know what it feels like to be a participant in the student's group. He lacks, in other words, the important quality of understanding, which derives only from living the culture of the people studied.

But ethnic scholars do not insist that their insider status solves all their research problems. For example, some admit that, like any sociologist, they sometimes have difficulty gaining access to a social setting or community in which they are racial and cultural members but social strangers. In such cases, they usually have to meet most of the same demands the alien does. But there is a general feeling that their ethnic credentials often make the task easier than it is for the researcher who is both an ethnic and social outsider.

Others acknowledge that their insider status sometimes involves serious constraints. Although they generally claim the double advantage of being more relaxed with informants who are in turn more relaxed with them than they are with outsiders, there are occasions when this is not the case. For those insiders who have undergone considerable acculturation, there is often a need to engage in an inordinate amount of stressful impression management. This is epecially so during periods when their minority group is in a state of enmity vis à vis the larger society. At such times the acculturated ethnic scholar is particularly liable to the suspicion and resentment of some ethnic fellows. Among Chicanos, the individual displaying too many out-group characteristics may be classified as a *vendido* (sell out), one who is Angloized or gringoized and therefore disloyal to his group and its culture. In Mexico, the equivalent betrayal is that of the *malinchista*, the individual who, like Doña Malinche, the Indian mistress and ally of Cortez, has been corrupted by foreign influences (see Paz 1961). American blacks and Orientals have similar epithets: The "oreo cookie" and the "banana" are, respectively, black and yellow on the outside but white on the inside.

There are other examples of conflict between research and in-group membership role requirements. The very fact of insiders' cultural and social credentials usually means that higher expectations are placed on their social and cultural performances; they do not enjoy the allowances made for the ineptitudes of outsiders. Nukunya (1969:19) makes this point: "As a local man [the insider] is expected by his informants to be knowledgeable in certain basic things, and certain queries which from an alien may be attributed to a curiosity 'to know things' may be considered irrelevant or even impertinent coming from him."

Insider status can also be a handicap regarding access to some kinds of information. For example, Srinivas, in studying such topics as the cultural constraints on the adoption of new farming techniques, or new landholding systems, or the operations of the *panchayati raj*, is better off than the outsider, if only because he can more easily perceive nuances than a European. But in studying problems related to untouchability he is, as a south Indian Brahmin, probably worse off. Even if he can distance himself psychologically from the subject matter, others may not be willing to give him the distance needed to be the recipient of certain kinds of information – in such matters he may not be defined as an impartial observer.

This also applies to ethnic insiders in the United States, especially during periods of interethnic conflict. At such times the insider is required to take a stand in intergroup political issues. Objectivity regarding such issues implies impartiality, which is, to some, tantamount to treason. One who is defined as an insider is also presumed to be a member of the group's moral community and political team and therefore is not permitted the distance needed to ask some kinds of questions. To seek the truth is to question what is known by every right-thinking partisan to be established.

Perhaps the most important criticism leveled at insider research is that it is inherently biased. In my experience in ethnic studies departments, I have seen evidence supporting critics' charges that ethnic studies researchers are biased in their selection of data and formulation of conclusions. But examples were few, and there seems to be little in these that I would label dishonest. Among those who showed signs of less than rigorous conformity to the technical norms of social science, some openly defined themselves as advocates. One individual, for example, admitted that he was primarily concerned to build cases, but cases based on fact. Nevertheless, he said that he was not interested in wasting time "proving" such cases. It seemed to me that he was so convinced of the truth of his research conclusions that any formal attempts to test them would be superfluous to him. He was morally committed, and out of his commitment arose a clear lack of intellectual impartiality.

It should also be noted that when ethnic scholars are biased, this bias is not always positive; it may in fact be negative. By virtue of their aspirations for class mobility – their level of educational achievement may be an expression of this – ethnic scholars tend to be more acculturated than the majority of their ethnic fellows. Some of these individuals may reject or feel ambivalence toward their group and its customs. A certain amount of this is to be expected in a society that depreciates its ethnic minority groups, especially those considered to be racially different. In order to achieve a sense of increased self-esteem and social worth, ethnic individuals have – in addition to academic advancement and economic success – two obvious options open to them: They can actively participate in ethnic-pride activities designed to enhance the status of their group (if not in the eyes of the larger society, at least in their own), or they can attempt, by means of psychological mechanisms, altered life style, and social practices, to divorce themselves from the group, to deethnicize themselves, and "achieve" assimilation into the larger society. In this attempt, the aspirants' own ethnic society may exist for them as a negative reference group. In any case, ethnic scholars – including those employed in ethnic studies programs – cannot be assumed to take the first option, which results in positive bias.

Bias is the human condition, a danger for both insider and outsider researchers. Whereas the insider might labor under a biasing chauvinism, all outsiders, by virtue of their primary socialization in one society, must make efforts to overcome ethnocentric bias. Similarly, the xenophilia of some socially mobile or ethnically passing individuals is also a possibility for the exoticist (outsider) who sees much virtue abroad and little at home.

As far as many ethnic studies researchers are concerned, the charge made against them of methodological dishonesty is hypocritical and, according to some, racist. One individual expressed the opinion that individuals who apply a procrustian treatment to their data in order to fit them to hypotheses and models are to be found in all groups. He singled out researchers working under the sponsorship of government agencies and private industries and in a cynical tone suggested that "grants sometimes buy conclusions."

Whether or not we share this view, it must be agreed that the problem of bias is general in scope: A lack of unfailing commitment to objectivity is not a quality exclusive to insider researchers in general or ethnic studies scholars in particular.

A common form of bias that all fieldworkers must guard against is, of course, sampling bias. Both insiders and outsiders, for example, must guard against the unwarranted generalization to an entire group the views expressed by a few favorite informants. But insiders have the unique problem of guarding against the projection of their views onto others of their community, of assuming that their orientation is more shared or representative than it is (Nukunya 1969:19). But these dangers can be mitigated with relative ease once one is aware of them.

Other biases, particularly those reflecting personality characteristics, and therefore often out of awareness, are more intractable. The now famous discrepancies noted in the works of such competent fieldworkers as Fortune and Mead (on the Arapesh), Goodenough and Fischer (on the Trukese), and Lewis and Redfield (on Tepoztlán) should dampen excessive enthusiasm about the objectivity inherent in the outsider's position. Subjective distortion and the usually unconscious transaction operating in data acquisition with informants are procedural pitfalls for all researchers. The naive empiricism underlying the claims of both the extreme insiders and outsiders reflects an inadequate epistemology that misguides most of us much of the time.

It has been suggested that the contrasting characteristics of insider and outsider researchers would have the value of being complementary in research teams consisting of both types of researchers. Of course, essential to such a cooperation would be a condition of mutual respect and appreciation on the part of insiders and outsiders for each other's strengths and weaknesses. The research on American racial problems in the early 1940s headed by outsider Gunnar Myrdal (Merton 1972:35) is an example of such an effort. For the value of their perspectives, Myrdal included within his research organization such insiders as Ralph Bunche and E. Franklin Frazier. And what American sociologist would not welcome the aid of a Tocqueville?

Nonetheless, few ethnographers would rest content with this division of labor. Paul (1953:442) stated the now widely endorsed view that the task of the fieldworker is "to gather and relate two sets of data, a description of the situation as he sees it . . . and a description of the situation as the native sees it." This dual perspective would be essential if, as Beattie (1964:84) notes, "the anthropologist's representation of the situation must bear some relation to the people's own actual (or potential) representations of it; it must be such that it could be presumed that if it were to be fully explained to a member of the society, he would recognize its validity. For in the last resort folk systems and analytical systems . . . relate to the same reality."

I agree that emic accounts and etic schemes should be analytically integrated whenever possible for a more thorough understanding of most kinds of situations. Even ecological studies are enhanced when they take account of how actors perceive the environments with which they interact. And emic data should be placed within an etic framework if the research product is to be more than a reproduction of folk theory. It would seem that if outsider and insider ethnographers are to accomplish this dual (and synthesizing) task, they must meet diametrically different demands. Thus, the outsider must to some extent get into the natives' heads, skins, or shoes, whereas the insider must get out of his or her own. Insiders must attain a necessary degree of distance for the sake of objectivity; outsiders must avoid too much distance lest they be ignorant of what it is they are being objective about (Dalton 1959:283).

Some features of the insider's training and research conditions may act to nudge, if not push, him into a partial transcendence of insider perspective. Nash (1963:149), for example, notes that "the novice-anthropologist is recruited into and trained by a group with a particular formal and informal ideology which, to a greater or lesser extent, he absorbs and carries with him into the field." Srinivas (1966:157) suggests that "after finishing fieldwork, the [insider ethnographer generally] goes back to his university to write up the results of his study. Physical distance from the field, as well as the necessity of describing and analyzing his experiences in terms that will be intelligible to his colleagues...forces him to emerge from his previous role of participant-observer and become an impersonal analyst." In addition the insider researcher normally will formulate the study problem at the university under the influence of colleagues. If he or she is a graduate student about to conduct a first field project, this formulation will occur under the influence of the thesis or dissertation committee. This might help to mitigate the problem of not noticing that which is too familiar, because if the researcher defines the problem and its empirical correlates before entering the field, many of the relevant objects of perception will be preselected according to theoretical criteria and therefore more likely to be observed regardless of degree of familiarity.

But there is a potentially negative side to this. The insider's socialization into the ideology of the professional community and the necessity of meeting the intellectual requirements of colleagues may combine to neutralize one of his or her principal advantages. These conditions induce the researcher to ignore much of what is already known about the study population and situation because it cannot be fit into the concepts of the discipline. This would, however, probably be less likely to happen for researchers working in ethnic studies departments, as their faculties are normally recruited from a number of disciplines. Insofar as this heterogenous group of colleagues serves reference-group functions for the researcher, his or her research may suffer a lack of influence from the conceptual framework of the particular discipline. In the ethnic studies context the corresponding pressures may be defined by notions of pragmatic and ideological relevance and the demands of a nonspecialized reading audience.

Conclusion

Up to this point I have focused on principles related to ideal types, without reference to the most critical determinant of success and failure for both insiders and outsiders – talent. Throughout the history of anthropology, many anthropologists have, as outsiders, provided us with peeks into the world views, attitudes, and behavioral strategies of people of other cultures. They have succeeded in this primarily because they have exercised powers of empathy and perspicacity and social skills that enable them to make use of the wider human condition. No doubt cultural differences present problems for cross-cultural communication and understanding, but cultural boundaries are not hermetic seals; given the commonalities that characterize humankind as a social and physical species, cultural boundaries can to some extent be permeated by individuals possessing the appropriate technical and personal skills. Talented insiders such as Srinivas (India), Obeyesekere (Sri Lanka), Uchendu (Nigeria), Mading Deng (Sudan), Kenyatta (Kenya), and Nukunya (West Africa), to name a few, have provided structural analyses of aspects of their own social systems, while some have demonstrated, as Goffman has for the United States, the ability to render explicit aspects of their own covert cultures. Given the role of individual talent, then, we must define the structural pressures described in this discussion as contributing to tendencies rather than as the absolute monopolies and exclusions they are suggested to be by the rhetoric of some insiders and outsiders (see Merton 1972).

Other factors also help explain the successes of many insiders. First, ethnic insiders are generally not as much inside the cultural and social settings they study as most of the discussion so far implies. For one thing, they are in important respects marginal to the majority of their ethnic population. They are, by profession at least, middle class, whereas most of their ethnic peers are of the working class. Ideologically they are set apart to some extent by their socialization into the scientific ethos of their profession, and, as I stated above, they are likely to be more acculturated and assimilated into the larger culture and society than most of their ethnic peers. We can expect these differences to be reflected in significant variations in cultural orientations and social alignments.

Finally, we should ask what it is that critics and proponents of insider research consider to be inside of: a homogenous culture and an undifferentiated subsociety? This is the implication underlying many of their assertions, but it is contradicted by the ethnological fact that all sociocultural systems are complex. Many societies are fragmented by class, regional, urban-rural, and ideology-related affiliative differences, and all cultures (including subcultures) are characterized by internal variation (Pelto and Pelto 1975).

Despite this, the extreme arguments both for and against insider research rest on an implicit model that characterizes all researchers as either absolutely inside or outside a homogenous sociocultural system. The facts indicate, however, that because no one participates in all segments (or levels) of a domestic population or shares with everyone in that population all ideational components of its culture (T. Schwartz 1978), a more realistic model of the situation would view the local ethnographer as relatively inside (or outside) with respect to a multiplicity of social and cultural characteristics of a heterogeneous population.

In principle, at least, this structural complexity provides researchers with the opportunity to retain some of the assets of insider status while minimizing some of its liabilities. They can strategically select among demographic locations and research topics – particularly with respect to cultural domains – in order to regulate the degree of their social involvement and cultural immersion. To the extent that they are successful in this attempt, they will approximate the ideal of enjoying aspects of both insider and outsider statuses. Whether or not they can have it both ways is something that can only be determined by experience.

If I have learned anything from the proclamations of insiders and their critics, it is that the problem has yet to evolve beyond the stage of hunches, rhetoric, and untested insights. I have also concluded, however, that instead of providing vituperation we should encourage insider research. As Srinivas (1966:154) points out, the insider's biases might very well be sources of insight as well as error. Furthermore, it has been reasonably argued that if we study only those aspects of a society's life that are open to foreign inspection, we will end up with a collection of skewed images of that life. This would apply especially to matters of what is considered important in the lives of the people studied. Insider research should thus be appreciated not only as information about various groups but also as information about the insider researchers themselves, just as studies of other cultures by American anthropologists can tell us, if we care to look, about American culture. We should, therefore, encourage insider researchers to reflect upon and share information concerning experienced advantages and disadvantages, so that their research may serve as "both a source of data and a datum itself of comparative methodology" (Cicourel 1964:54) as well as a contribution to the sociology of knowledge.

PART II Urban studies

The city is a focus of study for many anthropologists at home, and urban anthropology has become a major subfield of our discipline. In chapters 3 through 6, four different cultural settings within cities are described and a variety of methods are used to elucidate the issues and challenges of urban research.

Paul Bohannan and his team of researchers address the "unseen community" of the poor and the elderly in San Diego hotels (Chapter 3). Bohannan's emphasis is primarily on methods of inquiry. One of his most useful tools is a series of "debriefing sessions" that allows fieldworkers' data and the principal investigator's theoretical concerns to coalesce throughout all stages of the project.

In Chapter 4, John L. Gwaltney takes us to the urban Northeast, into the black neighborhoods of his upbringing, and into the research for his recent, award-winning book, Drylongso: A Self-Portrait of Black America *(1980). He pursues a style of native anthropology that relies on personal documents and folk field seminars conducted in the private homes, churches, taverns, and housing projects of the district. Core black culture, he tells us, "runs upon the oils of circumspection, reciprocity, and improvisation," and his presentation of those three expressions, occasionally flavored with bits of anger at the arrogance of majority social science, makes the issues of black life in America (and Gwaltney's own methodology) come alive.*

Urban cooperatives and the role of a consultant-cum-researcher are described by Richard Zimmer (Chapter 5). Contrary to the notion that so-called primitive and modern economic expressions are far apart, Zimmer shows us certain parallels in the context of Latino neighborhood cooperatives in San Francisco. His dual role as consultant and anthropologist had virtually no effect on cooperative structure, operations, or member commitment, he says, but it did affect leadership and group process. This is a discomforting admission for many researchers who strain to be detached, which their professional colleagues expect, while they are forced to be involved by the expectations of their subjects.

27

In Chapter 6 David Serber addresses the issues of accountability in two state insurance regulatory commissions and the methodological and moral quandaries that an anthropologist may face on the inside of a big bureaucracy. Because his identification as a researcher was suspect to many of his key informants, Serber's insights into gaining access and seeking cooperation in the quest for data are unquestionably important for any who seek to "study up" (Nader 1974) in the corridors of power in modern society.

3 Unseen community: the natural history of a research project

PAUL BOHANNAN

Anthropologists usually do not spell out in detail the processes by which they gather their data. Some describe the field situation in detail, but they too often assume that their readers will know what their processes of data gathering have been. The way anthropologists manipulate and analyze their data once they are collected is described even less often.

The primary purpose of this article is to provide information on how we went about data gathering and analysis for a specific research project in our own culture – The Unseen Community[1] – carried out by research associates of the Western Behavioral Sciences Institute.[2] In order to set that explanation into context, however, I shall first provide some background on the problem, its vicissitudes, and a summary of our results.[3]

The problems and the findings

In the course of research on the causes of poverty some years ago, associates of the Western Behavioral Sciences Institute (WBSI) were led to the residents of center-city hotels in San Diego. It soon became evident that this was a very special population. Therefore, at a later date, background research was carried out and problems formulated, which led to the submission of a research proposal to the Center for Studies of Metropolitan Problems of the National Institute of Mental Health. The project was called Unseen Community: Old Nonwelfare Poor In Urban Hotels.

The original problem

The original problem centered around the fact that the old people who lived in center-city hotels were poor, but they refused welfare even when they were eligible for it. They struggled valiantly and by and large successfully against what seemed to be immense odds. The small literature on the subject[4] discussed the bare and invisible kinds of social ties that held these people together in the face of immense social disorganization. We came later

29

in our research to think that the framework of social disorganization was an unfortunate one for describing this population – nevertheless, it was the one with which we started. We focused on the social ties that, we reasoned, had to be present in order for the people to make as good an adjustment as they had in fact made.

The timing of our original application was a key issue. Research began in the summer of 1974. The city of San Diego had been planning since 1972 to tear down many of these hotels in the process of urban renewal, and it then appeared that several hundred of these old residents would be displaced in the process.

Therefore, our original scheme gave us time to make a preliminary study of these people, after which the focus of our research was to have been on the ways in which the population was resettled. More specifically, the overall objective of the project was to discover, describe, and analyze the social and psychic situation of nonwelfare poor senior citizens living in single-room-occupancy hotels in downtown San Diego as the area was transformed through urban development. We wanted to determine the degree to which the informal social support systems sustain the mental health needs of nonwelfare poor residents in urban center hotels.

To achieve this objective, the research pursued the following aims:

1. To describe the formal and informal social structures of a hotel for nonwelfare poor.
2. To compare the social structures of middle-class and skid-row hotels to the subject hotel in order to isolate the unique characteristics of the latter.
3. To describe the adaptive mechanisms used by the residents to support their mental health needs and the way in which the mechanisms change over time.
4. To develop a set of recommendations for mental health delivery systems that emphasize the adaptive strengths of marginally subsistent individuals and the supportive strengths of the social structures of their residential units. Such recommendations would assist in making social policy decisions in metropolitan areas.
5. To provide basic information on an important type of residential arrangement so that a long-term project on American household patterns could be undertaken.

In addition to these aims stated in the proposal, the general thrust of the research was to assess how the hotel residents, who live under conditions of minimal subsistence, make sense of and organize their everyday lives, and how the social structure of their group quarters contribute to their well-being.

Recessions, postponement, and the vicissitudes of research

Our original proposal assumed that the time frame given by the city planning officials would see the progress they postulated. But these well-laid plans ran into difficulty with the recession of 1975 and the consequent financial concerns of the developer. This situation not only slowed down the timetable but led to rethinking of the entire redevelopment project.

Therefore, our original plans to assess the viability of the unseen social structures and their strengths and weaknesses under the pressures of dislocation and relocation were casualties of the total situation. Although changes have occurred in the area as a result of predevelopment activities, these have not as yet included massive forced relocation or the destruction of any hotels.[5]

In response to the slowdown in redevelopment, we decided we would carry out a thorough ethnography of the area, for by now we knew enough to believe that the social disorganization frame of reference that had been used for all the hotels studies in the literature was an inadequate one. We began to realize that the problem for our specific population was adaptation rather than disorganization. We expanded our sample of hotels from three to twelve, of all sizes and sorts. We still think that the original plan of studying removal and adaptation to urban development was a good one. But we also think that the job we did provides far better background than any we could have done if the city's timetable had remained on schedule.

Extensive field observations were carried out in the area from July 1974 until the spring of 1977. Anthony Gorman lived in the Golden West Hotel for almost two and a half years. Lisa D'Arcy, a degree candidate at San Diego State University, joined the fieldworkers after she completed her M.A. degree on the topic of the networks of elderly residents of the hotels. Kevin Eckert, a Northwestern University doctoral candidate with a National Research Service Award, joined the research team in the second year. He coordinated his research with the larger WBSI study. He lived in the study area from September 1975 to September 1976, studied the medical anthropology of the older hotel residents, and for several months worked as desk clerk at the Knickerbocker. In September 1976, after completing his field research, Eckert joined the project staff to assist in analyzing and writing up the findings of the study. After Gorman had completed his participant observation in the Golden West Hotel, Wayne Rauschkolb joined the research team to observe specific downtown behavioral settings. He lived and worked in two of the hotels.

In the middle of the third year, ethnographic observations and collections of new data were scaled down to monitoring status as energies were redirected toward the analysis of the data.

Findings of the study: theoretical points

The Unseen Community project has provided a rich store of information about the coping mechanisms, life styles, and adjustment of the urban elderly poor, as well as about the processes of urban decay and renewal. The findings are reported here in highlight form. More complete analyses and findings are to be found in the written reports cited in note 3.

Sociodemographic characteristics of the population. Residents are predominantly male (90 percent) and live alone. The average age is sixty-two years; this datum hides two important details: (1) there are a good number of very old people, but (2) because of injuries or disease, "old age" may start as young as forty-five. The mean level of education is nine years; most have been employed in unskilled and manual occupations. Only 17 percent of the population are employed, despite the fact that 41 percent of our formal sample were under the retirement age of sixty-two as defined by the Social Security Act. Respondents were not newcomers to the downtown environment, having lived there for an average seven and a half years; their mean monthly income was approximately $300; the majority received their income from Social Security, Supplemental Security Income (SSI), pensions, disability, or veterans' benefits.

Self-reliance. The elderly hotel residents are fiercely self-reliant individuals who refuse to be dependent on public or private social services. They persistently say that in times of need they do things for themselves. Their desire to be self-sufficient is taken to the extreme in some cases, in which vulnerable individuals go to considerable lengths to avoid help that seems to outsiders to be essential. In such cases, a fear of dependency becomes maladaptive.

Differences among groups. People in single-room-occupancy (SRO) hotels are different from those in both middle-class hotels and those in skid-row hotels. The middle-class group exhibits more intact primary social support systems. The single most evident difference in the middle-class hotels is the greater emphasis on sociality. Residents visit relatives, friends, and neighbors more frequently and are more interested and amenable to voluntary and organized social activity. The skid-row group is younger and much more mobile – they seldom stay in one hotel for more than a few weeks or months, as compared with the group in the working people's single-room-occupancy hotel.

Old-timers. The decision to live in the downtown area appears to be positively made. Inexpensive hotel rents, coupled with the availability of many goods and services, make the downtown practical for a considerable portion of the elderly population – probably for far more than actually live there now if adequate arrangements could be made for them.

Health. On the whole, older hotel dwellers are sicker than age peers in other groups. There is a large number of physical and emotional complaints present in the population. The older, postretirement cohort had nearer to normal self-perceptions of health, as measured by the Cornell Medical Index, whereas the younger, preretirement group perceived themselves to be in poorer health. While the overall level of disability among the SRO residents is high, those in the older cohort (sixty-five and older) deny many of their problems and minimize their needs. They avoid potential helpers from outside the hotel environment for fear those helpers (social workers, nurses, and relatives) will, in their efforts to assist, fail to honor or somehow undermine their self-reliance or their need for control over their own lives.

Infrastructure of services. The urban commercial zone provides the older residents with other important services. The area contains a number of cheap restaurants where they can get balanced meals – an important point often overlooked by planners who say one good restaurant will do, disregarding the need to make choices about running one's own life. Most of the older residents buy second-hand clothing at the Sally (Salvation Army) or Volunteers (Volunteers of America). These clothes are necessary in order to dress one's identity. When one is properly dressed, one is identifiable as a resident and hence not hassled as visitors may be. Discount drug stores were available in which to buy medicine, sundries, shaving needs, and the like. There are several laundromats in the area. Police and other safety provisions are close at hand. The urban zone also provides transportation that is both accessible and affordable. The hustle and bustle of the downtown further provides entertainment in the form of street theater. This infrastructure of services is vitally important to life in the hotels and is always in a very delicate balance.

The hotel itself provides the basic social structure. A resident can be said to rent a role with a room. As a part of the deal, he also gets many basic services, such as housekeeping. The hotel provides furniture, linens, heat, telephone, and security. The hotel staff frequently take a benevolent attitude toward the older residents and provides many services of a nonpersonal nature (and occasionally of a personal nature, such as trimming nails). Because the hotels are the major source of social support, the resident is not required to create a further social network to get many of his needs fulfilled.

The dyad is the unit of the informal structure. Because so many services are provided by the hotel and by the urban zone, the social needs of residents can be (and most often are) reduced to dyadic interaction. Some of the dyads are of superficial content (talking of sports, politics, or gambling). But helping relationships emerged early and consistently throughout the research. Helping relationships usually took the form of dyadic relationships among persons who appeared to interact only minimally under normal circumstances but provided care in crisis situations. When helping extended beyond a short period of time, hotel residents and staff disapproved. The fact that helping occurs at all means that the ethic of self-reliance can be breached. Therefore, helpers must be careful lest they be ostracized and blamed for the fact that those they help do not get better. The most common kind of helping is doing "runs" for the incapacitated. Others include lending money, radios, clothes, and other items. What little wealth is available is thus used maximally.

Sociality. The density of the social networks of residents (the number of people in one's network who know one another) is not high, and the degree of connection is singularly small. When viewing these shallow networks, however, it should never be forgotten that some people have more need for people than others. A large proportion of the hotel population created their characters on the basis of low need for social interaction. The hotels provide a social situation in which this low-need life style is the norm, so that adjustment is not terribly difficult or psychically costly. To an observer whose need for sociality is greater, this life style seems socially impoverished. But these people found it, and they continually re-create it, for it was already there when they entered it. It was an econiche into which they settled. This view should not be seen merely as blaming the victim. Some of these men are victims, in the sense that life has dealt harshly with them. But other people with no more money have found other adjustments. To live in a hotel is a chosen way of life – and it was usually, although not always, chosen before old age set in.

Informal social groups. A few social groups form in the hotels, usually around cliques – the few clusters in the network. These social groups are based on common interest, and, especially, on long-term residence. Interestingly, many have at least one woman in them, although women form only about 10 percent of residents – women seem to offer a kind of social cement that men do not choose to offer or else do not want to need. These groups are ephemeral. They form and disperse, even as others form. They have very limited functions, whereas the dyadic relationships often have important functions in maintaining independence and in mutual assistance. The social structure is simple for a simple reason: These are not socially minded people. The hotel and the environment offer a social world in which residents do not have to participate deeply or heavily.

Character structure. Many of the residents have suffered from physical or psychic catastrophes in their lives either as children or in their adult lives. Their response was to withdraw, to eschew intimacy, dependency, or dependability, even though some of them remain gregarious. Their lives have been built around escaping domesticity, the family, the Protestant ethic of job and success. Many, as they get older, wait almost impatiently for death. But a few have managed to age gracefully and to enjoy the process. We found, perhaps not surprisingly, that these latter were people who had taken one of three courses: (1) understanding themselves and their histories, to achieve what Erickson called "ego integrity," (2) dedicating their lives to helping others, or (3) remodeling their experiences into art (which need not be good art to be effective), particularly poetry and songs. The presence of all these kinds of character structures fit in well with the low-demand quality of the community. The people and the setting were made for each other.

Policy implications

Many of the numerous econiches in which people live are either little understood or are actively misunderstood by people from other niches of society, particularly the middle class (including some middle-class urban planners). Policy makers should be aware of the panhuman tendency toward cultural ethnocentrism – especially the policy makers' own. Policy and planning decisions must include judgments made on the basis of the character structures and adaptations of people on the ground, not just what they ought to be.

Hotels provide an immense amount of care for people, including old people, at a price and with a finesse that is not available in most other extended-care facilities. Institutions care for only about 5 percent of our old people; it is not possible to say what proportion live in hotels. If we expand our views to include all hotels, at all socioeconomic levels, the number is large. The care that people get there is good and it is cheap. A lot of people can live in hotels who do not in fact now do so. That does not mean, of course, that everybody can live so. The point must not be carried too far. But we have, in planning for the elderly, overlooked hotels – and we overlook any asset at our peril.

The processes of urban planning should be encouraged to take longer and wider views. Hotel dwellers in the city centers are a varied group – varied in background and current needs. However, they reflect – indeed, they almost caricature – the most cherished values of American culture. The hotels and commercial neighborhoods in which they are located provide sufficient services to enable residents to continue to live independent and self-reliant lives. Tearing down either the hotels or the surrounding business establishments threatens not only the way of life of these elderly residents but also an immensely valuable social asset – a way of life that, because it is neither family nor institution, is overlooked.

Of course these so-called deteriorated commercial zones have to be developed. But not at the cost of destroying the kind of community that exists within them – exists profitably for us all, because keeping people in hotels is more pleasant and vastly less expensive than other types of institutional care.

Fieldwork and data analysis

Neither anthropological fieldwork nor anthropological data analysis is natural. There are various styles of both. Indeed, separating the fieldwork and the data analysis is itself an analytical exercise. For that reason, it is important to state specifically what was done in any particular instance so that nonanthropologists can judge the exercise or anthropologists can replicate it.

The basic method used by anthropologists – participant observation – has been set forth in detail by Ross and Ross (1974). However, the processes of data manipulation and analysis – what some behavioral scientists call "massaging the data" – have not been equally clearly spelled out. I have drawn on Ross and Ross for the stages of participant observation data gathering. I have added a description of the kind of data analysis necessary at each stage and included a stage to describe the final data analysis.

Stage 1: initial introduction to the field

During this phase of the study, the fieldworker's task is to learn the community – who is in it, where the people go, and what they do. The fieldworker must learn about group differences and various values placed by the participants on their activities. What do people fight about or get angry about? How do they cooperate? This stage takes longer if it is associated with language learning, as it often is for anthropologists. The fact that there is no apparent language problem, however, does not mean that this stage can be avoided, and it may not even mean that it can be shortened.

One of the primary concerns of the initial stage is that the fieldworker take on a set of roles that is comfortable both for himself and also (just as important) for the people being studied. It takes a long time, sometimes several months, for a fieldworker to know his way around in the new cultural setting. And it takes just as long, sometimes longer, for the people in the setting to grant him the grace of familiarity and trust. An experienced anthropologist can shorten this period, but no amount of experience on the part of the anthropologist will do very much to shorten the period of time required for the informants to get used to the anthropologist.

All of the fieldworkers on this project said openly that they were carrying out research and explained the project to anyone who showed any interest at all. No lies were told at any time – an important point in maintaining trust.

Some of the fieldworkers, moreover, took on additional roles. When the project was begun, Anthony Gorman moved into the largest hotel. A man in his middle fifties, he needed no overt role other than resident. We learned that, in hotels, one can rent a role with the room, as it were. The fact that Gorman was working set him apart from others, but comparatively few people ever questioned him about why he was there. Whenever I went into the area, I went as Gorman's friend and co-worker. I never needed any other identity. I spent two weeks living in the hotels to get the feel of them, and I spent a lot of time, both in the daytime and in the evenings, in the area. I took notes. But it was the four fieldworkers who supplied most of the raw data.

Gorman and I immediately began regular debriefing sessions, a process to be spelled out below. Within a few weeks a second fieldworker appeared: Lisa D'Arcy was collecting information on the same community for a thesis at San Diego State University. She sat in on and contributed to most of the debriefing sessions for the next six months. When she had completed her thesis, she undertook to examine women in the area, specific group formations, and did an ethnography of one hotel on subcontract from the NIMH grant. She continued to sit in on the debriefing sessions.

About a year after the fieldwork had begun, Kevin Eckert (then on a predoctoral fellowship from NIMH) came into the area to study the health of the hotel population. He moved into one of the hotels and began participant observation. Eckert became a room clerk in the Knickerbocker Hotel a few months after his arrival; again, both his employer and the residents of the hotel knew that he was collecting material for a thesis. Being a desk clerk was an invaluable supplementary role, and it enabled him to learn at first hand the workings of the hotel and also to talk to many of the guests on business and then to extend such conversations if the residents were amenable – most were. Eckert joined the debriefing sessions. When his period of data gathering and his predoctoral fellowship were over, he joined the staff of Western Behavioral Sciences Institute and became a part of this study.

After still another year, Wayne Rauschkolb, who coded the diaries (see below) and who had assisted us earlier in carrying out a land-use survey of the area, joined us to make specific observations in the hotels. He too became a desk clerk, and he too sat in on the debriefings during the final few months.

Anthropologists at home sometimes are concerned because the people of their own society are said to be so similar to themselves that they either lose the good effects of culture shock, or confuse themselves with their informants, or both. At first, both Gorman and I felt, about our informants, that "There, but for the grace of God . . . " That feeling did not last long. I came to see that, no matter how poor or outcast I might become, I could not make that particular adjustment to poverty, because there are many other adjustments that require no more money but do have more social dimensions. I am not a loner. Gorman's longer stint in the hotels made it possible for him to see that he could make such an adjustment (indeed, for the length of the fieldwork, he did), and to consider it not too difficult a way to live. Watching the fieldworkers and myself during this period, I came to realize that the adjustment required for the fieldworker in his own society may demand a little finer tuning to sense and capitalize on the differences between self and informant but that it was no different in kind from the adjustments of the fieldworker who goes to the Bongobongo.

The debriefing sessions. Debriefing sessions are usually not a factor in anthropological fieldwork (both roles in the debriefing session being played by the ethnographer), but our use of them is vital to our approach in the Unseen Community project. They are a device that allows several anthropologists to work together with a greater sense of purpose than informal meetings among them or even seminars can. And they allow complete touch with the theoretical materials at the very time submersion in the data gathering process is going on.

Debriefing sessions, as we used them, provide an organization – both a social organization and a workflow organization – that allows the fieldworker's data and the debriefer's theoretical concern to come together overtly at all stages of the work. The minimal cast was one fieldworker and the principal investigator (in this case myself). Most of our debriefing sessions were attended by at least two fieldworkers. On a few occasions, other social scientists were invited as guest debriefers, and sometimes an informant would be invited, brought from the hotel by Gorman in his car. We found that the visiting social scientists asked good questions and that sometimes we were given new leads. Only a few informants were successful – most were uncomfortable with the high verbal level, and most had never before looked at their own social situation so analytically. In the debriefing sessions, we spoke our language, not theirs, but they were often quoted and the quotations set into context.

How a debriefing session works. At regular intervals that varied from three days to three weeks depending on the stage of the participant observation, the fieldworkers and the principal investigator got together, usually in the latter's office. Each fieldworker reviewed his or her notes in some detail with a tape recorder going. The need to explain the situation to the principal investigator made for greater detail than was ever achieved in written notes. The task of the principal investigator was to ask probing questions. Sometimes this process – both the fuller explanations and the questions – uncovered whole new dimensions in which the fieldworker might concentrate effort.

As items or whole areas began to show up as important, it was possible for the principal investigator to formulate questions of theoretical significance. Sometimes I asked for more information. For example, Gorman early reported his own concerns about security in the hotels. In order to allay his concern, we decided that he would ask specific questions about locks on the rooms, hotel policy for visitors and strangers, and coping mechanisms that other residents used. Sometimes the very fact that the kind of information I asked for could be the wrong kind of question was instructive. For example, the groups of old men who sat in the lobby of the Golden West Hotel had a limited membership. Gorman discovered, when he tried to join in, that these cliques resisted a stranger. He also found, however, that he could join them over a period of time by expressing interest and knowledge to group members, outside the group setting, about the discussion topics – racing in one case (about which Gorman didn't know or choose to learn much) and politics in another. The groups, nevertheless, seemed amorphous. My question was, "What is the leadership situation? Who holds them together?" Gorman could not answer the question; he said that there wasn't any. I pursued the point. Gorman returned to the groups and finally asked one member (when the two of them were alone) what he thought about the question of leadership in the group. The informant described one man as the leader, because he was the most helpful to all the others. This insight – that "leadership" is a wrong-headed notion (which we knew) and its place is taken in the formulations of the clique members by "helpfulness" (which we did not know) – became one of our important leads into what we eventually came to call "helping networks."

Thus, when an item or a whole area began to show up as important, it was possible for me to formulate questions about the possible theoretical significance at the same time that the fieldworker was looking into the importance of these data for the people themselves and hence for the ethnographic record.

Obviously, at one level, every fieldworker does this kind of questioning. Nevertheless, we found that having two minds and a social interaction made it far more efficient, and it kept us in touch with both ends of the process (the data and the theory) throughout the course of the fieldwork. I came to play for the fieldworker something of the same role a supervisor plays in psychoanalysis. Psychoanalysts, during their early cases (and later, when they encounter difficulties in their cases) have a supervisor with whom they can talk through problems. The supervisor can ask questions from a new viewpoint (in part because he or she can take the personality of the analyst into account) that allows significant reduction of error and speeds the enterprise. The debriefings, it has become evident, form a running preliminary analysis.

Running analysis of the findings. The debriefings were, at first, transcribed. However, transcription created some difficulties. It meant that all of the interaction among the participants, no matter how trivial or irrelevant, got into the record, making the record unwieldy. Attempts to hold such trivia to a minimum created a kind of self-consciousness that allowed no progress at all. It meant we could not explore one another's personalities to the same extent, and it meant that serendipity had been excluded. It was simply uncomfortable to know that every remark would appear on paper and even more distracting to try to turn off the recorder during the irrelevant interchanges, because they sometimes turned up important serendipitous discoveries.

Therefore, full transcription was stopped early. I took over the job of transcribing the tapes, taking down only relevant data, sometimes in full, usually in note form. Now, instead of eighty pages of transcript from a debriefing session, we had twenty pages of compact notes: All meat and no waffle.

These notes differ significantly from a fieldworker's notes. They contain not only data, but, clearly demarcated as such, formulations and preliminary analyses. Some of these latter points can be suggested to fieldworkers, more or less as assignments. Others go back to form the protodraft of analysis. We found only one possible difficulty. One must allow for the fact that the fieldworker's task is to discover what is there, not to bring in information to please the supervisor. It demands full trust between the two, including the very important capacity of the fieldworker to suggest that I was wrong.

Preliminary indexing. The annotated transcripts were then indexed. This task – like every other task in this process – cannot be left to clerical assistants. Obviously some of them could create an index. But the creation of the index is an essential part of the learning process for the person who is ultimately to write the reports. It is dull, but it is essential.

The indexing process is much the same as indexing a book. I often wrote the headings into the margins of the annotated transcript (but sometimes did not). Any time later it is possible to transfer the headings to cards. I found that doing this every three or four months was enough, and allowed me to review the notes while I was doing the transferring, thereby keeping them fresh in my mind. This is something that no fieldworker can take time to do. The fieldworker is not in the right "time frame" to do this job, because it takes attention away from what is happening right now, which is where the fieldworker's attention belongs.

The indexing categories were created as the fieldwork and preliminary analysis progressed. It was occasionally necessary to go back and insert new headings that had not seemed important when the information was first transcripted.

From these cards (and sometimes directly, without the cards), and from continually referring back to the transcripts, I typed up the basic information under each category on what can be called "subject sheets." These sheets had headings such as "crime in the streets," "food," and the like; sometimes they were all the references to an individual; sometimes they were about the desk clerks and policies of a specific hotel; the point is that the level of generalization in the heading is not important at this stage. What is important is to get together in one place all that is known about a specific subject.

The indexing process is carried out by many anthropologists, but when they work alone, it is necessarily done after the fieldworker returns from the field. Again, the advantages of splitting the task are obvious: The collation of information can be done efficiently while the fieldworker is still in the field. The fieldworker can go back to check on, enlarge, or extend findings.

An important point is that it is necessary to go over the debriefing notes and the case history transcripts several times, at several months' interval, so that new ideas can be worked through and old ideas rescued and all of it fitted together into a continually expanding view of the total problem.

Stage 2: focused research

At the second stage of the research, the fieldworker narrows the focus. A contextual background already exists. In this stage, the note taking also changes – the fieldworker does not have to take notes on many items, because they would be merely repetitive. Checking out to see whether matters have changed is enough. Having learned who the people are and what is important to them, the fieldworker can now zero in on those important points.

The narrowing and focusing of the fieldworker's activities means that, ipso facto, his or her role has changed somewhat. Both fieldworker and informants have some minor adjustments to make in this phase, because the fieldworker no longer pays as much attention to some of the activities that people think important in the first phase. However, by keeping in touch and checking out change as it occurs, the change in focus should be only minimally noticed by the residents. In this phase of the fieldwork, we kept in touch with all activities but focused our attention only on those that we knew would be part of our final report – food, psychological adjustment, medical problems and responses, and social organization.

It was also during this period that the greatest number of our case histories were collected, because the case histories provided an opportunity not only to obtain life stories (which were important at this phase) but also to obtain specific reactions to specific events in hotel life. The free-association interview was the primary method for gathering these data.

Case histories. As it became evident that certain modes of adjustment – sometimes whole character structures – were shared by many residents, our need for information about the earlier lives of residents and their views of such adjustment became pressing. Fortunately, we had built thirty case histories into our original design. We collected thirty-seven such histories, which we ultimately came to call "autobiographies." We asked specifically about respondents' childhoods – whether severe trauma in the childhood was of specific importance – as well as about their job and family histories. We knew that many residents had spotty job histories with little commitment and many changes of job; we knew that most were unmarried and that some had never married. We wanted to know more details of their lives and what their own evaluations of them were.

During the interview, we held to an out-of-sight program or schedule, but seldom was it administered like a questionnaire. In a few cases we did administer it purposely, to see how much loss of spontaneity would result. We decided that the loss was too great and so continued with selected informants in the free-association interview. The structure remained in the head of the interviewer, not overt in the interview situation.

Gorman, who did most of the interviews, talked mainly to people whom he had known for weeks or months and who had come to trust him. Most of the interviews were done either in Gorman's room or in the autobiographer's room in the hotel. Informants were encouraged to tell him about their lives and were paid a small amount, five dollars, for doing it. An occasional question asked when a subject had not been exhausted allowed us to cover the points on our schedule without turning it into a visible instrument, although it was nonetheless an instrument for that.

Analysis of autobiographies. The autobiographies were recorded and transcribed. I then indexed them in the same way I did the notes from the debriefing sessions and my own fieldnotes.

Such autobiographies are sometimes questioned by some researchers on the ground that they are false to the facts. That is, people adjust and adapt their autobiographies in the processes of adjusting to the present. Indeed, if they cannot do that, they are almost by definition mentally ill. Thus, the autobiographies must be analyzed in terms of the current situation of the respondent and what this particular arrangement of the facts, with its characteristic sets of emphases, does for the respondent. "God's truth" has no place in an autobiography (Collingwood, 1946). It is information about the present and about the processes of adaptation and adjustment, not a historical document about the truth of the past.

I edited fifteen of the autobiographies – in other words, I rearranged the material into approximate chronological order and changed the names of all persons and places, if the place names could identify the respondent. The edited version was typed up and shown to the autobiographer. He was paid another five dollars to verify the autobiography and make any changes in it he desired. Several changes were made, but we did not honor several requests that real names be used.

The first two stages of fieldwork are not separated clearly – one phase drifts into the other. One cannot say, "Today is the first of November, time to go into Stage 2." Rather, one finds oneself saying, "I know that already, I had better concentrate on such and such." Continuous analysis is essential, however, in clarifying just where one is and how much one does not know.

Stage 3: systematization and measurement

Stage 3 emerges when the focused attention of the fieldworker reveals precisely what details or quantities are needed to bring the research to a successful outcome. Thereupon, the fieldworker is likely to add new and subsidiary techniques to the continuing processes of participant observation. Thus participant observation, especially when it is accompanied by careful running preliminary analysis, gives rise to a number of problems for which the participant observation method may not be the best solution technique. Therefore, we built into our design a number of subsidiary techniques that we used to measure and systematize those aspects of the fieldwork on which we had focused, particularly matters of food, networks, and health.

Panel interviews. When we worked with autobiographies and with information that is taken from notes on participant observation, many questions necessarily arose about whether what we have seen (or what one or more of our autobiographies revealed) was typical, and, if so, for what population. Our design was such that we could turn to survey research techniques to find the answers to these questions once we had pinpointed the questions in the focus stage of our fieldwork. Survey research, on a properly drawn sample, is of course the method par excellence for answering the question "How many?" when participant observation brings the researcher to the realization that "Some do and some don't."

We administered three questionnaires to a panel of residents, a sample derived from all the men over the age of fifty living in twelve hotels (for details see Erickson and Eckert, 1977). These questionnaires were precoded, which allowed us to use traditional statistical techniques for analysis (Erickson and Eckert, 1977).

Although the tests of the questionnaires were carried out by the fieldworkers, the questionnaires, once tested, were for the most part not administered by fieldworkers. (The exception is that Eckert administered a portion of the second and third questionnaires, because they contained information specifically relevant to health, which he was working on.) This is an important point, because it avoids role conflict on the part of the fieldworker. Even more important, it avoids the informants' seeing conflict in the purposes of the fieldworker, who has come on as friendly and sharing, not as somebody who pays for specific information in a structured interview.

Three questionnaires were put to our panel. The first was about sociality and security and other important topics garnered from the participant observation. The second and third focused more clearly on health: The second was the administration as a questionnaire of the Cornell Medical Index, after we determined by testing that this population could not fill it out in written form, in which it is usually administered.

The questionnaires offered us hard data about the categories and ideas that had turned up in the participant observation. None of the quantitative material we obtained by means of the survey research techniques could have been obtained through observation alone, although the questions or their suitability could not have been determined without the observation. One needs both.

Diaries. Because we also wanted to know about what people ate and how they spent their time, energy, and money, and because we wanted detailed data over a period of time greater than recall in a questionnaire would provide, we obtained diaries from thirty-seven members of the sample for whom we had information on the questionnaires. These thirty-seven were the only people who either could or would participate. We soon discovered that this population could not keep a detailed diary without assistance. Those who tried only wrote of the weather and recorded a few clichéd good thoughts. That is an interesting datum, but it did not help us in determining how these people ate, slept, and associated. Therefore, we created a diary booklet of eight pages, including a series of questions. Some of the respondents could keep their own diaries, but most could not and had to be visited every day or every other day by either a fieldworker or an interviewer to ensure that the diaries were kept. This netted us thirty-seven diaries of one week each. The accomplishment was considerably greater than that summary sentence would seem to indicate.

The diaries were coded in an orthodox way: I created the codebook, after which Wayne Rauschkolb (who later became a field observer) took information from the diaries about the food that people ate, the number of hours they slept, and the people they interacted with.

Thus just as Stage 2 fieldwork allows one to set specific problems into the context that is mastered in Stage 1, so Stage 3 fieldwork allows one to be specifically detailed and accurate about those problems on which one focused in Stage 2.

The stereotype of the anthropological fieldworker often reflects only an inadequate understanding of Stage 1 – people who suggest that participant observation is subjective, or soft, are limiting their appreciation of the method to Stage 1. The number of anthropologists who limit their methods to Stage 1 is, today, very small; however, since it is the part that is most fun, it is often the part that they talk about.

Stage 4: final data analysis

After one leaves the field, the final stages of data preparation take place – the coded material is analyzed and the tasks of creating, completing, and in some cases cross-referencing annotated subject sheets and index is completed.

It is the process of these final stages of data analysis that dictates the form in which the data and analyses will be presented for publication. Just as it is a false exercise to separate (in any way except intellectually) the processes of data gathering and data analysis, so it is a false division to separate data analysis from writing. At least preliminary analysis of the data from Stage 1 of participant observation must be achieved in order to get into the second stage of focused research; the preliminary running analysis, when properly carried out, reduces the time period and increases the effectiveness with which the focused research of Stage 2 can be undertaken. Again, further analysis must take place before one can go from the focused research of Stage 2 to the systematization and measurement part of Stage 3. Collation of all this data, which has been proceeding all along, is completed in Stage 4, which overlaps with the writing – indeed, one might consider Stage 4 completed only when the writing of reports is completed.

The easiest way to examine the processes of data analysis is to put them on a timeflow chart, together with the stages of fieldwork and of writing, remembering that the distinction between stages is useful for explanation but that the several sets of processes cannot be kept completely distinct in the doing (Figure 3.1).

This leaves one major topic that, on the surface, appears larger when one is working in one's own society but which in fact is no different from what anthropologists have concerned themselves with traditionally: To whom is one responsible, to what extent, and how is that responsibility expressed? One owes it to one's informants to leave them at least as well off as one found them and not to misrepresent them. This is sometimes difficult with people who want to present themselves to the world in a way that does not bear up under scrutiny. Fortunately, we did not encounter this problem. We helped when we could, just as our informants help each other. And we found that our help turned out to be the kind of help that anthropologists traditionally give in exotic societies: rides, information, hospitality, small loans, food, tobacco. Our informants have checked their own autobiographies and made corrections. We have discussed our interpretations with them. We have been extremely careful to protect their identities.

We hope hotel residents can be made more comfortable in the process of urban development, and we would, if necessary, fight city hall for their rights to stay independent. Fortunately, in San Diego there is no need for that. Our rapport with officials was good after an initial period in which they feared we would try to stop the redevelopment as the Yerba Buena project had been stopped in San Francisco. When they discovered our true purposes and when we began to exchange information with them, they and we saw that our problems were all held in common, and we cooperated fully with one another.

No study in one's own society – perhaps none in the world – is without policy implications. But today we know that anthropological field techniques are among the best ways of illuminating the unseen places of the greater American social structure and that the variety of life-styles found in those places is what makes for freedom and self-determination for us all.

Epilogue

One of the readers of this manuscript wrote the following comments about the foregoing chapter:

Bohannan's paper . . . deals with a very interesting problem with major policy implications. Unfortunately, it slips too quickly over the problem/policy question into standard issues of research which should already be familiar to most students of anthropology. We would like to see this paper reorganized with less emphasis on methodology. It also disturbs us somewhat that the researchers were more interested in observing the consequences of forced dislocation, than becoming involved in attempting to stop it or impact on it, in view of the fact that they seemed to begin their project with the notion that elderly individuals had established support networks that should not be disrupted. We question the ethics of this kind of research and would like to see the issue addressed in this paper.

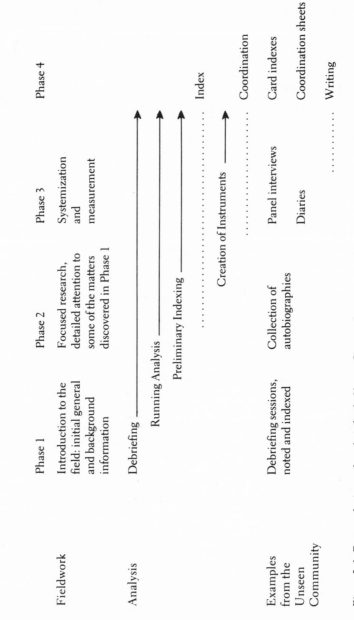

	Phase 1	Phase 2	Phase 3	Phase 4
Fieldwork	Introduction to the field: initial general and background information	Focused research, detailed attention to some of the matters discovered in Phase 1	Systemization and measurement	
Analysis	Debriefing ——————————————————————————→			
		Running Analysis ———————————————→		
		Preliminary Indexing ——————→		Index
			Creation of Instruments ——————→	Coordination
Examples from the Unseen Community	Debriefing sessions, noted and indexed	Collection of autobiographies	Panel interviews	Card indexes
			Diaries	Coordination sheets
			·············	Writing

Figure 3.1. Data gathering and analysis for the Unseen Community.

These charges are important enough that I would like to respond to them, for they seem to me to be misunderstandings of the issues involved in urban research.

First, the methodology section of this paper was first written in direct response to a request for such a paper from the administrators of our grant at the National Institute of Mental Health. They asked for such a paper because, they said, the overall quality of the methods sections of anthropological applications is miserable. Having read a number of such applications, I cannot but agree. There are, of course, many exceptions, but a clear statement of what anthropologists *do* when they are working in an urban situation appears in too few applications and nowhere in the published literature, as far as I know. If I am wrong, I hope that someone will correct me.

Second, it disturbs me that the reader wants me to "stop" or "impact on" the very process I should be studying before I have any information about it. There is a delicate moral (but scarcely ethical) situation here. I presume that the writer of the critique knows that the developer of every urban project is required by law to see that people who are displaced by the project are resettled, without cost to them, in equal or better accommodations, and that all American cities have special services to assist such people. We worked sympathetically and in detail with the people who run those services in San Diego. After their initial consternation that we considered them part of our research project was dispelled, we became colleagues in determining just what the costs might be. They and we both knew the hotels intimately; they, like us, interviewed people there; they and we compared notes and ideas about the impact of resettlement and how to make it profitable for the people who would be affected.

We did indeed begin this project with the "notion" (it was actually more formal than that – it was a hypothesis that proved wrong) that elderly individuals living in run-down hotels in the center city have established support networks. By and large, they have not. Their networks are shallow and transient. It is, by and large, part of the life adjustment of these people to run from the commitment that a support network implies. If we had taken action before we discovered the true situation, we would have created a hullabaloo for nothing, perhaps even forcing the old men into commitments they have spent lifetimes trying to avoid.

In my opinion, the city officials and the developer are as much a part of our study as are the hotel residents. If the city and the developer were in fact going to damage the residents, and if the anthropologists are to make a fuss about it, they must do so on the basis of provable fact. In this case, there were no such facts to prove.

As this note is written (June 1980), my colleague, Dr. J. Kevin Eckert, is in San Diego working with the people (fewer than fifty) who will be moved from the four hotels that will be destroyed – far smaller numbers than we originally thought. A full report on who did what to whom and the ethical issues involved will be forthcoming from him, once redevelopment is in fact achieved.

In short, I agree with the proposition that this issue should be addressed, but I seriously disagree with the premises on which this reader seems to have made the remarks.

4 Common sense and science: urban core black observations

JOHN L. GWALTNEY

My own communities of enculturation were among the beleaguered but undaunted northeastern United States black enclaves in which I conducted the research that informs this chapter. The year 1973–1974, which I spent at home doing my most protracted indigenous anthropology,[1] was the culmination of a lifetime of organic participant observation. As an outsider, I had attempted to gain a representative impression of variations upon the human cultural theme among peoples as diverse as Shinnecocks and Chinantecs (Gwaltney 1970, 1973). During the course of research among cultures that were often strange to me, I often wished for an opportunity to employ social science as an insider with the general view of drawing an indigenously derived description of salient aspects of Afro-American communal character that the prudent core black masses could recognize as a representative impression. We are a great and splendid people with all the virtues and vices requisite to that preeminence. Our survival on terms that obviously are not totally of our enemies' making is awesome evidence of our particular cultural genius. The Euro-American, for a plethora of conscious and unconscious considerations, has often chosen to deny the very existence of that cultural genius. (For a discussion of this phenomenon see, for example, Blauner 1970.)

The enclaves in which I worked, all things considered, were a part of the native world described by Fanon (1968).

In Sartre's preface to Fanon's *The Wretched of the Earth*, the use of the terms native and settler implies that racial distinction which is also reflected in the current inequitable distribution of the strategic resources of the world. Natives tend to be poor, powerless and non-white while settlers tend to be characterized by the arrogance of power and wealth. [Gwaltney 1976:236]

I share the common belief of the people of these North American "native" enclaves that their cultures have been traditionally misrepresented in the literature. The three prime purposes of this research, therefore, were indigenous, core black evaluation of some main premises of social science, indigenous definition of core black culture, and the use of anthropology as a means of "setting the record straight" (D. Jones 1970:258).

46

The setting

A number of environments exist within the cramped confines of the northeastern urban enclaves in which I conducted this research. Shelter for the hundreds of persons whose confidence and generosity made this research possible ranged from a large, clean packing case to castellated luxury apartment blocks. It is, however, no exaggeration to say that the dominant environment of town life in these black enclaves is that of peril. The inhabitants of these enclaves have the reprehensible and entirely unmerited distinction of residence in the closest North American equivalent to the insecurity of medieval towns or bombed-out modern cities. The current urban desolation is seen as an intensification of a diachronic reality. Many of my informants and I can remember when many of these enclaves were comparatively flourishing and infinitely less perilous places to live. But our grandparents knew very well the lessons of deadly force that are part and parcel of Euro-American castelike organization. The painful awareness of the occupied status of these black population centers is common to persons of all generations.

I'd be a fool if I thought that army was our army. If it's my army and guard and navy and all that, will you tell me why it was shooting at me here a few years ago? If anybody can be the president, why all them dudes look like they do? If you could see the money you would see that there just are none of us on it! It's their money just like it's their country and their damned army and their damned everything else. [fieldnotes]

The exotic, relatively accessible marginals, addicts, or those to whom welfare has become a way of life were minimal elements in the field populations I worked among. I wished to arrive at an indigenous explication of core black culture generated by the vast majority of Afro-Americans. I mean those whom Billingsley (1971:33) describes as "self-supporting," with "stable marriages," and who "despite the grossest kinds of discrimination and provocation . . . manage to keep out of trouble" and "meet the American test of family stability" – those whom my sister calls the "clean poor." This life style is seen as *core* black and is not imitative black bourgeois affectation.

Native anthropology

It has been said that the life history can be a bridge between common sense and science (Allport 1942). Minority scholars recognize a profound need for such a linkage between their cultures as they know them and as they often see them portrayed in the literature (see, for example, D. Jones 1970, Murray 1970, Galarza 1971, Willis 1973, Hsu 1973, and Ortego 1973). This disparity between native perceptions and formal scientific representations is generally held to be indicative of a bias that is as much a part of white approaches to science as it is endemic in all areas of Euro-American–directed life. Science is not seen as some ideal process but as a vehicle that can serve interested or objective ends. Black people, by and large, do not respect the so-called science of scientists they cannot respect. They are not surprised when formal portrayals of their reigning cultural styles are skewed to project core black culture as sick, sordid, and criminal. Glazer and Moynihan's (1963) view of blacks as having no culture or indigenous values to defend is just another indication that much of science is a part of the fixed game of caste, another permutation of the conspiratorial big lie that is crucial to the maintenance of white supremacy.

I know that science is what scientists make it. If the scientist is not a person of good will, and even nature, then he will produce a bad science. I would not condemn all white social scientists because I didn't like something one of them did. That, I do know, is what most white people have done to me. Worse even, they have condemned me because of what they think the black people who live only in their imaginations would do to them for what they have actually done to me. It is very complicated and it goes way back beyond our grandfather's times and the only way to end it is to end it. So I will end it insofar as I can by treating everybody in the same way that I would like them to treat me . . . To survive is not enough. You have to survive for something and I would like to see a world in which everybody stands on his own capacity. I know that white men are afraid of such a world but I don't really think they should be. [fieldnotes]

Indigenous elucidation of salient aspects of core black communal character and common-sense core black assessments of some main social science premises conspire to augment the currently minimal body of native anthropology. As a number of minority scholars have pointed out, native anthropology is not the incorporation of personnel drawn from previously underrepresented, power-deprived subordinate societies into the settler social science establishment. Properly understood, native anthropology is the incorporation of traditionally ignored perspectives into theory building. Many of the people who helped me to conduct this research were aware that the expression of their views might not only occasion honest controversy but might indeed provoke that critical reaction that arises from the traditional short shrift often accorded the native view simply because it is the native view.

You know that the whites will not thank you if you tell them the truth. The whites will punish you if you put what I have just told you in a book because the truth is poison to them. The truth should be written because the truth should be written, but it will not change them you know. Be careful. [fieldnotes]

Native anthropology is a reaction against the colonial model that looms so large in social science. The people of subordinate societies have traditionally produced crude data, and the social scientist, generally some kind of powerful stranger, has refined and analyzed this material. Personal explication of data by the donors of those data establishes indigenous perceptions of meaning. Donors of life histories quite correctly regarded their life histories as unique and vital. There is a general belief that everyone is his or her own best interpreter of the life he or she has led. Interpretive interjections were routine in these personal documents: "Now I said that to say this." "Now that's what I said, but this is what I mean." "If I'd 'a said what I meant, this is what I'd 'a said." Those who were gracious enough to donate life histories took it for granted, then, that their interpretation of their data was indispensible to the proper understanding of that material, and many people alluded quite specifically to the danger that outsiders would impose their own meaning on their data.

I wouldn't want to talk to any anthropologist or sociologist or any of those others if they were white because whatever I said they would write down whatever they felt like so I might just as well save my breath.

I don't think that a white interviewer would tell the truth about what I told him. The white women in the office where I work never really pay any attention to the answers I give to the questions they ask me. Sometimes I play a little game with them. I just say the first thing I happen to think of and they always go on just as if I had given them a reasonable answer. White people don't care any more for our opinions then we do for theirs, but we do at least listen to them. [fieldnotes]

Magorah Maruyama's (1974) belief in the capacity of natives to build theory in their own right is shared by every black scholar of consequence that I have ever known. Nobel Laureate Baruch Blumberg's observation that "science is not as scientific as people think it is" (*People* magazine, Mar. 14, 1977, p. 51) goes to the heart of the most unfortunate consequence of the social science colonial model.

The tendency to equate the settler social science establishment's imperfect, often arrogant, and partisan pursuit of the truth with verity itself has fostered the myth that science *is* what it is seeking. This widely held, erroneous assumption, together with the defensive, decorous pomposity that often forms a part of the ritual of established social science, affords only perfunctory recognition of the views of tribal, peasant, and other subordinate societies. The equally erroneous a priori assumption that the native view is possessed of some kind of intrinsic superiority simply because it is a native view was never maintained by the field populations with which I collaborated.

Francis Hsu (1973:6) has observed that the relatively unqualified preeminence of the Euro-American logical models imposes a "psychocultural bondage" upon many white social scientists. Alternate logical models derived from hitherto underrepresented, subordinate, and misrepresented cultures will introduce the often fruitful criterion of difference. The logical models of core black and other currently power-deprived cultures merit a more serious and sensitive reception before a more open and polyglot social scientific institution.

Methodology

As an insider I worked with friends and relatives and the friends of friends and relatives. The vast bulk of the data elicited by this research emerged from the dialogue of folk seminars (small discussion groups) and personal documents supplied by these gracious and sagacious donors. As the research was only tangentially statistical, concentrating primarily upon depth and reflection, I relied heavily upon these methodological media, because they permit a maximum of analytical refinement through the exchange of ideas and reflection. The recurrent cultural themes manifest in the individual and group contexts of the life history and the folk seminars produced an impressionistic, composite view of core black culture.

Many informants were prompted to participate in the research by that deference that core black culture displays toward blind people. Like all cultures, core black culture makes its own traditional kinds of room for people, places, and things. As a blind ethnologist, I was generally assigned a place in that capacious, ambivalent category reserved for the "sick and afflicted." The injunction to assist the sick and afflicted is rooted in traditional notions of theology and fair play. Arbitrary disregard of this injunction carries for some the prospect of divine retribution. In this culture, doing this kind of work, blindness often proved to be an asset rather than a handicap. Traditionalists know that this attitude is not universal among black people and that there are certain marginals who display a desperate disregard for the traditional civilities.

Now you take somebody in your condition, do you think the people out here who would rather get over than work would have any mercy on you? No, they would just as soon rob you as they would anybody else out here.

Be cool out here Rigo, you know some of these dudes have forgot everything their mamas ever taught them. They'd tap you in a minute if that shit told them to do that. I'm trying to get out from under this number, and if I make it you'll hear from me, and if I don't we best to stay apart. [fieldnotes]

For purely cultural considerations rooted in the transgenerational tradition of racism, the race of any social scientist is important in all the enclaves in which I worked. Color, however, is but one of a number of factors weighed by core black informants in their response to a request for assistance from any social scientist. In core black culture the prudent masses are as meticulous in their choice of an anthropologist as a social scientist should be in the selection of an informant.

The assumption that I would take personal responsibility for the security and anonymity of the people who consented to assist me was, of course, instrumental in any decision to cooperate with me. Implicit in the mutual confidence that made the project possible was the certainty that I would not shun the drudgery attendant upon the proper maintenance of that confidence and anonymity. I could not, of course, farm out the data to secretaries, graduate assistants, or anyone likely to have knowledge of any of the enclaves investigated. Being a professional in the eyes of those field populations in no way excuses me from the more mundane tasks of my calling. Given my own grounding in both the ethics of the core black variant of common sense and of science, it was equally unthinkable for me to turn this material over to strangers. I have spent years transcribing the data amassed by this research project.

Core black culture runs upon the oils of circumspection, reciprocity, and improvisation. Getting beyond the barrier that is the bane of so many outsiders requires relatively untrammeled access to the considered but unguarded thinking of a justly suspicious people who are normally quite content to say infinitely less than they really mean.

Personal documents and folk field seminars

The folk field seminar is a child of many parents. It is rooted in the tradition of fending and proving (the art of clandestine slave exegesis), and there is a direct line of dialogue and debate that extends from brush arbor to barbershop. Children ingest notions of propriety with their mother's milk, and enculturation is grounding in the logic of one's culture.

Given the climate of race relations in the United States, it is certain that the undue emphasis placed upon street-corner culture and the preponderant exotica that looms so large in the literature is in part caused by the avoidance of whites by the prudent black masses. Black core culture has never believed in black powerlessness or subscribed to the notion that it is some kind of subcultural tail on an Euro-American dog.

Ain't nothing ours but us and they tried to say we didn't even own ourself . . . I get tired of that one nation under God boogi-joogi. We are ourselves. We are our own nation or country or whatever you want to call it. We are not no one-tenth of some white something! [fieldnotes]

Knowledge of any culture is a prime factor in the relevant translation of anthropological data into profoundest meaning. The life history, then, is made intelligible by what is already known. All anthropology strives for the inside view. If, as almost always happens, the outsider cannot be an insider, he or she must take more than deliberate speed to enlist some insider and indirectly acquire field data. A corps of natives assiduously contributing and moiling for the paydirt of research is an indispensable fixture of anthropology.

There was general agreement in folk seminars that the insider-versus-outsider question was being debated unrealistically among white social scientists. Anthropological field-work was seen as an effort to become an insider. Outsiders endeavoring to acquire insiders' perspectives in black culture have reported a "gulf" (Keiser 1970:229) or "fence" (Liebow 1967:250–251) beyond which they could not go. But it is plain that they would penetrate this cultural barrier if they could.

There is a pervasive preoccupation with the weight of the unjust social order that rests upon our backs, and that concern leaves little time for such disembodied abstractions as universal access. Under the conditions actually obtaining in the real world now, the insider position is imperative for profoundest research in black communities.

I came over here because I wanted to help you if I could. But I can't see what good it would do me to help some white man do your job. They don't worry much about my troubles. You see I got the same ones I had the last time you saw me. Luther, me, you, anybody out here has the same problems and are dealing with the very same shit that our foreparents had to deal with. The man is evermore talking about changing but do you see it? No, and you ain' gon' see it either! [fieldnotes]

A generative nucleus of friends, relatives, and their friends were contributors of personal documents and organizers of folk field seminars from which other donors of personal documents emerged. Folk seminars were small discussion groups that met in places as diverse as private homes, barbershops, churches, vacant lots, the courts of housing projects, taverns, and hospital rooms. As few as three and as many as twenty of us met in informal discussion groups that were roughly analogous to Hessler and New's (1972) research commune. We were, however, all insiders preoccupied exclusively with the evaluation of some main premises of social science generally, ethnology particularly, and the nature of core black culture. A high level of pertinent, often profound, inter-change was generally sustained. Life circumstances and particularity of interests oc-casioned shifts in the complements of folk seminars. Many groups, however, retained a nucleus of dedicated personnel from which many of those who elected to give life histories were drawn. In a very real sense, many participants in folk field seminars chose to associate themselves with the project. People who had heard about the research from me or some other participant came and often interested others in the research.

Many of the most active donors of personal documents and organizers of folk field seminars were chronically ill. Chronically ill people are often obliged by the circum-stances of their lives to make profound assessments of the quality of life in its individual and group manifestations. Chronically ill people often have extensive ties with local theological and fraternal organizations that are of great value in research of this nature. Most of the chronically ill people I worked with seek employment whenever they can and are consequently in a position to offer personal accounts of the quality of ameliorative programs and indigenous ideas about the improvement of such services. Chronically ill people often have larger blocks of time to devote to participation in field seminars and the donation of personal documents.

The main tendency of this research was from the commonality to the particularity. The cultural vector formed by the convergence of life histories is impressionistic and only incidentally statistical. The vector produced by the interrelation of these life histories is a bridge between indigenously perceived concepts of common sense and science. Indigenous notions of the self-evident, the supernatural, the lessons of history, and the nature of humanity are at least as valid as any other cultural views of these vital concepts. From these internally derived traditional analyses of the heavens, nature, and humanity, blacks have been building theory on every conceivable level.

Securing access and establishing rapport

The quality of access in the black enclaves in which this research was conducted is intimately bound to the general national condition. The more onerous the restrictions of caste organization, the more reluctant subordinate populations are to cooperate with powerful strangers. Slavery is a common heritage of these enclaves, and taxation is consequently generally held to be simple extortion. Many informants expressed the view that their thoughts were about the only thing they had that the powerful Euro-American center could not commandeer: "You can read my letters but you sure can't read my mind."

A general feeling that they would not be accorded access to the environing Euro-American ethnic communities engenders an opposition to according social scientists from those communities serious entrée to core black enclaves. Neither access nor social science are perceived as abstractions devoid of crucial considerations of reciprocity. The shock waves of the violence and intolerance that are necessary elements of unjust social organization do, of course, intensify the reluctance of the prudent core black masses to cooperate with the foreigner. In most of the black enclaves I studied there are considerable numbers of Euro-American runaway children and young men and women living as uninvited but generally unharassed guests. The civility that these strangers are generally accorded is in marked contrast to the uncivil surveillance accorded many black people in the white residential communities that often ring black towns.

The insolence and programmed inadequacy of the very institutional offices that are ostensibly designed to render community services, and the entrepreneurial legerdemain and brigandage common in these enclaves, strongly militate against anything like general access. In this context, the use of the social science devices upon which this research relied almost exclusively, the folk seminar and the personal document, would certainly have been impossible for foreign observers. I chose the life history and folk seminar because they are social devices that foster a maximum of self-expression. The sense of security requisite to any protracted expression of personal and social expression was augmented by listening to life histories in the homes of donors or in the homes of donors' friends or relatives. Indigenous concepts of civic responsibility were important in the decision of many donors and seminar participants to cooperate with me. The desire to assist a native career and to facilitate a project of indigenous relevance was instrumental in the thinking of many donors. The vast majority of the people who participated in this project equate ethnic solidarity with civic responsibility. A few members of folk seminars declared their willingness to talk to any social scientist but subsequent discussions made it abundantly clear that most of these people were not really prepared to discuss their feelings, convictions, and philosophy with anyone perceived of as the shadow of the shadow of castelike coercion.

I give everybody a break who will not hang me up for being nice. There are probably many white people who are as honest as we are. Well, there are certainly some. I guess there can't be many or the country would not be as rotten as it is. Anyway, since I can't tell the good ones from the rest, I have as little to do with any of them as I can.

It's hard to say what you would do until it's time to do it. I have the feeling that I would much rather talk about something important with a black person. It has been my experience that white people don't really want to talk to me. [fieldnotes]

Listening, that indispensable element of rapport and analysis, should be even more attentive to the unconventional. Amamu Amiri Baraka's (L. Jones 1967:66) observation that "bums know at least as much about the world as Senator Fulbright" would not be regarded an an especially surprising view in any black enclave I know. But it is the kind of statement that might be dismissed as extravagance or mindless militancy by some out-siders. An observant scholar would consider the matrix from which this statement proceeds. What does it indicate about indigenous concepts of self-confidence and world view? What does it say about indigenous perceptions of the quality of statecraft? To what extent is this fairly common ill opinion justified, and why is its existence a surprise to anybody?

The stock folk caveats in the weighing of evidence and the assessment of reliability run through the discourse of folk seminars and personal documents. "It wasn't told to me, I only heard." "If what I'm gon' tell you is not what God loves, then Heaven ain' clean, crackers ain' mean, and Jericho's wall is stannin' tall." There is a demonstration of that same concern for the truth in that admirable life history of that admirable black hero, Nate Shaw, when he told his biographer (Rosengarten 1974:3): "If I tell any kind of story that I think was just something told to entertain, I'll say, 'That's what I heard So-and-so say, and so on.' But my daddy told this for the truth."

Core black culture has a long tradition of extreme aversion to the gratuitous lie that is not plainly offered as an element of signifying, woofing, or some other variety of nonveracious discourse.

Miss Elva said that she couldn't figure out why a professor would want to talk to her because she didn't believe in what they were teaching her niece in school and she was not going to lie for anyone. [fieldnotes]

The allegorical antihero of slave sermons, "long tongue liah," is the slave image of the composite security risk whose desire to perform imperiled internal security.

There is an equally venerable tradition that has it that "oaths freely taken are binding." So anyone donating a personal document freely is under an especially strong cultural and personal injunction to strive for the rendering of a true account. People who donated personal documents generally went to great lengths to establish their accounts as veracious. Most seminar members and personal document donors were plainly aware of the harm that might be done a native career by lying. The stock phrases that express this recognition that their data, as the stuff of analysis, had to be as pure as they could make it, are interspersed generously through their life histories. "If I can't help you I won't hurt you." "I didn't come all the way over here to tell you no lie and I will not uphold anybody else in no lie." "I don't want to give 'um anything to shoot you down with." The consistent and general striving for profound veracity was often the occasion for chagrin, rueful reflection, and tears. Rare indeed is the black informant steeped in the customary admonitions and values of core black culture who would contemplate anything like that degree of intimate defenselessness before any outsider.

White people are interested in what we think for the same reason they are interested in all these foreign countries. See, if they can figure out how somebody thinks then they can figure how to git over with that person or that country . . . Now we would be some fancy fools to tell this man anything that would help him to sock it to us. I'll talk to the dude all day long if he'll pay me, but he won't know as much about me when we finish as he knows now and let me tell you that is not a hell of a lot! I mean, that's how the black man makes it you know because white folks don't know a damn thing about us and that is the way it should stay.

Lelly King[2] do not lie to anybody! If you were white, I would not mislead you. I wouldn't say a thing to you and then if you were not as dumb as most of them, you would just go on about your business and leave Lelly King to take care of hers. White folks think that because they are their mama's pride and joy they are Jesus to you and me. That devil of a madam of mine is evermore telling people how "deevoted Lelly is to the children." Now nobody but a fool would waste her time hating or loving kids like that. She doesn't know how I feel about anything and that's a good thing too. She don't even know how she would feel if she was me. No son! You are just the right color for Lelly King to talk to. I don't stir up no sweetbread for no whitefolks and I don't give them none of my day off! [fieldnotes]

Reciprocity

The compensation I offered was probably of greater use in helping to piece out the extremely low and variable incomes of the chronically ill than it was with the generality of others, but in no instance were purely monetary considerations instrumental in anyone's decision to organize a seminar or give a life history. I was often obliged to rely upon indirect strategies of compensation, and it was only by great exertion that I was able to keep even remotely abreast of the formidable hospitality of my people. I did not wish to be identified with that swarm of junketing assessors with a "handful of gimme and a mouthful of much obliged." My failure to pay people for their time, to provide some part of the feast, to give of my own time with something of the same grace with which people extended themselves to assist me would have been justly fatal to rapport. As one senior lady put it as she purveyed the customary feast: "It is right that you pay people. Now nobody's goin' to be able to buy no farm with that, but it shows you mean well."

Indirect strategies of compensation depend, as do all the vital methodological considerations of fieldwork, very largely upon a knowledge of the cultural complex you are attempting to describe. One of the more unfortunate consequences of the refusal of much of the white social science establishment to believe that there is such a thing as black culture is, of course, a monumental, cavalier ineptness. All fieldwork in core black culture must begin with the assumption that there is a culture system to investigate and that that system has survived because there are men, women, and children who live by it.

If you wish to be trusted with people's life histories and serious thinking in the context of the folk seminar, you must be seen as a person worthy of such consideration. Core black culture, like all others, has its standards for the exemplary. Individuals who are knowledgeable in this particular culture system and who are known not to have departed significantly from its tenets are deemed sober men and women. In black culture one is much more likely to recommend oneself with a good reputation than to command or persuade by high status as that term is understood among middle-class-oriented Euro-Americans. One's job does not define a person's status in core black estimation nearly so much as it does in the congeries of Euro-American ethnicities. Miss Hannah Nelson, a domestic worker who is locally admired as a prudent, incredibly talented "racewoman," enjoys a much higher status than does Mr. Kenneth Swanson, whose income, derived from indigenously despised sources, is at least thrice hers. A dozen people either participated in or organized folk seminars simply because Miss Nelson asked them to help in the research. Three of the persons who assisted me out of respect and admiration for her eventually volunteered splendid interviews and personal documents.

John Oliver, a wise, redoubtable urban countryman, asked the five members of the Olijambra, his quintet,[3] to cooperate with the project, and three of them gave personal documents and interviews. Two of them provided extensive transportation, and all participated in at least one field seminar. Harriet Jones, a seventeen-year-old respected by her neighborhood for her uprightness and judgment, asked her mother, her playmother, her best girlfriend, and several of her peers of both sexes to participate in the research. She and her playmother contributed excellent narratives and only one of the score or more people she attempted to enlist in the research was unable to participate. Janet and James McCrae asked their formidable extended family to help in the work, and many members of that family were kind enough to widen the net of participation.

The research would have been impossible without the kind of quiet sharing of resources that renders life in all the black towns I have ever known more than mere survival. Mrs. Surry not only contributed a lengthy, absorbing personal document, but contrived to be at church cake sales and women's club meat feasts when I needed a comfortable, secure home site for critical initial interviews and personal documents. A request from Mrs. Surry was sufficient to inspire no fewer than eight people to seek me out and offer their cooperation. By loosely scheduling interviews, personal document recording, and field seminars in places regarded as positively familiar, the indispensable criteria of security and anonymity were mutually satisfied. A third of Mr. Jonathan Melton's admirable life history was given in Mrs. Surry's home. The remainder was taken in his own home. Portions of Harriet Jones's eloquent, sombre life history were recorded in her own home and in three other secure locations in which she feels at home. Both Othman Sullivan and Nancy White host intimate social groups that meet in rotation in each other's homes to talk, eat, and drink, as they used to do in neighborhood taverns before such places became the habitual haunts of desperate marginal youths. Both these groups became large folk seminars in their own rights and were the sources of other such groups. Both Mrs. White and Mr. Sullivan are reckoned *primus inter pares* in the large kindreds to which they belong, because they are seen as preeminently "straight." Their own interest in the research, coupled with their subtle recruitment of others, was of immeasurable assistance in four enclaves.

Miss Elaine Young, a twenty-year-old art student who is, on principle, opposed to the practice of black studies programs she has observed, has the respect of a large student constituency. Through her assistance, a number of her peers and members of her large extended family – spanning four generations – volunteered invaluable data and analysis. Washington Arias, a middle-aged electrician, at home in North American core black culture and in Afro-Iberian Caribbean culture, organized a series of multiethnic folk seminars that yielded valuable data. Mrs. Yula Moses, a domestic worker whose high indigenous status is derived from her reputation as a devout faith healer and upright person, was also very helpful. Both Mr. Arias and Mrs. Moses provided me with transportation, interview sites, and superb data.

Conclusion

This is a people preeminently capable of self-expression, and to that end I have relied upon them heavily to speak for themselves. They knew what they wanted to say, and they had pronounced opinions about what I ought to be doing as a social scientist. Neither the goad of caste nor the weight of empire have been sufficient to destroy equanimity in core black culture.

The general striving for balance and veracity is a tribute to the human spirit under egregious, unwarranted social stress:

Please describe us as we are. We will still emerge as good as any other people. It's like making a cake I guess. Some things cannot be enjoyed by themselves, but taken all together, they make a good thing which is just as good as any other good thing. Only a fool would try to prove that black walnut cake was better than Baltimore cake. [fieldnotes]

Until that disparity between core black and standard settler views of black life is substantially diminished, a vital part of the black anthropologist's responsibility must be to serve as a vehicle for the expression of indigenous core black cultural definition: "I know what is going on out here because it has gone on over me!" (fieldnotes).

The ethical professions of social science will not be taken seriously in any core black enclave until the social sciences acknowledge and rectify, to the extent that they are able, their own gross racist theoretical aggression. Black anthropologist William S. Willis's conjecture that "ethnographic monographs are simply novels and that theoretical concepts are but daydreams" (1973:462) is a professional statement of a widely held core black lay dissatisfaction with the literature of social science. Ethnology is rarely viewed as a disinterested discipline, and fieldwork is not seen as a generally "independent and dispassionate" endeavor (Wax 1978:94, 98). Social science is not seen as possessing a great deal of power to promote positive social motion, even if it were universally committed to the amelioration of caste. Social science is generally perceived of as a part of an essentially unjust political and social system with the same traditional tendencies of the inegalitarian matrix in which it is embedded. Ethnographic fieldwork is seen as a relatively high status job because its pay scale is high in comparison to prevailing core black minimal rates. Core black culture's passion for its own variety of individualism, its general aversion to fragmentation, and its detestation of the close supervision of caste also render anthropology an attractive job because of its relative autonomy. In all the black enclaves I investigated, people were generally aware that they were doing me a favor.

I liked the idea of talking to you about my life but you want me to do that more than I want to do it. I'm just talking but you are working and if nobody will talk to you, you will be out of work. Now that's how it is with the white anthropologist too. That's where that is. Nobody is going to give him money to talk to himself. The white man has worn out his welcome everywhere. Those Africans will tell him where to go in a minute! We are just about the only natives he has left. The Indians are always running him off some reservation. If you have to watch every little thing you say, talking is painful. That's why me and white people have practically nothing to say to each other. [fieldnotes]

Indigenous analysis

Among the pieces of social science literature evaluated by many folk seminars was a 1974 letter to the American Anthropological Association's *Anthropology Newsletter* ("Correspondence," vol. 15 (January):2) denying the existence of a serious crisis of access and affirming that the colonial model of fieldwork was a source of gratification to minority peoples. When the possibilities of satire and irony had been dismissed, the premise that settler access to native field populations remains essentially untrammeled because natives have some kind of need to "perform" for settlers occasioned mild amusement. This inversion of the colonial fieldwork model was attributed most often to that curious combination of wishful thinking and reasoning by decree that characterizes so much of caste management. This wishful thinking is a common-sense elaboration of a concept of social science known variously as non-knowledge (Simmel 1950:312) and romanticism (Gwaltney 1976). The tendency to delegate drudgery and to avoid unpleasant or unwelcome realities is held to be a pervasive prime element of helm segment settler cultures. The distorted views of core black culture and denial of its very existence that characterize so much of the largely outsider-generated literature of social science is thought of as just another manifestation of this romantic tendency. There is general concurrence with Matthiasson's (1974) assertion that anthropology owes a massive debt to minority and oppressed people. Most people I worked with thought that a representative impression of their life styles would be evidence that this massive ethical debt was beginning to be reduced. My concentration upon the reigning core black life styles was designed to contribute to that representative impression. The marginal people who did participate in folk seminars and contribute personal documents were, far more often than not, expressly concerned that the atypicality of their life styles be duly noted.

Look man, you been knowing me since high school so you know I'm into some wrong action out here, but that's me! Everybody ain' into what I'm into.

I brag on my sister because she is one straight woman! I wish I could live that life but you know what I'm into. [fieldnotes]

We are a classical people with a high regard for reality. Most informants recognized that the desire to seem better than one actually is is a weakness that contributes to distortion. Caveat phrases that served as a brake on the kind of rampant romanticism that most people were at pains to guard against were commonly employed.

Now right is right and it don' wrong nobody so let's tell this thing like it went down.

We ain' God and whitefolks don' have to be devils. There's salt in that sweet bread you are eating too you know. [fieldnotes]

Such admonitions were not born of self-deprecation but of a profound conviction that the people are at least as good as any other people we ever heard of.

Somebody should write a book about Jim. He's the kind of person that keeps everything going. Most people don't really give people like Jimmy much credit, especially if they are black. You never really hear about black people like you or Jimmy or me. Not that there is anything so special about me but everything I read about us is sick or, yes I guess I do mean sick in one way or another. I'm an ordinary black person. I have never spent a day in jail. I'm polite to everybody who is polite to me. I don't take drugs and I can save my money. I can say three sentences without "man" and "like" and "you know." I am not on welfare and am not about to get on welfare as long as I can work. [fieldnotes]

Native anthropology and its practitioners are certain to be charged with lack of objectivity and excessive idealization. Their findings are, of course, at variance with much of the standard settler social science reporting on our communities. A proper regard for the veracious account is shared by good people of all the ethnic communities of this castelike commonwealth. Stan Steiner (1972:102), in his critical commentary on Charles A. Valentine's approach to the study of black communities, seems to be saying that the insistence on the necessity for immersion in black American culture in order to understand it accurately may have made Valentine "less of an anthropologist and more of a man." Most people with whom I discussed this notion were at a loss to understand how better people could fail to be better ethnologists. Core black culture tends toward the holistic view of human character. There are insiders and insiders, outsiders and outsiders, and most of the people I worked with are secure in their capacity to distinguish among them. It is difficult to imagine anyone speaking as well and as knowledgeably for themselves from their own ignored perspectives as did Andreski's (1970) Ibibio informants or Ashenbrenner's (1975) black Chicagoans. It is a tribute to these outsiders that they had the wit and healthy humility to permit their informants to speak for themselves.

It is certainly possible that native investigators may be privy to more privileged information than are nonnatives, but they are likely to acquire it only if the people they are working with esteem them as persons of requisite discretion. It is axiomatic that dealing in trivia is the key to the safest relations with the powerful, unprincipled stranger.

I know some people you should speak with. My part of Virginia is Prophet Nat's country and there are still people there who revere him and fear him with a clean fear. They would never tell any white man anything of importance. [fieldnotes]

Trust was an indispensable element in the cooperation of the field populations I worked with. The fact that some of my informants had known me since the hour of my birth certainly did not prove a hindrance. In other cases I was checked and cross-checked by many before a decision was made to take part in the research. In this connection the opinion of a member of the community perceived of as reputable was infinitely more valuable than purely professional credentials. Implicit in the decision to take part, of course, was the faith most people had in their own ability to reveal only as much of themselves as they wish. It has been said that

the Negro, in spite of his open-faced laughter, his seeming acquiescence, is particularly evasive. You see we are a polite people and we do not say to our questioner, "Get out of here!" We smile and tell him or her something that satisfies the white person because, knowing so little about us, he doesn't know what he is missing. [Hurston 1970:18]

Dealing, the virtuoso improvisation on the traditional themes of personality defense in the transgenerational cold war of caste, has made black people masters of the necessary art of "telling some and keeping some." The people say that "the truth is the light,"but they also know that the "truth is a razor." So we keep our cool, watch our mouths, and keep our business out of the street to avoid those "messes that are hard to clean."

Black people are, of course, aware that a conspicuous strain of Euro-American thinking dismisses them as ignorant, inconsequential witnesses to their own core black tradition:

Now I told you that to show you what I am going to teach you. Now I wouldn't say that to a white man because he think I can't teach him a thing. [fieldnotes]

Science, especially social science, is not held to be some kind of pure abstraction above racist arrogance but rather the product of the endeavor of women and men who may or may not attempt to follow the truth wherever it leads them. The personal documents and the proceedings of folk seminars yield many of the same sovereign dissatisfactions with social science to which many professional scientists have directed public attention. These data plainly indicate that the gap between the considered reflections of the dealing natural man or woman – the carrier of core black culture – and the thinking of responsible scientists is often more apparent than real.

Common sense and science

The myth that common sense and science represent irrevocably differing qualities of thought serves to elevate the latter to a position of uncritical eminence and to debase the former to a place of indiscriminate denigration. Joan Cassell (1977) lamented the relative absence of a body of data treating the role of the anthropologist as peer while conducting fieldwork among her own white middle-class indigenous constituency. The status gap she alludes to applies as much to natives' and settlers' theorizing as it does to the natives and settlers themselves. In both forms this status gap is identical with the traditional social science colonial model. In fact, common sense and science display many significant congruities. There is often considerable convergence between the considered common-sense reflections of core black culture and the conjecturing of social scientists of most allowed sufficiency.

Core black culture has a tradition of fending and proving and rapping and a concern with the profound issues of the human condition that still inform daily dialogue. We are a people who still like good talk, and once the indispensable conditions of security and trust were met, many informants welcomed an opportunity to exchange views and expound their ideas about the nature of humanity. The profundity that emerged from this volume of reflection and exchange was couched in a variety of speech forms. Secure, on their own ground, dispensing their own tasteful and bountiful hospitality, people employed what-ever speech code or codes they felt at home in to speak their minds. As the categories dealt with by common sense and science are often the same, most people could and did come to terms with the elemental linguistic formalities of social science.

I used to think that there was a great deal to everything. I think that's a trick now. You know, a trick done by the people who run things. They have to make everything look like it's much more complicated than it is . . . It's not really that big a thing. If something is so big, I mean, if how to do something is so big that ordinary sensible people can't do it, then maybe we have no business doing it. [fieldnotes]

Here Miss McCrae was voicing the same reservation about rampant technical naiveté expressed by the president of MIT when he observed that

[Americans have] outrun our technological base and certainly our intellectual base. [The United States is now seeing] the consequences of becoming too cavalier about what we do and trying to do too many things. [*New York Times*, September 28, 1975, 1:34]

This feeling of deep dissatisfaction with the subordination of the individual to fancy packaged, inorganic technical tyranny surfaces in the personal document of Miss Nelson.

A car is not greater than a person's foot . . . a radio is not so great as an ear, or a television greater than one of the multitude of eyes that watch it. The human hand has made all these things and they are all less than the wart on the human hand. Nothing that I can make can be any better than I am. [fieldnotes]

Miss Nelson is drawing attention to the same flaw in the quality of industrial existence deplored by Marvin Harris when he points out that

Lee found, for example, that his Bushmen worked at subsistence for only ten to fifteen hours a week. This discovery effectively destroys one of the shoddiest myths of industrial society – namely that we have more leisure today than ever before. [Harris 1977:227]

Both Miss Nelson and Dr. Harris have been led by common sense and scientific observation to substantial agreement with Arnold Toynbee's view that "there is no correlation between progress in technique and progress in civilization" (1934:173–174).

Both the language of common sense and that of science have their respective grammars. From whatever vantage point we listen, it is imperative to listen for the unconventional. Preoccupation with style must not obscure meaning and a due regard for the character of the speaker or source. When Othman Sullivan, a man reckoned as deliberate, circumspect, and wise by his neighbors, says, upon reflection, "I think this anthropology is just another way to call me a nigger," his remarks should not be summarily dismissed. The fact that Malinowski (1967) did think of the Melanesian field populations that were instrumental in his ethnographic prominence as "niggers" does lend some weight to Mr. Sullivan's view. Mr. Sullivan's view excited no particular curiosity in the many folk seminars he hosted and attended. His premise is in no wise diminished by Gunnar Myrdal's (1962:928) opinion that "American Negro culture is a distorted development or a pathological condition of the general American culture." Mr. Sullivan's common-sense observation is an adequate précis of William S. Willis's professional social scientific statement that

white exploitation of colored peoples has been crucial to the prosperity of white societies. This cruciality is the key to the persistence in anthropology of negative perceptions of colored peoples, and it has insured that positive perceptions have been seldom, if ever, devoid of some kind of negativism, for instance, paternalism. [1973:461]

The pathological distortion of core black culture is seen as the social science manifestation of a general tendency to suppress the truth and tailor history to fit the requirements of a castelike inegalitarian society.

If the president of the white nation would alter the taped historical record of his people and lie about his own historical record, what kind of accuracy could this black girl expect from any American boy who might grow up to be an anthropologist or social psychologist? [fieldnotes]

Miss Young's common-sense question arises quite logically from Guillermo Bonfin Batalla's social scientific observation that

to state that science is universal is only part of the truth, because science is also an institution and a cumulative tradition, and, after all, a social product; as such it necessarily reflects in some way the conditions, values and orientations of the society that produces it. [1966:92]

Miss Young was implying a generally held premise of every field population that collaborated with me.

Scientists are people. They cannot escape values in the choices they make nor in the effects of their acts . . . We cannot divorce ourselves from the consequences of our scientific acts any more than we can from those of any other of our acts as human beings. This is a fact of existence in human society, and it is a tenet of democracy. [Berreman 1968:392]

Native anthropology will have more than justified its existence if it facilitates the significant increase of what Maruyama calls "polyocularity" in anthropology:

"Objective" agreement to one view impoverishes our perception. On the other hand, cross-subjective comparison of differentials enables us to calculate the dimensions which are not directly observable or measurable. [Maruyama 1974:320]

The American Anthropological Association's own Committee on Minorities and Anthropology came to essentially the same conclusion in its report:

The pursuit of science demands that we accept and explore new insights, and accept the possibility that alternative ways of thinking and communicating the subject matter of anthropology exist. Including the minority perspective can be a way of forming a new paradigm. [1973:84]

Mrs. Yula Moses put it this way:

There is a woman's understanding and there is a man's understanding. And there is wisdom.

5 Observer participation and consulting: research in urban food cooperatives

RICHARD ZIMMER

The 1960s and 1970s have seen a renewed interest in organizing small-scale retail food cooperatives in the United States and Canada. The same period of time has also witnessed a change in the role of anthropologist as traditional participant observer of so-called primitive peoples. This paper explores the ways in which these two developments converge. It is a description and analysis of my place as an anthropologist-cum-consultant working with three cooperatives in San Francisco from 1972 to 1973.

Cooperatives

Small-scale food cooperatives are also called buying clubs or food conspiracies. They are purchasing unions whose members buy grocery items in bulk from wholesalers and redistribute them to each other in a variety of formats. Members might use a parking lot and lay out the food just bought, or they might have a small store, a garage or storefront in which they stack cans, dry goods, and other items. The underlying cooperative principle is to substitute one's own labor for the grocery-store middleman's labor and to pass the savings on to each other as co-op members.

Modern food cooperatives are a utopian experiment of people working together for a given purpose. They are the children of the first cooperative, begun by the weavers in Rochdale, England, in the 1840s (Abrahamsen 1976). The Rochdale experiment became a social movement and spread to North America in the 1860s (Knapp 1959). Cooperative markets prospered in the 1870s and 1880s under the impetus of the Knights of Labor and the Populists. Many small cooperatives remain from this period; they dot small towns all across the United States and Canada. Some markets were started later and have grown to be as successful as the fourteen-store California Consumers Cooperatives in Berkeley.

Because cooperatives save members money and because they are community responses to felt needs, the federal Office of Economic Opportunity tried to promote them in poverty areas, particularly in the years 1964 to 1971. Residents in poor rural areas faced the same food problems as inner-city people: Few chain stores operated to serve them, prices were high, and quality was low. Co-ops seemed an ideal solution. Groups of people could get together, pool their resources, and buy directly from wholesalers. Despite the impetus, many co-ops failed again and again, although a good deal of money, technical assistance, free labor, and other forms of support were poured in from various government agencies.

The usual explanations given by the agency for such failures were either that poor people could not operate cooperatives or that the venture was not worth the economic effort.[1] These reasons seemed inadequate. First, the Rochdale weavers had been poor and they had succeeded. Secondly, the savings were worth it. I knew this from my many years of working in cooperatives – from being a member to being a president, from organizing a score of buying clubs in inner-city areas of Los Angeles to helping start two at different universities.

Cooperatives presented both an intriguing domain and a theoretical question worthy of study. I wanted to find out why some cooperatives succeed and others fail despite the real need for the savings and services they can provide. Only in a field study in an inner-city area could I begin to answer that question, by focusing on the ways in which base groups organized co-ops and in which these co-ops dealt with external agencies and solved day-to-day problems.

In the year 1972, there was a hitch in defining the problem in terms of a field study. Anthropologists customarily find a people to study and try to remain neutral observers. By 1972, however, residents in American inner cities were hostile to any outsiders coming in to study or work with them; they felt they had been exploited by such observers in the past and given little in return for their cooperation (T. Wolfe 1969). They might condescend, however, to allow someone in who gave them something in return. Obviously, I could give them my technical expertise and co-op experience. But would it be possible to do an anthropological study that was also dispassionate, objective, and focused on a larger issue?

What follows is my answer to these questions. It is a history of how I defined a suitable research question for my dissertation, an account of the consultation and research performed, and an analysis of that type of scientific methodology. It is, to a large extent, the story of two cooperatives in San Francisco's Mission District, a low-income Latino area of the city. I helped the co-op members organize and operate their cooperative while studying them in 1972 and 1973. Throughout this study, while dealing with the basic question of why some co-ops have succeeded while others failed, I learned some strong lessons about remaining a neutral and scientific inquirer. Until this study began, I could not have anticipated all the questions or the anthropological and technical problems involved. Nor would I have obtained access to the co-ops if I had not provided the members with something they valued – my experience with and knowledge of wholesalers, distributors, and government agencies – as a form of reciprocity.

Defining the research problem

My original research concern was to find out why some co-ops succeeded and others failed. That, however, was not a sufficient anthropological research question. Anthropologists concern themselves with issues central to human social organization. My research question would have to be framed in larger, more fundamental terms.

I found these terms in typical anthropological fashion, by considering an analogy between co-ops, the Pygmies of the Iturbi rain forest, and the !Kung Bushmen of the Kalahari Desert in Africa (Turnbull 1962, Thomas 1965). Pygmies and !Kung Bushmen hunt in bands and bring home the kill. There, surrounded by their kin, they divide up the meat. A similar pattern exists in all small-scale food cooperatives: Several members go out to the wholesalers and bring back sacks and boxes to a garage or storefront, where, surrounded by co-op members, they divide up the food. The Pygmies and the !Kung Bushmen obviously need the meat from the hunt for their own survival. They also value both the hunt and the distribution, reinforcing both in ritual and myth. It is clear that many co-op members need grocery items. It is less clear that all of them value the acquisition and redistribution of these items in the same way the Pygmies and the !Kung Bushmen do. The analogy suggests that social factors, such as the nature of member participation and the value put on the entire process, affect the success of the food acquisition – distribution enterprise. My first goal was to determine if the analogy was sufficient to explain co-ops.

Co-ops do not appear to have the same central role in people's lives as does the hunt, nor do they have any of the color, excitement, or romance of the outdoor markets found throughout the Third World and in parts of Europe. Small co-ops are typically fragile mutual benefit associations, dependent upon each member performing his or her task at the right time. They demand emotional commitment to and patience with the enterprise, even in the face of disaster, as when the meat buyer does not show up with the "kill." The research question became, in effect, an analysis of the ways in which organizational and ideological factors affected marginal groups.

The two Mission-area cooperatives in San Francisco provided me with a starting place. These co-ops were organized by Latinos under the aegis of the Roman Catholic church to meet the grocery needs of parishioners in the inner city. Both comprised the same ethnic and religious membership. Yet they were different enough to provide an adequate control and comparison situation for research purposes. Moreover, their underlying similarities allowed me to test the hunter-gatherer co-op analogy by focusing on the specific commitments members had made to the operations and mission of each co-op. I could then explore the ways in which the co-op worked as a grocery operation, setting it in the context of the Bay Area grocery industry, and as a political organization, viewing it in the context of poverty-area politics and governmental regulations.

Defining an anthropologist-cum-consultant role

In order to answer my research question, I was confronted with a second challenge, that of refashioning the participant-observer research role of social anthropology. Traditionally, social anthropologists have been neutral observers in alien cultures, participating in events just enough to obtain relevant information.[2] This role presumes that there are people who will allow the anthropologist to maintain a scientific, detached, and interested objectivity. Most anthropologists who work with certain groups in the United States do not have that possibility. Women, homosexuals, and various ethnic groups tend to resist outsiders, whether they are from government or the university. Moreover, these groups do not want to be researched. Anthropologists need to find new ways to gain access to these groups.

Some have solved this problem by sharing a special quality of their own with the group under study. Amador, for example, was a homosexual studying homosexuals (1973). Schensul was a researcher interested in providing background information to improve the services of drug treatment programs (1974). Pilcher was a longshoreman who worked on the docks to get his information (1972). Spradley collaborated with Mann to study cocktail-waitress culture (Spradley and Mann 1975). Anthropologists have had to be sensitive to the politics and issues of the groups they study and have realized the need to provide their informants with something in reciprocity.

I faced the same problem as these other anthropologists. The only cooperatives operating in San Francisco's inner-city areas in 1972 were organized by Latinos. Various contacts cautioned that Mission District residents were wary of outsiders and that I should not approach them in the role of anthropologist asking merely to watch their activities. They would expect me to provide something in return. In my case, that return could be my fifteen years of experience in small-scale retail food cooperatives. Perhaps I might then be able to do some applied or action anthropology (see Beckhard 1971), but I was more interested in obtaining a larger perspective.

I also realized that the role of social anthropologist and technical consultant had to be reexamined to find their points of compatibility and conflict in the contemporary setting. Traditionally, the social anthropologist working alone in the field finds a group suitable for study, makes contact, seeks its permission for the research, and then begins a long period of familiarization with group members. In time, the anthropologist might find some terms of acceptance by the group. He or she might be tolerated, as Evans-Pritchard (1970) was by the Nuer, or be ritually included as Cushing (1970) was by the Zuni. For the most part, however, the anthropologist remains a "marginal native" (Freilich, 1970). Whatever the terms of eventual acceptance, the anthropologist has first to ask the group for permission to enter. Dealing with one's marginality vis-à-vis the group being studied comes a little later.

The technical consultant faces some of those same problems in the field. The consultant, too, is an outsider and must find procedures by which to get acquainted with the group and gain acceptance by group members. Technical consultants, however, are asked by the groups with which they work to help them deal with the specific issue (McGrath 1964). Social anthropologists usually ask groups for permission to study a range of issues. And whereas the anthropologist has a wide field of movement to study the totality of social life, the consultant contracts to focus only on selected aspects.

Neither social anthropologist nor technical consultant knows the politics of the groups with which he or she will be working on first gaining entry. The social anthropologist must take a long time to learn them; the technical consultant must do so more quickly in order to get on promptly with the main work. Both, however, may affect their groups in the process.

Social psychology has shown us that any observation of a group under study, regardless of purpose, changes the behavior of individuals within the group as well as the group as a whole, often in quite unpredictable ways. In one case, workers in a control group increased their production during the course of the study, suggesting that subjects under scrutiny may alter behavior in response to what they perceive to be the expectations of the observer or of the experiment. This is known as the Hawthorne effect (Roesthlisberger and Dickson 1939).

In another set of experiments, observers were given a set of expectations about subjects that were not true. Nevertheless, the observers reported results from their subjects conforming to these expectations. The data were valid, not fabricated, suggesting that the observer's expectations of behavior strongly affected the performance of the subjects. This is known as the Rosenthal effect (Rosenthal 1966).

Social anthropologists have become increasingly aware that they, too, may unavoidably affect the groups they study. Malinowski noted giving double messages to the Trobrianders but did not explore the consequences of his actions (1961:11–12). Kloos (1969) and Jarvie (1969) have stated in general terms the problems of role conflicts with specific informants but have not suggested any ways they affect data collection, except in terms of skewed samples. The anthropologist may sometimes precipitate major social change within the group (see Gluckman 1969: xviii) or become the object of factional contention (Bowen 1954). The social anthropologist, however, does not study a group to change it.

By contrast, the technical consultant works with a group to effect change (Mann 1971). He or she is contracted to provide assistance in a given area, whether it be with the whole group on a particular task or with individuals in specific situations. Despite this contract, the technical consultant may see only a partial picture of the group and as a consequence may affect aspects of organizational structure other than those of his or her design.[3] Thus the technical consultant may inadvertently bring about changes beyond the limits of the contract.

The consultant's contract is specific, and it is mutually and formally decided upon before entrance to the group. By contrast, the social anthropologist's permission is more open ended and informal. The consultant may study the group with a specific purpose; the anthropologist usually studies the group for diffuse ends. The former is contracted for his or her expertise; the latter must initiate efforts to gain entrance and movement, as Whyte (1943) did when he participated in bowling activities and did precinct work in an Italian neighborhood in Boston.

The anthropologist and the consultant face similar problems as outsiders to the group, but in different ways. The anthropologist can claim ignorance of the group; he or she wants to learn the culture (L. Bohannan 1973). The researcher can make mistakes and thus gain valuable insight into organizational activities, as Whyte did when he tried to approach an Italian woman in an Italian bar. His rejection convinced him that there were better ways of making contact with Italian women (Whyte 1943). The consultant cannot make mistakes in the area of contracted expertise, but is expected to stay within the contract. The consultant may have to fight for acceptance by the group outside the area of expertise. The consultant gives the contractor group something they say they want; the anthropologist provides little beyond his or her personal presence.

The result is that the anthropologist has an advantage over the consultant in becoming familiar with the group and dealing with the fact that he or she is an outsider. The group must exercise greater patience with the anthropologist than with the consultant. The anthropologist is usually with the group for a long time and is expected to learn – and respect – the group norms but is not there to change them. The consultant is with the group to change at least some group norms. The anthropologist has the time and the research excuse to meet all individuals within the group, despite original entrance through the leadership. The technical consultant may only be meeting with the leadership or fulfilling the goals of the leadership when meeting with other individuals. Even for the anthropologist, however, it may be necessary to assert an independent stance from the leadership to gain entrance to any factions within the group (see Bowen 1954).

Anthropologists and consultants both deal with their marginality, whereas group members do not – members have their own lives to lead; the anthropologist and the consultant are preoccupied with their work. The group must still learn to deal with them, but the obligation is a bit one-sided, except when the focus of the study forces group members to reevaluate their relations with one another, as Komarovsky found when she interviewed blue-collar couples in New Jersey (1967).

These different problems, however, do not make a combined social anthropologist-technical consultant role unfeasible. An anthropologist who brings to the group under study some expertise can justifiably ask for data on a wide range of issues, in part by claiming that such data are essential to the consulting role. If the group wants the anthropologist-consultant's expertise, then that is a fair contract. Moreover, the holistic approach that social anthropologists usually take concerning group studies and the tradition of spending a long time in the field checking initial impressions (Freilich 1970:34–35; Malinowski 1961) may in fact provide them with greater insights into how their particular expertise and their own research role affect group actions.

Those anthropologists interested in development who have focused on social change from a holistic point of view (e.g. Goodenough 1963) may in fact be bringing about change too unpredictably (see Cochrane 1971). A social anthropologist who provides a group with technical expertise may be able to work more effectively with that group for several reasons; for example, he or she may speak in terms the group can understand about issues the members want to change. In addition, the holistic approach allows for greater perception with which one can anticipate problems within other areas of social life that a technical consultant lacking that expertise may not perceive. Moreover, the approach allows the anthropologist to collect data in other areas as well as the primary one and to place those data in a theoretical framework emphasizing change.

Considering all this, I decided to pursue this joint role of anthropologist-consultant with the cooperatives of the Mission District. As an anthropologist, I knew that I had to initiate the contact with the cooperatives in order to study their operations. I could offer them my experience as a technical consultant, specifying clearly the contributions I could make and the data I would want. Because of the novelty of the role and the limits of research opportunities on this topic, I saw my primary role as that of an anthropologist who could help. The data I wanted to collect from a holistic perspective – such as group structure and values and the nature of the grocery industry – would not necessarily be affected by my presence. The success of the group might; I felt I could be objective enough about both to present a picture of cooperatives that could answer my research question. First, however, I had to work out a fair contract.

The study: gaining access

In the fall and winter of 1971 to 1972, I tried to find out what groups in the poorer neighborhoods of the Bay Area were considering the development of cooperatives. People in community action agencies, the government, and the cooperative movement told me that there were only a few, located only in San Francisco in black and Latino areas. Most of these groups were receptive to the study and my offer of technical help but decided, for different reasons, to pursue other goals.

The last group I contacted was a cooperative in San Francisco's Mission District, a largely Latino section and one of the worst poverty areas of the city. This group, known as the Cooperativa, was sponsored by the Catholic Council for the Spanish-Speaking (COCLA), a lay social agency of the Roman Catholic Archdiocese of San Francisco. The council is a multiservice agency for Spanish-speaking Catholic Latinos.

According to my sources, the Cooperativa had not yet begun any grocery operations. No problems with the group, such as internal conflicts or fights with any other groups, were known. On paper, the group seemed ideal to study – a serious, emerging cooperative comprising an interesting membership.

I did have some reservations about approaching the group, since I was neither Latino nor Catholic. Still, my technical expertise and my extensive work with Latino and Chicano co-ops could serve as my credentials. Would the Cooperativa agree? This was my most pressing problem when I first tried to make contact with the group.

The Catholic Council and the Cooperativa: an unwitting pawn

I tried to reach the director of the Cooperativa, Señora Avelar, for several weeks during April 1972, but to no avail. She simply could not be reached, and I could not find out why. In desperation I finally decided to visit the Catholic Council's offices to see whether I could reach her through the sponsoring agency.

That decision was an important one, for it put me in the middle of a dispute between the Catholic Council and the Cooperativa. The council's secretary asked that I speak with Señor Roger Hernandez, the executive director. He took my message for Señora Avelar but also seemed interested himself in talking about cooperatives with me.

Only after meeting with Señor Hernandez and Father James Hagen, a member of the executive board of the council who joined us, did I realize that the council and the Cooperativa were at odds. I also realized that Señor Hernandez probably would not forward my message to Señora Avelar.

At this point I faced the first challenge in my combined research – consultation role. If I were to continue this research topic in the Bay Area, I had to make contact with the real members of the only inner-city cooperative operating at the time. I did not want to take sides in any dispute and wanted to meet all the people involved with the co-op. As a social anthropologist, I needed this first-hand contact.

I had come onto the scene ignorant of conflict. When the conflict became apparent to me, I met with Señor Hernandez, Father Hagen, and other council board members and told them that I would neither involve myself on their side of the dispute – they had wanted me to intervene as a program evaluator – nor work with them or the Cooperativa while the groups were so embroiled with each other. The reasons were straightforward: As a cooperative organizer and activist, I had learned that grocery operations are so time-consuming and exhausting that no energy can be spared for intra- or intergroup bickering. Following my Pygmy–Bushmen analogy, it would be as if, for every step of the hunt, each person stopped to reassess work roles and whether to do a particular task. I had visions of the elephants and giraffes escaping – or the groceries spoiling – while everyone argued. Furthermore, as an anthropologist, I felt that the dispute prevented the groups from actually starting a cooperative and that if that happened I would not have a research problem.

Learning the background of the dispute and presenting cooperative alternatives with my offer of technical consultation took several weeks. The issues of the dispute were not clear nor were council members able to focus on what they hoped to accomplish in organizing a cooperative. To help clarify these issues and address the disputants' needs (for their benefit as well as my own), I followed a technique called "mirroring," in which a person actively listens and repeats to another what the listener hears the other saying. Mirroring is used among mental health professionals and community workers to resolve problems and conflicts with clients or in the community (see Singh 1971). Mirroring enables the listener to build up another's picture of what is happening as well as to understand that person's problems by listening for difficulties implicit in that picture. The listener then mirrors the picture so that the other person can check whether the picture presented represents his or her understanding. In addition, the listener simultaneously presents feedback to the other person on the problem he or she has perceived from the conversation. The other person can then choose to act on these difficulties. The procedure is consonant with change in a democratic society and fits in with information-gathering needs of organizational development in social anthropology.

What emerged from applying this mirroring technique in my instance was a confused picture. The Catholic Council had decided to establish a cooperative, the Cooperativa, a year earlier, after receiving a grant from the Campaign for Human Development. They had thought little about the difficulties of such a project, concerning themselves with the Christian mission and service it could offer Latino parishioners. Señora Avelar had been hired as director, but she had been given almost no instructions and little support.

She managed, somehow, to organize an informal cooperative board and several committees. She enlisted eighty members and amassed a bank account of several thousand dollars (shown to me by Señor Hernandez, who served as the Cooperativa's treasurer as well as the council's executive director). The Cooperativa organizers had established a committee structure and were teaching cooperative principles to members. Like many other beginning cooperatives, the Cooperativa had built up its resources preparatory to engaging in grocery operations.

By April 1972, the Cooperativa had grown far apart from the council. Despite the fact that her salary was paid by the council, Señora Avelar had (in the name of the Cooperativa) taken political positions in the community that opposed those of the council. This proved embarrassing for the council, as it had lent its good name to the Cooperativa and was its parent organization.

It became evident to me that the two groups were too much at odds to start food operations successfully. All this left me in a position in which I could do no work as a technical consultant and only a limited amount of research as an anthropologist. Nor was I consoled by the fact that I could not have known of the dispute beforehand, or that, like the Pygmies or the !Kung Bushmen, the disputants had to achieve a stable working–trusting relationship in order to engage in grocery operations.

Two changes soon occurred, however, as a consequence of my conversations with the council, which enabled me to proceed with the research. Both had implications for the council–cooperativa fight. In May 1972, Father Hagen, a council board member, decided to organize a buying club within St. Peter's parish, in which he served. The following August, the Cooperativa severed its relationships to the council and the council decided to proceed with organizing a buying club under its own direct control. As a result of these changes, I was finally able to establish a joint anthropologist-consultant role.

Research methods for a dual role

Shortly after my meetings with the council board members in April 1972, Father Hagen told me that he had been thinking of my suggestions about various cooperatives. He wanted to start a buying club, he said, and he invited me to work with him as a consultant. He assured me that I could also pursue anthropological research at the same time.

Father Hagen made this offer for several reasons. First, he wanted a suitable project for his Bible class, a group of forty Latino women, to undertake. The women all had low incomes and would benefit from any food savings a cooperative could provide. Second, he was impressed by the small-scale cooperative formats I offered as suggestions. He felt that a small, grassroots movement could succeed among his parishioners and in the district in general. He had previously been dismayed by the failure of a medium-sized cooperative in Hunters Point, an adjacent black area, just two years before. An even more ambitious proposal for a $150,000 supermarket, conceived of by Stanford Research Institute (SRI) in 1970, which was to be located in the Mission District, seemed even more unworkable to him. It would be neither grassroots-based nor acceptable to Latinos, who, he felt, would react strongly to the presence of large numbers of non-Spanish-speaking Anglo consultants. Some kind of group-based small store seemed ideal. He accepted my need for data collection, he pointed out, only because I would be providing him and the Bible class with expertise and help. I could start working with him in June 1972.

I noted earlier the sorts of resources I could offer as a technical consultant. In my new role with St. Peter's buying club, I worked alongside the members as they learned the tasks of food purchasing and redistribution. During the early stages, I compiled lists of wholesalers and obtained their prices. I accompanied Father Hagen as he began purchasing foodstuffs, reviewing the grocery orders with the suppliers. I also helped him load the goods into his truck or my VW bus. I accompanied other members to relevant government agencies, such as the food stamp program, and helped them type a constitution at that agency's request.

At the distribution end, I aided in setting up a procedure for selling groceries to members and worked with the distribution itself. I taught the women to use an adding machine and helped the club accountant develop bookkeeping procedures for club operations. Because Father Hagen was the leader of this group, I spoke with him at length about club operations. This helped him clarify his own goals and provided me with important research data as well as helped solve other problems within the group.

Father Hagen's offer to me to live in the rectory during the summer of 1972 meant that I would be able to use participant-observer fieldwork techniques with the base group for the buying club, the Bible class, as well as with the religious leadership within the parish. Because the parish was promoting social change, my secondary goal was to determine why the personnel of this parish were involved in that task. I wanted to ascertain, from a cooperative viewpoint, the relationships between the base group and the cooperative that it would organize. I interviewed parish personnel and observed meetings of a variety of parish groups during that summer and on a weekly basis in the ensuing year.

While working with Father Hagen and living in St. Peter's church, I continued to meet with the council and finally met with Señora Avelar. I wanted to learn as much about the background of the dispute as possible and hoped ultimately that it would be resolved. Unfortunately, it was not: The two groups split in August. Everyone involved was badly shaken. It turned out that the Cooperativa never engaged in any grocery operation and eventually disbanded. As a result, Señor Hernandez almost lost his position as executive director. Subsequently, he and other council board members decided to continue with cooperative development and to organize a buying club, whereupon they asked for my help just as Father Hagen had done.

Many of the same research procedures used earlier were also followed with Señor Hernandez and the council club in the fall of 1972 and throughout 1973. But my new role differed somewhat from the one I played at St. Peter's. First, I could more easily provide the council club with grocery information, as it was already obtained. Second, they had more people power to do the work; hence I could focus on goal clarification and implementation difficulties. I visited the council club twice weekly throughout that year.

At both St. Peter's and the council club, I had access to all members and to documents of the groups concerning cooperative operations. This amount of trust was rewarding, because it meant that I could visit anyone involved in the cooperatives and as well as examine records at my leisure. This was necessary for my work as consultant and as anthropologist.

Some degree of acceptance by co-op members was also necessary for my work as an anthropologist. All of them, except for Father Hagen, were Latino Catholics. I was not Catholic, but the issue of religion never arose. And although I was not Latino, Father Hagen (an Irish-American who speaks flawless Spanish) reassured me by saying that even though he had worked in the parish for five years and was well loved by his people, he still felt himself an outsider. My research–consultation contract focused only on cooperative operations and related issues; that is, on what I was doing, not who I was. Members gave me enough group acceptance to do my work, and by the end of the first summer I knew I was well received when I was given a warm going-away party by the members of the St. Peter's buying club as a "thank you" for my help.

Conclusions about cooperatives: factors for success

During the period of research from 1972 to 1973, I worked with the St. Peter's Bible class and with the Catholic Council as they tried to develop buying clubs. I also tried to keep informed about the progress of the Cooperativa. St. Peter's Bible class started its co-op in June 1972 and the Catholic Council in October 1972. Both groups operated cooperatives during the period of the study. The St. Peter's club was the more successful of the two because Father Hagen organized the co-op within a strong social group and exercised forceful leadership from the start. That club has continued to the present, a major achievement for a small inner-city cooperative with no government help. In contrast, the council club limped along from the very start because its social group was weak and its leadership divided. Because of this, it folded in 1975. The third group, the Cooperativa, never started operation, because it was devastated by its fight with the Catholic Council, to whom it eventually lost most of its members. It finally disbanded in 1973.

In the case of St. Peter's buying club, perhaps the most important reason for success is that the base group for the co-op was a cohesive group of people whose interests could develop its cooperative directions. This group was St. Peter's parish Bible class, approximately forty low-income immigrant Latino women, who had been meeting for a long period of time for religious and social purposes. When Father Hagen approached them with the idea of a buying club, they saw its usefulness in terms of savings to them as well as something enjoyable to do. As they developed the club, they came to see it as a part of their Christian endeavor, a sort of return to the meaning of the early Christian church. St. Peter's class club became a sharing community, exchanging food both ritually and practically in potluck dinners and grocery redistribution.

The second reason for St. Peter's success was that the format of operations meant a minimum of work and difficulty for all members. The club used Father Hagen's garage stall. Members stacked nonperishable dry goods, such as rice and beans, on shelves and in bins. They tended store (as they called it) three times a week, selling each other grocery items. The store was opened on weeknights and after Sunday mass. Within a short time, they extended operations to some perishables, such as cheese, eggs, and butter, using donated second-hand refrigerators. Father Hagen helped by exercising a strong leadership role at the beginning and doing much of the work the women did not have time or knowledge to do. He gradually removed himself from those tasks, however, as the members took them on.

The women of the club also found secondary benefits from the cooperative. They had a chance to meet each other in an informal, work-related format rather than a religious setting. Many of them established new friendships. Second, they were able to socialize without their husbands and children. This was important, as many of them were otherwise apartment-bound all day long. And finally, they had a chance to learn useful new skills, such as accounting, bookkeeping, and ordering from wholesalers. In many ways the cooperative became a rich, socially integrative, and varied experience for its members. Members confirmed its significance by holding monthly potluck dinners and occasional religious retreats (one of which was held at my house). At the time I finished the research, they had even begun a catering cooperative.

On the other hand, the council club ran into problems from its inception, although it had followed the St. Peter's model of operation. First, it tried to build a co-op using its own council executive board as a base. Unlike the women of St. Peter's buying club, the council board members were not low-income people and did not need the savings the cooperative could provide. Hence they had less incentive to make it succeed. Second, the council club involved men, most of whom did not value working on food-related projects and who saw anything connected with food as women's work. Third, they confused personality and work-related issues. The club, for example, started in Señor Hernandez's garage. Other club members resented the fact that it was in his (and not their) house, unlike Father Hagen's garage which was considered neutral. As a result, the club was moved to a $160-a-month storefront. That was neutral enough but the club ultimately could not generate enough business to pay the rent. Finally, the council club degenerated into a male social group, as distinct from a co-op. Members preferred getting together to socialize to doing business. Consequently, the group lacked real commitment.

Viewing the failure of the council club co-ops in terms of the Pygmy–Bushmen analogy, the council club did not work well because it was neither central to members' food needs nor did it become central to their social needs. Moreover, the group never developed a reason for being together which could balance work-related or personality difficulties. In the most basic terms, the Council Club was not important to its members. It failed long before it ran out of money.

As a suitable contrast, the breakaway Cooperativa was too conflict ridden to do any grocery operations. Because its members could not live on some future hopes when it came to something as necessary as food, and because the leadership conflict could not be resolved, they eventually lost interest. Most members eventually joined the council club.

These three co-ops succeeded or failed not because there were no savings and not because their members were incompetent to operate them, but for specific social, structural, and leadership reasons. It is clear that small-scale retail food cooperatives are very difficult to start and keep going, because they are both fragile and economically marginal. A person who saves five dollars a week may not be able to afford the time, energy, and emotional commitment to participate in a co-op, particularly in an inner-city area where there are other more pressing priorities and constraints of jobs, crime, and housing. It was only in the St. Peter's groups where there was real need and a group commitment to working in a cooperative format (expressed in religious terms) that a cooperative succeeded and flourished.

Like the weavers of Rochdale, who worked together as weavers and cooperators, the successful co-op may be not only the one that keeps its business operations afloat but also the one that finds ways for its members to share tasks equally. The St. Peter's buying club members had not only come to value their redistribution; they had also encouraged interaction with each other in diverse and complementary ways. They alternated work tasks in the club and in the class at the same time they socialized with each other. Furthermore, they celebrated their interdependence much as the Pygmies and Bushmen do, in dinners and religious retreats.

Unfortunately, the St. Peter's buying club represents one of the few successes in inner-city cooperative development. The club answers what is, in effect, a pressing need for most low-income residents – quality foodstuffs that are cheap and easily obtainable. Yet most inner-city residents do not organize cooperatives. These people face even more pressing needs than obtaining low-cost meals, such as finding safe housing and employment and securing personal safety. It is too much to expect them to participate in a time-consuming operation that does not save that much money.

Furthermore, like other Americans, their food habits are changing because they eat more meals out – in schools, cafeterias, or fast-food shops. In general, inner-city people today do not prize their hunt for food as do the Pygmies or the Bushmen. St. Peter's is an exception in more ways than one; its members still continue to buy groceries and eat mostly at home.

There are other groups like St. Peter's in most American inner-city areas, ones that can develop small-scale retail food cooperatives. They are the stable base groups found in churches, child-care centers, and mutual benefit associations. Their members can take on the additional tasks of a food cooperative and provide a needed service for themselves. But, as has been shown, developing a working cooperative is not an easy process.

Discussion: the relationship between anthropology, consultation, and co-op leadership

The data collected on each of the co-ops' structures, operations, and group commitments, as well as the material obtained on wholesalers and government agencies, were not affected by my consultant role. What was affected was leadership within the groups and its consequent effect on group processes. This is an unavoidable result of the sort of consultant role I had developed. I was, in effect, contracted by the leadership to help them develop co-operatives. The fact that I was ultimately invited in by Father Hagen and Señor Hernandez to their respective groups minimized the impact of my original approach to them and allowed me to play a more straightforward role.

What I did find was another dilemma, however, when I realized that the leaders were pressing me to broaden, not narrow, my contract and to solve too many problems. My combined role meant that I was not only an expert on everything cooperative but also on anything social. Resisting these pressures while trying to obtain data and help build the cooperatives meant that I had to walk a very narrow line.

This balancing act was made apparent when Señor Hernandez urged me to provide policy, rather than technical, alternatives. At the time I lunched with Señor Hernandez in March 1973, the council had received a six-thousand-dollar grant from the Campaign for Human Development to promote buying clubs. Señor Hernandez was the officer of the council with legal responsibility for disbursing the funds.

As we began lunch, he turned to me and asked: "What do you think I should do with the six-thousand-dollar grant?" I did not know how to reply and did not see it as a technical question, so I turned back to him: "What do you think?" During the remainder of the meal, he explained to me that the council wanted to use the money to subsidize its own club. As he answered my questions, he realized that, as grant officer, he would be violating the terms of the grant if the council implemented that desire.

My questioning had changed his awareness and some of his actions. It was an unavoidable consequence of trying to get data on how leaders intend to implement programs. Such interference data are acquired as a result of asking people to think things out; Komarovsky (1967) found this out in her counseling, when married couples, after her interviews, sometimes started divorce proceedings. In such cases the information and the consequences may be inseparable.

Sometimes research pressures can be handled by periodically withdrawing from the scene, as Bowen did (1954). I also wanted to see how Señor Hernandez – and the council – did without my presence. So, following the budget meeting, I did not visit the club for a month. Señores Hernandez and Chavez, the two leaders of the council club, spent some time during the summer of 1973 working out their policy differences on their own in a religious retreat. The same pressures to solve internal difficulties appeared as well in the St. Peter's club and the same withdrawal procedures were followed there as well.

The anthropologist-consultant role engenders other difficulties as well. This kind of anthropologist must learn to work closely with leaders and yet be independent of them in the group. He or she must have the leaders' trust and obtain reliable assessments of group operations when necessary yet must also be able to offer constructive criticism to the leadership regarding the contract expertise or other data being collected.

Hagen. The council club, in contrast, never progressed to the extent that I was working alongside the members.

The anthropologist-consultant role engenders other difficulties as well. This kind of anthropologist must learn to work closely with leaders and yet be independent of them in the group. He or she must have the leaders' trust and obtain reliable assessments of group operations when necessary yet must also be able to offer constructive criticism to the leadership regarding the contract expertise or in relation to other data being collected.

I was genuinely accepted as a helpful outsider by the women of the Bible class. More time and a female research assistant might have brought me additional data on the relationship of home life to club and Bible class life, but I did manage to establish enough legitimacy and independence from Father Hagen to collect data from members on leadership within St. Peter's church.

As for the effects of my technical expertise, I helped accelerate the time in which leaders and members solved problems peculiar to co-op activities. Father Hagen, for example, learned to work more effectively with the wholesalers as a result of my help. Similarly, the members of St. Peter's buying club learned to do their tasks faster. The result was that Father Hagen's leadership was probably strengthened, and members' difficulties in learning to adjust to a new and different type of work were minimized. More than likely, my technical expertise expedited the organizing of both clubs. Leadership works well when it can act effectively. Membership becomes more involved when it performs tasks easily. Father Hagen could not have organized his club, however, if he had not had the requisite leadership and organizational skills, and the women could not have done the work without the ability and interest needed to do so. Nor could any help I could have given Señor Hernandez compensate for the lack of viability in the council base.

Epilogue

It has been several years now since this study was completed. In retrospect, I still feel that I could not have worked in inner-city areas with a group that felt itself under attack if I had not reciprocated with something. I feel that the data I collected were, and still are, extremely valuable in understanding small-scale retail food cooperatives.

Anthropologists working in inner-city areas and among marginal groups are presented with even more complicated challenges than merely adjusting to an anthropologist-consultant role. They must research groups whose fortunes are affected by the research itself. Sometimes the change is for the better: Groups use the data provided to improve their operations or to press for additional funding. Often it is for the worse: Intragroup conflict may intensify because of the study, funding may be cut, or there may be political retaliation from other groups. The anthropologist is, for all practical purposes, an information specialist whose data may have unanticipated consequences.

Thus anthropologists face serious ethical problems in doing research in inner-city areas, and they must shape their theoretical concerns and methodology to accommodate this sensitive social and political reality. They may have to give quid pro quo in order to gain access – their services to a group which may specify what they may research and how the research is to be done. Some input from the group on conclusions and some restrictions or dissemination of information may have to be accepted.

These constraints may discourage anthropologists. Yet research needs to be done, because our understanding of all social problems is incomplete. Inner-city residents and policy makers both need reliable information on which to act and make policy to solve problems. Anthropologists must find ways of gaining access to marginal groups while respecting their informants' needs and their own commitment to scientific truth. The data collected are valuable as anthropological and historical records, despite these limitations.

6 The masking of social reality: ethnographic fieldwork in the bureaucracy

DAVID SERBER

The dilemma of research in government bureaucracy

One assumption of critical social research is that social reality is rarely what it first appears to be. Institutions of government, particularly regulatory agencies, often directly demonstrate this principle. They are publicly represented as doing one thing (protecting the public from abuses of the marketplace by private enterprise) while, in fact, they are doing something quite contradictory (stabilizing the profit-making environment). What is true of any social situation – that its complexities and causal mechanisms are not apparent – is even more true of what the French philosopher Louis Althusser has called the "ideological state apparatus," especially because elements of this apparatus have as an important part of their task the masking of social reality.

The state in a democratic capitalist society must appear to be neutral, or its legitimacy will be challenged (O'Connor 1973). The state's institutions must be perceived by the people to whom they are accountable as attempting to make decisions objectively, considering the interests of all social and economic sectors of the society. Regulatory agencies are some of the clearest examples of government organizations, ideally held as neutral (standing between consumers and corporations), that actually tend to minister to needs of regulated industry rather than to maintain balanced policies and practices. The ideological function of regulation is to demonstrate the state's neutrality by regulating industry in the public interest (see Offe 1973a).

The jurisprudential scholar Louis Jaffe (1954) argued that "industry orientation" and "capture" of the agency by the regulated industry are conditions endemic to both state and federal agencies that seek to regulate industry. Variations of the capture theory are widely held by economists (e.g., Posner 1974, Stigler 1975) and political scientists (e.g., Bernstein 1955, Edelman 1964). Lawyer-economist Bruce Owen, although developing a theory of regulation based on understanding the function and operation of the administrative processes, advises: "No industry offered the opportunity to be regulated should decline it. Few have done so. Railroads, airlines, telephone companies, radio stations, and other industries have warmly embraced regulation when it was offered and have strongly resisted efforts to remove it" (Owen and Brautigan 1979:2). We find much discussion but little research, however, on why this apparent capture is endemic despite agreement among scholars that contradictions exist between the agencies' ideal functions and actual practices. James Wilson (1974) offers an explanation based on Olson's *The Logic of Collective Action* (1965), suggesting that when the benefits of regulatory policy can be concentrated to a small group (industry) and the costs distributed widely (consumers) we find industry-oriented policy. When costs are concentrated and benefits widely dispersed, however, Wilson argues that such regulatory policy will be stalled. Therefore, the bulk of regulatory policy that is implemented will benefit industry.

Few have discussed the question of power as exercised by the regulated industry within the agency as well as in the environment of linking governmental institutions. To date there is little empirical research focusing on the organizational process of such agencies, despite the enormous impact that they have on our economy and overall quality of life in America: "Our thinking about the regulatory process and the independent commissions remains impressionistic, and the need for empirical research is largely unfulfilled" (Bernstein 1972:16).

Organizational researchers, although they have developed interesting frameworks that are potentially useful for better understanding regulatory agencies, have not yet studied regulation. The notion richly exploited in the literature, that some organizations can be best understood as responsive to their environment when they are dependent on resources outside the organization for survival (see Wamsley and Zald 1973; Aldrich and Pfeffer 1976) is particularly useful when thinking about regulatory agencies that appear to be completely dependent on outside organizations for budgetary allocations, appointments to leadership positions, legitimacy, and content and scope of regulatory power.

The lack of first-hand empirical organizational research on regulatory agencies may indicate that these agencies are uniquely difficult to study, in part because a structural requirement of such institutions is to conceal the actual organizational processes that generate industry orientation (Offe 1973b; see also Bachrach and Baratz 1963). It would seem highly probable that any publicly accountable institution violating its fundamental mandate (in this case, regulation in the public interest) may resist an attempt to observe empirically the way in which it operates. The use of interview and participant observation methods, however, techniques that allow us to penetrate the masks of social reality, depend on the cooperation of those being studied. Even in a research environment not characterized by such fundamental contradictions, we know that people and organizations are often reluctant to cooperate with social researchers whom they see as nosy and interfering and that neither individuals nor organizations have any formal obligation to cooperate with the independent researcher.

Many of the anthropological accounts of fieldwork describe how ethnographers have had to contend with varying degrees of cooperation in every field site (see particularly Whyte 1943:279–358, Berreman 1962, Powdermaker 1966). Yet in a research environment where there is a fundamental conflict between the public goals and actual behavior of the participants the question of cooperation may become even more problematic.

This paper describes some of the problems encountered in such a research situation (see also Blau 1963:269–305). I will discuss some of the ways in which my research design was successfully and unsuccessfully adapted to the environment of the regulatory agency as an ethnographic field site.[1]

My research problem – an ethnographic attempt to focus on the actual process of state regulation[2] of the insurance industry – required that I have access to many different organizational settings, individuals, situations, and written records. I needed, first of all, to be able to observe the process itself, through both conversations and negotiations between all parties, including regulators, industry representatives, and legislators. I needed to discuss specific cases as well as general conditions and aspects of work within the regulatory agencies. In addition, I needed to examine documents and records maintained by the participating organizations. Therefore, the process of gaining access was a continual activity.

The following discussion focuses on access in two central sites worked on during my twenty-six months of fieldwork on regulation of the insurance industry: the California Department of Insurance and the Pennsylvania Department of Insurance.[3] Although the two situations were quite dissimilar, the different sorts of access problems encountered reflected the degree to which inquiries attended to real, rather than ideal, regulatory processes.

The specific methods employed were largely determined by the degree of access available. The extended interview was the principal tool of the research. Because I was interested in developing a general ethnography of the process of regulation, interviews were based on a set of 250 questions, but they were not carried out in a rigorous fashion. The questions served as guides to the issues and areas studied as well as a means of redirecting often rambling and personal discussion by informants. Observation – or presence in the agency – was critical to the project and to developing an understanding of the agency and its relationship with industry. Focused observations, observation of meetings and of one-to-one interactions between staff, consumers, legislators and their agents, and industry representatives were employed throughout the research whenever possible. Such meetings were followed by interviews of the participants to get background and their perception of what took place. Also, the examination of documents provided a major source of my research hypotheses and data.

Access and cooperation in California

The California Department of Insurance was composed of approximately 260 employees, one-third of whom were professional staff. The agency has the responsibility of regulating business practices, scrutinizing rates, granting charters, examining for financial stability, and drafting and evaluating industry-related legislation. It is headed by the commissioner of insurance. The commissioner is appointed by the governor, but historically the choice has been determined by the recommendations of the larger campaign contributors in the insurance industry. I initially approached the commissioner of insurance, with my request for access. Despite my impersonal and academic presentation, it became clear that he was concerned that my efforts to understand the department might go beyond a description of standard operating procedures to what actually goes on in the Department of Insurance. My request included a summary of the proposed project and the kinds of interview, observational, and documentary access I would need. In addition, I made it clear that I would not be a participant in any regulatory activities and that I was independent from any state or private institutions associated with insurance regulation and would remain so throughout the research period. The commissioner responded by permitting interviews with employees who voluntarily agreed to talk with me during work hours. I was also permitted to observe day-to-day regulatory activities. This observation consisted of hours of sitting in the offices of regulators while they conducted their review of documents and consulted with co-workers and industry representatives. For example, I spent nine weeks observing officials process complaints about insurance companies brought by consumers to the Department of Insurance. I also had access to documents related to my observational material (for example, records of the disposition of consumer complaints).

As my research progressed, I became increasingly aware of the importance of informal procedures in routine regulatory practices as well as in policy formation and administrative decision making. For example, potential disciplinary problems with companies were identified and processed through confidential letters, telephone calls, and off-the-record meetings. Disciplinary matters were always under consideration; yet during the two-year period in which I followed the activities of the Department of Insurance, not a single formal disciplinary hearing proceeding concerning an insurancy company took place. It must be noted that this point implies not that company violations were never attended to but only that the means of dealing with these cases was informal and not subject to public review. I also found that regulations that originated in insurance company legal staff offices and subsequently revised at informal meetings between the company and the department were frequently and smoothly implemented. I became aware that the civil service hearings for advancement were symbolic confirmations of informal decisions made by top-level administrators in conjunction with representatives of industry. It became increasingly clear after an extensive period of exploratory research that if the process of insurance regulation was going to be understood, the inquiry must focus on the informal level.

Therefore, I began to construct a series of preliminary hypotheses concerning the relationships between various types of informal practices and regulatory decision making. These hypotheses served to guide further research activity. As my work progressed, my interview questions and observations must have clearly reflected this redirection in my research concerns. Informants began to volunteer information and documentation related to my interests in the informal; at the same time, however, they warned me that some of the higher-level administrators were observing me carefully and considering barring me from the agency. One informant commented:

You know, people around here are getting paranoid. They've got a pretty nice thing going and they don't want to get it screwed up by somebody makin' trouble in the newspapers . . .

I've been asked by ——— [chief legal counsel] to report all your questions to her; they don't know what you're up to, but they're worried. [interview 427-A]

Soon after this conversation, the commissioner summoned me to his office and severely restricted my access, explaining that it was not a question of "disapproving" of my research, but simply of the amount of staff time I was utilizing. Permission to examine documents, records, and correspondence not expressly designated under the law as public was withdrawn. I was informed that all such material was legally confidential under Clause 12919 of the California Insurance Code:

Communications to the Commissioner or any person in his office in respect to any fact concerning the holder of, or applicant for, any certificate or license issued under this code are made to him in official confidence within the meaning of subdivision 5 of Section 1881 of the code of civil Procedure. Liability shall not exist and no action or proceeding shall lie for, or on account of any such communication or the making thereof, but the existence of such communication shall not be deemed to dispense with or nullify any requirements of notice, hearing or production otherwise required by law.

This all-embracing protective clause guarantees to the regulated companies and the commissioner of insurance (meaning the Department of Insurance) that all internal memoranda, department – company communication, investigation reports, and files on company disciplinary matters that have not reached the stage of public hearing are confidential. The Department of Insurance officials who were responsible for overseeing my activities broadly interpreted Clause 12919 to include nonwritten material having a confidential character, thereby restricting my observation of informal meetings of the staff and between staff and company representatives. I was told that I could attend only public hearings (of which there were few), as specified under the law. I was also instructed to limit my questions to matters of public record; workers were instructed not to answer any questions that were not of this nature.

The basic goal of the research, to describe the actual regulatory process, became clearly associated with my fundamental methodological-theoretical problem: Because the public mandate for the representation of the regulatory agencies conflicts with the actual behavior of the organization, various barriers are established that serve to conceal and obscure the decision-making and administrative process. These barriers restrict access to state institutions and various types of state documents and records through both legislative and administrative regulations that guarantee the confidentiality of day-to-day regulatory practices and policy-formation processes. Because informal procedures are the substance of regulation, they were of primary interest to me, yet I found them easily protected or concealed by these barriers to information.

As the institution withdrew its cooperation, particularly by limiting opportunities to study informal regulatory processes, I was forced to develop alternative access strategies. The research was continued as unobtrusively as possible within the restrictions placed on me, but I began to arrange to interview regulatory workers outside the workplace. In addition, I constructed a list of all former professional employees of the department's northern California office and began to contact and interview them extensively. I also began to focus more on industry executives and lobbyists who frequently had dealings with the Department of Insurance.

As the research continued, the level of suspicion on the part of particular bureaucrats grew. A memo circulated throughout the department warning employees that they should be extremely cautious in their conversations with outsiders and reiterated the restrictions on the subject matter discussed. I was told that a set of files I had been working on (which were not legally confidential) had been removed from the office for storage and later destruction. After several months more research, the paranoia of certain officials became comical, as I was followed from office to office and into the bathroom by the chief administrative officer.

When I inquired why my briefcase was being searched repeatedly when I left the office and why I was now being observed routinely as I performed some of the most private bodily functions, I was curtly told: "We are instituting some new security procedures here because some confidential documents have been discovered missing." An informant later explained, as I suspected, that it was "simple harassment," designed to discourage my research:

They just want you to go away. They've tried to make it as difficult for you as possible to get the data you want, and you're still around, so now they're harassing you. They're standard methods bureaucrats use to "subtly" communicate their disapproval. [interview 137]

As I interviewed regulatory workers outside the department, I found that the contradiction between official rhetoric and actual regulatory practice (which had resulted in my interest in the informal and eventually restricted institutional access) promoted and enhanced my access and rapport to many individuals. A handful of workers, particularly some of the higher-level bureaucrats, refused to grant outside interviews, or, if they consented, they restricted their answers to safe areas of public record. Most professional regulatory workers, however, particularly attorneys whom I sought to interview in this fashion, not only consented to interviews but also saw departmental restrictions as not applicable to interviews on their own time. In fact, I discovered that many of these workers resented the limitations placed on my attempt to study the department and viewed these restrictions as violations of their own personal and professional autonomy. As one attorney articulately explained:

I wanted to do this interview despite [attorney's supervisor's] objections and the general attitude around the office. These types of restrictions are part of a general pattern to keep attorneys in their place. I think that there is an effort, conscious or otherwise, on the part of the administration to denigrate the attorneys and to sap them of their independence, to make them more susceptible and more willing to be overruled. Many methods are used to bring this about – the first is to treat attorneys in a manner that one could only call demeaning. They constantly chide attorneys for taking coffee breaks and lunch breaks that are five minutes too long. Or treat their suggestions for improvement in regulatory procedure or working conditions as being totally impractical, and not giving them any consideration. This is because they don't want attorneys taking an active role in determining procedures or establishing working hours or suggesting innovations . . . And they will often tell an attorney who tries to exercise independent thought and action that he is politically unrealistic or politically naive, rather than encourage him to pursue an unpopular cause or try to forward a new idea. . . . Often attorneys are treated as errant children or school boys instead of dealing with us on a professional level. [Serber 1976:119–120]

Other informants further confirmed my notion that formal restrictions placed on my research and the tendency of department supervisors to maintain absolute control over the activities of their subordinates are outgrowths of the administration's fear of public exposure. As my work in California progressed, I developed a large base of informants who extensively and frankly discussed the realities of insurance regulation. They volunteered information and documentation of informal procedures that characterized regulation in the state. Therefore, although the administration's attempts at limiting my access succeeded in preventing much direct observation of informal decision making, it failed to discourage the cooperation of the regulatory workers and in fact helped to generate much richer data that I had actually expected to gather. In this sense, institutional restrictions placed on my research in order to mask the contradictions of regulatory activities served to increase my access to information on the regulatory practices.

Access and cooperation in Pennsylvania

The problems of access in the Pennsylvania department were remarkably different. In California, the top administrators were closely associated with the insurance industry but had a strong interest in maintaining a neutral public image. The administration's restrictions on my access and the repressive work environment for the professional staff were both outgrowths of the conflict between ideal regulatory neutrality and actual regulatory practices (Serber 1975). In contrast, the commissioner of insurance in Pennsylvania, Herbert S. Denenberg, acknowledged the traditional industry orientation of insurance regulatory agencies and vowed publicly to reform the Pennsylvania department. The official motto of Denenberg's Pennsylvania Department of Insurance became: *Populus iamdudem debutatus est* (the consumer has been screwed long enough).

My initial request for access clearly delineated my interest in informal processes and outlined the type of observational and documentary access my work required. In addition, I provided the commissioner (who formally held a chair at the Wharton School of Business, University of Pennsylvania) with the papers and proposals I had prepared on my California study. The commissioner's response was to grant me unlimited access to the agency. I was given absolute freedom of movement and the administration's guarantee that I could interview anyone who consented to being interviewed without limitations on subject matter, I was also extended the privilege of observing all meetings of staff and between staff and industry, providing the agency's participant did not object. Workers were urged in an official memorandum to cooperate with me. All documents I requested were to be available for my examination with the restriction that details of a confidential nature (names of individuals and companies) would not be published. I was even permitted to use an unoccupied office as a base for my research both inside and outside the Department of Insurance. The commissioner's assurance of complete access was maintained throughout the research period.

The administration's guarantee of open access to the Pennsylvania department, however, created a set of access problems different from those encountered in California. Many of these problems developed from the unique set of circumstances surrounding Denenberg's flamboyant attempt to reform insurance regulation in Pennsylvania. Other access problems were a result of the same set of regulatory contradictions that generated formal barriers to access in California.

Rather than adopting the more conservative and professional mannerisms and language characteristic of the head of a state bureaucracy, Denenberg employed a colorful style and street vocabulary that attracted the press but was disturbing to other state officials as well as the industry. During the first three years of his administration, over 2,000 press releases were prepared and distributed and more than seventy-five articles appeared in local and national magazines; Denenberg also made dozens of television appearances during that period.

While the brunt of his public assault was directed at the insurance industry, Denenberg made public statements mercilessly criticizing physicians, dentists, lawyers, and state legislators, whom he referred to as "bungling do-nothings." *Time* magazine dubbed him "Herb the Horrible" as he rapidly became the most famous insurance commissioner in the history of the country. A poll taken by the governor's office revealed that he was better known by Pennsylvanians than either of the state's U.S. senators; only the governor's recognition rating was equal to Denenberg's.

While Ralph Nader was acclaiming Denenberg as "a true public servant" (*Harrisburg Evening News*, Oct. 4, 1971, p. 11) the insurance industry, organized medicine, and the Pennsylvania Bar Association were all calling on the governor for his dismissal. In a public letter to the governor, the Pennsylvania Medical Association stated: "There are, we believe, several options. You as appointing authority, may replace him. This would be the quickest and easiest." The letter further threatened "to accede to the growing demand of our member physicians for a withdrawal from all bureaucratic aspects of the state-operated medical care plans. The thought is to continue to take care of people but to withhold all paper work until Mr. Denenberg is removed from office." (*Sunday Patriot News*, Oct. 12, 1972, p. 1).

The demand for Denenberg's removal was echoed by the Pennsylvania Bar Association and, of course, by insurance company executives throughout the nation. Denenberg's direct attacks and issue-oriented reform attempts threatened these groups, but they were most disturbed by his successful strategy of public exposure. When asked by one journalist how he could "take on the entire insurance industry, legal profession and the medical profession," Denenberg's response was, "Yea, though I walk through the valley of the shadow of death I fear no evil, because I am the meanest mother-fucker in the valley" (Frederick Ferretti, "Horrible Herb," *Viva*, 1(November 1973), p. 67).

I thought he [Denenberg] was a clown, and many others thought he was too. He said the present auto insurance industry was a consumer fraud. He used powerful and seriously indicting language. He called businessmen the kinds of things he did. *And many members of the public believed it.* So they say, "If it is true, the whole thing ought to be done away with and the federal government should take over." Because of this I think Denenberg is extremely dangerous. The more regulation, the less competition, and before we know it they will nationalize the whole goddamn industry. [interview 601 with a company president; emphasis added]

As Denenberg seriously threatened the industry, it fought him by every means available to them. The Insurance Federation of Pennsylvania, the major industry trade association and one of the most powerful lobby organizations in the state, orchestrated the industry's efforts to undermine Denenberg in the legislature, through the media, and within Denenberg's own agency.

The agents' trade association and at least a dozen large insurance companies in the state also independently assaulted Denenberg and his policies. The Senate Insurance Committee, whose chairman was financially linked to the largest insurance company in the state, violently opposed Denenberg. The House Consumers Affairs committee (responsible for insurance legislation) was Republican-dominated and publicly investigating "improprieties" in the Denenberg administration with impeachment in mind. The governor's office was also active in continually attempting to tighten the reins on Denenberg.

In addition to these external forces working to undermine Denenberg and his attempted reform, the Department of Insurance itself was dramatically torn; although many factions existed, the principal conflict was between Denenberg and his appointees and the civil service staff of professional regulators.

Enter the anthropologist who wants to study formal and informal regulatory process. The notion of independent research was no more a legitimate concept to the actors in this field environment than it is to the group of Truk islanders who poisoned one of my former colleagues because they thought he was paying informant fees to members of the other clan on the island.

I always knew this was a zoo, but when you came here, I was sure. I thought, "Anthropologist my ass," what's this guy up to? I was sure you were working for ——— [the executive assistant for the consumer affairs committee] and when I was told you were meeting with him, I was sure. Everybody thought you were a spy for somebody or other. Even ——— [an insurance lawyer] said he "knew" you were working for Ralph Nader . . . I remember getting a call from ——— [principal lobbyist] . . . He's not really a zoologist or anthropologist? He said "Who the hell is this Serber? He's got to be working for Denenberg?" [Denenberg appointee, interview 731–3C]

Each faction within and without the Pennsylvania Department of Insurance suspected I was a spy for one of the other factions.

As my research was not limited to the agency, it became known that I was spending time with the Insurance Federation, House Consumers Affairs Committee, Senate Insurance Committee, and various companies and lobbyists; speculation about my loyalties was rampant. As paranoia grew, complete cooperation and acceptable rapport were difficult to achieve. To further complicate matters, at a later point, after I had gained access to the highly confidential weekly meetings of the Board of Directors of the Insurance Federation of Pennsylvania and had established some rapport with prominent industry representatives and lobbyists, I became the subject of suspicion by those loyal to Denenberg. Not only did most of them suspect me of some sort of political espionage, but the key actors, including the lobbyists for the federation, members of the House Consumer Affairs Committee, and Denenberg himself attempted to recruit me as their own personal informant.

Despite my refusal to provide information and my careful maintenance of the posture of the professional, and objective researcher, the participants often appeared so convinced of the correctness of their positions that they seemed to suspend their suspicions and assume I was their ally. This often became awkward, as in an informal meeting I attended between Denenberg, his top aids, and powerful industry representatives. I recall Denenberg making a very strong statement about company practices and sending a glancing look toward me as if to say, "I really told those bastards," while the lobbyist for the Insurance Federation looked at me with an expression that clearly read "I told you this guy was crazy." I soon became disturbingly aware that other participants in the meeting noticed what had occurred.

Despite such setbacks to my professional image, the strategy of openly associating both formally (by interviewing and observing behavior in interactive situations and interviews) and informally (by bar hopping and poker playing, etc.) with all factions in the regulatory community, yet never disclosing what others told me, slowly began to establish my reputation as an independent researcher. After four months in Pennsylvania this was acknowledged; one morning I came into the department and found an official Department of Insurance plaque on my office door that read "David Serber Outside Spy." That plaque remained there throughout the balance of my research.

The most difficult problem I had within the Department of Insurance in Pennsylvania was obtaining the active cooperation of the civil service staff who had long histories of industry orientation (see Serber 1975:96–103). Despite Denenberg's loud fanfare,

Day-to-day regulatory activities of civil service staff were relatively unaffected by the new regulatory policies of the reform administration; the loyalties of the civil service staff and administration remained with industry and previous regulatory patterns prevailed. Industry representatives were constantly seen in the Department. Throughout the agency, attempts at more aggressive regulation and new regulatory policies were met with intense internal resistance. In the division which was headed by a non–civil service Denenberg appointee, some minimal controls and checks were developed to moniter the performance of the civil service staff, but again, this was met by tremendous resistance. Wherever possible, staff would revert to informal accommodation of regulatory process. [Serber 1976:208]

The barriers I encountered were unofficial manifestations of the same contradictions and tendencies that officially restricted my access in the California Department of Insurance.

Organizational ethnography is highly dependent on informants' cooperation in order to get access to various kinds of situations. In a complex, formal organization so much activity takes places that it is impossible for a single researcher to become aware of every significant situation in which observation might be desirable. Therefore, even in a situation in which access is guaranteed, unless participants actively inform the researcher of what is taking place, he or she misses many observational opportunities. For example, as I discussed above, informal meetings among staff members and between staff and industry are at the core of the process of regulatory activity; notification of such meetings is more than likely equally informal and not a matter of public record. In order to obtain access to situations, I needed to be aware that they were being planned. Therefore, my access depended on informants notifying me in advance that such meetings were going to take place. In this sense, access was largely dependent on rapport. For example, in Pennsylvania, I would frequently receive notes on my desk like this one:

Meeting next Friday at 2:00 on Safeguard in Denenberg's office. Informant 2C.

While there was some humor intended here, the meeting was a pivotal one, and my attendance was dependent on a participant's assistance.

While the commissioner and his appointees were attempting to transform the ideology of insurance regulation into a reality, career civil servants were successfully maintaining the industry orientation of regulatory practices:

Part of the problem of reorganizing the Department of Insurance is that the staff fights you. When you try to regulate the industry, they have an instinctive feeling that one way or another, this is the only thing that could eventually cost them their job and career possibilities in insurance they might have. And in most cases they are right. [interview 204]

The old guys around here have a way of really putting a crimp in this operation. It's like guerilla warfare. They sabotage us, but we can't see their faces. [interview no. 181]

In this situation, civil service staff, particularly those in top supervisory positions, had to conceal their regulatory practices and activities. The contradiction between rhetoric and actual practice operated on an unofficial or informal level within the department to restrict my access. These informal barriers took the longest to break down. It was only after the civil servants were aware that industry welcomed me to their private meetings and informal leisure activities that many of them confided in me and actively aided my research efforts.

Concluding note

The research experiences discussed in the Pennsylvania and California regulatory agencies demonstrate how attempts to obtain and maintain access on various organizational levels reveal conflicts and contradictions that operate within the organization (see Heydebrand 1977). It is likely that the state institutions, which often have contradictory goals and procedures, are most likely to exhibit these as researchers attempt to gain access to various types of data. Public–private and individual–organization conflicts create serious access problems and require the researcher continuously to develop strategies to maintain access on the individual level. Because individual access is central to the process of organizational research, cooperation or rapport is the key to maintaining access and making access pay off. An ethnographic approach allows the social researcher to exploit various alternatives as unforseen situations arise that threaten the research. Those of us who attempt organizational ethnography must remain flexible enough in our research design so that we may adapt to, rather than turn away from, access problems generated by the internal conflicts and contradictions that are often fundamental characteristics of such field sites.

PART III Rural studies

A study of ecology and regional economic forms is the topic of John W. Bennett and Seena Kohl in their joint research in rural Canada (Chapter 7). This discussion of the Saskatchewan project describes the methods and theory employed in their already well-publicized work (Bennett 1969, 1976b, 1980b; Kohl 1976). As a regional study, it is an expansion of the more traditional community-study approach. Well into the paper, the authors ask themselves if what they are doing is really anthropology. They conclude that it is, as it uses established methodology (cultural ecology and in-depth fieldwork) and reflects local perspectives throughout.

Susan Brandt Graham's dual community study in Arizona (Chapter 8) demonstrates the application of the network approach to contemporary anthropology. This study integrates important methodological and theoretical insights into questions of class and community structure. Graham also describes what it is like to be in a small company town, living out the contradictory roles of company employee's spouse and research anthropologist. Her solutions to problems of method, theory, and role are especially revealing of the creativity of anthropology at home.

Can the researcher be his or her own key informant? This potentially divisive issue is addressed by Lawrence Hennigh in a study of a rural Oregon town (Chapter 9). Hennigh describes his problems pursuing a field assignment (part of a large research contract) that did not fit the field situation. He then describes and justifies becoming one of the townsfolk and using his own insights into community life as a principal research tool. In the end, he says, researchers in their own society cannot avoid being their own informants, like it or not.

The methods of ethnographic semantics focus Agnes M. Aamodt's inquiry into neighboring behavior in rural Wisconsin (Chapter 10). Aamodt's interests combine nursing with anthropology. Here she has focused on her own kinfolk to elucidate various categories of caring for one another, or "things neighbors do for neighbors." In consequence, her professional involvement brings her home on a personal quest, exploring her own rural Norwegian-American-Lutheran roots.

7 Longitudinal research in rural North America: the Saskatchewan Cultural Ecology Research Program, 1960–1973

JOHN W. BENNETT and SEENA KOHL

The Saskatchewan Cultural Ecology Research Program (SCERP) was conceived in 1960 as an attempt to explore the relevance of anthropological cultural ecology for the study of contemporary agrarian society in North America.[1] The choice of a North American setting was based upon the conviction that the anthropological study of contemporary societies is an important area of research because the tribal cultures, long an anthropological specialty, were fast disappearing. Contemporary rural societies seem a natural compromise: They lack the bewildering multiplicity and large populations of urban areas, yet they are close to the soil and subsistence and retain many social features, such as personalistic relations, of smaller, multifunctional societies.

In 1961, when the study began, existing research in anthropological cultural ecology consisted entirely of studies of tribal and peasant communities and was influenced by the ethnological conception of discrete cultures based on a subsistence economy.[2] In the North American context, attention had to be paid to the changing pattern of incentives and constraints imposed by the market system and the various government and private agencies that control the resources needed for production.

The culture of these North American agricultural communities is strongly characterized by public orientation toward production and by a concern for the monetary nexus of social organization. Instrumental concerns may dominate daily activity and conversation, although this emphasis may be modified in private social contexts, such as the family, the church, social ceremonials, and social relationships. Both of these relationships – instrumental and expressive – are diffused across an extensive geographical territory in the typical North American rural society, and especially so in the western half of the continent, with its sparse populations and limited productivity. *Community* is hard to define; what takes its place is a series of overlapping functional spheres of social and economic participation. In order to obtain an adequate sample of these overlapping contexts of life, it is necessary to focus on relatively large geographical-social regions rather than nucleated communities.

The region we call "Jasper" was located in Saskatchewan, the center of the Canadian section of the North American Great Plains. It was selected mainly because of its variety of natural environmental features, resources, and ethnic and occupational groups.[3] The region also had environmental constraints that imposed definite limits on the conduct of commercial agriculture. Settlement was relatively recent, and first-generation pioneers and rich historical data were available for study. The inhabitants, with a few exceptions, possessed general North American middle-income standards that were difficult to attain given the economic and climatic constraints. The general mix of characteristics seemed appropriate for a cultural-ecological study, providing the approach was defined in general terms as an investigation of the interplay between the physical and social environment in the process of making a living. The fact that the society was producing for the market rather than for subsistence made necessary a conception of a complex social environment which had to be manipulated – adapted to – very much as physical resources are managed.

The presence of a large component of contemporary institutional structure and process required a wide range of methods: Survey techniques as well as depth interviewing; documentary analysis; media analysis; investigatory tactics designed to penetrate the vicissitudes of legal and administrative regulations; the full use of local people as participants and advisors, making the relationship between researcher and subject really one of collaboration. Above all, there was need for time depth in the study, as the essence of adaptation to both the social and physical environments was the behavioral process of coping with continual change and fluctuation. A simple synchronic approach, if made during a period of high market prices, or unusually favorable weather, would seriously distort the findings or fail to note existing adaptive strategies used in less fortunate episodes. Although the project was not initially proposed as a longitudinal study, within the first year or two of research it became apparent that this would have to be done. SCERP used methodological elements borrowed from anthropology, sociology, economics, geography, and agronomy; however, the methods with crucial significance for the study of cultural ecology were those associated with longitudinality.

Longitudinal research requires dedication to a single research site and repeated visits over many years. It permits the researcher to follow a population through time to assess factors of continuity and change in both the individual and the social structure. Change is, in fact, one of the central themes of this kind of research.

Longitudinal research also permits a continuous and continually deepening understanding of a given social system. Most relevant is the serendipitous character of repeated visits in which data collected at one time serve to illustrate a later topic of research. Similarly, longitudinality permits reanalysis of data, the reinvestigation of problems, and above all allows for field-defined questions to be resolved at leisure. Although these attributes sound so attractive that one may ask why all field studies are not longitudinal, it should be remembered that each of these features imposes severe burdens of time, effort, and technical complexity on the researcher.[4] Longitudinal research is most easily accomplished when the researcher has a stable professional position and is not concerned with rapid or abundant publication. Longitudinal research requires at least two items of data for every one needed by a single time-slice study – a feature that seems of minor significance until the data begin to multiply through the years, and the second, third, or fourth data item differs radically from the first. Longitudinal or diachronic research is cumbersome and requires a level of theory that transcends that of synchronic studies, which need not cope with the problem of both segmental and vectorial (secular) change.

The fieldwork setting

The region, named for its major service center town of Jasper, was defined as a flexible area of from six thousand to seven thousand square miles (15,000 to 18,000 square kilometers) located in the southwestern portion of the province of Saskatchewan. The dominant economic activities of the region were cattle and grain agriculture, occurring in pure and mixed contexts and at different levels of scale. The region was sparsely populated, with about 1.7 persons per square mile (.66 persons per square km). In general, cattle ranching was located on the slopes of the hills and mixed grain and cattle farming on the plains. The region also included six Hutterian colonies (total population 540 in 1970) and a small nontreaty Indian reserve with about 110 persons.[5] There were as well five small village and town settlements which, with the exception of one, Jasper town, a multipurpose service community, could be defined as specialized service centers.

This entire geographical, demographic, and social entity was defined locally as the Jasper region in conversation and in printed documents and maps, such as those produced by commerical and civic bodies in Jasper town and in the villages. Local people also viewed themselves as residents of this region, and often spoke proudly of belonging to this historic old western pioneer area. The conceptual unity of the region was also shared by other people in Saskatchewan and by the provincial government. Our demarcation of the Jasper region was determined by ecological considerations of terrain and habitat, economic activities, and political, social, and symbolic boundaries. We used definitions of the region as given to us by residents and by various bureaucratic agencies.

Jasper, the first town settlement in the region (founded in 1883 as a camp for Canadian Pacific Railroad laborers) is the site of the region's hospital, consolidated high school, major banks and post office station, and major religious groups. Contrasted with the small specialized service-center villages, which might consist of a bulk-oil dealer, grain elevator, gas station, and perhaps a store or cafe, Jasper represents a functional social community with a small business district and a population of some 2,500 persons (in 1970).

Because settlement of the region was late and economic stabilization of agricultural enterprises recent, the accepted conveniences of urban life were late in entering the region. Electrification of rural areas in Saskatchewan was accomplished by 1956. Other amenities, however – plumbing, phones, and passable roads – were in the process of entering the region when fieldwork began in 1961. By the end of the decade of our research, all these amenities were available and expected.

In traditional ethnological conceptions, fieldwork consists of the time spent with informants whose culture – the community culture – one is trying to find out about. But in a study like SCERP, the boundaries of the culture are impossible to establish other than arbitrarily, because the people of the community are nodes in networks radiating out over a whole continent and their ideas and actions are continuously influenced – are really part of – much larger systems.

Consequently, the conception of fieldwork had to be extended to include communication with experts and officials, agents of change outside the region, keepers of the gates to resources wherever they might be, and sources of information coming into the region. SCERP made full use of these agencies, and Bennett spent at least three weeks of every major field season traveling between Jasper and other parts of Saskatchewan, Alberta, Montana, and North Dakota, tracing lines of influence and connection and seeking information and expertise. Traditional fieldwork and "background" research – as the latter has usually been called by anthropologists – merged. A range management specialist might furnish technical knowledge that enabled the researchers to analyze data, but this same person might also be a relative of local Jasper people, bound up in status and influence networks in the region. Hence, he was an informant as well as an expert.

Because of the nature of government, many bits of vital information in a study emphasizing adaptive behavior cannot be obtained locally, as they are analytically separable only in a bureaucratic context. For example, in our studies of land use and adaptation to resources, we found it necessary to study the mechanisms and kinds of allocation of leased grazing land in government offices hundreds of miles from Jasper, because the local people often did not know this information or could not see the big picture. Therefore, some of our fieldwork consisted of sitting at desks in government offices and participating with government, university, and trade association officials and members. While much of this work came under the heading of background interviews, it is impossible to make detailed assessment of the time and effort, since so much of it was informal and part of it unrecorded or recorded only in informal notes.

Other styles of fieldwork emerged due to the nature of the study and of the locale. The traditional anthropological field experience took place (or was supposed to do so) within a clearly defined community with social and natural boundaries. These boundaries, set by natural features – the village, barrio, or neighborhood – served as containers for social life and lines that the fieldworker could stay within. Where there were no simple geographical boundaries to the Jasper community, there were nevertheless fairly well defined social boundaries that demarcated the interaction between group members. In SCERP research, the rather vague geographic boundaries of the study region surrounded an area of over 6,000 square miles (15,500 square km). Thus, the long interview, acquired by automobile travel to the respondent, assumed key importance. The region was sparsely populated, and because people played different roles in different places, individuals who were interviewed in one context, for example, as enterprise operators, were met and interviewed in other places and contexts, for example, as schoolboard members or 4H Club leaders. Since there were several members of the research project, it was possible to interview the same individual several times in varying contexts. This made it possible to check perceptions and share information. Further, the longitudinal nature of the research meant that these same people could be re-interviewed as their life situations or organizational positions changed.

Roles of the researchers

Roles played by the fieldworkers were, on the whole, standard for fieldwork[6] social science. The diverse sex, age, and status roles of the researchers were important elements in the process of information collection. The contrast between the rights and obligations of the male members of the research group with those of Kohl, the female member, led to different sets of friendships and consequently to contrasting views of social relations and of the region's friendship networks. [7] Similarly, the different status positions of professor and graduate student permitted contrasting views of the fieldworkers by Jasper folk. The more formal role was assigned to Bennett as the "professor," and a less formal (and more ambiguous) set of expectations assigned to Kohl, both female and "student." The fact that the latter had a more junior role, and a sympathetic one as the friend of families, however, meant that she was more privy to the ambivalence felt by many people in Jasper towards the highly educated and urban person – attitudes reflected in mixed feelings about the research project. [8]

SCERP methodology combined individual exploration of congenial topics with a constant central synthesis. This approach worked, in that the research was not confined to a one-shot field session but was a continuous and evolving process building from one fieldwork session to the next. The individual projects were conceived as complementary, and they moved along paths representing the key ethnic and institutional areas of Jasper society and economy. Continual conferencing, in the field and back home, permitted us to keep the central focus on socioeconomic and ecological questions in view at all times. The research roles of the several fieldworkers were thus independent but nevertheless coordinated.

No attempt was made to deceive Jasper people, although the objectives of the study were often described in somewhat simplified terms: "economic history," "economic development," "family life and history," "the development of natural resources," and so on. Kohl, primarily concerned with social relationships and the relationships between family and agricultural enterprise, emphasized topics concerning the history of the family, development of the enterprise, and goals for the future. [9] Kohl, as a woman, was expected to be concerned with family and children – the woman's world. Her own status as wife and mother was an important element in the exchange of information about children and aspirations for children. There seemed to be less apparent concern and anxiety about her discussions with family members on family roles and obligations and the expectations held for children than there was about the economic topics. Common experiences and problems were shared, and differences between rural and urban situations were discussed. In some situations Kohl was asked to act as arbiter, a role she filled by attempting to rephrase the questions and arguments so the disputants could begin to communicate.

Bennett, with previous research experience in rural North America, [10] followed the direction of local male interests in his interviewing, emphasizing the topics of management, economics, and politics. As one way of rendering the social exchange between researcher and resident more fruitful to both parties, he trained himself in agricultural and development economics. Thus he was able to repay his informants for their time by discussing their problems with a certain amount of (it is hoped) helpful knowledge. Bennett probably did not play the role of anthropologist as often as he performed as a somewhat authoritative and sympathetic partisan of rural life and affairs – a role representing genuine commitment and interest.

One of the ways the traditional role of the anthropologist has been defined is as the learning of a different way of life (or language, myths, etc.). Such presentation of self and one's intentions has been on the whole explicable and understandable in the context of exotic peoples. In a setting where the researcher already occupies a certain status in a known national or continental social system and is not unfamiliar with the culture, the stance of learner is not an obvious one, even though it may be precisely the one the researcher desires to assume. It must be validated and explicated before the residents can respond to teachers.

We found it necessary and true to point out to Jasper people that they had particular expertise that the researcher as an urbanite did not have. This consisted of their experiences in managing a difficult and capricious environment that was different from other rural and certainly urban situations. However, these people also maintained their connection with and were also able to manage aspects of the urban world that might be considered difficult and capricious, such as bureaucratic regulations. The interviews and subsequent conversation with residents commonly included discussion of urban life compared with rural life. Thus, the Jasper residents were assured that their expertise was real, and this enabled them to view researchers at least in part as learners. In addition, there was continual reaffirmation of the fact that only through the collection of individual agrifamily histories could the researchers ever hope to complete the social history of the region, and that completion of this task was dependent upon the residents' help. [11]

The collection of data on economic and technological matters proceeded as a mixture of interview and observation. Westerners are known for their taciturnity, especially toward urban outsiders, and Jasper farmers, ranchers, and resource agents were no exception. Before detailed information was communicated, it was necessary for the fieldworkers to exhibit, in subtle fashion, their preliminary understanding and appreciation of the complexities of the informants' lives, and this required, whenever possible, actual participant behavior. Thus, Bennett and the other male fieldworkers frequently assisted in branding, inoculation, haying, harvesting, planting, irrigation, extension services, and other key features of the year's round of activities.

Once the knowledge of the fieldworker had been demonstrated, collaborators became free with details, complications, and exceptions. They also became able to analyze the operations of their neighbors and associates, permitting a protocol of multifaceted portraits of the scale and skill of the conduct of agricultural management by a large sample of family farm and ranch enterprises. This emerging body of data began to have theoretical implications rather early in the study, and we shall describe these in a later section of this chapter.

Because the technical and economic information was highly specialized, it became necessary to consider many of our key informants as true research collaborators. This collaborator role was informal in most cases, but in some it took on formal associate status in SCERP. Such persons assisted the fieldworkers in locating interview respondents, constructing samples or correcting the grosser census sampling categories, providing expertise on technical and geographical matters, delivering lectures on Jasper history and culture and filling in gaps in genealogies, providing skill assessments of farm and ranch operators, and helping in many other contexts of research. SCERP owes a considerable debt to these collaborators, and field research in North American society must recognize the necessity of this type of interrelated research operation. It is fundamentally different from the classic image of the lone anthropologist investigating nonliterate or unsophisticated native peoples.

Public statistics and media documentation

Field studies of particular sectors of politically centralized, record-keeping societies have an important advantage over research in tribal and peasant communities insofar as a large body of documentation on social phenomena is available in public offices. These data do not always substitute for detailed field surveys, because the criteria for microsocial research are almost always finer than those designed for governmental surveys of various kinds. Nevertheless, certain important subjects are well covered by these resources, and they save much valuable time.

Our use of census data for Jasper increased as time went on. By 1971, the census of Canada made available printouts of data for various small areas. This refined our presentations of district and township demographic information over and above the level available in *Northern Plainsmen* (Bennett 1969, 1976b), which used data from the early 1960s. In some instances, we combined our field data on families, households, and migration with the census data, using the two sets as checks against one another. For example, where census data for a particular small area showed a net loss for a certain census interval, our genealogical and migration data for that area would be searched to see if the loss was a real one or resulted from difference in the various sources. When the discrepancies were unresolvable, we took a median point. In any case, the level of accuracy was close enough for our purposes, which were to show trends and patterns (see Bennett 1976b:107).

In some cases we supplemented published statistics with our own data. This was true for weather data, which, with the usual exception of temperature, is rarely collected for small areas. Because we were concerned with microclimatic and microedaphic differences, it was necessary to acquire information of our own for particular localities. We made full use of local weather observers – usually farmers – and we consulted the tax records of the rural municipalities for precise data on soil types for particular spots (rural land taxes are based on soil types in Saskatchewan).

All of our local collaborators in the study of the contemporary country population were literate and all paid close attention to the information and recreation media typical of North American culture. Their images of the Jasper region and the immediate community around Jasper town were shaped by the attention given the area by Canadian television, radio, magazines, and newspapers. The media conceptions of the old West, ranchers, homesteaders, and Indians had formed a layer of symbolism in Jasper thinking that had reshaped the authentic anecdotes and history of the frontier. More importantly for our study, with its instrumental emphases, Jasper enterprise was influenced by the outpouring of technical and economic information produced by the provincial and federal departments of agriculture, and by the agribusiness companies.

We found it necessary to study these informational and symbolic inputs into Jasper mentality, because they formed a significant part of everyday discourse and entered into key concepts and explanations of why people did what they did. We found that the most convenient method was to collect documents, clippings, lists, program schedules, manuals, and pamphlets: The collection in the SCERP office fills three file drawers. It was not always possible to know just what documentation was influential for what purpose, so this operation, like others in fieldwork in any society, inevitably suffers from redundancy. But it is redundancy in a good cause; more is never enough, and new meanings and significance are constantly being found in old documents as data analysis continues and as reinterpretation of social process and cultural meaning proceed in a longitudinal research program.

The sampling procedure

Studies that focus longitudinally on a particular region and a particular problem differ from sociological and attitude-survey research, whose objectives are to sample an existing human population at a particular point in time. The socioeconomic aspect of SCERP was concerned with sampling the relevant socioeconomic units within the natural population and the roles of the people within these units. Because these interests represented a combination of economic and ecological criteria, our basic units ere economic enterprises, or rather, that combination of kin, friends, and agricultural enterprise we now call the agrifamily. From the beginning we anticipated at least two years of fieldwork. We knew that as our knowledge accumulated our ability to sample relevant sections of the universe would improve and that opportunities for correction of earlier attempts would be available. Figure 7.1 lists the relevant populations that evolved during the study.

The first effort towards gaining a representative population centered on the construction of the regional schedule, a thirty-five page comprehensive instrument consisting of many types of questions – open-ended, precoded, discussional, fill-in – administered to a set of farm and ranch operators and members of their families selected to match the categories of farming and income levels enumerated in the 1960 Canada Census of Agriculture for the region (although we did modify the census categories because we found them too crude). The census classifications for income, type of farming (mode of production), and acreage were based largely on central Canadian agriculture and did not clearly represent a typical plains grain–livestock region such as Jasper. The case population developed by administering this regional schedule represented our major attempt to sample the country population of the region.

The second continuing effort at sampling consisted of selecting cases designed to test particular hypotheses or pursue particular problems (for example, housewives, small ranchers, teenagers, a special panel of enterprise managers, people of a certain religious affiliation). As our work with such groups of cases proceeded, we related the accumulating lists to the regional schedule population to check representativeness. In other words, the original regional schedule case population was gradually transformed into the regional sample. This sample of 216 enterprises and families forms the basis of the book *Of Time and the Enterprise* (Bennett 1980b).

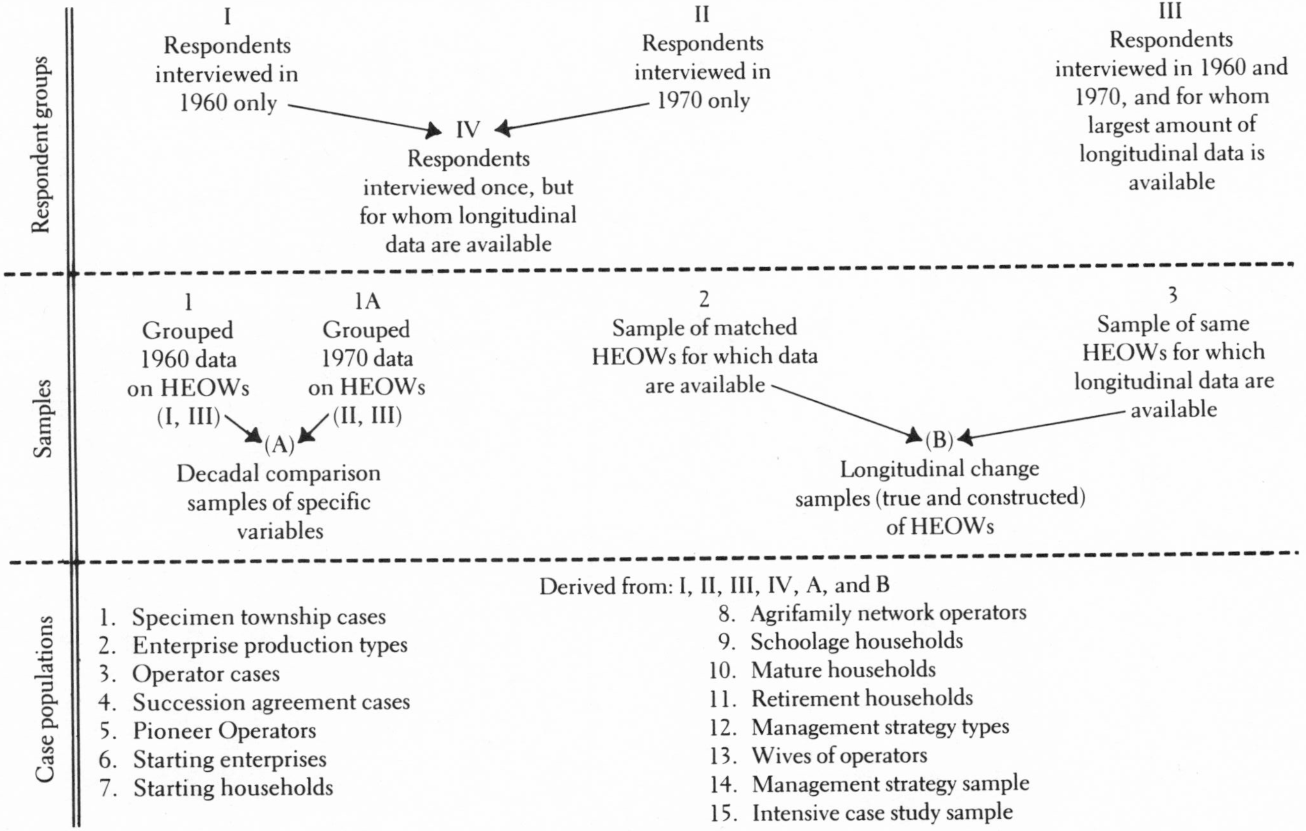

Respondent groups

I
Respondents interviewed in 1960 only

II
Respondents interviewed in 1970 only

III
Respondents interviewed in 1960 and 1970, and for whom largest amount of longitudinal data is available

IV
Respondents interviewed once, but for whom longitudinal data are available

Samples

1
Grouped 1960 data on HEOWs (I, III)

1A
Grouped 1970 data on HEOWs (II, III)

(A)
Decadal comparison samples of specific variables

2
Sample of matched HEOWs for which data are available

3
Sample of same HEOWs for which longitudinal data are available

(B)
Longitudinal change samples (true and constructed) of HEOWs

Case populations

Derived from: I, II, III, IV, A, and B

1. Specimen township cases
2. Enterprise production types
3. Operator cases
4. Succession agreement cases
5. Pioneer Operators
6. Starting enterprises
7. Starting households
8. Agrifamily network operators
9. Schoolage households
10. Mature households
11. Retirement households
12. Management strategy types
13. Wives of operators
14. Management strategy sample
15. Intensive case study sample

Figure 7.1. Saskatchewan Cultural Ecology Research Program: heirarchy of household, enterprise, operator, and wife samples for computer analysis.

The third step in our sampling procedure was the construction of a true longitudinal sample of between 90 and 130 enterprises and families, depending on subject matter. These were enterprises and families for which we had the most abundant data for both the 1960 and 1970 periods.

As time passed, we also found it necessary to construct a number of specialized samples (case populations on Figure 7.1) serving specific purposes, although all of these were derived from the accumulating regional sample entity. One of the most important of these special samples was the management strategy sample, a group of thirty enterprises and their operators and families, studied intensively at selected intervals to determine the dynamics of decision making, the changing fortunes of the enterprise, and sociological parameters.

These sampling methods are appropriate, we believe, for a long-term study of a relatively small population with less diversity than would be typical of urban areas. All in all, we interviewed more than 400 persons in a total regional population of about 7,500, of which about 3,000 lived in villages and one town. Of the 400 people interviewed, all but about 60 were country people, and of the country population, about 100 were interviewed more than once, some as many as 20 or 30 times. Of the total of 475 interviews, 365 were taken with members of 166 agrifamilies. These agrifamilies constituted a sample of the regional total of about 1100 agrifamilies and associated agricultural enterprises in the early 1960s (about 1000 by 1970).

The emerging model of analysis and interpretation

As SCERP proceded through the first three field seasons, the parameters of sampling and data collection served to identify the major organizing concepts of the study. Most fundamentally, SCERP focused on instrumental concerns; that is, the ecological, economic, social, and cultural aspects of making a living. This orientation was felt appropriate not only because of the predilections of the research but also because of the nature of Jasper society. North American rural society evolved in a climate of commercial enterprise; the rising costs and prices of the continental agricultural economy has necessitated ever closer concern for the enterprise and its relations with the outside world. To a large extent, Jasper was an instrumentally guided society, or one in which most of the activities of daily life were shaped by the conduct of a production system. In contrast to anthropologists who prefer to view such activity as a stable characteristic of all cultures, we recognize that such thematic emphasis is a matter of degree and a historical creation, and that if North American rural life is strongly instrumental, other societies and cultures may be just as strongly expressive, or less preoccupied with making a living or beating the market.

As we proceeded, we found it possible to identify two major organizing concepts: the idea of the agrifamily as a systemic unit of research, and the notion of temporal cycles and rhythms of change – time frames – in the agrifamily and associated subsystems.

The agrifamily was defined as the most significant context of social experience for the country population. It consists of two internal subsystems, the household and the enterprise, and several external subsystems, the instrumental network, the community, and the national structure. These are diagrammed on Figure 7.2.

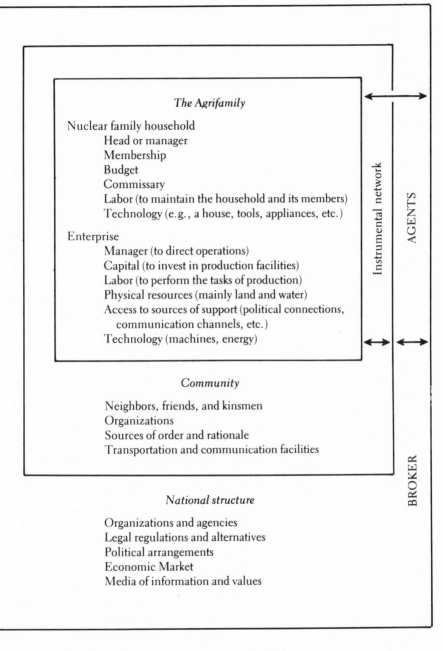

The Agrifamily

Nuclear family household
    Head or manager
    Membership
    Budget
    Commissary
    Labor (to maintain the household and its members)
    Technology (e.g., a house, tools, appliances, etc.)

Enterprise
    Manager (to direct operations)
    Capital (to invest in production facilities)
    Labor (to perform the tasks of production)
    Physical resources (mainly land and water)
    Access to sources of support (political connections,
        communication channels, etc.)
    Technology (machines, energy)

Instrumental network

AGENTS

Community

Neighbors, friends, and kinsmen
Organizations
Sources of order and rationale
Transportation and communication facilities

BROKER

National structure

Organizations and agencies
Legal regulations and alternatives
Political arrangements
Economic Market
Media of information and values

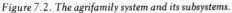

Figure 7.2. The agrifamily system and its subsystems.

The enterprise subsystem provides a crucial link between the family or the household and the outside world. The temporal rhythms of the household unit coincide or clash with the stages of the enterprise, and the maturational experience of the several household members are likewise interdigitated, for better or for worse, with these cycles and stages. Some of the key rhythms are diagrammed on Figure 7.3. By reading down the columns, one can see the possibilities of cycle intersection.

The intersection of the family development cycle with enterprise stages features the transfer of resources from one generation to the next (or from one owner-operator to another, in the case of the sale of an enterprise). The analysis of this transfer process highlights the longitudinal orientation of the study: Succession becomes the central focus of the time-depth study. The external system, represented by the market and the physical environment, provides other sets of temporal rhythms with which the internal social subsystems must cope.

These and other models of social and behavioral components of Jasper country life emerged late in the study, after the decision was made to make the study a longitudinal undertaking. This occurred in 1970, when enough data had accumulated to permit a glimpse of the processes governing Jasper existence. The appearance of early versions of these models prompted a new round of field studies that required additional major financing. These studies took place through 1973, but fieldwork has never really ceased. Once the decision to make longitudinality a formal project was made, it became necessary to devote major attention to methods of data analysis and interpretation. Up to that point – through the 1960s – analytic procedures were painstaking but largely descriptive in nature. Tabulations of the regional schedule data were made, and some of these materials appeared in books and papers. These were all synchronic items, however; the new approach required much more rigorous methods.

By 1973 it was clear that the very large volume of accumulated data concerning several points in time required a computerized analysis. Some means had to be found to select the key variables and test them against each other for different time periods in order to elucidate causal and temporal processes. We had to do this in such a way as to make it possible to compare the results with the descriptive materials not amenable to quantification. Two years were required to select the variables, code them, test and revise them, and then begin running the program (one of the familiar SPSS instrumentalities). This operation also served to test and refine the interpretive models. We were able to make predictions from our models and earlier explanations and then test these with our analysis of variables. The results of this operation were satisfactory on all counts and we felt that we had successfully combined quantitative and interpretive or integrative methods. (Some portions of the computer analysis appeared in Kohl 1976, but the full fruits of the study will be found in Bennett, 1980b.) The analysis of the computer and observational materials also created a number of additional models and concepts, the most significant one being *management style*: a way of grouping a number of factors in the behavior of agricultural operators to define a temporal vector or pattern of management and its changes in time. This is a wholly anthropological pattern construct obtained mainly through the use of computerized variable analysis.[12]

Component and Functions	Cycles			Process
Enterprise manager Decisions and task-accomplishment	Bachelor "starters" → Establishes → Develops → "Slows down" → Retires → New operator: develops			Aging
Enterprise Economic and technical	Establishment phase → Development phase → Maintaining phase → Redevelopment phase			Developing
Nuclear family household Reproduction and socialization	Courtship → Marriage → Birth and training of children → Transmission of headship → Courtship marriage			Expanding and contracting
Instrumental network Reciprocal exchange	Wife's family added	(various events will influence)	Offspring's family added	Ramifying and attenuating

Figure 7.3. Temporal rhythms of local components of a typical Jaspar agrifamily system.

All of these methods of data analysis served to trace the changes and development in family life and the agricultural enterprise over various periods of time. The key interval was, of course, the eleven or twelve years of actual field observation of a particular sample of agrifamilies (along with more segmental data on townspeople and organizations, government agencies, and the like). However, our methods of genealogical analysis also permitted a reconstruction of the full history of many enterprises – the thirty we called the management strategy sample – back to the date of founding (from sixty to thirty years, depending on date of entry into the region). We were also able to trace the relationship of changes in management to the key events and intersections in the family and community society. All this permitted an appreciation of the dynamism of the entire system. Although the North American agrifamily system is a highly regularized, institutionalized entity, the people behaving within it manifest typical adaptive flexibility and capacity for change. Jasper people, like humans everywhere, constantly cope with their own social system, just as they do with the physical environment, the external society, and all other reference structures. Culture is an instrumentality, a constraint, an opportunity, as well as a mold for behavior.

In its final manifestation, SCERP's studies of the farm and ranch population in Jasper became a study of the family farm, possibly a passing kind of socioeconomic structure that is under grave pressure in the modern world. In viewing our work in this context, we were aware of the fact that studies of the family farm by specialists in the agricultural establish-ment were focused on rather limited economic concerns and largely excluded the full social context of agricultural life and management. Although we shared many of that establishment's interpretations, particularly the focus on instrumental concerns in North American agricultural society, we were more interested in showing how economic phenomena were both shaped by, and also were shaping, the dynamics of behavior in the family, the community, and the general culture and its symbols.

The cultural-ecological approach, or the study of the use of physical resources to make a living in a defined institutional context of national as well as local provenience, used longitudinally, permitted us to see how a social system emerges and how that social system provides the tools to cope with institutions (Bennett 1969, 1976b; Kohl 1976). This approach culminates in the study of the management of the agrifamily as a combined social, economic, and ecological undertaking (Bennett 1980a).

Management – or decision making writ large – is an adaptive system insofar as past decisions determine future problems. Although personality and situational factors give consistency to the behavior of agrifamily members, they must maintain considerable flexibility in choices and decisions in order to adapt to, or be successful within, a total environment that is characterized by considerable uncertainty and risk, marginality of basic resources, and continually changing economic values.

Consequently, family-farm management in an entrepreneurial society can be seen as a system of behavior in which idealized goals of profit, or of conservation of resources, must always be qualified by reality considerations. These considerations include the goals and desires of the family, the community, the nation and its institutions, the vicissitudes of the economic market, and the past experience of the manager. In more general social science terms, this model assumes that time is crucial for the understanding of human activity and that no satisfactory answers can be provided for questions of development and change and society unless some way is found to incorporate the effect of time – that is, to view human behavior as a temporal or adaptive process.

Postlude

We feel the need to make some general statement about the academic locus of our study. Questions can be raised: Is this an anthropological study? Can anthropologists retain their professional and intellectual identity when studying a familiar slice of their own culture? SCERP was anthropological at least in two senses: (1) it used a cultural ecology frame of reference, especially in the earlier years, and this was derived from anthropological writings, and (2) we did intensive fieldwork, generally an anthropological specialty. We also were concerned with obtaining the residents' own view of their lives and activities. Our assumption was that Jasperites, a literate, contemporary population, held important reflexive skills necessary to tap an understanding of their social world.

But beyond these factors, we did what the subject matter required; hence we adopted and adapted a variety of analytical and theoretical tools from a variety of fields: agricultural economics, resource management and conservation, climatology, demography, rural sociology, agronomy, and hydraulic engineering, among others. Perhaps, in the final analysis, this was the most anthropological aspect of all: our willingness to be eclectic and to learn everything there was to learn and to acquire the skills or the knowledge necessary to learn it.

8 Social networks and community administration: a comparative study of two mining towns

SUSAN BRANDT GRAHAM

Pioneers in the anthropological study of American life often assumed that the conclusions drawn from research in a particular empirical community could be applied to American society in general. This assumption is an early anthropological bias, the result of a longstanding emphasis on the study of what were believed to be homogeneous groupings in so-called simple or primitive societies. This is a dangerous assumption, however, insofar as it obscures important variations in complex societies such as the United States – and perhaps in the simple societies as well. If anthropological study of American life is to contribute to an understanding of American society, anthropologists must describe the richness of variation and attempt to explain it, using traditional methods when they are useful and developing innovative methods when they are needed.

Community administration is an important dimension of variation in community life in complex societies. Determining the effects of different forms of administration on the daily life of local communities was the major goal of a comparative study of XYZ Mining Company[1] employees living either in Townsite, a company town owned by XYZ and administered by its officials, or Red Butte, a neighboring incorporated town administered by an elected town council (Graham 1975). In the initial stages of research, participant observation, the traditional anthropological field method, was the major field method employed. Over time, however, the need to utilize other methods for the fuller comprehension of similarities and differences between the two towns became obvious. Although prior to the present study social-network analysis had not been formally used in a comparative community study, it seemed to offer a method by which some of the effects of different community administrative forms could be measured. Thus the study provides a test of the utility of a comparative network approach for the analysis of community life.

The approach proved useful not only for the purpose for which it was employed but also for suggesting some important factors in class differences, another important dimension of variation in American society (as well as in other complex societies). Ethnicity, occupational status, education, and income level are usually included in definitions of class, because social scientists regard them as major factors in behavior in general and

106

patterns of social interaction in particular. Yet the comparative network data revealed that, for XYZ employees and their families, none of these factors was as important as residence in either Townsite or Red Butte. As will be seen later in this chapter, this finding helped to illuminate some fundamental factors that influence both the heterogeneity of so-called working-class behavior and the homogeneity of middle-class behavior in American society.[2]

Entrée and rapport

I first saw Townsite in January of 1969 when a friend took me there to meet his family. Instead of the highway from Tucson, which goes around the mountains, we took the old road over the mountains. Looking out from near the top of the mountains, I got my first glimpse of Townsite – a large smokestack with billowing clouds of smelter smoke dominated the landscape and the town, and in the background was a range of wild and rugged desert mountains. The sun began to set as we descended into the town, and the mountains, clouds, and smelter smoke turned a flaming orange, then a glowing red, and finally a dark velvet purple. It was the most fantastic sunset I had ever seen, but my friend said sunsets in Townsite were always like that. He was indeed correct, but I have never ceased to marvel at them nor at the way they would always renew my spirit at the end of a day.

Although I had never before seen a company town, I had definite expectations. My mental image of such towns was as dirty and ramshackle, of unpainted and dilapidated frame houses with old washing machines and unkempt children on front porches watched over by women who were thirty but looked sixty. As we drove into the town, I was struck by the fact that the company hospital was the first building one passed. Then, almost immediately, I was struck by the appearance of the town itself – it looked like a neat, clean, middle-class neighborhood in Tucson. The houses were of concrete block, a typical construction material in the Southwest, and all were freshly painted in a variety of bright colors – pink, green, yellow, white, and brown. The yards were meticulous, and some even had winter flowers blooming. The inside of my friend's parents' house looked very much like that in which I had grown up. At first, I could hardly believe this was a company town.

I was soon reminded, however, that Townsite was indeed a company town. A loud whistle blew at 9:00 p.m. – the company whistle. Earlier I had gone outside, but after a few minutes my eyes began to burn and I could hardly breathe. My friend's mother called out, "Oh, Susan, come inside. Sometimes the smelter smoke blows into the town, and you have to come in and shut all the windows. But don't worry – it never lasts for more than a few hours." Back inside, the evening's conversation centered around "the company." As we drove back to Tucson that night, I resolved to return as an anthropologist to study Townsite.

In the following months I married, completed my master's degree, and had a son during the semester in which I finished coursework for the doctoral degree and my husband completed his degree. At that point we had to make a decision: My husband needed a job and I needed to begin dissertation research. We agreed that Townsite might be able to accommodate both these needs.

A general characteristic of company towns is restricted recruitment of residents, and Townsite is no exception. To obtain a house in the town, the renter must be both employed and married. In order for me to live in Townsite during the course of fieldwork, it was necessary for my husband to become an employee of the XYZ Mining Company. This was fairly easily accomplished – he was ready to go to work somewhere, and XYZ was expanding operations and hiring employees with his qualifications. He began work in June 1971 and we obtained a house and moved to Townsite in October.

Another general characteristic of company towns is that the employee and his family's place in the community is defined by the employee's place in the occupational hierarchy. These are communities of single function, and one's relation to that function is of supreme importance. Throughout our five-year residence in Townsite I continually and completely explained the nature and goals of my research. Nonetheless, few residents fully accepted my identity as a student and anthropologist; rather, I was defined as "the wife of one of the Graham boys – you know Gordon, he's in purchasing" and the in-law of men who worked in payroll, computers, and in the mine itself. These identities proved to have both advantages and disadvantages.

Not surprisingly, a major advantage of my community-defined identities was the freedom to come and go as any other woman in the town would. Indeed, not only was I allowed to behave like other women, it was expected. This was ideal for participant observation of all activities in which residents ordinarily participated. At this stage of fieldwork, because the residents perceived no conflict between my behavior and that which was expected of other women in Townsite, few people even seemed to hear my explanation of what I was doing. I was not disturbed that so few people took my explanation seriously, because my comings and goings as a participant observer were unhampered.

This is not to say, however, that personal conflicts did not arise during this stage of the fieldwork. The most serious conflict at this time was over how to handle information that was given me in confidence by people who understood what I was doing and that was given openly by other people who did not fully comprehend my activities. Once I had begun research, my husband would preface virtually every statement he made about the goings-on in XYZ's administrative offices with, "This is information for you, not for your study." Other information given by in-laws and a woman whom I came to regard as a friend rather than as an informant would not have been given to me had I been perceived as an anthropologist rather than as only a relative or friend. Although none of these latter informants requested confidentiality for their statements, I nevertheless felt an obligation to keep them confidential. But at the same time, I felt an equal obligation to the completeness of my research. After long hours of grappling with the problem, I resolved the conflict to my satisfaction by deciding to use this information in much the same way that archeologists use ethnographic analogy; that is, to generate hypotheses that could be tested against information collected from other sources. This is the only way in which information given by my husband, his family, and my friend was used, and for a time I had no further conflicts.

As soon as I began formal interviewing for the network portion of the study, however, I came to know exactly why Fischer (1970:272) had said, "It is surprising to learn that field work in one's own culture can be as traumatic for a woman, if not more so, than field work in a foreign culture." In my case this was so because up to this time I had thought I was indeed working in my own culture, failing to comprehend completely the vast subcultural differences between the residents and myself. I should have known better. Long before I began my research and while I was living in Tucson, a Townsite resident once pointedly remarked, "It's too bad that women are taking up space in college that would be available for more men if the women weren't there." This succinctly states the view of many Townsite residents toward education for women. Here women are expected to support their husbands' careers rather than develop their own. This subcultural view diametrically opposes that with which I was raised, and it led to a lot of personal conflict.

When I began the formal network interviewing, an unheard-of activity for women in Townsite, the initial gossip was that I was lying about being a student carrying out a research project – "Everyone knows that students go to classes at the university" – but it soon became obvious to all that I actually believed I was doing exactly what I said I was doing. The gossip then concentrated on the state of my mental health. My strange activities came to be explained as the result of frustration and depression over what the residents perceived as my inability to have a second child in a town in which children come in pairs. This folk explanation of my behavior can be interpreted from the perspective of symbolic structuralism. First, because my self-defined role did not fit into the framework of possible roles conceptualized by Townsite residents, it was an ambiguous role. Second, because I violated the expectations that a woman should have at least two children, the role ambiguity was transformed into a statement of sexual ambiguity. Through my perceived inability to conceive a second child, the residents defined me as lacking an important component of "femaleness" and thus as an "inadequate," "partial," or "ambiguous" female. This sexual ambiguity was perceived as causing a frustrated and depressed mental state, which then "explained" my behavior. At the point at which this gossip came back to me, I experienced culture, or more precisely subculture, shock.

This was not the only subculture shock I experienced during the course of fieldwork. It was more difficult to cope with the expectations the academic subculture held for academic women. In Townsite a complete woman did not have a career; at that time in the academic world a complete professional woman did not have a family. To Townsite residents I was a marginal female because I was also an anthropologist; to many of my professors, women as well as men, I was a marginal anthropologist because I was also a wife and mother. To this day, very few of my professors realize my husband became an XYZ employee so I could study Townsite, believing instead I chose to study Townsite because my husband was an XYZ employee. The academic subculture may have allowed a woman to have a career, but only if she gave up a family in exchange for that career. The realization of this expectation made me very angry; after all, it seemed to me, men were allowed to have both careers and families, so why couldn't a woman have both? But it was as inconceivable to professors as to miners that a husband would support his wife's career. Fischer (1970:279) has observed that "most professional women have been in conflict about the professional role at other points in their lives; carrying out field work in places where women's status is low may serve to renew the conflict." In my case, conflict arose not only in the field setting, but also within the academic setting. Only my commitment to anthropology and the faith my husband and parents had in me kept me going at this stage of research.

On the positive side, norms are clearly revealed when their violations are sanctioned. As Fischer (1970:278) had noted, "One of the most insightful aspects of being a woman in the field is the stimulus she offers for comments on what should be her appropriate role in life." Furthermore, because the residents perceived me merely as a distraught housewife rather than as a threatening outsider, they did not hesitate to answer my questions; indeed, they seemed quite willing to humor me. In time I came to realize that both the amount and content of the gossip about me were reflections of the extent to which I was integrated into the community; that is, I was ambiguous precisely because I was perceived as a member of the community rather than as an outsider.

The question that now arises is: How can a fieldworker carry out scientific research in a setting in which she or he is so highly integrated? The answer is: through use of a research design addressed to specific issues and planned to answer specific questions.

The research design

Community administration

Based on variations in community administration, communities can be placed on a continuum. At one extreme would be an ideal type in which the people themselves make all the decisions that affect them, and at the other extreme would be an ideal type in which the people make no decisions that affect them. Communities of the former type are internally administered, whereas those of the latter type are externally administered. Although externally administered communities have been termed "administered communities," all communities are in some sense administered (Weingrod 1962, Kushner 1973). The defining characteristic of *administered communities* is the residents' lack of substantive participation in policy making. The administration is not representative, and the administrative positions are not filled by the consent of the residents. In internally administered communities the residents set standards for the administrators, whereas in externally administered communities the administrators set standards for residents.

Kushner (1973) developed a general model of administered communities based on his fieldwork in a *moshav olim* in Israel and others' descriptions of Japanese-American war relocation centers and American Indian reservations. Although he was concerned with communities in cultural contact situations, Kushner's general model applies to another variety that can be termed the *administered occupational community*. This variety differs from those in cultural contact situations, in that residence is based on achieved occupational criteria rather than ascribed ethnic criteria. Examples of this variety are company-owned towns, armed forces bases, and national-park towns.

Some additional important characteristics of administered occupational communities are the following:

First, employers are the administrators. No local elections are held, and there are few opportunities for substantive participation in policy making by the majority of residents.

This is in contrast to internally administered communities, in which residents are able to participate in community decision making either directly or through elected administrators. As a result, administrator-employers control to some extent those services and material goods usually controlled by residents themselves in internally administered communities. Examples of such services and goods include local government, housing, schools, health-care facilities, churches, utilities, recreational facilities, police and fire protection, community upkeep, and local newspapers.

Second, there is a dichotomy of status between members of the administrative portion of the occupational hierarchy and those outside this portion, even though membership in the administrative portion does not necessarily imply substantive participation in the making of policy. Specific examples of the dichotomy in various administered occupational communities would be the distinction between white-collar and blue-collar workers in company towns, National Park Service employees and those of the various concessions in national parks, and officers and enlisted personnel in the armed forces. Internally administered communities may have a variety of status distinctions, but these are often based on other or additional criteria.

Third, administered occupational communities have a single purpose, with the fulfillment of this purpose taking precedence over the wants and needs of residents. Company towns are built to meet the demands of economic success in a given industry. National-park towns are built to meet the demands of conserving natural areas, just as armed forces bases are built to meet the demands of defense and national security. In contrast, most internally administered communities tend to fulfill a variety of purposes.

Fourth, residents are recruited on a restricted basis, so that only those people involved in maximizing the single purpose for which the community exists are allowed to reside in it. This is in contrast to internally administered communities, to which virtually anyone may move.

Administered occupational communities are organized quite differently from internally administered communities. Spicer and others (1969:20) have said that "public policy involving the future of human communities *must be made by those communities,* or the destruction of some of the most important human qualities is certain to take place, resulting in frustration, apathy, and dependency." This belief is probably held to some degree by nearly all American-educated social scientists. Although studies of administered occupational communities dot the literature, however (see, for example, Cleland 1952, Epstein 1958, Allen 1966, Buder 1967, Bradwin 1968, Lucas 1971, and McLaurin 1971), very little detailed data on daily life in such a community has been published.

The present study was especially concerned with examining daily life in an administered occupational community and comparing it with that in an internally administered community. The fieldwork was undertaken to compare the daily life of XYZ Mining Company employees and their families who lived either in Townsite, a company town owned by XYZ and administered by its officials, or in Red Butte, a neighboring incorporated town administered by an elected town council. Initially, the towns were compared and contrasted in the various aspects listed above (see Graham 1975). This ethnographic comparison suggested some important qualitative differences and similarities. As fieldwork progressed, however, I began to seek some method that would allow a more quantitatively precise statement of similarities and differences in patterns of social interaction of the residents of the two towns.

Social networks

In recent years the concept of the *social network* has received a great deal of attention in the social sciences. Mitchell (1969:50) had stated that "the uniqueness of particular empirical communities can be comprehended through the structure of network linkages within them." And as Fischer and others have said,

individuals are linked to their society primarily through relations with other individuals: with kin, friends, co-workers, fellow club members, and so on. We are each at the center of a web of social bonds . . .our personal *social networks* . . .In sum, to understand the individual in society, we need to understand . . .how the structural circumstances that individuals face influence the formation and maintenance of social ties. [Fischer et al. 1977:vii]

Network analysis, however, has not yet fulfilled its promise as a methodology that will allow us better to understand the individual in society. There are several reasons why this is so.

As Bax has said of networkers such as Barnes (1969), Whitten (1970), A. Wolfe (1970), and Neimeyer (1973),

a considerable number of them are almost completely involved in technical problems. They are busy refining existing concepts and enlarging the arsenal; they try to make elaborate classifications, and they attempt to inject network analysis with mathematical concepts and procedures in order to give it a more "scientific" tone. Evidently for these network "technicians" (or butterfly collectors, as Edmund Leach might call them) there is not much time left for realizing that network analysis is meant to solve anthropological problems. [Bax 1977:3]

Network analysis merely for the sake of network analysis contributes little to anthropology and to our understanding of social behavior.

Bax has also recently pointed out that network analysis, although developed to emphasize the interdependency of individuals, "has been hampered by the frequently misconceived issue of 'Individual and Society' " (1977:1). He states that "network structuralists have systematically underrated the freedom of the individual, while actionists have overemphasized it" (1977:2). Examples of the former would be Bott (1957) and Kapferer (1973), whereas examples of the latter would be Mayer (1966), Boswell (1969), Blok (1973), and Jongmans (1973). If network analysis is to contribute to our understanding of the individual in society, both structural constraints and individual action must be analyzed and related to each other.

Before the present study, social network analysis had not been formally used in a comparative community study; however, it seemed to offer a method by which some of the effects of different forms of administration on the daily life of local communities could be measured. Thus, the study was first of all an attempt to use network analysis to study a specific problem: the relation of forms of community administration and the social behavior of community residents. Second, the nature of the problem itself demanded that the study specify, analyze, and relate both structural constraints and individual action.

Nearly all network researchers believe that any given aspect of a network can influence all other aspects of a network; however, they also realize that a large amount of time and energy must be spent to gather data on all aspects of even one individual's network. Therefore, the present study was limited to the first-order zone (Barnes 1969) of personal social networks. Boissevain (1973:125) defined the first-order or primary zone as "all the persons to which a given person (ego) can trace a social relationship, and has personally met, and the interconnection between these persons." His study (1973) of a countryman and townsman dealt with *all* persons whom the individuals had met directly, regardless of whether recurring relationships had been established. He states (1973:126), "I began with two informants, on a pilot study basis, planning to branch out and test findings more systematically on a wider sample. Collecting these data proved to be very difficult, as did its analysis. Hence, I have data on only two first-order zones." Because Boissevain's effort appeared to produce diminishing returns, the present study was further limited to those persons with whom the individual had established recurring interactional relationships. Further, data collection was limited to those aspects that could be expected to be influenced by differences in community administration.

Comparison of Townsite and Red Butte

As pointed out earlier, because the XYZ Mining Company owns Townsite, the company's administrators control a wide variety of the town's services and resources. Control of goods and services, such as local government, housing, businesses, health and recreational facilities, police and fire protection, schools, churches, utilities, the local newspaper, and community upkeep, allows the administrators to ensure that the town does indeed fulfill the single purpose for which it was built, the profitable exploitation of a large body of ore. Control of these also allows administrators to set standards for residents. In Red Butte, on the other hand, residents set standards for administrators who are elected and who retain their positions only as long as the majority of voters are satisfied with their performance. Administrators in Townsite must be responsive to the wants and needs of the company rather than to those of the residents, whereas administrators in Red Butte must be responsive to the wants and needs of the electorate, the residents of the community.

With the exception of some upper-level administrators, XYZ employees are not required to live in Townsite; indeed, housing exists there for fewer than one-fourth of company employees. Residents of the towns are very much aware of having made a choice between two different styles of life in their choice of community of residence. It is not an overstatement to say that the residents of the two towns, although they are employees of the same company and thus co-workers on the job, are contemptuous of each other.

The typical view of Townsite residents toward Red Butte was expressed in an editorial in the weekly newspaper published in Townsite but distributed in Red Butte as well:

Residents of the [Red Butte] community have been asked to begin the clean up of their community
. . . There is no crime in admitting that maybe that old car or that small wooden apple crate in the front yard could be moved to help make the town just a little nicer place to live in. For the past several years [Red Butte] has had a slow but steady increase in population which could only mean that [Red Butte] has something to offer these people. Most likely it's the quiet, slow life . . . [Red Butte's] Town Council is offering a real bargain to its residents in that they will have all

the junk cars towed away for a tiny fee of $10 per car. All it takes is a phone call to the Town Hall and your yard can be free for grass to grow where that ugly car is now parked. [*The Miner*, January 2, 1975, p. 2.]

A Townsite resident stated the typical view toward Red Butte even more succinctly than did the newspaper editor: "I don't allow my teenagers to say, 'Go to hell.' But when they say, 'Go to [Red Butte],' everyone knows exactly what they mean" (fieldnotes).

Red Butte residents, however, are equally contemptuous of Townsite residents:

I know they have better houses in [Townsite] and all the streets are paved. But I'd be damned before I'd move to [Townsite] – it's the same thing.

[Townsite] is like they've got everything, and we don't here. But everything we have got here, we have provided – we built it and we financed it. Nobody has to hand us anything on a silver platter.

I don't like [Townsite] because it is a company town. In [Red Butte] you can do anything you please.

Here you have people that are independent of the company. The independence is the great thing. You have no voice in [Townsite]. [fieldnotes]

It can thus be seen that the freedom of XYZ employees and their families to choose a place of residence results in a process of self-selection: Those who value material goods and chances for occupational advancement more than independence from company control choose to become Townsite residents, whereas those who value independence from company control more than material goods choose to become residents of Red Butte and other towns.

Anyone who chooses to move to Red Butte may do so. This is not true of Townsite, where in addition to self-selection there is also administrative selection of residents. XYZ administrators want only the more stable employees to become Townsite residents. They are able to accomplish the goal of selective recruitment of residents by imposing stringent rules for obtaining a house, which is possible, of course, because XYZ owns the houses. In addition to selectively recruiting residents, however, these rules also imply many behavioral standards valued by administrators. For example, the rule requiring a renter to be both employed and married emphasizes the value placed by administrators on steady work and stable marriages. This rule has certainly affected the behavior of at least some Townsite residents. As one person summed it up, "In other towns people stay together for the kids; in this town they stay together for the house."

A widely shared belief in Townsite is that occupational advancement can be achieved by conformity to the rules and expectations of administrators; that is, by being good community members. Given the emphasis on stable marriages, good residents must at least appear to be happily married, whether in fact the appearance has anything to do with reality. Being seen socially as a couple tends to support the appearance of a stable marriage. Furthermore, if conformity to the expectations of employers is to lead to occupational advancement, the employee must be noticed by company officials. That is, the conformity must be observable within the community. As has been noted elsewhere,

given the administrative practice of systematic exclusion of all but necessary workers in administered occupational communities, it is not surprising that career goals sould be expressed in increased social interaction within the community of residence among residents of a company town. Social interaction outside of the community cannot serve to enhance one's position in the occupational structure (except possibly at the highest levels of administration), just as an improvement in one's place in the occupational structure has little meaning outside of the community (again with the possible exception of the highest levels of administration). It is quite possible, however, for social interaction within the community to result in a rise in the job structure, just as such a rise has meaning to residents. [Graham 1978:120]

Among Townsite residents, many of the numerous examples of promotions from within the ranks are at least partially attributed to the fact that both the employees and their spouses were socially active within the community. In this respect it is important to note that the behavior of the spouse can be as important as the behavior of the employee: Company standards must be supported by the family as well as the individual.

Not only individuals and families but also many voluntary organizations in Townsite support and reinforce company standards. For example, many clubs allow only married couples to become members. And even the fraternal organizations have many activities in which spouses and other family members may participate; in fact, they are encouraged to do so. One such organization held an indoctrination meeting for wives during the initiation of the husbands, the point of the indoctrination being that wives should not only participate in activities with their husbands but also that they should appear to be happy while doing so. As the wife of one of the club's officers put it, "It just doesn't look good if you come down to the club and have a fight with your husband. So when you're here, try to act happy even if you can't stand him" [fieldnotes].

Townsite residents conform to the behavioral expectations of employer-administrators in order to enhance occupational mobility. In contrast, the residents of Red Butte set their own behavioral standards. They have chosen to live in Red Butte precisely because they do not want to be required to conform to the expectations of employers when off the job. They seem to value personal freedom and independence not only from the company but within marriage as well. Because activities in the community have little connection with the job, just as the job is not a measure of one's place in the community, interaction within the community and with the spouse is not used for occupational advancement.

Comparison of social networks in Townsite and Red Butte

Given these major differences between Townsite and Red Butte, network differences in certain aspects of range and jointness could be predicted. These are terms that have been used in a variety of ways by various researchers. "Range" here refers to the place of residence of network members in relation to that of the respondents and has been divided into four categories: (1) community – residence in the same community as the respondent; (2) area – residence within a ten-mile radius of the XYZ mine; (3) state – residence within Arizona; and (4) out-of-state residence. "Jointness" here refers to whether or not the network members are also seen socially by the spouse of the respondent and has been divided into two categories: (1) shared – also seen socially by the spouse; and (2) unshared – not seen socially by the spouse. Specifically, it could be predicted that if community administration did affect aspects of social networks, then residents of Townsite could be expected to have a larger number of joint networks members and a larger number of community network members than residents of Red Butte. That is, stable marriages are desired by administrators, and joint social interaction with the spouse enhances the appearance of a stable marriage, whether in fact the appearance is a reflection of reality. Furthermore, if conformity to administrative standards is to help one, then the conformity must at least be visible within the community. Interaction at the community level promotes visibility. A second prediction was that in the categories of range and jointness with other than shared network members and community network members, Townsite and Red Butte residents should not show significant differences.

Formal interviewing was the main field technique used to gather the network data. Forty women, representing slightly more than 3 percent of the households of XYZ employees in Townsite, constituted one sample, and twenty women, representing slightly less than 6 percent of the households of XYZ employees in Red Butte, constituted the other sample. The Townsite sample was selected from a list of addresses using a table of random numbers. Because the list of addresses obtained from the Red Butte town clerk bore no resemblance to the numbers on houses when the houses indeed had numbers, and because only about half the households in Red Butte have a member employed by XYZ (the remainder are employed by other mining companies in the area), I abandoned the random sample drawn from the listing of addresses and instead just went around the various sections of Red Butte knocking on doors. Although the Red Butte sample is not a true random sample, I believe it is representative of women in households in which at least one spouse is employed by the XYZ Mining Company.

Each respondent was asked to name the personal acquaintances outside of the household with whom she had contact (in person, by telephone, by mail, etc.) about once a day, about once a week, and about once a month. For each person named, the respondent was asked a series of questions such as where the person lived, how long she had known the person, and whether her husband also had social contact with this person. Although the study was concerned with recurring social contacts within the framework of one month and less, the field techniques employed recorded only those network members who could be considered kin and friends. More casual recurring social contacts were not picked up, nor were purely instrumental relationships such as those with store clerks, physicians, and so forth. As an artifact of the interview technique, the networks appear rather small compared to some other network studies.

T-tests were used to assess the significance of differences between means of network members in the various categories of range and jointness. These tests indicate that the residents of the towns differ significantly in numbers of community and shared network member (see Tables 8.1 and 8.2). Townsite residents interact significantly more within their community of residence and jointly with their spouses than do the residents of Red Butte. In the other categories of range and jointness the residents of the towns are virtually identical.

To determine whether the differences in numbers of community and shared network members were in fact the result of community administrative forms rather than some other factors, additional t-tests compared the means of community and shared network members by respondents' length of residence in the community, ethnicity, and educational level, and occupational status, work schedule, and income level of the household member who was an XYZ employee. Importantly, the only significant differences noted were those based upon length of time in the community (see Table 8.3; for a fuller discussion of ethnicity and occupational status and their relationship to networks, see Graham 1981). The results of these *t*-tests indicate that established Townsite residents

Table 8.1. *Comparison of means of aspects of range by community of residence*

Range aspect	Community	Mean of network members	
Community network members	Townsite		6.85
		P	0.05
	Red Butte		4.10
Area network members	Townsite		1.25
	Red Butte		1.25
State network members	Townsite		2.18
	Red Butte		2.55
Out-of-state network members	Townsite		3.45
	Red Butte		3.15

Table 8.2. *Comparison of means of aspects of jointness by community of residence*

Jointness aspect	Community	Mean of network members	
Shared network members	Townsite		11.10
		P	0.05
	Red Butte		7.10
Nonshared network members	Townsite		2.63
	Red Butte		3.95

Table 8.3. *Comparison of network means by times of arrival in the community of residence.*

		Time of arrival				
Network aspect	Community	Before 1967				After 1967
Range						
Community members	Townsite		10.87	P	0.05	4.44
		P	0.05			
	Red butte		4.92			2.88
Jointness						
Shared members	Townsite		14.60	P	0.10	9.00
		P	0.05			
	Red butte		7.17			7.00

interact more within the community of residence and jointly with the spouse than do new Townsite residents or both new and established Red Butte residents. That is, interaction within the community and jointly with the spouse appears to increase with length of residence in Townsite.

XYZ officials have never explicitly stated a desire to change the behavior of employees in Townsite; however, these results do suggest that certain aspects of employees' behavior did change with increasing length of residence in the town. Furthermore, those patterns of social interaction noted for established Townsite residents are often regarded as characteristic of the middle class, while those of new Townsite residents and all residents of Red Butte are usually considered characteristic of the working class (for example, see Young and Willmott 1957, Gans 1965, and Berger 1971). Ethnicity, occupational status, education, and income level are dimensions often included in definitions of social class and often regarded by social scientists as major factors determining patterns of social interaction. Yet, compared with length of residence in Townsite or Red Butte, they appear to be of relatively minor importance. Why should this be so?

The behavioral expectations of employer-administrators in Townsite are aimed at assuring a stable supply of steady workers. A steady worker is welcome to live in the town because she or he produces a profit for the company. XYZ officials apparently believe that married workers are more stable than single workers; hence, houses are rented only to married workers. Furthermore, an employee who obtains a divorce can be required to vacate the house and move out of Townsite within ten days of obtaining the divorce. Because the married worker has dependents who rely upon his or her income for their livelihood, she or he is perceived as more likely to remain on the job taking orders than is the single worker, who is perceived as much more likely to quit the job if she or he dislikes company directives. XYZ officials see married workers as more stable than single workers, and only married workers are allowed to move to Townsite.

The differences between Townsite and Red Butte in patterns of social interaction can be explained as a reflection of the visible conformity of Townsite residents to the expectations of employer-administrators. Because XYZ employees can choose not to live in Townsite, those who do not wish to conform to the expectations of employers when off the job simply live elsewhere. Furthermore, administrators have the power to require employees whose behavior does not meet their expectations – for example, an employee who obtains a divorce – to move from the town. But, generally speaking, the majority of residents who remain in Townsite for more than five years willingly conform to these expectations. This is because they value occupational advancement and believe that visible conformity can produce promotions within the occupational structure.

In a classic work, Gans outlines what he considers to be some important class differences. He suggests that for the "middle class . . . work is not merely a job that maximizes income, but a series of related jobs or job advances which provide the breadwinner with higher income, greater responsibility, and, if possible, greater job satisfaction," while for the "working class . . . identification with work, work success, and job advancement – while not absolutely rejected – are of secondary priority" (1965:245). In other words, according to Gans the middle class is career oriented, whereas the working class is not. As has been pointed out, this is an extremely important difference between residents of Townsite and Red Butte. Furthermore, given that patterns of social interaction identified in Townsite are those that have been considered typically middle class, I suggest that behavior that is generally agreed to be middle class reflects conformity to the expectations of employers, whether found in an administered occupational community or in the larger society, and that behavior generally agreed to be working class reflects conformity to the expectations of others than employers (e.g. peer groups, family), regardless of where it is found. This would account for the widely reported homogeneity of middle-class behavior, which is then easily explained by the fact that behavior that is considered desirable by one employer is quite likely to be that considered desirable by other employers. On the other hand, it could be expected that working class behavior would be much more heterogeneous, as conformity is to the expectations of a much wider variety of others.

The significance of the network comparisons lies in the demonstration that aspects of personal social networks differ significantly between residents of Townsite and Red Butte, and that they differ in definable ways that can be directly related to community administration and structure. The network methodology proved useful in illuminating not only important differences betwen the two communities but also some significant factors in so-called class differences in American society.

Research in one's own society: a personal view

The traditional rite of passage from graduate student to professional anthropologist has typically involved field research in a society not one's own. Today, this is no longer necessarily true, as North American anthropologists in increasing numbers turn to the study of American life and field research here at home. Because we have held some false assumptions about the homogeneity of our society, we have often been surprised to discover that fieldwork within it can be as difficult and traumatic as fieldwork in a foreign society. There are several reasons why is this so.

Because we are in our own society, we are not received as privileged strangers, as we often are in foreign societies, but rather as ordinary people who are assumed to be properly socialized to the prevailing norms and standards and who are, therefore, expected to conform to those norms and standards. However, because of subcultural differences, we may be unable to meet this expectation. First, we may indeed initially be as ignorant of local customs as we would be in a foreign society. Second, the expectations our own academic subculture holds for us may be in direct opposition to those that the subculture in which we are working holds for us. But because we are received not as privileged strangers but rather as ordinary people, our behavioral mistakes may not be as easily forgiven or excused as the result of either ignorance or professional commitment as they might be in a foreign society. I believe this is especially true for women, who, regardless of subculture, have traditionally had a narrower range of behavioral options from which to choose than have men.

Weidman (1970:262) has observed that fieldwork in a foreign society can be "a powerful source of both satisfaction and frustration." This is equally true of fieldwork in American society. More than ten years have passed since that day in January of 1969 when I first saw

Townsite. As I reflect on those years, I am amazed that I am doing just what I would have said then I would be doing today. But I am even more amazed how much the events of those years changed my self-image as an individual in society. I agree completely with Weidman:

The field experience revealed to me, in a way nothing else could, something vital about the relationship of the individual to society and the meaning of culture at the gut level.

The barriers to entering a new cultural system head on are just as formidable as if they were made of bricks and mortar. By grappling with what at first is an unyielding structure and by gradually becoming able to move easily within it, I learned more about the freedom of the individual within culture than I could have otherwise. Because I was also an observer, however, and not just a participant, I could include these two kinds of systems among all others to achieve a perspective that, by its very range and depth, allowed me to tolerate with greater equanimity the pressures to conform within my own tradition. Furthermore – and perhaps this is the most salient point of all – I had a much firmer basis for continuing to explore various dimensions of relationships between individuals and societies. [Weidman 1970:262–263]

Given a wide variety of lifestyles within the United States, doing research in that society does not necessarily mean that the anthropologist is at home. Indeed, only when anthropologists have described its richness of variation and attempted to explain it will the anthropological study of American society contribute to an understanding of that society. The challenge is there, and any anthropologist willing to assume it will discover that the frustrations and rewards of doing research in one's own society, rather than in a foreign society, while perhaps somewhat different, are at least as great.

9 The anthropologist as key informant: inside a rural Oregon town

LAWRENCE HENNIGH

This chapter uses the perspective of a key informant to argue that fieldwork in one's own culture is not simply a transfer to a familiar setting of skills, experience, and academic traditions developed in studying alien cultures. It has been frequently argued that experience in alien cultures is a valuable, or even necessary, prerequisite for studying one's own culture (Kluckhohn 1949:9, Spindler 1973:16, Wolcott 1975a:114). It does not follow that such experience is also sufficient preparation. The two types of fieldwork are inherently different; they require different types of rigor, produce different results, and should be judged by different standards. By implication at least, research in one's own culture requires different graduate training than is being offered many students.

A case history of four and a half years of fieldwork in a rural Oregon community is used here to make a point: The methods developed to study alien cultures may be imposed on the study of one's own culture, but the result is a false rigor that may do unmeasured damage to the fieldwork and unreported psychological harm to the fieldworker. The specific arguments are: (1) A fieldworker in an alien culture must seek out people familiar with that culture to provide the vital functions of key informants; (2) a fieldworker in a familiar culture may become a key informant and use himself or herself as such; (3) becoming one's own key informant is personally and professionally rewarding; (4) not becoming one's own key informant is personally and professionally costly.

These arguments do not seem to have been made previously. They are based on an adaptation I made to a difficult field situation without considering the alternatives. It was only after I discovered that other anthropologists used different methods than I did, or expected me to do so, that I concluded that becoming a stranger to familiar people is an arbitrary contrivance. In this paper I will try to make a case for treating familiar people as familiar and applying the resulting insights to the analysis of an unpredicted community–school crisis.

Fieldwork situation

In 1972, Abt Associates, Inc., a private applied-research firm in Cambridge, Massachusetts, received a contract from the National Institute of Education to study federally funded educational innovation in ten rural school districts. The plan, called Project Rural, called for permanent resident fieldworkers to be present in each district for the entire five years of the project. The fieldworkers' tasks were to complete socioeconomic histories of the districts, write ethnographies of them, and assist the Cambridge staff in conducting community change studies, pupil change studies, and organizational change studies of each district (Herriott 1977). For reasons that were not made clear to the fieldworkers, we were heavily committed to the community study components in the research design. We were to become experts in the ethnography and social change in what was assumed to be the community served by the school district under study. It is the community study aspect, especially social change, that is dealt with in this chapter.

I was assigned to the South Umpqua school district in southwest Oregon, a mountainous, forested area, characterized by outdoor scenic grandeur, mild climate, and easy access to urban conveniences an hour and a half away on Interstate Highway 5. The schools served 8,000 people in a 350-square mile (906 square km) district. Students came from four voting precincts, two of which contained small municipalities, and a third that was a large unincorporated bedroom community. The district had come into existence several years earlier when snow on election day kept many conservative voters from the polls and allowed a consolidation measure to pass by six votes.

At the time my wife and I arrived, the area was recovering from an economic slump caused by the closing of some lumber mills. There was both rapid population growth and population turnover. For a variety of reasons, newcomers tended to settle in South Umpqua, and new industry developed in surrounding districts.

This brief sketch should be enough to show how the research design differed from traditional anthropological fieldwork in several ways: (1) It required long continuous presence in the field, rather than short intense interruptions of academic routine; (2) the subject matter and research problems were selected for the fieldworker; and (3) the unit of study was not a natural unit. In Oregon, school districts as administrative units resemble timber tracts or areas zoned for agriculture more than they resemble communities. There is a strongly felt sense of community in southwest Oregon. People from the cities come there looking for community; they find it and often remain in spite of greater economic opportunities elsewhere. The frequently heard term "the community" refers to a valued way of life more than to a shared sense of social boundary. A community supporter might be heavily committed to an area much smaller than the school district, such as a volunteer fire department in one of its municipalities, or to one much larger, such as the Douglas County Historical Society. Only occasionally is a community member's social life prescribed by the school-district boundary. The field assignment, in other words, did not fit the fieldwork situation.

During my first few months in the field I proceeded much as I had during my earlier research on Eskimo culture (Hennigh 1970, 1972). I conducted formal and informal interviews, acted as participant and nonparticipant observer, combed through records, and took voluminous notes. I continued traditional research the entire time in the field. Some local residents identified this work as my job and complained if they were not interviewed or observed. At the end of each interview I asked for names of other possible informants. Often the reply was, "Well, if you want someone whose opinion is exactly the opposite of mine, you might talk to ———."

Within six months, my emphasis had shifted heavily to participant observation. Both my wife and myself became active in community affairs, often in leadership capacities. I played Santa Claus for the Myrtle Creek Chamber of Commerce, in which I was an active member, and was president of the Canyonville Breakfast Club and parade chairman for both the Myrtle Creek Wood'n Nickel Days and the Canyonville Pioneer Days annual celebrations. I later became overall chairman of Pioneer Days, an annual festivity, or rather an annual crisis, as failure is interpreted as loss of community spirit. My wife was a part-time reporter for two local newspapers and active in her church and women's organizations.

In effect, I gained a key informant's perspective of the community by becoming my own key informant. Local residents began using me in a small way as a key informant. When newcomers asked about school financing, local history, or other matters, they were sometimes advised to "talk to that anthropologist who hangs around meetings a lot."

As I shall point out, my active participation did not seem to influence the action any more than would more conventional fieldwork, although the effect I did have was perhaps different. The community had an acceptable place for active newcomers and did not need to make special accommodations for the fact that the newcomer happened to be an anthropologist. If anything, informants made a special effort to make sure that I understood them. Accurately conveyed information was their defense against an active newcomer disrupting the smooth flow of their daily lives. School personnel used the term "community resource" for people such as myself who might be called upon to chaperone field trips or to provide other services an investigating anthropologist ought to do anyway. They treated me as any other community resource, because doing so was natural to them.

If my involvement in activities for survival strategy and for objective observation could be separated in practice, then I would have been conducting traditional research at a high cost. I tried at first to separate active participation from the research problem. I found that members of the community recruited not only help but also supervisory leadership. Being a key informant requires a certain amount of work. I also found that my participation was not outside the research problem. School–community relations were more comprehensive than had been suspected. Both school and community were being influenced by unrecognized processes. I learned things that at best would have been poorly identified if observed from a narrow focus.

I am quite sure that I, and therefore my results, were affected by my survival strategy. It has been noted elsewhere, and not always approvingly, that I seemed to enjoy being in my alien setting (Herriott 1977:111, Wolcott 1978:160). Presumably, my attitude affected the published results, either for better or for worse. I will suggest possible implications for the quality of results at the end of this chapter. Here I will only emphasize that it seems natural to do fieldwork differently in one's own culture than in an alien one. Once these differences have been identified, they may become predictable.

My role as key informant did not develop as a result of any unfolding rational plan, but, more than anything else, as a response to research requirements. The traditional anthropologist sets out for the field to get all the information possible and can quit when the field time comes to an end without having solved the problem originally posed. Data-gathering requirements were severe and frustrating in my case (see also Clinton 1975; Firestone 1975). Under these conditions I drifted into unconventional data gathering practices.

Looking back, it seems that there were at least three motives that led me to become active in community affairs and assume leadership roles. The first was that it was highly efficient. An interview appointment can take days to arrange and then be cancelled at the last moment, or it may interfere with observation of something more significant that develops unexpectedly, or information so obtained can quickly become obsolete as situations change. To observe the many formal meetings that are forever going on in the district is to see cheerful people accomplishing a great deal with seemingly little effort. To participate in those meetings, where exact knowledge of what stands or falls with each decision is a requirement for membership, is to obtain an enormous amount of information in a short time.

A second, and sociologically more real, motive for becoming civic minded was that I did not have a great deal of choice in the matter. Residents of southwest Oregon have a sure test – and cure – for potential troublemakers: They try to put them to work, on the assumption that those who would do wrong are basically lazy. This test was not invented for the anthropologist. Branch managers of businesses, professional people, and others commit themselves heavily to civic betterment programs. As one branch manager put it, "You don't have to be civic minded to survive in this business; you have to *enjoy* being civic minded."

A third, more psychological, motive for becoming publicly active did not become apparent until the project was nearly over. Civic involvement was a psychological defense against the abrasions of long-term fieldwork. So much has been written about the need for long-term fieldwork that it came as a surprise to me when anthropologists studying different districts on the same project stated that they found the personal cost of remaining on site unacceptable (Wacaster and Firestone 1978:269–275, Wolcott 1978:160; other fieldworkers' personal communications). Some other anthropologists on the project applied field methods developed for studying foreign cultures to their own culture. They were objective and neutral, even on subjects about which they felt strongly; they solicited other people's opinions but withheld their own, year after year. The basic difficulty with long-term fieldwork seems to be that the anthropologist may lose academic social stimulation but does not replace it with other social stimulations.

The difference between traditional field methods and my own were noticed by members of Abt Associates and consulting reviewers, and at one time I was required to give written justification of why, given my heavy data-gathering schedule, I allowed so many local people to "order me around." One reviewer of an interim report wondered in a friendly manner, how, since I was so socially active, I ever found time to "do anthropology"? He added that he did not object but that he had never heard a justification for such an approach.

One justification for becoming a key informant was that the heavy workload itself required some sort of efficiency. Not only does the key informant have more information than does the marginal native, he or she also has greater access to further information. The key informant knows whom to ask for information. Because he or she has interacted with knowledgeable people in a meaningful manner, a key informant can approach other key informants without laboriously negotiating for their confidence, and he or she can understand what might otherwise be Delphic answers, because they are given by personalities rather than subject. A second closely related justification was that joining took less time and energy than did withdrawing. To show interest in an organization is to be asked to join it, and token membership may be offensive. A third justification was that there was little likelihood that my active participation would change the community in any significant way. The roles I filled in South Umpqua have since been filled others who are proceeding quite as if I had never lived there. Southwest Oregon has a national reputation for political, economic, and social conservatism (*Newsweek*, Dec. 13, 1976, p. 72; *Time*, Dec. 20, 1976, p. 67, Sept. 5, 1977, p. 19). One discovery I made as a key informant was that this conservatism is not a function of personality but of social structures into which individuals can easily enter and leave without changing the structures.

As Everhart has pointed out for his study of an urban school, the traditional anthropologist has to struggle to gain some insight into a foreign culture. The fieldworker in his or her own culture can so easily fill roles in it (e.g., evaluator, administrator) that, to have the same perspective, he or she must struggle to withdraw from the subject under study (Everhart 1977:1–15). Everhart also found long-term fieldwork to be debilitating. These deprivations never occurred in my case, because the people of South Umpqua had an effective assimilation system and a willing new rural resident.

After four years in the field, I was sought out by a career anthropologist and interviewed as a key informant. The interviewer was professional, friendly, and unthreatening. He asked open questions that did not imply an answer and that required a great deal of introspection. I found myself almost abusing the interviewer's quality as an attentive listener by going into what, for me, was a rare monologue. At the same time I found myself holding back on certain types of information. It was not that the data would be favorable or unfavorable to the community, but that I had a vague feeling of loss of control over how the information would be used. It seemed that familiar information would be incorporated into a foreign body of knowledge and would become strange.

That the other anthropologist's information would in fact become strange was perhaps inevitable. In 1977, *Time* (Sept. 5, 1977, p. 19) published a brief report on Oregon Senator Packwood's response to a report "penned by a social anthropologist" which "characterized Douglas County as being 'provincialism carried to the extreme, the redneck capital of the world.' " Actually the anthropologist had not called the people rednecks but had included the term in a long list of comments made by people who had lived in Douglas County for various lengths of time (U. S. Dept. of Agriculture 1977:104).

My own informants stated that they objected not to any specific statements in the anthropological study but to what they felt was the distant and therefore aloof tone of the entire report. The anthropologist was defended by his employers as having used "accepted research methods" (*Roseburg News-Review*, July 8, 1977). In defense of both the researcher and the people of Douglas County, anthropologists also become irritated when traditional objectivity is applied to subjects about which they could apply the test of psychological reality. As Yanagisako (1978), following Wallace (1969) and Schneider (1965), points out in relation to the study of American kinship, "American anthropologists, I suspect, like natives everywhere, find it irritating – to say the least – to have someone tell them how they think."

To summarize thus far, members of Project Rural either observed, confirmed, or discovered a number of dangers of applying traditional fieldwork techniques to a familiar setting. These dangers are not necessarily fatal to a fieldwork project, but they are well worth guarding against. In our case at least, previous fieldwork in the Arctic had not prepared my wife and me for research in mainstream America. We adjusted, without fully realizing we were doing something "unusual," by accepting local expectations that newcomers prove themselves to be useful citizens. This is a field approach we could not have taken in the Arctic because of our ineptitude, and could not have avoided taking in South Umpqua without great effort and the loss of the perspective of key informants.

In addition to doing everything a fieldworker in an alien culture does, the anthropologist at home must do more, and he or she must pass more tests of adequacy with more people. A corollary is that the student of one's own culture has a more difficult time in justifying procedures, because they are more complex. In the case of documenting community–school relations in South Umpqua, my most significant findings were unpredicted and theoretically unlikely. Justification for studying the unlikely was difficult to come by, and the temptation was to reject the significant for the traditional. To illustrate this, I shall return to the fast-changing situation in southwest Oregon.

The significant data

Although my wife and I did not realize it when we arrived in South Umpqua, we were participating in the beginning of a national movement that came to be called the flight from the cities. Historically, migration has taken place from rural America to the cities. In the 1950s, a net total of five million people left nonmetropolitan America. This migration slowed in the 1960s and then dramatically reversed, with a growth in nonmetropolitan areas of 4.2 percent between 1970 and 1973 (Beale 1975:3–7). This reversal caught the experts by surprise. As recently as 1975, rural sociologists were being criticized for not having begun to study the phenomenon (Capener 1975:398–410).

In South Umpqua the population of about 8,000 was growing at 4 percent per year, in spite of declining family size and continued emigration. There was much building activity, a housing shortage, 10 percent per year real estate inflation, and rising rents, which forced some of the extremely poor out of the area.

Newcomers ranged from left-wing hippies, who settled in communes in the hills, to one recorded case of an extreme right winger who came to the area because of its all-white population. A shorter list of types who quickly rose to positions of influence ranged from conservative patriotic retirees, who would be quick to notice if a parade were not led by the American flag, to members of NOW (National Organization for Women), who kept their family names after marriage. Reasons for moving to rural Oregon varied but almost always fell into at least one of the three overlapping categories. One type of newcomer objected to racial tensions, drug abuse, and general decay of the urban environment, as contrasted to the perceived self-discipline, honesty, and hard work of rural populations. Another type objected to the hypocrisy, impersonality, and materialism of urban life, as contrasted to the freedom, slow pace of living, and chance to get close to nature available in rural America. That is, one type objected to the permissiveness of urban life, another to its regimentation. A third category, which might or might not overlap the first two, included those who came from the cities after a family tragedy or career setback. It was not at all hard to find loggers or mill workers who came to southwest Oregon after a harsh divorce, loss of a child to drug abuse, or loss of upward mobility.

Regardless of their background, newcomers who successfully adjusted to small town life almost invariably emphasized rural life style more than did locally born residents. Newcomers made quilts, entered homemade pies in annual contests, joined civic betterment drives, and remarked spontaneously, "We never had this type of opportunity in Minneapolis," or wherever. As the local saying went, "They out-Oregoned the Oregonians." Newcomers were never insulted if mistaken for locally born residents of pioneer background. Long-established residents always corrected the error if mistaken for a newcomer. Newcomers who did not make the adjustment left quietly, and their absence was not noticed. They blamed what they supposed to be an almost uniformly long-established population for their dissatisfaction with the community and were equally likely to describe it as overly conservative redneck or overly liberal "permissive" that let their children run wild.

Contrary to social science theory, a *gesellschaft* folk society was assimilating a *gemeinschaft* urban population. It was obvious from much building activity that dramatic changes were occurring. It nevertheless came as a shock when a 1975 housing survey showed that half the families in South Umpqua had lived there for five years or less (Umpqua Regional Council of Governments 1976). The complex, but efficient, mechanisms of assimilation have been described elsewhere (Hennigh 1978). Suffice it to say that this would have been an extremely difficult process to record without having participated in it, even to the point of rising, with other newcomers, to positions of some influence.

The fact that so many of the defenders of a valued way of life were new to the area caused rapid social change. These changes appeared dramatic, even to the traditional anthropologist, but they did not conform to preconceived theories and patterns were therefore hard to discern until toward the end of fieldwork. Then it was the key informant who imposed some order on the welter of data the anthropologist had collected. Some social changes which accelerated during the years of field observation are noted here.

First, lines of authority were becoming blurred. During the 1930s, parents were embarrassed to send their children to graduation because they could not afford graduation clothes. Mr. Bates, the banker, set an example by sending his daughters to graduation in homemade dresses. Mr. Bates had authority to set an example, and his name is never recalled without the title "Mr." As recently as the 1960s, almost all positions of authority on town councils, schoolboards, and civic committees were held by either merchants or professional people. School teachers and other leading citizens were always seated together at social occasions as special people, and children were taught to put them on pedestals.

During the 1970s the sharpness of these lines of authority was dimming rapidly. Even mill owners could be voted out of public offices they had held for more than a decade. Organizations that might once have been called exclusive came to be called "cliques," a disparaging term. A standard reply by members of such organizations came to be, "Come on and join the clique." Business and fraternal organizations, such as the Lions or Elks clubs, not only accepted laborers but actively recruited them. Loggers who did not own suits or ties sometimes borrowed attire for initiation into important decision-making organizations. Long-established residents as well as newcomers took advantage of rapidly increasing choices of conduct and association. Traditional local leaders often welcomed and encouraged increasing public participation.

That a responsible minority lost ability to establish public consensus may be illustrated by two public hearings on a proposed Days Creek Dam. In 1970, only two residents spoke out against the dam, and a parade of prominent citizens spoke in favor of its construction. Several skeptics who had been present recalled that they were against the project but had been embarrassed to speak out against such a strong showing by local leaders. A 1976 dam hearing was dominated by the opposition. The People Against the Days Creek Dam wore green shirts in a show of unity, passed out handbills, and entered their opposition into the public record for hours. Opponents of the dam ranged from headband-wearing hippies to conservative housewives who noted that the area would become "another asphalt jungle like I remember in Los Angeles," that "since I have been here, we have had the same family of doves return three years in a row," and that "anyone stupid enough to build on floodplain deserves to be washed down the river."

Second, the communications system was becoming eclectic. Young adults recalled that whenever they had gotten a licking at school, their parents knew about it by the time they got home. During the 1970s notices of school events were sent home with students. If the mimeographed announcements got lost along the way, parents might never suspect what they had missed. Many things contributed to this scattering of communications. The housing shortage forced families to live where they could rather than where they preferred. New businesses, churches, and clubs recruited regionally, rather than locally. In the 1970s it was becoming not uncommon for a locally born resident to live in one municipality, work in a second, shop in a third, worship in a fourth, and belong to three or four regionally composed organizations. The effect of this scattering of associations on shared public knowledge may be illustrated by two unprecedented events. In 1974, the voters of South Umpqua elected a resident who taught in another district to the school board, in spite of a tradition that such a situation, with its many potentials for conflict of interest, should not occur. Many voters did not know that the candidate was a schoolteacher. In 1975, national commentator Paul Harvey told of the nearby town of Winston, which elected a city councilman who could not be located. Nobody in town had ever seen the candidate.

Third, the sanction system was changing. Although friendliness had always been valued in South Umpqua, loud outbursts did occasionally occur. A mayor might tongue-lash a city council for holding informal meetings outside the council chambers. In the 1960s such exchanges seldom resulted in resignation or withdrawal. To be out of the decision-making process was to be ineffectual and possibly lonely. In the 1970s, withdrawal was far more threatening to an organization than to any of its members. Most influential residents were overcommitted socially. One school principal, for example, attended meetings of formal organizations for as many as 18 evenings in a row but was nevertheless criticized for not keeping the public informed. Under these circumstances it was easy to lose interest in any one organization, as an individual had abundant social resources elsewhere. The 1973 and 1974 Wood'n Nickel Days were something less than successful. Some church groups disliked a Jaycee-sponsored beer garden; some charitable fund-raising organizations disapproved of allowing commercial carnival outfits to participate. The 1974 parade consisted of three floats and five fire trucks. A committee was organized to revive the event. Old timers and newcomers worked hard for most of a year, not only contacting but recruiting more organizational leaders than they had known existed. The 1975 parade had ninety entries, and a record heat wave did not keep crowds from the midway.

Under certain circumstances withdrawal can be self-defeating, as it allows greater autonomy to decision-making groups. Under these conditions organized grassroots protest movements can develop. Two such protest movements occurred before 1970. One was against the schools after they were consolidated in 1965, the other was against economic leadership in 1935. Eight grassroots protest movements developed in South Umpqua between 1973 and 1977. These were against the schools, a police department, a publicly elected sewer committee, a utilities company, the state Department of Environmental Quality, and the proposed Days Creek Dam.

Fourth, the costs of rural assets were rising. Conventional wisdom had it that rural living was inexpensive and that distinctively rural assets were least expensive of all because they were readily available. This belief was based in part on the assumption that people are moving from rural America to the cities, leaving homes, municipal facilities, and outdoor recreation areas for those who remain. With the reversal of the migration patterns, these suppositions are challenged in two respects. The first is that the sense of the great outdoors that newcomers find so attractive is deceptive. In Douglas County 90 percent of the land is forested. The remaining 10 percent is contested for use by agriculture, industry, and housing development. The resulting real-estate shortage makes once marginal flood plains and dry hillsides increasingly attractive for development but brings both newcomers and established landowning residents into conflict with outside authorities. The most enduring grassroots rebellion, for example, has been against the Department of Environmental Quality, which has the task of enforcing septic tank regulations enacted when almost all home building was on level farmland. Seemingly arbitrary regulations, which add to the already high cost of building on marginal land, force an alliance between long-established landowners who would benefit from real-estate inflation and home-building newcomers who want to buy as low as possible.

The second unexpected cause of rural inflation stems from the conflict between the need for expanded public facilities and the need for restrictions on their use. Growing population creates needs for expanded water, sewer, police, and other facilities. Often urban solutions to the problems of growth are the least expensive in dollar terms but most expensive in terms of quality of life and rural freedom. When the choice is between maintaining a valued way of life and paying higher taxes, the taxes are paid. Canyonville has long had an antiquated water system. Thousands of hours were spent over many years searching for a solution to the water problem, and the question of what to do about it was asked of every candidate for city council. By agreeing to chlorinate South Umpqua River water, Canyonville could long since have had an inexpensive, efficient water system. This option was so unpopular it was almost never considered even as a logical possibility. Instead, in 1975 the voters approved a $620,000 bond intended to ensure a supply of fresh spring water. Similarly, the residents of Tri-City, an unincorporated area, pay higher taxes for fewer public services than do residents of nearly municipalities but benefit from lack of zoning restrictions, city ordinances, or other restraints on personal freedom. There was not the slightest groundswell for incorporation in Tri-City during the 1970s. In some areas of southwest Oregon, burgeoning industry has had the paradoxical effect of making the goal of keeping our town small realistic by providing abundant tax revenues.

These changes are all part of the same process. An interesting analysis could be made of how a study of any one of them led to each of the others and, eventually, to American disenchantment with urban life styles. Such an analysis would have been extremely hard to justify during Project Rural. The funding was for the study of federal aid to education. The community study aspect was intended ultimately to increase knowledge of community–school relationships. It was not at all clear how information received while first participating in the assimilation process and then performing as a responsible citizen would contribute to the goal of the project. A necessary penalty for conducting fieldwork the way I did was that the research was unfocused. It was not until close to the end of the fieldwork that data already collected became vital to explaining unpredicted events in community–school relations.

Discovery of significance of data

In October and November of 1976 and twice in January 1977, viewers of the national evening television news watched four districts in rural Oregon close or open their schools as a result of school budgets failing or passing during the school year. The so-called Oregon taxpayers' revolt received national press coverage and was attributed to conservative locally born residents who objected to higher taxes and to modern education (*Newsweek*, Dec. 13, 1976, p. 72; *Time*, Dec. 20, 1976, p. 67). A total of seventeen rural school districts, including South Umpqua, began the school year without voter-approved budgets. This situation was so unprecedented that as recently as two years earlier knowledgeable residents could not have described the legal and financial implications of such a happening. The banner headline of the Myrtle Creek *Mail* (Sept. 16, 1976) read: "Schools Have Funds For Less Than Month." The budget in South Umpqua passed handily, but in other districts the schools were locked or they got by with drastically reduced expenditures.

It was immediately apparent that the taxpayer revolt had not been spearheaded by locally born conservatives and was not a campaign against high taxes. One opposition group campaigned against the school budget on the grounds that it was too small. A more powerful group, which did demand a smaller budget, readily agreed that the result would be higher taxes because of loss of state matching funds, damage to the local economy, and other reasons, but, as they put it, "That's the price we'll have to pay."

The taxpayers' revolt had not even been against the schools, but against traditional authority (Hennigh 1978). Briefly stated, newcomers and, increasingly, oldtimers also, accepted rural life styles but not traditional social control. Traditional leaders in most sectors of the society adjusted readily, often welcoming and even recruiting help from "responsible people" who were "not afraid of a little work." School administrators, however, were under considerable legal and accreditational constraint to maintain the firm-but-fair policy and high professional standards that had been expected of them when they were hired.

As the traditional school administrative system came to be seen as politically powerful and arbitrary, people began to complain that the schools were showing objectionable films, teaching immorality, permitting delinquency, graduating functional illiterates, and wasting money. Organizations such as the Concerned Citizens for Education, the Volunteer Parent Patrol, and Citizens for Responsible Education formed. Once the structural changes demanded by the public were accomplished, complaints about the quality of education ceased, and record high-school taxes passed easily.

Protests against the schools began as soon as the new federally funded research program was announced in the traditional way during teacher orientation in the fall of 1972. A teacher leaped to his feet and demanded, "You dared agree to this program without consulting the teachers?" Then other teachers joined in an unprecedented debate. The protests ended the day the federal research funds ran out on the last day of school in 1977. In between, many of the public protests had been directed against educational innovations I had been hired to document. It would have been extremely tempting, and internally consistent, to describe the federal program as a causal factor in the organized protest movements. But eighteen school districts had faced voter rejection of their budgets; some of them were receiving federal funding and others were not; some were educationally conservative and others, like South Umpqua, had long held progressive educational policies. What the school districts had in common were the same scenic grandeur and friendly small-town atmospheres that were attracting newcomers to South Umpqua. Because of my experience in community decision-making processes, I was able to document that the protests would have occurred anyway; they were symptomatic of general social change. By implication, detecting such general changes in the future will increase the predictability of success or failure of projects anthropologists are employed to study.

Conclusions

During the four and a half years of fieldwork in South Umpqua, I observed, heard about, or read about several dangers of conducting traditional fieldwork on familiar people as if they were foreign to the investigator. One danger is social deprivation, resulting from self-imposed marginality. Another danger is being seen as equally foreign to the people being written about. Neither of these dangers is necessarily fatal to fieldwork, but they are both worth warning against.

The conclusion of this chapter is that a fieldworker in his or her own culture has at least one research opportunity not available to marginal natives in an alien culture: The fieldworker may become his or her own key informant by becoming a significant member of the community under study. It seems that key informants provide vital functions that students of foreign cultures cannot provide for themselves but that fieldworkers in their own culture have difficulty not providing. Among these are:

1. Perspective: The anthropologist as a stranger learns details of the fragments of the culture under investigation before comprehending their places in the larger system. The result is likely to be an exaggerated sense of the importance of these fragments (Guemple 1972:7). The key informant comprehends the entire system and is therefore able to place component parts into their proper perspective. In the case of South Umpqua, public protests against the schools were placed in the context of general social change, of which the changing community–school relationship was one component.

2. Hypothesis reduction: Most accurate explanations of alien behavior appear implausible to the anthropologist as stranger. Therefore, the number of implausible but equally probable hypotheses is incapacitating (D'Andrade 1976:161). The key informant can quickly reduce the hypotheses to a researchable few. In South Umpqua, for example, it became apparent that public protest was not directed against the federal project I had been hired to document.

3. Objectivity: The objectivity of an anthropologist as a stranger is the dispassionate rejection of strong social stimuli (Nash 1963:149–152). The objectivity of a key informant is the testing of reality by responding significantly to strong social stimuli. It is the resulting sense of significance that allows the key informant to test hypotheses and to provide perspectives for the anthropologist as stranger. In South Umpqua, my wife and I were assimilated into the community and therefore realized that the schools had to deal with many active newcomers similar to ourselves.

The advantages of becoming a key informant were sharply increased data-gathering opportunities, increased tolerance of long-term fieldwork, and, I hope, a more useful study. I stress that the methods used in South Umpqua were not the result of intelligent planning but were an adaptation to a difficult research assignment. I suggest that the unplanned nature of the adaptation be taken as evidence that it was natural, whereas traditional field methods would have been unnatural. Pelto (1970:92) has stated that fieldworkers are participant observers whether they know it or not. I would add that fieldworkers in their own culture are their own key informants whether they know it or not.

10 Neighboring: discovering support systems among Norwegian-American women

AGNES M. AAMODT

My project began on a spring day in 1975 as I was writing a brief paper for health professionals to illustrate my conceptualization of health and healing systems. I was using data from a field experience in a Papago Indian village in southern Arizona (Aamodt 1976). As I tried to make explicit the human condition defined in the Papago cultural system, the complexities stirred my senses to carry the question to a second culture, my own. For the next two years, I put seemingly disparate pieces together – my heritage of Norwegian emigrant *bønder* (farmers), homemakers, and theologians who settled in Wisconsin in the 1840s, 1850s, and 1860s; conceptualizations of life-supporting rituals and care that serve as the hallmark of nursing practice; a projected sabbatical leave; and a growing curiosity to learn a set of formal procedures for collecting cultural knowledge. [1]

Getting my world in order

The study that emerged from this sequence of events was based on the assumption that "taking care of" can be a culturally relevant domain that organizes human experience (Aamodt 1978). At first my research question was stated roughly: What patterns can be identified in cultural solutions of Norwegian-American women when someone (themselves or others) needs help, support, assistance – in other words, care?

The methodology drew from the work of Spradley and McCurdy (1972) and the strategies of the ethnographic interview. Culture was conceptualized, following Spradley and McCurdy's definition, as knowledge that generates behavior and interprets experience. My choice of the methodology of the ethnographic interview set forth several problems that were to give direction to the research. A first problem was finding informants who were knowledgeable about caring activities in a Norwegian-American community. Women who had cared for others during their lifetimes were potentially most desirable. Another problem was to decide on a circumscribed domain of information. The cultural scene was to be the unit of analysis as conceptualized by Spradley and McCurdy (1972) as "the information shared by two or more people" that defines for them

133

selected experiences in recurring social situations. As an example, another form of the study question was: What cultural scenes could be identified in a Norwegian-American community and how were they defined by the women members of the community?

A final problem of the project was to organize the information or invent a structure (taxonomy) that would meet the approval of the informants whose cultural system was to be represented in the taxonomy. This structure would eventually serve as the basic framework for an ethnography of the cultural scenes in the domain "taking care of" among Norwegian-American women.

As my research activities developed, the way in which I conceptualized the elements in the question became more refined. "Taking care of" was translated to "taking care of others." "Others" was translated to "neighbors." Thus the focus of the research became "things neighbors do for neighbors."

Conceptualizing neighboring as care has not been reported in the nursing literature. Honigmann and Honigmann (1978) report on nurturance and its conjunction with the patterning and learning of responsibility in rural Austria. Nurturing behavior, they found, was strongest within household groups; it was more intense with neighbors and less intense with more remote individuals. Litwak and Szelenyi (1969) point to the difference between kinship and neighbor interpersonal relationships. Neighbors, they report, are likely to share problems in the immediate environment. That is, neighbors were called upon for short-term favors; whereas family members and friends were depended upon for long-term problems. In contrast, Turnbull (1972) writes about the Ik, among whom he saw few, if any, behaviors that suggested a caring relationship with another person, neighbor, or family member. An important feature of the neighboring relationship for nursing or any applied field is the difference in the set of obligations and the social distance among actors as neighbors as distinguished from actors as family members.

This chapter focuses on the problems and solutions of doing anthropology in a Norwegian-American community in western Wisconsin where I was relative, stranger, friend, and acquaintance. I will attempt to make explicit the complexities in becoming legitimate in a community of cousins, aunts, and uncles; the realities for me in the researcher-informant experience; and the strategies necessary for following the data and finally settling on the domain of neighboring.

Preparations for my project proceeded at various levels of consciousness: three weeks of traveling in Norway; reading *Kristine Lavransdatter* (Undset 1942), a novel of twelfth century Norway; a casual attempt at Norwegian language lessons; program planning for a faculty conference on ethnographic methodology and pleading with James Spradley or David McCurdy to meet with us; writing a sabbatical research proposal and submitting a grant to the American Nurses' Foundation (rejected); accepting an offer of sponsorship from James Spradley, Macalester College, for my fieldwork in western Wisconsin in the winter of 1977–1978; writing to relatives about living with and learning about Norwegian-Americans; and finally traveling in and around Pierce County, Wisconsin, for a preliminary field visit in May 1977, three months before the study was to begin.

Emotional commitment and logistics for the project shuffled back and forth. A sabbatical contract, willing cousins, aunts, and uncles, and approval from my university's human-subjects committee labeled the project worthy. On a Sunday morning in August 1977, I drove into Ellsworth, Wisconsin, to meet cousins who were to be one of the strong links in a chain of fieldwork brokers. My project to learn about Norwegian-American women – my people – began.[2]

The world of my kin: getting into the field

My mother and father grew up in a rural community in Wisconsin approximately fifty miles (80 km) east of the Twin Cities of St. Paul and Minneapolis, Minnesota. My father's family came in the 1860s from southern Wisconsin, where they had farmed for twenty years or so after emigrating from Norway. My mother's mother grew up in southern Wisconsin, the daughter of an emigrant Lutheran minister. She met my grandfather when he served as an intern in her father's parish in Pierce County, Wisconsin. Eventually, they were called to the church where the Aamodts, including my father, were members. When she was in her late teens, my mother boarded in the Aamodt home and taught Norwegian summer school for the local township.

A core of community members had stood fast for sixty years. The Norwegian Lutheran Synod churches that had formed the nexus of community life in this area had been amalgamated into the American Lutheran Synod in 1960, and the identity of being Norwegian was disappearing. Membership in the church had changed, as people moved in and out of the county, villages, and townships. The first Sunday I attended my father's old church, the new Sunday school teachers were being sworn in and the remark was made that not one of an approximate dozen had grown up in and been confirmed in this congregation.

Because I had experienced getting into the field on a previous fieldwork trek on an Indian reservation, where I was unmistakably an outsider by color, ethnic background, language, and religion, I knew some of the complexities of working and living with people who vacillate between wanting you as a family member, not trusting you, and viewing you with outright aggressiveness. The community members I knew and who knew me were my father's sister, her son, and my father's brother. In close proximity to the township lived two other cousins, their children, and multiple cousins, all of my father's family. This had seemed a reasonable setting to begin the research, especially because of the limited time I had for the fieldwork. If I could begin where I knew the people and they knew something about me, getting in might be facilitated.

When I had learned my sabbatical was a fact, I sent off letters post haste to members of my family to tell them of my idea and what I hoped to do. As it worked out, I was able to plan a trip about three months before I would attempt the serious live-in fieldwork. My intent with the letters and the visit was to give family members a chance to talk among themselves, choose whether or not I should come, and, furthermore, find out what kind of a person I was. For me, this was fair. I was encouraged by letter, conversation, and phone calls. The advantages of doing anthropology at home were emerging. On the other hand, given the obligations and rights of our family system, they really did not have a choice.

My position in the system was crucial to their sense of obligation. When my mother and father were living we traveled to my grandparents' home at least once a year for summer festivals and visits. My mother and father were buried on the family plot in the cemetery of the church where my mother's father had served as the preacher and my father's grandfather and father had served as charter members and strong monitors of the congregation. I had visited off and on for short visits during the past thirty-five years, but since we had grown, my cousins and I had not taken the opportunity to learn to know each other. The obligations of the family system enjoined them to do right by me. The rules were, and continue to be, that family members are mutually dependent in the sense that they help each other in any way they can. On the other hand, the rights were such that members of the family do not infringe on the privacy of other members. They live in different neighborhoods and have different friends but participate in activities of good fellowship on holidays, anniversaries, baptisms, weddings, and funerals.

During my preliminary visit, I had announced a need for living quarters where I could be more or less alone. Two weeks before I was to leave for Wisconsin, I received word by telephone that a small house owned by a teacher who worked out of the area was available and if I wanted it I probably could have it. This was a typical sabbatical arrangement. The owner was a professor in a nearby university and would be coming by from time to time, but for the most part, I would have the house to myself. The house would be left stocked with sheets, dishes, soap, an iron, and so forth and I could just move in.

My plan was simple, my project innocuous. When I drove up to the house where I would stay, I thought that surely such a worthy project as learning about taking care of others could only be looked on with favor. The house was located on the main street of a small town, the county seat of the area I wanted to learn about. The day I arrived, one Sunday morning at about 11:30, my cousins met me and we drove to the house and from there to a restaurant for a Sunday dinner to get acquainted. Later, the homeowner and I talked about arrangements for the cost of the house, general house maintenance details, and so on. Everyone was gracious, kind, and welcoming. Importantly, I was not to live in with close relatives. Although relatives were strategically clustered all around me, I preferred not to be locked in to any one segment of the community. In this way, I hoped to be able to give both to them and myself the social and geographical distance that would preserve their rights yet facilitate my aims.

Gradually, as I did the normal things one does in any new community – meet the neighbors, become a regular customer at the post office, grocery store, drug store, bank, and gasoline station, and attend church – I built up a cadre of people who knew my name and knew a little about me. Eventually, I joined the church choir and added to my list of acquaintances. The woman whose house I was renting was a native; her mother and father had lived in the community during their lifetimes both on a farm and in town. So I became known as "Louise's renter." Aamodt was a name well known to many of the natives in the community, and as time progressed I was able to trace a relationship with almost every person of Norwegian ancestry that I met. Either they knew someone I knew or were related to someone who had been a neighbor of someone in my family. My world became smaller and smaller. People were saying how glad they were to have me around.

Nonetheless, I was viewed with suspicion in various ways. Could I be trusted to live alone in a home that had not been cleared of private possessions and papers? Did I have money to support myself? What secrets did I need to know? What interpretations was I making of my observations?

For the first several months I was referred to as "that woman." As it turned out, the community members were somewhat divided as to whether an unknown person should be allowed full reign of a house containing all the personal possessions of Louise's mother, who had died no more than six months before. Could it be I would not look in personal papers and private drawers? A sense of privacy among most people is a highly valued commodity. In this small town the questions were endless.

Initial inquiries of community members highlighted another area of concern – my money. Where was it coming from? (Gloss: "Will you be asking us for welfare funds?") For a stranger to move into this community without a job to go to every day suggested a potential welfare recipient. In this largely northern European locale, persons who live off the government are carefully monitored. Another area of concern was, who are you doing this for? When I could say that I was working with some teachers at Macalester College (about forty miles away, or sixty-four km) the questioners were appeased.

Another question focused on the nature of my data-gathering techniques. To be an anthropologist meant more than digging pot shards and gathering prehistoric information to these rural Wisconsin inhabitants. Especially, I answered to the male members of the community, husbands, brothers and sons, "No, I wasn't taking notes on this conversation" (we were eating Sunday dinner in a private home); "Yes indeed, some things are very personal," "No, I was not interested in whether the Indian way of life was better than how the Norwegians did it." (Many non-Indians are preoccupied with the Indian way of doing things. Others were certain that better-or-worse comparison was my conceptual base.) As my research became more focused we could all relax. An important strategy in resolving this problem was to go public and explain and reexplain the kinds of information that would be useful to the aims of my research.

Possibly the single most useful strategy in becoming legitimate was the services of fieldwork brokers; that is, members of the community who facilitated the work of myself, the fieldworker. A fieldwork broker serving as a link between researcher and informant provides a backstage for conversations with informants that can clarify the motives and the personal value system of the foreign fieldworker and help to reduce the ambiguity about the research for the community. I accumulated a team of five fieldwork brokers who served as a support system for myself and most of the seventy or so women I interviewed from time to time. One of the brokers also served as an informant. Spradley and McCurdy (1972) speak of a middleman as a kind of go-between who helps to create and, ideally, maintain a trustful relationship between researcher and informant. Golde (1970) refers to her chief informant as a "pivot" from which she built a social network of informants and friends. In most field studies, the individual who serves in the role of interpreter serves as fieldwork broker whether "interpreter" refers, in the strict sense, to translating conversations when actors are informed by mutually unintelligible coding systems for speech or to translating meanings of social behavior and expectations of behavior.

Reducing ambiguity and becoming legitimate also focused on my multiple identities among community members. Among my referents were niece, cousin, writer, learner, nurse, professor, someone interested in Norwegian-Americans, someone who had lived with the Indians, Arizonan, Aamodt, aunt, visitor, friend, customer, neighbor. My identities and personal community expanded as I acquired a social network of acquaintances and friends. After several months of initiating social interaction in order to become known and to know community members, I found myself unable to maintain the expected circle of activities. In consequence, I had to choose and to withdraw from, or not promote, some relationships that were both personally and professionally tempting to me. The process was not much different from that everyone experiences in day-by-day situations. In my ordinary life in Arizona, the constraints of my job, being a woman, being white, being interested in Papago children and transcultural health care made it necessary to make choices every day to follow or not follow leads that would bring rewards to me in the form of intriguing insights and questions and new friendships.

The researcher–informant experience

Relationships between fieldworker and informant necessary to the ethnographic interview experience are frequently more intense and more dependent upon actors liking one another and always require more of the informant's time than do casual encounters of participant observation or single encounters of survey-gathering techniques. Criteria for the selection of informants for this study followed those reported by Spradley and McCurdy (1972); that is, that the informants know the culture, be willing to talk, and be able to communicate in a nonanalytic manner. I hoped for one or two informants that I could work with throughout the winter months.

From September 1977 until the end of April 1978, I participated in family gatherings, birthday celebrations, holiday festivities, funerals, auctions, ladies aid meetings, church services, coffee parties, dinner parties, choir rehearsals, senior citizen devotions and tours, and so on. In one way or another, everyone I met, ate with, visited with, and with whom I attended social gatherings contributed to my corpus of information. Typically, as I explained my project to those around me, I was greeted with comments of interest supplemented with recommendations of persons who could help me.

One of my informants was suggested by the local minister, who, serving as a fieldwork broker, arranged our initial meeting and then left us to manage for ourselves. A second informant was a friend of a cousin of mine. We met as a threesome. From time to time, visitors came upon us during our conversations and I solicited information from them as well.

An unexpected source of support developed in the availability of the Norwegian grapevine. Televisit, a program for inexpensive telephone service within Wisconsin during off-peak hours, allowed continual communication among various groups of informants. Families visited one another and my presence and my project were discussed.

Through the generosity and tolerance of cousins and aunts, I collected my first formal taped interviews six weeks after I entered the field. Two months later, I was systematically interviewing two women over eighty years of age who had grown up in a rural community within ten miles (sixteen kilometers) of each other. With their help, I was able to begin to construct questions appropriate for the domain "taking care of others." Problems that developed in this ethnographic interview experience focused on finding good informants, training the informant, and training myself.

Finding good informants meant long hours of participation and observation and casual interviews with people who were generous of time and information. Often I was referred to a knowledgeable woman only to be told by her of another person who "really knew." Similarly, the purposes of the research were frequently misunderstood and I was expected to be interested in the lives of important Norwegian women or the history of family members. Often after I made contact with an informant our interviews were not good, in the sense of an ethnographic interview, until the fourth or fifth encounter. Before this time, we often were unsure if we really liked each other, the informant did not yet understand the nature of taxonomic rules, and I was groping for questions and struggling to listen to what she had to say. When the informant and I liked each other, if she had the patience to stick with the repetition of questions, and if she liked the kind of detective work the ethnographic methodology demanded, the quality and the quantity of the data were enhanced.

Recognizing tradeoffs or reciprocities for time consumed is an important principle in developing a cadre of persons who are willing to serve as informants. Companionship was one useful bargaining item. Human beings isolated from the larger world for one reason or another are often ravenous for company and news. During the Papago experience (Aamodt 1976), my presence with a mother and her young children was desired, in part, because she had someone with whom she could talk over daily events. Man is a social animal, and whether Norwegian, Papago, or whatever, the response is largely the same. The elderly, the home-bound handicapped, mothers with small children, as well as children themselves represent a population of observers and critics with time available to trade for someone's interest in what they have to say about their world.

A researcher–informant encounter went something like this: Upon meeting, our casual conversation focused on the elements in our immediate experience, for example, the ice on the porch, a feeling of chill as the wind came through the door, or a slight cough. These exchanges created a sense of acknowledgment that we had met. After we decided how and where we were going to sit, I would attempt to set the stage with a review of where we had been at the last interview, what I had done with the data, and where I saw us taking ourselves that day. Generally, about one hour of formal interviewing was a tolerable amount of time for the two of us. The presence of a third person encouraged diversions into secondary topics, reducing the intensity of the conversation. On these occasions, it was not uncommon to continue an interview for two hours. For many informants, a visit following the formal interview was the important stage in the encounter. Thus, for another hour or so, we often sat around drinking coffee, eating Norwegian cookies, crackers, and cheese, and chatting about the community social history.

The tape recorder was off, my notebook was folded in place, and the formal interview was over. We were relaxed, and our social hour could begin. Anything I could remember from these conversations was quite all right. I would be reminded that we had talked about it if I touched on a subject from these conversations another day. It was, however, against the rules to use any of the interviewing tools at this time. This meant recording at night after I returned home. With some informants I stayed for a meal or overnight. Often, one or the other of us would remember something we needed to share long after the interview. In some cases I used a notebook or a scrap of paper. In other instances I kept a running notebook in my purse where brief reminders later served as an outline for more extensive fieldnotes. This was often when the "good stuff" emerged.

During a visit to Macalester College, James Spradley had provided me with a formula for the interview and analysis of data. For two hours he interviewed and analyzed data from students in an undergraduate course on methodology. Within this short space of time he developed a taxonomy and a beginning format for a componential analysis of what students do for students when they are "down." I was impressed. As I talked with potential informants in my own research, however, I was equally impressed with the work needed to train an informant. The students Spradley interviewed were knowledgeable about the need for detailed accounts and the format of subsequent structural questions. What an informant needed to know became a challenging task.

The sequence of events from the first encounters to the concluding interviews moved from casual conversations to focused discussion on what it meant to be Norske and the kinds of things Norwegian-American women did day by day. Generally, we had two or three of these sessions as I began to develop a sense of the vocabulary and the kinds of general questions that would elicit information related to the concept of care. Not infrequently I would be told, "We've said that before!" Often initial conversations focused on the nebulous character of "doing something for others" and the low priority given to care taking in the American economy in comments like, "I don't think I've told you anything," "This is just what we always do," "I can't understand why you could want to learn about this." Later as we moved to more specific data, their commentary was critical of what they were giving me and they would say, "Now, this is only the way I see it!," "Someone else might say it differently," and "Could I sort that again, I've thought of another way it might work."

Initially, some women did not like the idea of a tape recorder. The strategy of the ethnographic interview, however, required that I record conversations in order to develop questions rooted in their language. These verbatim accounts were crucial to the beginning analysis of the data. Whereas several informants took it as a matter of course, others refused to have the tape recorder on. Sometimes it took several interviews before an informant would concede. On some occasions an informant would remark, "Oh, is the recorder on?" Yet at other times, an informant would look from time to time toward the recorder out of the corner of her eye. No one wanted to listen to the tape or hear her voice.

I was reminded of the Papago, who are not supposed to talk about certain aspects of their power. One young Papago woman repeated a sequence of events about her puberty ceremony in one breath. What I could remember, she said, was all right, but I could not tape her recitation or take notes. The phenomenon of the tape recorder can be a difficult barrier; that is, fear of the recorder itself, fear of the power that develops or dissolves when one's voice is preserved recording secrets, and fear of saying something in not quite the right way are fears that I found inhibited people from agreeing to a tape-recorded session.

Recurring ethical problems concerned sensitive issues in many past, as well as current, social relationships. Emotionally loaded information came in bits and pieces and could not be pursued for long periods of time. "Love and shame are gone!" was the laconic remark of a nursing-home resident in a commentary on family care of the elderly in today's Norwegian community. This brief allusion communicated a crucial breakthrough into the value system. Most of the elderly, many of whom had cared for their own aged parents, were living out their last years in nursing homes. There was not enough love or enough shame, they explained to me, among the young people to continue this commitment.

Reliving the past often became a painful and exhausting ordeal for informants, and I found myself shortening interviews, delaying introduction of topics, and implementing other strategies that would change the pace and preserve the integrity of the informant yet get the story. Often relatives who desperately wanted to help me with information found themselves reliving tragic deaths, mistakes in judgment, and forgotten obligations that could not be amended. Despite my intentions and the safeguards I had built into my modus operandi for getting into and maintaining myself in the field setting, I found I was unable to refrain from exploiting relationships with family members and friends of family members. Getting the information for my research goals often held a higher priority.

On the other hand, it was with good cheer and support that a group of family informants talked about their ability to cope with whatever it was we needed to talk about. I was telling them of changes I had had to report to the Human Subjects Committee of my university. Their curiosity provoked me to tell them of the nature of social and psychological risk in my kind of research and how the federal government and universities attempted to provide procedures to preserve the integrity and anonymity of human subjects. The reply was terse, "You just tell them that we're made of stronger stuff than that."

Training myself in some aspects of the ethnographic procedures was something I had not quite counted on. I was familiar with most of my biases. Sensitive issues relating to abortion, family gossip, religion, and politics emerged and dissolved. In this field setting I did not have to watch for slips of the tongue, as I did among the Papago, when using names of "people who had gone on" could have invoked the presence of a ghost-soul or referring aloud to safety measures prior to an automobile trip could have precipitated the thing I was trying to prevent (Aamodt 1976).

Problems with my behavior were of a different order. The ethnographic study requires a sequence of questions that elicit language samples and subsequently the development of logical relationships between categories and subcategories (Spradley and McCurdy 1972). General questions such as "Tell me about a time when you were a child and went to the neighbors'," "Tell me about things neighbors do for you" on the surface appeared casual and nondemanding. Procedures for acquiring language samples with these kinds of questions were somewhat easier to monitor than were the structural questions required in the formal organization of the taxonomy. Between interviews I sifted through written notes and tape recordings for reference to "things people do for people" that could be developed into a framework of care among Norwegian-American women. Structural questions were, "What kinds of neighbors are there?" "What kinds of things do neighbors do for neighbors?" "Visiting and serving coffee are a kind of———? "Why are 'telling them things' and 'praying for them' more alike than 'sending someone to help' and either of the other two?"

The purpose of such questions was to get at the way informants conceptualized their neighboring experience and generated their behavior. Sometimes the questions were misunderstood, sometimes the informants would qualify what they had said or provide alternative ways of organizing the domain we were working on. To concentrate on these kinds of exacting activities for more than an hour without diversion often produced fatigue and lack of interest. The combination of work and casual conversation needed to be monitored to keep us on track of the goal and give us both a feeling of satisfaction – that we had accomplished a job.

My own strategies needed continual review. Bringing us back to the job was most frequently accomplished by inventing specific questions (e.g., " Tell me about a time when you visited") that, in themselves, insisted on detail relevant to the research goals. Furthermore, I found it was important to maintain the posture of a slow learner. This needed to be done without appearing rude and offending informants. In my past field-work, informants had often expected me to remember and know what they had said after telling me once. The process of remembering enough to be able to ask for more detail is also an important strategy. As I reviewed the taped conversations, however, I was surprised to learn how often I used "yes" and "uh huh" and "I understand" (as an empathetic nurse) instead of pausing and saying "oh?" or "and?" I had to learn not to anticipate, not to expect that I would understand, and to look more perplexed, at least about those things that honestly made me curious.

Following the data

Following the data in the language of the informant is probably the most important principle in the procedures for the ethnographic interview. As I have said, my purpose was to develop a taxonomy using domains derived from the way informants phrased their answers that could serve as the structure for ethnographic statements on how Norwegian-American women take (or took) care of others. This information would represent a cognitive structural pattern of their view of social behavior related to the care concept. At the same time, I was collecting information in the spirit of participant observation and recording data (that is, interviewing myself) about what I observed. What was culturally relevant to Norwegian-American women was crucial. According to Spradley and McCurdy (1972) developing the "grand tour" questions that made sense to the native was what led the researcher to the culturally relevant domains of the human users. I anticipated problems that could develop in differences between what I wanted to learn about (i.e. the care concept and Norwegian-American culture) and what was culturally relevant in the knowledge system.

As it turned out, "care" was indeed an inappropriate referent. For example, whereas what people did for each other was easily understood, almost everyone was unwilling to say that she had taken care of someone. A grand-tour question using the word "care" did not elicit the kind of information I hoped for. It was as if I, as a nurse, was placing a meaning on "care" equivalent to a kind of nursing care; that is, taking it to mean taking care of someone because of a special need. Another meaning attached to the idea of care was the value of consciously caring about what happened to something or someone. Both of these interpretations seemed to elicit the wrong connotation. The alternate verb "did" was less value laden. What someone *did* for someone else made sense.

Another grand-tour question focused on the Norwegian dimension of the study: What do you have to do to be Norwegian?" As I conversed with various family members, I learned that I was not alone in growing up with biases about the cultural and genetic heritage of a Norwegian family. For example, I was told that learning to be Norwegian-Lutheran in the 1920s and 1930s meant believing that all people were Norwegian and all Christians were Lutheran. On the other hand, one informant remembered holding the view that Norwegians were not as good as anyone else – that Norwegians wouldn't admit to being Norske, because schoolmates laughed at their dialect and shunned the body odor, that is, the barn smell, that came from milking cows before school.

Speaking, reading, and writing Norske were often identified as the major criteria for "being Norwegian." This was true when I talked with an eighty-year-old cousin in Norway and was equally true in rural Wisconsin. A potential informant said to me (in Norske), "How is it you call yourself educated and yet can't speak Norwegian?" Although I couldn't speak the language, I had learned the table prayer *Jesu navn* as a child. This, and the multitude of ways to say "thank you" (*mange takk, tusen takk, takk for sist:* "many thanks," "a thousand thanks," "thanks for the last time we were together") became a part of my everyday language. The relevancy of "thank you" was probably more obvious to me because in my fieldwork with the Papago I had had such a difficult time with their way of showing appreciation, which did not include a phrase similar to "thank you."

In my first months of general conversations and participant observation I gathered an assortment of information about such things as the Norwegian view toward holiness, the Triune God, how to raise chickens, the social order in a herd of dairy cattle, and so on. All of these ideas helped me to organize a framework of what it was like to be Norwegian and more specifically be Norwegian-American.

My rural informants were brimming with details of incubating, feeding, and watering chickens; gathering and baling hay; games they played when they were young such as "last couple out" and "two old cats"; what to do when someone dies (ask is there anything at all you can do, fix casseroles, salads, pies and cakes); food to eat in cold weather (custards, honey, chili stews); chores they did when they were young (picking rocks off the field and putting them in a stone boat pulled by a horse, washing clothes, carrying wood, bringing in water from the well); worshiping (evening devotion, listening to Norwegian sermons); foods that were Norwegian (*søtsuppe, rommegrød, fløtegrød, lefse, rullepulsa*); things to do for children (bedtime rituals, sick time rituals, rituals to keep from getting sick); what to do for dying people (talk Norwegian, read old gospel hymns, promise to stay); how Norwegian women behave when something is wrong (don't reveal about themselves and endure); and things neighbors do for neighbors.

Understanding the Norwegian-Lutheran view of what was holy became an intriguing task. In the early 1900s, I learned, a woman was known to have said that Jesus was wrong on one occasion, that He should not have changed the water into wine. The relationship between doing something unholy and against God and drinking wine or any liquor was strong in some families. Furthermore, God was linked with the weather. Indeed, the weather was of God's making and to say bad things about the weather was just the same as complaining about God – a violation of the first commandment.

I learned that in the early 1900s the belief was held that the Bible was written in Norske. To these descendants of immigrants, the Norwegian language carried a sense of holiness. In the 1920s, a father, for example, requested that the minister repeat the vows in Norwegian at his daughter's confirmation into the Lutheran Church "just to be sure."

Three months after I began the research, I was ready to list potential domains related to the questions "What kinds of things do people do for others?" and "What kinds of things do you do when you are Norwegian-American?" Examples of some of these data are presented in Figures 10.1 and 10.2.

As the focus of the research became clearer to me, several questions emerged that demanded attention before I could progress to the development of taxonomies. Initially, I had to choose between "taking care of self" and "taking care of others." Directing attention to others appeared to increase my chances of obtaining what might have been sensitive data. In addition, the idea of sharing information (a criterion basic to the culture concept) and be caring for (a criterion basic to nursing) was implied by the domain "things people do to take care of others." Who the others were frequently occupied my mind during these early months. As I viewed the cultural scenes of the Norwegian-American women I was talking to, I could see others in children, husbands, relatives, friends, chickens, God, cows, gardens, the church, and so on. During the first months of the fieldwork, my eighty-four-year-old aunt had repeated on almost every visit I had made to her, "I miss my neighbors. I don't know my neighbors anymore." The idea had been all around me but I was unable to conceptualize it. Other informants were reporting on various chores they exchanged with their neighbors – for example, checking on persons who lived alone, taking in the mail, bringing food, and so on. Some neighbors were known to one another, but in recent years some continued to be strangers after living side by side over a period of ten years. The changing patterns of neighboring highlighted its importance as one culturally relevant domain in the culture of Norwegian-American women.

Information on differing time periods presented a second problem to me. As I pursued relationships between elements such as God and the weather (from the 1930s) and women, pollution, God, and childbearing (from the 1860s) and variations in rules for visiting neighbors with the advent of the automobile, telephone, radio and television, I felt inundated with seemingly disparate pieces of information that I knew intuitively were somehow related. I continued following the data, discovering what made sense, and inventing a way of looking at the culture of Norwegian-American women. Kinds of things, kinds of reasons, kinds of privacy, kinds of ways to "be there" represented different dimensions in the explicit and tacit culture that informed and informs the behavior of Norwegian-American women.

Developing the domain: things neighbors do for neighbors

Settling on this domain was advantageous for several reasons. First, neighboring (etymon: "near farmer") emerged as a culturally relevant phenomenon in this Norwegian com-

Read, write, and speak Norske	
Fix "Norwegian" foods	Boil potatoes Make *flatbrød* Make *tykmelk* Cook *flødegrød*
Take care of other Norwegians	
Take care of yourself	Have a stockpile of food in the house Buy things when you have money Be responsible for your own actions Cut wood one year in advance
Worship God	Pray Have family devotions Go to church Give money to church Participate in the sacraments
Be ashamed of a Norwegian heritage	Speak English with a Norwegian accent Smell like cows from the barn
Be proud of a Norwegian heritage	Believe Leif Ericson discovered America

Figure 10.1. A taxonomy of things to do when being Norwegian-American.

Sit with someone who is sick or dying
Open up a grave
Bring *søtsuppe* to a new mother
Visit
Ask if there is anything at all you can do
Exchange field help
Give a ride to church

Figure 10.2. Preliminary domains of things Norwegian-Americans do for others.

munity for seventy-five years or more. Families who lived in close geographic proximity were dependent upon each other for survival. As the data developed from the interviews, it became apparent that the moral and value system of the Norwegian-American culture was played out in relationships with neighbors – rules for visiting, sending someone to help, telling neighbors how to do things, giving neighbors things, praying for neighbors, helping with barn raisings and chimney fires. The value system made explicit the simultaneous value of privacy and the importance of being present, as well as simultaneous respect for people in trouble and the value placed on endurance and taking care of oneself. Neighbors gathered together to respond to reported wife beatings. A group of men, so it was told to me, met with a husband and threatened him with tar and feathering if he repeated his acts of violence toward his wife. In another example, an eight-year-old girl was directed by her mother to give the best she had, her first and only store-bought dress, to a neighbor girl whose family was burned out by a house fire.

A second advantage of neighboring as a domain was its heuristic nature for the unknown dimensions in the concept of care. The social distance of neighbor to neighbor could be viewed, I thought, as isomorphic to that of nurse to patient. The set of obligations and rights and the kind of emotional involvement that emerged in neighbor-to-neighbor interaction appeared to be different in kind from obligations, rights, and long-term emotional involvements in family relationships. Such a conceptualization of care might, as I viewed the possibilities, provide direction for a different set of principles for patient–nurse interaction.

Finally, there was a third advantage that facilitated the process of data collection. Neighboring provided cultural scenes somewhat distant from personal thoughts and feelings, which might prove sensitive and confidential and difficult for informants to express. Furthermore, the rules for neighboring involved a wider social network. The shared meanings of multiple families were needed. Rather than focusing on one family, with all of the attendant methodological problems, neighboring allowed me the privilege of eliciting information from a wider assortment of community members who might or might not belong to the same family group.

Three kinds of relationships have been identified in the domain of neighboring (Figures 10.2 and 10.3; Table 10.1): First, X is a kind of Y; that is, "kinds of things neighbors do for neighbors." Second, an analysis of definitions of contrast: "things women neighbors do for women neighbors when there is trouble." Finally, stages in "visiting a neighbor." Each of these analyses highlight a different segment of details in the cultural pattern of neighboring.

One of the most pervasive features of things women neighbors were found to do for women neighbors was to be present. Being alone characterized many of the kinds of reasons for neighboring. To have another human being to talk with, to have someone arrive during a time of crisis, to feel something living and hear the sound of breathing nearby was important. During the time of being there, what occurred, such as what kinds of things were talked about, what kind of food was served, what chores were done, and where people sat were all important to the cultural scene. To be around, to be present, to be available, however, fulfilled a culturally defined need in this rural community.

Ask if there is anything at all they can do		
Go to them	Visit	Stop in Spend a day Go for coffee
	Help when there is trouble Sit with them	
Send someone to help	Do chores Clean the house Care for children	
Watch out for them	Look for a light Stop by to check	
Give rides		
Pray for them		
Make them feel welcome	Set a table Serve coffee Pump water from the well	

Figure 10.3. A taxonomy of things neighbors do for neighbors.

Although being there emerged in the definitions of contrast in Table 10.1 "when there was trouble," it was repeatedly reinforced in activities of participant observation. I probably could not have learned to appreciate the irresistible nature of neighboring without listening to my aunt, who said, "but I miss my neighbors so." Furthermore, to be alone was not viewed as a desirable state. Bachelors, spinsters, and others who preferred a somewhat solitary life were recognized as belonging to the community but were considered marginal Norwegians.

To like being alone did not appear to be a well-understood conceptualization. Today in Norway, the solitude found in a mountain hut is viewed as a way of rebuilding courage and peace in one's soul (Kinn 1978). In other Scandinavian countries most families have a sauna, but in Norway they do not. Instead, families choose to have a little place in the mountains for weekend or vacation retreats. What solitude or being alone means, how these domains contrast, and what the links are between the perceptions of Norwegians in Norway and Norwegian-Americans in Wisconsin might tell us something about variations in interpreting experience and generating behavior related to care.

Other themes of tacit (out-of-awareness) culture emerged in the analysis of contrasting dimensions in the taxonomy "things women neighbors do for women neighbors when there is trouble." These were "serving the Lord," "privacy" and "sickness and death." Whereas religious beliefs of Norwegian-American women permeated their day-by-day activities, including *husandakt* (house devotions), mealtime prayers, and Sunday church, activities related to religious beliefs were not incorporated into neighboring activities except when associated with praying. (Praying for neighbors was a private activity done in

Table 10.1. *Componential definitions of contrast in things women neighbors do for women neighbors when there is trouble*

	Being there	Serving the Lord	A private thing	When sick	When dead or dying	Because they are alone
Sitting with them	Yes	No	No	Yes	Yes	Yes
Ask if there is anything I can do	Yes	Maybe	No	Maybe	Yes	Maybe
Talk to them	Yes	No	Maybe	Maybe	Maybe	Maybe
Pray for them	No	Yes	Yes	Maybe	Maybe	Maybe
Take food to them	No	No	No	Yes	Yes	Maybe
Care for children	No	No	No	Yes	Yes	Maybe
Send someone to help	No	No	No	Yes	Yes	Maybe
Clean their house	Yes	No	No	Maybe	Maybe	No
Wash dead bodies	Yes	Maybe	Yes	Maybe	Yes	No
Watch for a light	No	No	Maybe	Yes	Yes	Yes
Feed chickens	Yes	No	No	Maybe	Yes	No
Help put out fires	Yes	No	No	Maybe	Maybe	Maybe
Staying with them	Yes	No	No	Yes	Yes	Yes
Take care of orphaned children	Yes	No	No	Maybe	Maybe	Yes
Pay respects to family members	Yes	Yes	Maybe	Maybe	Maybe	Maybe
Take things out of a house when there is a fire	Yes	No	No	Maybe	Maybe	Maybe

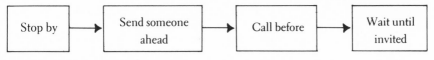

Figure 10.4. Stages in visiting a neighbor.

the presence of neighbors, but silently, especially at times of sickness or death.) These kinds of contrasts sort out sets of things neighbors did for neighbors and provide a pattern for neighboring activities.

Stages of visiting a neighbor (Figure 10.4) illustrate changing patterns of ways non-friends and nonrelatives have gotten together since the 1920s. Before there was mechanized transportation and easy communication, the rules for visiting neighbors were limited by the time it took to move from one place to another. When neighbors had reason or time, they might stop by without warning to talk about the weather, crops, cattle, family activities, and so on. Sunday church was a time for similar exchanges of information. The tacit or unspoken rule prescribed a visiting pattern that did not require advance warning. The advent of cars and telephones decreased the time and distance between neighbors, and the pattern changed. Whereas in the past neighbors sent word of a possible visit with family members, tradesmen, or clergy, in recent years they have called on the telephone before coming. Thus, visiting neighbors became more formalized, until today visiting selected neighbors (who may be family and friends as well) continues to be casual and unexpected.

Summary

This has been a sketchy analysis of a complicated human experience – doing anthropology at home in order to learn about doing things for others who are neither friends nor relatives but are neighbors. Neighboring is conceptualized in this Norwegian-American community as a kind of activity wherein people living in the same geographical locale help each other out in a variety of ordinary everyday activities.

Conducting ethnographic research in a community that represented home was facilitated by the availability of fieldwork brokers among relatives. Activities of persons who served as middlemen are well documented in the anthropological literature and are familiar to most, if not all, fieldworkers. Doing anthropology at home among members of my own extended family did not simplify the relationship of myself to informants. Aunts, uncles, and cousins served in many ways as sensitive, perceptive spokespersons, however, and promoted many opportunities for data collection.

"Taking care of others" or "doing things for others" was a culturally relevant domain in this rural community. In contrast, the domain "taking care of self" emerged as having limited relevance. Further systematic research is needed to learn more about culturally defined scenes in which women sacrifice themselves – that is, endure hardships – to provide for others.

Being present, a major theme in the neighboring process, was discovered by means of the analytical tool of contrast. Presence is a provocative concept for further work by students interested in the care dimension of a health and healing system.

PART IV Health systems

Health and medicine are the topics of another fast-growing subfield within modern anthropology. Chapters 11 and 12 are examples of contemporary research into alternative health and healing systems in North America.

Craig Molgaard and Elizabeth Byerly have studied a New Age health commune in central Washington as medical anthropologists in the modern context (Chapter 11). The topic of their inquiry is health care in a low-income, highly mobile, rural subculture. Their method is ethnoscience. Their overall approach encourages linkage between theory and application. They present us not only with a neat example of one direction in which anthropology is going but also with the basis of a potentially important statement about social policy and health-care planning. By concentrating on native theories of health, illness, and healing, they are able to determine and integrate culturally specific causes and effects that are mediated by unique traditions, values, and roles into the larger therapeutic process of coping with disease.

Linda Light and Nancy Kleiber demonstrate yet another approach to medical anthropology in their study of a women's health collective in Vancouver, British Columbia (Chapter 12). Openness and close cooperation between researcher and researched is their goal. As social scientists, they demonstrate a laudatory commitment to engage in fully reciprocal research interaction from planning and data gathering to final report. Their initial problem of dealing with the inherent power imbalance that typically exists between researcher and subjects led them to share control and access to that power and was more than offset by the remarkable results they obtained. There is tremendous potential in their approach for a true insider perspective on sociocultural reality.

11 Applied ethnoscience in rural America: New Age health and healing

CRAIG MOLGAARD and ELIZABETH BYERLY

The New Age communities

During the 1960s and 1970s, rural America became the residence of numerous groups of young (and some not-so-young) adults who sought refuge from the stresses of urban living in a return to the relative quiet of farm life, where rural lifestyles were often patterned after those popularized by the Foxfire books (Wigginton 1972) and the Whole Earth publications. New styles of living, in communes, extended families, single nuclear families, or liaisons, were based on living off the land and finding temporary and seasonal work. Most frequently Caucasian, or Anglo, in ethnicity, members of these groups were usually viewed by their fellow citizens as drop-outs from society, hippies, or flower children.

Partridge (1973) described the hippie culture as deriving core values from the cultural heritage of Western civilization and Judeo-Christian mythology. Definition of hippie groups is impossible, however, as Partridge noted, because they consist of a conglomeration of Christian mysticism, Vedic teachings, revolutionary tracts, Madison Avenue pop psychology, pseudo-American-Indian religions, hedonism, and some traditional American values such as individualism, independence, and frontier courage. Although each group selects from these different choices the one to which its energies will be directed, a predominant theme in recent years has been that of health and healing (Molgaard 1979, 1982; Molgaard, Byerly, and Snow 1979; Byerly, Molgaard, and Golbeck 1979a, 1979b; Byerly, Molgaard, and Snow 1979; Byerly and Molgaard 1982).

Health problems of counterculture groups living in rural areas are similar to health problems of other low-income rural residents. Housing and sanitary facilities are often inadequate. Dietary habits tend toward use of natural foods, including native plants and herbs, low protein intake, and foods with low nutritive value. Medicinal herbs are used as substitutes for synthetic prescribed or over-the-counter pharmaceuticals. Family transportation may be nonexistent, so that hitchhiking to centers for health care is not uncommon.

153

Many such families assist in harvesting soft fruits and apples in Washington state. Many are eligible for and make use of the services of migrant health programs in regions where they live and are employed. This chapter focuses on the use of ethnoscience methods in the study of health and healing among New Age counterculture seasonal agricultural workers in north central Washington.[1]

The problem

Delivery of health care in America in the 1970s has become a complex policy issue. Although some segments of the population receive high levels of specialized diagnosis and treatment, levels of health care for other segments are not only inadequate but are far below minimum standards in many underdeveloped nations (Horn 1975). These inequities have been attributed to an inadequate supply or maldistribution of professional expertise, variation in availability and accessibility of health facilities, extreme inflation in the cost of health services, and inadequate health education of the poor minorities. Explanation of the causes of these inequities is still largely problematic.

Migrant farmworkers experience many of the same problems as other minority and low-income groups: shortages of health personnel, inadequate emergency and primary-care facilities, and long distances to travel for medical care. Strenuous physical labor, long hours of work, and high rates of work-related injury further characterize farm employment. A high rate of mobility accentuates many of these factors. Seasonal agricultural workers experience unique problems in obtaining and maintaining continuity in health care. That section of the seasonal work force that is transient for at least part of the year is often highly mobile during the greater part of the growing season. The extent of mobility depends on the types of crops harvested (fruits or vegetables, field or orchard, stoop or ladder work, manual or partially mechanized labor), regional location of the work, timing of jobs available, weather conditions, and a variety of additional social and political factors. Family or individual preferences for the type and location of the work also influence mobility. When family members become ill, they may receive emergency or temporary care in one locale and then move, if able, to the next place of work. Communication of diagnostic or therapeutic information has been generally inadequate or poor between health personnel and facilities in one location and those where patients seek followup care. Health education under these circumstances is sporadic and difficult at best.

It is generally accepted that health care to low-income, highly mobile, predominantly rural subcultural populations has been a major problem. It is a problem that has been assigned high priority through federal health legislation and has resulted in the establishment of a number of action type migrant health-care programs throughout the country. Families to whom these services are offered have used them on a variable basis. Health planners and health professionals need to understand how minority and subcultural groups handle matters of health and illness in order to avoid gaps in health care due to misunderstandings or lack of client trust in the practitioner, the diagnosis, or prescribed treatments.

The setting

The setting for the research was a four-county area in north central Washington state. The eastern half of this region is separated from the western half by the Okanogan and Columbia rivers. West of the rivers lies the Cascade Range, and much of the land there falls within the boundaries of the national forests.

East of the rivers, the climate is drier and the terrain more barren. The southeast section is an area of field crops (potatoes, onions, sugar beets, carrots, beans, corn) that are processed at local packing plants. Most of the workers in the southeastern half of the region are Mexican-Americans from Texas, many of whom are now permanent residents of Washington.

The focal point of the region is the rivers. They are the dominant force in the region's economy, which falls or rises with the ebb and flow of the Columbia. Along the banks of the river and its tributaries, the earth is planted in fruit trees as far up the hillsides as it is practical to irrigate.

Most orchards are planted in apples, cherries, peaches, apricots, and pears, but the apple theme pervades the local scene. The region's largest city, Wenatchee, claims to be the apple capital of the world, and schoolgirls march in the Apple-ettes pep squad or strive to become Appleblossom Festival queen. "Apple Valley" is locally synonymous with the Wenatchee Valley.

Most of the Spanish-speaking workers in the western half of the field are from Mexico, and although some of them now make their permanent home in Washington, the majority do not. Native American and counterculture agricultural workers are mainly found in the northern part of the region. The former are usually local Indian residents or come from Canada to work the orchards along the upper Okanogan River. Counterculture workers are most heavily concentrated in a number of communes or houses near the Canadian border.

Entrée and rapport

Access to New Age or counterculture groups has traditionally been difficult for a variety of reasons. The youth movement of the 1960s was characterized by an antiintellectualism (Needleman 1970) as well as a self-righteous stance toward the Establishment that included liberal doses of hostility (Yablonsky 1968). Heavy use of drugs and concommitant paranoia toward anyone connected with "the Man" in any way exacerbated a reluctance to talk with social scientists, whose research was often directly or indirectly federally funded.

These factors generated some anxiety concerning our ability to contact and work with New Age groups. In order to establish initial contacts, which proved much less difficult than we had expected, we utilized existing bureaucratic structures in the field area. Specifically, the plethora of county, state, and federal social service agencies that operate in north central Washington were utilized in a discriminating fashion. While the top echelons of social service agencies were often too busy or indifferent to assist anthropologists with their research, many of these agencies employed full-or part-time outreach workers who, in our case at least, were of immense help in making initial contact with a New Age group. Much of our early time in the field was devoted to explaining our research methods and goals to such workers, some of whom found it either exciting or worthwhile to donate some time to aiding a research team. Eventually, local social service agency outreach workers placed us in contact with two members of a New Age community, who in turn introduced us to the rest of the community. This resulted in ten months of study of a New Age Healing Circle, or family, representing over 140 hours of taped interview time. Twenty-three individuals were interviewed with both ethnoscience and open-ended techniques, and the interview data were supplemented with participant observation.

We identified ourselves to our informants as exactly what we were: anthropologists interested in health beliefs and health-seeking behaviors. We explained that we were not focusing exclusively on the counterculture but were also interested in Mexican-American and native American health beliefs and practices.

An advantage of doing research with the counterculture is the level of education of many of its members. Most of our informants had been to college, many had bachelors degrees, and a few others had graduate degrees or some graduate work. Unlike informants in other cultures or even other subcultures in this country, they had a good idea of what anthropologists are and what they do.

The initial two interviews were not without hostility and defensiveness on the part of the informants. It proved difficult to convince the informants that we were interested in their beliefs and not testing them in some way. On the other hand, our own interviewing skills were somewhat rusty, as it had been months since we had been in the field. It might have been impossible to do any interviews, except that we had agreed before interviewing began that we would pay our informants an hourly fee. We were convinced, and we still are, that an informant's time is worth as much as our own. We were also convinced that for ethnoscience interviewing, in which the informant's classifications are of paramount importance and the interview is often grueling and boring, the expedient of payment not only makes up for lost time and hard work but serves to reinforce the notion that the informant and his or her ideas are our main interest.

Members of the Healing Circle were individuals whose social histories placed them as members of the youth movement of the 1960s. Participation in the movement and its associated drug uses seemed to have precipitated much of the concern with healing. As one member of the group, a former alcoholic and speed freak, said:

Most of us that have been through the sixties and the seventies and have done a lot of drugs and what not, we're really spacey people, I mean we are really. People talk about going to Venus and folks living underwater and real ethereal things, tend to forget that we have a physical body to take care of . . . I see my brothers and sisters, and we're a bunch of space cases. We forget to take care of our business down here, our heads are so far in the clouds . . . It's real hard, where I come from, where most of us come from, we come from a real loose place, a real wild place. Trying to learn to slow down, to calm down trying to take care of the kids' needs, your brother's and sister's needs, is a real hard thing to do. We are just real wired up. Coming down, slowing down, trying to remember everything you need to do, is quite an experience. [fieldnotes]

Another member of the Healing Circle, in tracing his movement to a concern with health, stated:

I got interested in health back in the sixties like a lot of people, just finding out what is happening. First there was drugs and everything that kind of separated us from everybody else. Then there was the food. The food was like . . . I guess all the drugs were saying is like you are not limiting your consciousness, you can go where you want to go. All of a sudden we're just more evolved and divine beings, and doing the food made it more understandable. Yeah, what we're here for is to be natural, we're not here to be on any of your trips anymore . . . It's real good that the foods are there. Food was the final trip that just made me realize, "Wow, like how different we are . . . " Years from now they will know the whole truth behind it . . . They'll find that none of the sacramental drugs that they called drugs weren't really drugs at all, just an awareness lifter for a lot of people that needed it. A lot of children, and a lot of us were caught up in it. [fieldnotes]

Maintenance of the identity of researcher was not difficult. Once it became clear that we were ultimately concerned with improving the health care of agricultural workers and not interested in any possible drug use in the group except as medicinal therapy, the New Age community's interest in health was an aid to our research. Specifically, the medical philosophy of the Healing Circle included a superficially confusing array of Ayurvedic, Chinese, native American, chiropractic, and homeopathic beliefs. By the fact that we took time to study their beliefs, we served to validate the somewhat esoteric health and illness concepts of the group and the commitment of individual members of the group to these beliefs. Several informants mentioned, "It was good that you talked to us. It makes us feel like our commitment to healing right now is serious and not just temporary." Others said, "Talking with you has helped me to organize my own beliefs better. It's a good thing."

Throughout our research with the Healing Circle, our own identities altered and became plural as informant–researcher interrelationships changed. Originally we were just "those people with the tape recorders," but our willingness to produce rides, tape record a child while a harassed mother tried to make bread, and take meals with circle members served to establish some degree of rapport. This was enhanced by our lack of interest in hallucinogenic drug usage. Eventually we were not only researchers and friends of a sort, but students of, patients of, and resource persons for the Healing Circle.

Assumption of the role of student was necessitated by the often confusingly intertwined beliefs of the informants. As in fieldwork in other societies, the entreaty "Please teach me about that; I want to learn" was often the most effective approach. Not only does it serve to massage the ego of the informant, but it also helps to equalize any perceived status difference between researcher and informant and thus to spur informality. Willingness to endure platitudes such as "Well, we are made up of cells" was eventually balanced by explanations of why all successful acts of healing are accompanied by fairy energy beams (Molgaard 1979, 1982).

When one is researching a deviant health delivery system (Hayes-Bautista 1976), the role of patient serves to lessen the chance of informants' fearing stigmatization for esoteric beliefs and again encourages rapport. For example, the first author was evaluated and given a New Age therapy called Bach's flower remedies at his own request. Early informants who mentioned the therapy had avoided discussion of the theoretic rationale for its use. Once one of us was acutually using the therapy, the topic no longer was avoided.

The role of resource person was assumed by both researchers. This involved explaining Mexican and Latin American health and illness concepts, which the New Age group had no knowledge of but expressed interest in learning about. For the second author, who is a nurse-anthropologist, this also involved Healing Circle members using her clinical knowledge of specific illnesses to round out their own knowledge. In one case, we encouraged the Healing Circle to take a member who had a seizure to a clinic for examination, and we aided in arranging the clinical appointment at the request of others of the circle.

It is somewhat misleading to discuss multiple researcher roles as if they were the key to our limited success with this New Age group. More than anything else, what worked was the time-honored anthropological tradition of participating, observing, and, in general, being noticeable in the environment until the familiarity factor induced the most knowledgeable and articulate informants to agree to be interviewed. In our case, our three most valuable informants, after sufficiently casing us, solicited us to interview them. Their interviews served to integrate and make understandable what had been until then a confusing array of diverse therapies, preventions, and illness concepts. As usual with anthropological reseasch, whether within this society or another, the key informants materialized when we had nearly finished working with the group. We were then at a point when they believed we had a firm grasp of their medical philosophy and health-seeking behaviors, even though this was not the case.

Methods and techniques for data collection

Our main research tools were an interview schedule and participant observation. The questionnaire contained twenty-four biographical questions and forty-one questions about health and illness. Of the latter, twelve were open ended, designed to elicit narrative concerning health seeking. The remaining twenty-nine were ethnoscience question–answer frames.

Sample selection

Worker families and individuals eligible for the services of the North Central Washington Migrant Health Project formed the sample population. Actual statistics on the total number of persons in the universe, by ethnicity, were not available, as official reporting of statistics on ethnic representation according to occupation and temporary/permanent residence in the state was either incomplete or inconsistent. In 1975, an estimated 91,000 workers entered Washington during the active growing season; latest reports from the North Central Washington Migrant Health Project indicated a potential clientele of 25,000 resident and migrant workers. There may be approximately 12,000 migrants in the region during the year.

The ethnoscience method mitigates against precise statistical representativeness, in that the cultural or subcultural code in the domain of health can only be approximated through in-depth interviews, during which the informant's statements are recorded according to his or her classification scheme and then checked and rechecked. Such interviews take a considerable amount of time. Articulate subjects tend to answer questions with small, highly informative texts (Werner and Fenton 1973:573). Given the slowness of the methodology and the time constraints of the research project, sample selection was not random but involved the convenience method (Abdellah and Levine 1965), in which all willing counterculture people were interviewed. An attempt was made to reasonably approximate one sampling criterion – equal distribution of males and females. Further divisions to obtain equal distribution of persons by sex in three age groups (12–20, 21–49, 50 and over) was not possible, because all but one of our New Age informants fell within the second age group.

Participant observation

Although participant observation in one's own society precludes the role of privileged stranger, it is an ethnographic mistake bordering on insensitivity to assume (see Freilich 1970) that in doing research in one's own society one is a native. Such a notion can lead to a serious mistake on the part of any researcher: believing that research in his or her own language is somehow easy.

When doing research in a foreign language or in one's own language, the linguistic variables, whether morphological, syntactic, phonological, or intonational, that carry social information are always network specific (Blom and Gumperz 1972, Cook-Gumperz and Gumperz 1976). The ethnographer's awareness of and partial facility with network-specific referential, situational, and inferential meaning is possible only after a lengthy period of participant observation. It is a mistake to assume that because words are recognizable their meaning is transparent.

An example from our research is the use of "brother" and "sister" as terms of address. In general, members of the Healing Circle consider everyone on the planet a brother or sister but use the terms of address only for members of the circle: for example, "Brother Mike" or "Sister Sara." We assumed that the use of these address terms denoted in-group solidarity, as has been noted in black American or Puerto Rican groups. Subsequently, however, one of our key informants gave us the following information:

I am sure that we were attracted here . . . This group has been drawn together here, and we have a lot of work to do together. We have worked together before . . . We talk about how rarely your family, your *true family*, are born under the same roof, how we attract *our brothers and sisters, people we've lived with in past lives.* People we have work to do with in this life. I see it every day. [fieldnotes]

It seems from this passage that, for this New Age group, "brother" and "sister" as address terms denote not only synchronic in-group solidarity but also a spiritual diachronic solidarity based on notions of reincarnation.

In general, most of the constraints on the participant observer in other societies also operate in one's own society, such as competence in the subcultural dialect, the ability to develop rapport, and guarding confidences. What is different about research in one's own society and in another society is that it is much harder to cover up poor fieldwork in the former.

Ethnoscience

The principles of ethnoscience, and field and eliciting procedures for the methodology, have been most lucidly explained by Sturtevant (1964) and Black (1969).[2] Briefly, informants delineate the boundaries of a major classification system, or *domain*, for the ethnographer. For our research, the major domain was health or healing, which, as defined by our New Age informants, is an aspect or by-product of spiritual progress.

Within this major domain we developed questions that we hoped would be productive in eliciting responses about health or healing. These are known as *question–answer frames*. The original set was developed from an evaluation of preliminary conversations and observations of migrant workers in both health-care and informal settings. These were then used in a series of pilot interviews, at which time informants were asked if each question made sense in terms of his or her own beliefs, and, if it did not, how it could be improved. This procedure produced a second set of subculturally valid questions that were then used for all subsequent interviewing.

In general, the question-and-answer method proceeded as follows. A cultural domain X was identified. A question frame, "What kinds of X are there?" was asked, eliciting a list of Ys, which in turn revealed kinds of Ys. In this fashion *segregates*, or labeled categories, were elicited, usually from the more general to the more specific. These labels, whether morphemes, words, or phrases, are called *lexemes*.

After eliciting lists of lexemes per subdomain (for example, illnesses, causes, curers, and therapies) the informant performed a card-sorting task in each. The card sort and the question–answer frame are the two basic methods of ethnoscience. While the latter generates lists of lexemes, the former is a means of determining how informants mentally organize the segregates within a domain. Separate statements by the informant were placed on individual 3-by-5 cards. The informant was then asked to sort the cards into piles in any way he or she saw as meaningful. No limitations were placed on the potential number of piles. Each initial pile of cards was then sorted a second or third time, refining each previous category into triadic or diadic dimensions of contrast. After each sorting the informant was asked why cards in each group were placed together and if there was a label for the group.

The results of the card sort were used to delineate the types of semantic contrast relations (direct, indirect, inclusion, and contrast) within the individual taxonomies of each domain (Kay 1966). Validity of taxonomies was checked by presenting them to key informants, who were asked if the resulting trees were an accurate representation of how they viewed each subdomain (Werner and Fenton 1973).

Figure 11.1 is an example of the product such a procedure generates. The data are from a thirty-eight-year-old counterculture woman. We were able to elicit ninety-eight therapy lexemes from her, which she then grouped into thirteen major categories during the card-sorting task. It should be noted that this figure represents only one-thirteenth of her total therapy taxonomy.

At this point, depending on whether one's theoretic position is discrete-feature or nondiscrete-feature semantics, one can either engage in a componential analysis or not.[3] For discrete-feature theorists, a lexical domain is analyzed in terms of the underlying

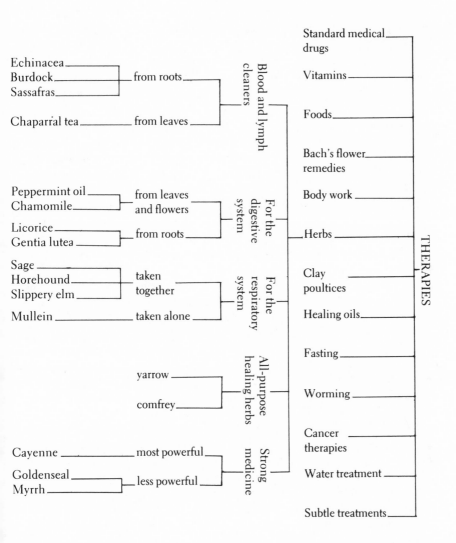

Figure 11.1. A taxonomy for the segregate "herbs," "domain," "therapies," elicited from a New Age woman.

dimensions of meaning and their component features (Kay 1966). Specifically, a category or class can be defined either by naming individual members of it or by distinguishing the criteria for membership in it. The latter is a componential analysis of the underlying covert semantic principles of organization for a domain.

For our research we assumed the stance of nondiscrete-feature or frame semantics. As a theory of cognition, frame semantics has the advantage of focusing not only on the structural interrelations of categories, that is, taxonomies, but also on the internal structure of categories per se. It also formalizes the common-sense idea that categories do not have sharp boundaries but graded ones which overlap. Our rationale for the frame semantic approach involved our understanding of folk medical systems on the one hand and the goals of our research on the other.

In terms of the latter, all traditional ethnoscience data are fundamentally decision-making data; that is, lists of lexemes that label concepts that are constructed on the basis of decisions about how to classify the biological and social environment. Frame semantics allowed us to consider the fuzzy areas of medical belief, where overlap between standard Western medical concepts and folk medical concepts can be seen to influence decision making and health seeking. Individuals can move easily from one medical system to another or else stay in one folk system throughout an illness episode, because, for example, no perceptual or cognitive overlap exists for such a subculturally defined illness as the "heebie jeebies."

Our understanding of folk medicine led us to believe that nondiscrete semantics is more appropriate for modeling the integration of cultural components into a folk medical system (Clark 1970). Specifically, because medical systems are affected by the major categories of culture (economics, religion, social relationships, education, family structure, and language), "only a partial understanding of a medical system can be gained unless other parts of culture can be studied and related to it" (Clark 1970:1). Nondiscrete semantics allowed us to place aspects of causation, illness, therapy, and curing firmly in the sociocultural scene in which they were meaningful, which discrete-feature semantics could not easily do except in terms of gross correlations (Conklin 1964).

The three fundamental analytic notions associated with nondiscrete or frame semantics are *prototypes*, *schemata*, and *frames*. Modeling in terms of these notions involves the use of narrative data concerning health seeking, lists of lexical items generated by ethnoscience question–answer frames, and informant judgments concerning degrees of set and category membership produced by question frames such as "What is the best example of X?" and "What is the next best example of X?"

A prototype is a perceptually salient point in a domain, around which a category is formed. The structure of such categories is an analog rather than clearly delineated criterial attributes; thus the internal structure of a category is composed of one exemplar and various other category members that more or less approximate the exemplar (Rosch 1973, 1975, 1976).

Complementing the notion of prototypical or graded category membership is that of prototypical or graded set inclusion (Kempton 1978). An example of the latter is that for the domain of New Age curers. When presented degree-of-membership question frames, New Age informants typically answer that the best or most effective curer is the patient

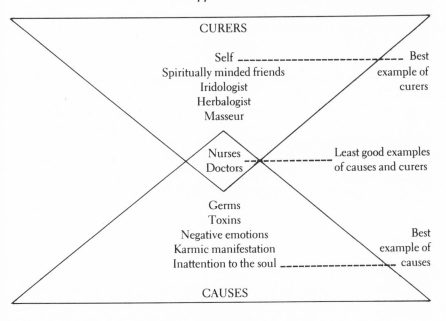

CURERS

Self ------------------------------ Best
Spiritually minded friends   example of
Iridologist   curers
Herbalogist
Masseur

Nurses ----------------- Least good examples
Doctors   of causes and curers

Germs
Toxins
Negative emotions   Best
Karmic manifestation   example of
Inattention to the soul ------------------- causes

CAUSES

Figure 11.2. Overlap in inclusion relationships between curers and causes.

himself. Only the individual actually heals; all other curers merely help to do so. In terms of semantic contrast relations, "self" is the most fully included within the superordinate set of "curers." The next best example of a curer is the patient's spiritually minded friends, because they are the most effective helpers during the healing process. Further removed are holistic healers such as iridologists, herbalists, and masseurs. Professional medical people, such as doctors and nurses, are poor members of the set of curers, because their ministrations often cause health problems, such as iatrogenic illness. Graded degrees of inclusion within the set of curers and the overlap in inclusion relations between the sets of curers and causes is shown in Figure 11.2.

The schema (Fillmore 1975, Kay 1975) is any kind of organized segment of actions or experiences that is mentally represented. Such scenes can be prototypical and also can be either dynamic (events) or nondynamic (things). Examples of nondynamic and dynamic schemata from the counterculture are "herbal kitchens" and "pendulum diagnosis", respectively. The prototypical schema of a herbal kitchen consists of the mental images and associated experiences a member of the counterculture has of a type of kitchen stocked with a large variety of individual and combined herbs and the necessary equipment for preparing poultices, teas, and so forth. Less prototypical herbal kitchens have a smaller selection of herbs, less systematic storage of them, or only commercial herbal combinations as opposed to individual herbs collected from the immediate area.

Pendulum diagnosis involves the use of a symmetrical crystal attached to a string to diagnose negative emotional states and energy blockages. As a dynamic schema, it involves the healer and patient in a series of ritualized positions and movements. The healer may either diagnose by holding the pendulum in his right hand above the patient's left hand, or by moving the pendulum along the three major currents of energy flow in the body. In both cases the direction of rotation of the pendulum, clockwise or counter-clockwise, determines whether the patient is healthy.

Frames are systematic sets of concepts and terms that impose coherence on human experience (Fillmore 1975, Kay 1975). Rules of indexing indicate the way in which lexical categories may be applied to parts of the schema. The frame for the schema "herbal kitchen" includes the lexeme "herbal kitchen" and all other lexemes associated with it. This would include the names of the herbs stored in the kitchen and rules for applying the correct name to the correct herb. The frame for the prototypical schema "herbal kitchen" would contain at least the following lexical items:

cayenne	garlic
goldenseal	blue cohosh
kelp	ginseng
chaparral	rhubarb root
burdock root	marshmallow root
sassafras	black walnut leaf
echinacea	yellow dock root
comfrey	blessed thistle
chamomile	fennel seeds
spikenard	fenugreek
chicory	wormwood
rose hips	pumpkin seeds
gentian	thyme
spearmint	basil
white oak bark	nettle
Oregon grape root	boneset
flax seeds	black cohosh
psyllium seeds	pennyroyal
yarrow	coriander seeds
mullein	raspberry seeds
licorice root	calendula
sage	Irish moss
horehound	aloe vera
slippery elm	turkey rhubarb

For the schema "pendulum diagnosis," the frame would include the lexeme "pendulum diagnosis" all other lexemes associated with it, and rules on how to use them correctly. This would include, at least, the following terms:

amethyst crystal	counterclockwise
energy blockage	pendulum
negative emotions	auric field
satvic blockage	prana
rajasic blockage	satvic current
tamasic blockage	rajasic current
clockwise	tamasic current

Doing anthropology at home

There are a number of specific similarities between fieldwork at home and abroad. Included are the location of a strategic research site, variability in researcher roles, competence in the subcultural dialect, the ability to develop rapport, the guarding of confidences, and the determination of methodological procedure by theoretical premise. For the ethnoscientist doing applied research in his or her own society, the general question of the relevance of traditional anthropological research styles in complex urban-industrial societies such as the United States refers to the basic assumptions and specific advantages of ethnoscience as an applied research tool.

Applied ethnoscience

The cognitive rationale for applied ethnoscience health research rests on three main assumptions. The first is that the environment is a cognitive construct, that is, a mental representation of biological, material, and social phenomena exhibiting distinct structural features and variable content. The second is that culture, as both an information-processing system and a set of rules for behavior, derives culturally and subculturally specific practices of decision making from such a cognitively realized environment. The third assumption is that the ethnoscientific study of native theories of health, illness, and healing practices allows a cognitive assessment of the effectiveness with which a human group combines biological and cultural resources in adapting to such a cognitively realized environment.

Whether he or she does applied or pure research at home or abroad, the ethnoscientist is committed by such assumptions to the search for cognitive classification systems, predispositions and styles at the culturally meaningful or emic level of cognitive sharing. The process of understanding any group's preferred world view and associated cognitive schemata involves a willing suspension of disbelief on the part of the researcher.

An example of this process is that of New Age illness concepts. Disease concepts have been a standard target for ethnoscience techniques since Frake's (1961) work with the Subanun. We also focused on disease concepts, and initial informants willingly coped with question–answer and card-sorting techniques. Our first key informant balked at the initial question–answer frame for disease, however, saying:

I don't know how to separate it into categories. Sickness of my left hand, sickness of my left foot. Sickness of my nose and eyes. Wherever my energy is blocked it's going to manifest in that part of the body. Or that part of the body that relates to that block. It can come out in many different ways . . . I keep thinking in the back of my mind that I want to say things that are going to help you out with the defining of the sicknesses, doing all these different things, but I just don't know how I could separate them . . . It doesn't matter if, you know, you call it stone rock disease or call it the red brick shit house disease. It's just *not* important, the important thing is energy. [fieldnotes]

Not only had we not yet reached the emic level of disease categorization and lexicalization but also, for this group, the subculturally meaningful classification system involved a rejection of the entire domain of disease. The group considered individual disease concepts and labels as irrelevant to the pursuit of health. What was important for them was the nature and flow of energy and the kinds of energy blockages that resulted in physically manifested illness. This domain orientation, in turn, was dependent on a world view in which spiritual progression was valued over physical well-being.

The primary advantage of applied ethnoscience research is in the placement of domain-specific attitudes, classifications, and decision-making practices within the sociocultural milieu of the people studied. This is accomplished by the use of open-ended interviewing and longitudinal participant observation in conjunction with ethnoscience data-generating techniques. Individual social histories, group and institutional histories, interactive patterns, role and status variability, patterns of leadership and authority, economic adaptations – all of the standard ethnographic foci contribute time depth and context to ethnoscientific data. For health policy, the advantage of frame semantic ethnoscience research over the traditional need survey is that the latter is too often solely concerned with how a human population perceives available biomedical resources or biomedically defined illnesses. The frame semantic ethnoscientist is able to determine the importance of culturally and subculturally specific illnesses and the way in which human groups utilize their perception of their societies' traditions, values, and roles as part of the larger therapeutic process in coping with biomedically defined and culturally or subculturally defined disease. This, in turn, allows a commitment to "determining what people want and aiding them to get it rather than how they can be persuaded to do what people in another culture think is best for them. The latter too often is a rationalization really concealing what is thought best for the dominant culture" (Beals 1962:182).

Some suggestions

We would like to suggest that a crucial area for ethnoscientific research in complex societies is that of the relationship between official and popular modes of cognitive classification (Sanjek 1976). For example, during a health-seeking encounter between a licensed physician and a New Age rural hippie, we have the interaction between a professional, officially sanctioned, legally reinforced health and illness classification system and an alternative (lay) system. The interaction between the bearers of two diverse health and illness cognitive organizations will probably result in the New Age person's placing constraints on the amount and type of information conveyed to the professional practitioner concerning culturally defined maladies and therapies as a means of avoiding a stigmatizing encounter. Cognitive nonsharing at this point can result in a misdiagnosis by the physician, failure to follow the prescribed treatment by the New Age person, and a failure in health care.

Whether the domain is health, education, law, or any other, the disparity between official and alternative (lay) classification systems both reflects principles of subcultural adaptation to the urban-industrial environment and determines behavioral strategies at the interface of professional and lay groups. The significance of ethnoscience research in alternative institutional structures such as a New Age Healing Circle is in the accurate description of the slippage of shared symbolic assumptions at such an interface (Wertz 1973). Only then can social policy makers and planners judge the efficiency, desirability, and humanity of the delivery systems that professional groups utilize in providing services to lay groups.

12 Interactive research in a feminist setting: The Vancouver Women's Health Collective

LINDA LIGHT and NANCY KLEIBER

The issues and the context

Issues of power and control are integral to every research situation. In the context of most traditional social science research, the greatest share of power rests with the researcher. The researcher sets the research goals, makes the research decisions, carries out the research techniques, and considers herself or himself to be the owner of the data collected. A good deal of the researcher's power depends on control of information, in the form of both professional expertise and the data generated by the research. Much of the researcher's power, therefore, depends on a lack of openness with those who are being studied.

The thesis of this paper is that such a restricted, asymmetrical relationship between researcher and researched is neither desirable nor inevitable. Openness and close co-operation between researcher and researched will result not only in more moral research but in research that more clearly reflects the reality it seeks to study.

The research experience discussed here was part of a project, which took place between February 1974 and November 1977, to describe and evaluate the Vancouver Women's Health Collective as an alternative structure for the organization and delivery of preventive health services to women.[1] The collective, established in Vancouver, Canada, in 1971, is an innovative feminist group composed of lay women. It is committed to the equitable distribution of information, power, and responsibility both within the group itself and outside the group between doctors and patients and between women and men. The collective has translated this commitment into an organizational structure (collectivity) and a structure for the delivery of services (lay participation and self-help).

The commitments of the group and the feminist orientation of the researchers quickly forced the issues of the distribution of information and power to the forefront of the project. These problems were not unique to our particular research situation but underlie every research undertaking, whether or not they are articulated or confronted. If anything was unique in our research context, it was the way in which we were able to work out with the group a truly cooperative way of doing research, in which information, power, and responsibility were effectively shared. The nature of the collective shaped not only its reaction to our initial research approach but the development of what we have here called our interactive method. In response to the group's concern, we expanded the egalitarian and participatory model to include a symmetrical relationship between researchers and those who were studied.

From February 1974 to July 1976, the Health Collective was funded by a demonstration grant from the Department of Health and Welfare of the Canadian government. In order to be eligible for this grant, collective members agreed to have two researchers, paid by the same grant, describe and evaluate the collective's organization and services. We, a sociologist and an anthropologist, were hired to carry out this research. Although, as stipulated by the government, we had not previously been involved with the Health Collective, we shared many of the collective's concerns and goals. We were young feminists, similar to collective members in life style and outlook. This similarity made it both difficult to maintain a traditional research relationship with the group and relatively easy to work out the problems that occurred as a result of our initial attempts to keep distance between us and the collective.

One important purpose of the interactive method is to make the research responsive to the needs of the researched group as well as to those of the researchers and the funding bodies. The goal of describing and evaluating the Health Collective's structure, for example, was in the beginning of the research seen by most collective members as quite distinct from any of their own goals. The researchers perceived that the research was viewed by some members as mere theory opposed to their real world of politics and service. To a few, the research was somewhat interesting, to some it was a nuisance, and to a small number it was an outright hindrance to the fulfillment of the group's goals. As researchers and collective members began to work together to formulate research goals and methods and to carry out data collection and report writing, however, members were able both to appreciate and to increase the usefulness of the research for themselves and their group.

There is no doubt in our minds that this interactive method was the best one and probably the only possible one in our research situation. There is some question as to the appropriateness of this model to other research situations that, for a variety of reasons, may not be conducive to close cooperation and open communication between researchers and researched. However, if we are were to consider consciously the issues discussed here every time we did field research, we would probably find many ways in which we could step down from our stance of professional objectivity that places distance between the researchers and the researched.

Collective members' contributions to this chapter

Collective members' perceptions of the research and its effects are quoted from two sources: (1) a transcript of a meeting of researchers and collective members in 1976 to discuss the research process and its effects on the group; and (2) a paper written by four collective members in 1977, in which they discuss the collective's experience of being researched. This discussion formed the collective's half of a presentation made by both researchers and group members on the interactive method. Both sets of comments were made in the latter part of the research period when some perspective on the whole experience was possible.

The Vancouver Women's Health Collective

During the research period, the Vancouver Women's Health Collective consisted of a group of twenty to twenty-five members at any given time. The staff members, including both paid and unpaid workers, were trained with the collective as health workers and counselors. They offered routine gynecological care, health education, and birth control and abortion counseling, serving a wide range of (mostly young) women in the Vancouver area. [2] There is no formal hierarchy in the group, jobs are rotated, and decisions are made by consensus. In common with other groups oriented to medical self-help, this group emphasizes the importance of shared knowledge and power and opposes a professionalism that defines information as the property of the few. The collective's focus on preventive health care, self-help, personal responsibility, and lay participation in health-care delivery contrasts with the focus of the traditional health-care system on crisis care and professionalism.

The collective provides all its services free to clients. When it operated the self-help clinic, if a client was covered by medical insurance and if the service provided was eligible the collective billed the appropriate medical insurance plan, usually one of two provincial government plans. Revenue from such billing accounted for only a very small proportion of the Health Collective's total income, however, which now comes mainly from a provincial government grant. In British Columbia, almost all residents are covered by provincial government medical insurance and receive medical care without paying for it directly. Aside from the moral issue of charging individual consumers for health-care services, the collective simply would not have been used by consumers if it had charged fees for service.

The demonstration grant

Demonstration grants like the one that funded the Health Collective are offered by Health and Welfare Canada to innovative groups providing health or social services in nontraditional ways. The purpose of these grants is to fund the groups' operations so that they may be researched, in order to discover those aspects of the nonestablished groups that can be applied in other settings. The intention of the demonstration grants is not to provide continuing funding for these groups; the federal government makes it clear from the beginning that it will not fund groups on an ongoing basis.

The research: methods, data, and findings

The purpose of the research was broad, and the government gave us a surprisingly free rein in what and how we researched. When we made what we felt was a radical shift from a traditional approach to our interactive approach, the government did not even look askance. The only major directive ever handed down to us from government officials was to stop collecting data. They felt that, after two and a half years, we had more data than we would ever be able to handle.

Our data included detailed observations of all collective activities; tape recordings of collective meetings, clinic consultations, and individual and group counseling sessions; twenty-seven intensive tape recorded interviews with collective members; over 300 personal-history questionnaires completed by collective clients and staff; over 300 medical history files from the collective's self-help clinic; forty-three tape recorded interviews with clinic clients regarding their experiences and satisfaction with the clinic; questionnaires from all fourteen available doctors who had worked at the clinic; and records of the collective's public-speaking engagements.

Some of our data were obtained by traditional methods, such as structured questionnaires and participant observation. Some data were obtained by close personal involvement with the actual processes of the collective – by becoming a patient at the clinic, a staff member in training, an assistant in counseling groups, and a friend and confidante of collective members.

None of our data could have been acquired without the fullest possible cooperation from collective members – cooperation that allowed us access, indeed welcomed us, to all of their activities. Such a welcome would never have been extended to researchers who had insisted on operating in the traditional closed manner of professional researchers. Early in the project it became clear to us that research that really sought to understand why the collective existed, how it functioned, and what made it succeed where so many other alternative groups did not would require as much perceptiveness and insight into the group and its members as we could attain. Such insight would not be possible if a great deal of emotional or intellectual distance separated us from collective members, if we were excluded from any collective activities, or if collective members did not talk as freely when we were present as they did when we were not. The decision to become more closely integrated into the collective, then, was a practical as well as an ideological one.

The findings of this research were published in the form of a book (Kleiber and Light 1978) that contains a detailed description of the activities and services of the Health Collective and an analysis of some of the problems and the usefulness of such a model in social organization and service delivery. The most important findings of the research were that collectivity, self-help, and lay participation, in spite of their imperfections, are very much better than the hierarchical, professional model for sharing information, power, and responsibility within an organization. Their usefulness in the organization and delivery of services cannot be doubted. Their implications for the research enterprise form a central focus of this chapter.

The initial relationship between Health Collective members and researchers

It is important to reemphasize that the relationship between the researchers and the researched group was largely a supportive one. Collective members made this point in their paper: "Although here we concentrate on the problems and how they were resolved, most of the interaction between the Collective and the researchers has been warm and positive" (Harriman et al. 1977:1).

We, as researchers, did not enter the group in an insensitive manner, make unreasonable demands on group members, or in any obvious way alienate those whom we sought to study. In a group so self-consciously concerned with the power-sharing implications of feminism, however, nothing short of total openness and cooperation in research was enough. The reason that what follows places such stress on the difficulties in the relationship between the researchers and the group is that the researchers took the collective's criticisms seriously.

A situation of compulsory research such as ours contains obvious problems for both the group and for the researchers. The research did not arise spontaneously out of the needs of the group but was the string attached to the money the group received for operating costs. Futhermore, as outsiders, we had to prove ourselves in the face of some suspicion from group members. Members themselves wrote:

In the words of one woman who worked at the Health Collective, "It felt like the researchers were watching a warm, cosy family that they were not a part of, and the Health Collective felt like it was being watched." Consequently, the atmosphere was occasionally tense. This initial mistrust led us to fear that the researchers would see us inaccurately and come up with negative reports. We felt particularly vulnerable since we talked about personal issues, as well as Health Collective issues, while they took notes. [Harriman et al. 1977:2]

In the beginning, our presence at meetings inhibited some members; our interviews promised to be time consuming and members feared that our questionnaires might offend their clients. Their lack of interest in the research meant that collective members were not motivated to invest much time in the research.

Members' difficulties in being observed and their feelings that their performances were being judged were discussed with researchers:

Being observed . . . offered me shades of school and tests, and one's performance as an "expert."

It's competitiveness that makes it seem like performance, but if the research is being done for good reasons and everybody feels comfortable with what's going on, then we can all learn from it. It ceases to be a test when everybody is there to help everybody else, instead of to get one up on anybody.

I think the performance aspect was changed by the fact that we read [the researchers' papers as they were being written] and we were involved in the research, too. If you just did the research and observed me, I would feel a little on the spot, but if you talk to me about it, then it's different.

In the beginning, everybody was really defensive about the stuff you were saying. As time went on, everybody came to trust you more, and it felt like you were really becoming incorporated into the collective. Then people would sit back and listen to you, and your perceptions [of the group] were probably a lot more accurate then too. [fieldnotes]

Another point of tension centered around members' fear that by revealing information to us about the workings of their organization they might be endangering their cause of feminism and political change. Members became more relaxed as they came to trust us and our politics. For our part, we learned to respect these fears and to become more sensitive to some of the dangers of collecting information about a group opposed to the mainstream of society.

Everett Hughes writes of this difficulty:

I think it is clear by now that most of us believe that on principle anyone can study anyone else and that anyone has a right to protect himself against the effects which come from giving up information. We then must understand what set of threats we can create when we go into any organization; what risks will come to the people whom we study from the fact of our having studied them . . . There are many situations where the mere presence of an observer causes danger to people being observed. It can also cause danger to ask certain questions. If one asks a question, he implies that there may be more than one answer to it. And if it is a question to which, in that circle, there is only one accepted answer the questioner puts his listeners into jeopardy, or may do so. [Hughes 1974:331–332]

The fact that collective members were asked to alter minor record-keeping practices and to incorporate questionnaires into some of their activities and services also caused some slight tension in the group.

Another problem was that the researchers received higher salaries than did collective members. Members wrote, "We also felt hurt because the researchers kept their full salaries, while we struggled to divide up our money amongst members, in order to provide the most possible salaries" (Harriman et al. 1977:2). This issue was never satisfactorily resolved but faded in significance as the research progressed.

The most critical problem in our initial relationship with collective members was rooted in the clash between professionalism on the one hand and lay participation, feminism, and collectivity on the other. In their paper, collective members summarized these difficulties:

Nancy and Linda . . . had professional backgrounds while we were lay people (with and without professional backgrounds) striving to demystify professionalism . . . While the researchers and the Health Collective were all feminists, Nancy and Linda had not seen sharing information as part of feminism in the same way that we had . . . Withholding of information was not suitable to our collective philosophy. It would be inconsistent to work for the demystification of the medical system without opposing mystification in the research process as well. [Harriman et al. 1977:2]

We began our research task in accordance with the basic traditions of social science research: We wanted to ensure that our results would be objective and uncontaminated by too much interaction between us and our subjects. Collective members not only found our relatively close-mouthed approach difficult to understand but also mistrusted our motives for withholding information from them. Collective members were ambivalent about the ethics and usefulness of our stance, and we were made increasingly uneasy by their challenge.

One incident may serve to illustrate this unease. Very early in the research, during a Health Collective meeting attended by one of the researchers, a collective member with whom the researcher had become friendly leaned over curiously to read the researcher's notes. The researcher hastily and with some embarrassment shielded her notes from view. What followed was a half-joking, half-serious debate about whether or not the collective member could read the researcher's notes. The collective member found it difficult to believe that the researcher, with whom she had up until then enjoyed an open and trusting relationship, would prevent her from reading notes she was taking on a meeting in which they were both participating. And the researcher was hard pressed to explain why she didn't want her to see the notes. The researcher felt extremely awkward in the abrupt shift from her role of friend to her role of professional researcher. She felt instinctively protective of her data and of her professional privacy, defensive of her professional role, and yet unable to justify logically her reaction to the situation. To her protest, that if collective members could read all that the researchers wrote about them and saw happening in the group they would be influenced by the research and the group processes would change, the collective member replied, "So what? We're bound to change with your presence anyway, and why shouldn't we? Why shouldn't we learn from what you have to say about what you see here?"

This encounter left the researcher deeply concerned about the position she had taken. It marked the beginning of the process that reached a crisis in the events described below and resulted in the development of an interactive method of research.

The turning point

Early in the research, we conducted in-depth interviews with each of the twenty-seven Health Collective staff members. These interviews were tape recorded and fully transcribed. Their purpose was to provide the researchers with data on the kind of people who made up the collective, why they joined it, the processes of their involvement, and their feelings about the collective. To encourage each member to be as open as possible with us, we assured each respondent of the confidentiality of her interview. It never occurred to us to do otherwise.

After the interviews had been completed and transcribed, we found ourselves in possession of a large amount of intriguing data. For example, we learned a great deal about collective members' ideas concerning their collective structure, decision-making processes, and patterns of leadership and about their political and feminist goals for themselves and for the organization. We were excited by the prospects of sorting through this wealth of information and eventually presenting the Health Collective with a useful report. Our enthusiasm extended beyond just a research report. We also wanted to use the interviews as a basis for a book about the Health Collective, and we tentatively outlined these plans at a collective meeting. The Health Collective's excitement did not match our own. Members had found their interviews interesting and thought provoking and wanted to share these experiences within the group, immediately, in their original form. They did not want to wait until the material had been distilled and adulterated by us. They felt that any book about the collective that utilized such personal data should be written by them, not us. They resented our usurping of their right to share with each other and challenged us on the ownership of information contained in the interviews.

It became dramatically clear to us that our professional stance as outsiders was a shield behind which we could no longer comfortably hide. Quite aside from the ethical questions, it was evident that our concern with confidentiality was neither relevant nor useful but tended instead to alienate us from the collective and prevent our access to data. If we were not going to be open with collective members, why should we expect them to be open with us?

By means of this incident, an issue that had lurked in the backs of the researchers' minds as a moral dilemma was forced into the arena of everyday working relationships. It was a practical problem that demanded direct and immediate attention. Professionalism and confidentiality clearly became negative concepts that supported an unequal distribution of information and power between the researchers and collective members.

At collective members' request and subject to permission from each individual respondent, it was decided that all interview transcripts would be made available, in their entirety, to the collective as a whole. The fact that all collective members readily agreed to make their interviews public pointed out to the researchers how unneccessary was our assurance of confidentiality.

What ensued was a learning experience for both researchers and collective members. Members found reading one another's interviews exhilarating and enlightening. One woman commented:

One of the first ways I felt the researchers' influence was in reading the interviews. I was new [at the collective], I wasn't around at the beginning of the collective, and just having in front of me everyone's background, and how they got involved, politicized me a lot. It gave me what wasn't being spoken, like why we were here, why people were doing what they were doing . . . It took me out of being a newcomer to the Health Collective. It had a really strong influence on me. [fieldnotes]

These interviews were kept in easily accessible files at the health collective's offices, and they became valuable historical documents for the collective. They were used as material to educate new members and served as a catalyst for self-reflection for individual collective members, providing members with a basis for tracing the processes of their own development.

Another member said, "I found my own interview an interesting piece of the archive. I was quite new when I was interviewed, and reading the transcript a few months ago was really interesting to me, to see the changes that I've gone through" (fieldnotes). This material also formed one of the bases for the researchers' analysis of the collective and for further discussions between researchers and Health Collective members.

The issues

Although the open and interactive methodology continued to evolve throughout the research period, its basic principles were established in direct response to the above interaction. The ongoing results of this incident can be distilled into several different but intricately related issues.

Power

Both the internal structure and the external goals of the collective are directed toward the sharing of information, which is in turn directed toward the sharing of power. By hoarding information and thus power, the researchers violated the most basic tenet of the organzation we sought to enter and to understand. Our work there forced us to make our professional practices consistent with our personal beliefs.

Once the issues of information and power sharing had been confronted, we all became more free to talk about our fears and resentments and our needs and hopes in this regard. We all became more aware of our sources of power in the group and felt able to deal with them fairly and openly. Our power as researchers became a positive rather than a negative force within the collective. One group member told us, "Your analyses are very powerful . . . You came from a powerful position in meetings because we were aware of what you were doing, and therefore we really listened to you . . . you had that personal respect and power" (fieldnotes).

Ownership of information

The question of ownership of information also emerged from these events. Did the data belong to the researchers, because they had collected them, or did they belong to collective members, because they had generated them? Given a commitment to openness and shared information, was the issue of ownership a relevant one? The answer, of course, in this context, was that no one owned the data, and everyone owned them.

In both incidents described in the preceding sections, it was clear that we, as researchers, had felt that we had a right to keep private the information we collected from our experiences at the collective and to distribute it how, when, and to whom we chose. Collective members, accustomed to openness and immediate feedback and self-conscious about their practice of sharing knowledge, took it for granted that they had every right to the information we collected as we collected it.

Once we were faced with and had accepted the moral and the logical arguments in favor of openness in our research, we had to deal with the other source of our desire to claim ownership of our data. We had to recognize that we felt threatened by Health Collective members having inside knowledge of us and our work. We had to overcome these fears, just as members had to overcome their feelings of being threatened by our inside knowledge of them. Openness on both sides helped resolve these questions of ownership and personal vulnerability.

Research objectivity

A concern with objectivity was the primary justification for the researchers' initial attempts to distance ourselves from the collective and to exclude members from the formulation and execution of the research. The choice for us became whether to maintain objectivity and professional territory and ignore the interests of the group, albeit as delicately and as covertly as possible, or to be open and truly cooperative with those we studied. We chose the latter; we feel that the loss in professional distance and objectivity was matched by a gain in perception and in sensitivity to the realities of the situation we were studying. Trust was placed in the integrity of both researchers and group members and in their ability to be honest and clear headed in spite of their involvement with the project.

By initially denying the intimate relationship between researcher and researched, we prevented ourselves from learning from the perceptions of collective members. We set ourselves up as experts and denied that collective members had crucial contributions to make in the observation and analysis of their own organization. Their perceptions as insiders were different from ours as outsiders, but they were no less valid. This sharing of information shifted the research process from an external evaluation to an internal and external evaluation.

The researchers, as outsiders viewing the organization from a different perspective, had a special role to play in the evaluation of the organization. In addition to our time and our research skills, both crucial contributions to the research task, our position did offer the advantages of a certain kind of clarity that results from a relative lack of involvement.

The lack of emphasis on traditional researcher objectivity did not mean that all caution was abandoned in a laissez-faire exchange of information. Traditional research methods, such as questionnaires and in-depth interviews, provided a necessary structure for data collection. The absence of such structure might have left the research unfocused and lacking in critical perceptions. Both the collective and the researchers carefully guarded the integrity of the research and were realistic in conforming to at least some basic standards of research, however open these were to discussion.

Feedback

As stated earlier, the original fear of the researchers was that if we gave information to the collective prematurely, while the research was in progress, the collective would change as a result of this feedback and our research would no longer be reliable. It became clear, however, that by forcing the collective to wait for the final report, the researchers were holding the collective back and preventing it from developing in response to the research.

Any organization, and especially one as innovative and flexible as the Health Collective, changes as a result of the presence of researchers. We could influence the collective by maintaining our separation from group members, collecting information that we did not reveal to them, and inhibiting them by our presence. Or we could influence them by becoming active participants in the group and feeding back information to them as we collected it. The latter approach appeared to be the most productive one. Furthermore, to make the process of change an overt topic of discussion served to demystify it and make its results amenable to observation, analysis, and documentation.

The constant process of feedback and change presented problems of keeping the research findings up to date. These problems were not insurmountable, however, and would have occurred to a considerable extent in any case, given the innovative nature of the collective. They were dealt with as difficulties that arose from an interactive approach to research, and they were not seen as sufficient cause to abandon that approach. As one way of dealing with this problem, we included in our research design the observations of collective members' responses to our findings.

Process versus product

The collective communicated to us by its own example the importance of process, or the means whereby an end is attained. The amount of physical, emotional, and intellectual energy members spend on working out the best way to do things, their desire to demystify processes, their constant concern with members' feelings and satisfaction, and their insistence on maximizing the human content of every situation all influenced our decision to alter the processes of our research. In turn, in what became a major learning experience for us all, we articulated and reflected back to the collective this concern with process. Health Collective members wrote about this exchange:

It is our view that the product is not more significant than the process by which it is attained. We feel that openness of discussion, feedback, support, and equal participation are crucial to, and as important as, arriving at the end result. This feeling brought us into conflict with the researchers who, in the beginning, were more concerned with the product of the research than with the process. This conflict was resolved by developing a co-operative method of research among Collective members and researchers. In fact, the researchers helped us to consciously identify the importance we placed on this process. [Harriman et al. 1977:2]

There is no doubt that such a concern with process and demystification is time consuming and entails a sacrifice of efficiency. In common with the collective and many other alternative organizations, however, the researchers came to appreciate the value to the individual and to the group of an emphasis on process. We thus made a moral commitment to pay as much attention to the way in which we did the research as to what we produced.

Rothschild-Whitt comments on this concern:

This process of demystification . . . so well distinguishes the ethos of . . . collectivist organizations from that of bureaucratic organizations. For demystification entails, in its essence, the negation of the process of professionalization which occurs in most service organizations. The central purpose of this demystification process is to break down the usual division of labour and pretense of expertise, and to thereby allow all members of the organization to participate more equally in its control. [Rothschild-Whitt 1976:82]

Her comments are as relevant to our relationship with the collective as they are to the group's internal functioning.

Another aspect of the dichotomy of process versus product emerged in relation to our plans to show the collective only the products, or reports, of our work. For example, as a result of discussing the problem of feedback with the collective, we decided at one point to conduct the research as a series of miniprojects and to provide the Health Collective with feedback at the end of each project. None of us were satisfied by this decision, for we still did not report immediately what we observed and our tentative interpretations of it and invite discussion. To present the collective with the product of observations and analyses and not to reveal the processes whereby conclusions were reached was to continue to withhold information and mystify our techniques. We were still preventing the collective from participating in its own evaluation and retarding the group's development.

The need to shield the evolution of our methods and reports from view reflected, at least in part, a need to protect ourselves. To reveal the processes of our work was to make ourselves vulnerable. To present the research as a fait accompli was to show only our shiny exterior. As a result of increased openness, we as researchers became free to discuss our doubts and problems with the group and to ask for feedback on thoughts and on papers while in progress, thereby strengthening the research. A fear of vulnerability is not unique to the research situation, but is a condition of human relations in general. It should be dealt with as such, not elevated to the realm of professional necessity.

Onus on researchers

Inviting collective members to ask us questions and to give us suggestions about the research was not sufficient to ensure their participation in the process of the research. In order to involve collective members in the research, we had to take active steps in that direction. We had to call meetings with members to discuss the goals and the design of research tools. We asked them specifically to comment on, correct, add to, or delete from our reports. It was the responsibility of the researchers to share our knowledge, skills, and perspective. Without this conscious sharing on our part, Health Collective members would have been less able to participate effectively in the research.

The research: Who is it for?

The foregoing discussion culminates in this final and crucial issue: Who is the research for? Is it for the funding body, in this case the Canadian Department of Health and Welfare? Is it for the researchers, who depend on it for their livelihood and for their status and career enhancement? Is it for the public in general, or for specific interest groups within that public? Or is it for subjects of the research to help them understand and develop their group and its processes?

In the development of our interactive method of research, we did not alter whom we intended to benefit from the research, but we did alter the priority we assigned to each beneficiary. Our original target was primarily the funding agency; we wished to please the group that paid us. Through the process described here, we came to realize that the primary recipient of our research must be the Health Collective. It was the collective that provided the raw material and contributed most to the research, and collective members could benefit most directly both from the processes of the research and from our findings.

If people are to have power to control their lives, they must have information with which to do so. The researchers' evaluations and recommendations constituted such information. In order to build up trust between researchers and researched, research must be not only on the group but also for the group. This concept may be broadened to apply to social science as a whole. Dorothy Smith asserts that "in sociology it means I think constructing a sociology *for* women rather than *of* women." She says:

Insisting on constituting women as subjects . . . raises questions about the relation of women members of the intelligentsia and their work to the existence and experience of other women. [This leads to] exploration of what it means to be *responsible* to women in the society as *subjects*; what it means to develop forms of thought and knowledge capable of expressing their experience. [D. Smith 1975:35–36]

By sharing our skills and our approach, we may contribute to the eventual assumption of the evaluative task by the group itself. If research is to be truly for those who are researched, then they must be included from the very beginning: They should help decide whether research should be undertaken, who should do it, its goal and focus, and how it should be done. These, of course, are ideal specifications; we must work within the confines of our own practical situations to achieve this ideal as closely as possible.

In our own situations, once we had adopted an interactive approach, we consulted collective members as soon as a new idea had taken form. Although we were open to the collective's initiating research activities, in practice the original impetus always came from us; group members responded to and criticized what we put forth. The time and energy that we were able to devote to the research task and our unique perspective as researchers made this somewhat predictable. As groups learn more about research and become more articulate about their own needs and more critical of their own processes, research ideas will come from those being researched. In the meantime, early consultation between researchers and group members can help researchers avoid inappropriate decisions, improve research by including input from various perspectives, and ensure that the research is relevant to the group. One of the most useful tasks researchers can accomplish is to help a group define its own goals; only then can research be directed toward these ultimate objectives.

Research that is for the group being studied must not entail unacceptable risk for that group. Researchers who cause such danger for the group by their presence must either withdraw or change their approach to ensure that neither the research nor the researchers place the group in jeopardy.

The effects of the interactive method

The effects of the change in our methodological stance were far reaching. For researchers and the collective, the effects were both practical and psychological, immediate and long lasting.

For the researchers and the research

We were infinitely more at ease employing an interactive methodology than we would have been had we continued to separate ourselves and our findings from collective members. We challenged and were challenged, developed as people and as researchers, and learned to do research as a human enterprise. We had full access to all aspects of the collective's operation and received cooperation from all collective members. Members contributed their experience and insight to the design of questionnaires, helped administer them, tape recorded counseling and examination sessions for researchers, participated in meetings called specifically to update or comment on reports, and read and made contributions to all drafts of papers and reports. Members talked freely with the researchers and shared insights and perceptions about their own and the group's philosophies and activities.

For the collective

"The research had been going on for some time before the Health Collective realized that we could benefit from the research. We learned that we could have a trusting relationship with Linda and Nancy. Our initial apathy then developed into interest and involvement" (Harriman et al. 1977:3). Collective members gained a new image of both research and researchers and new insights into the research process: "We gained experience, information and appreciation for the time and energy the researchers have spent on us" (Harriman et al. 1977:4). They gained a perspective on themselves and their organization that was more contemplative and analytical than it had been prior to the research. "We gained by seeing ourselves from the outside point of view so that we could be more self-critical, more analytical, and make clearer decisions" (Harriman et al. 1977:3–4).

One member said:

It has been helpful to have somebody here observing in the collective. We get so caught up in getting things done, and in our daily tasks, that we don't sit back and look at the dynamics [of the group]. Having someone around who was concentrating on the dynamics and on the directions we were going helped me to look at that, too. The research has changed the collective in the sense that it's made us more self-aware of the kinds of directions we're moving. in [fieldnotes]

Ironically, although it was the questionnaires more than any other research tool that collective members resisted, it was the construction and use of the questionnaire that comprised the major technical legacy left to the collective by the researchers. Through the research "we came to understand more fully the value of tape recordings and questionnaires. We have further incorporated these methods into our structure" (Harriman et al. 1977:3). Collective members designed and administered their own questionnaires in order to obtain feedback on doctors and on their own services and information about clients' diaphragm use.

The ease of the methodological shift

The reason that the shift from a traditional closed research policy to an innovative open one was relatively easy in our situation was at least fourfold:

1. The researchers had much in common with collective members: We were all roughly the same age and social class and shared life styles and sociopolitical outlooks. Most important, perhaps, we were all feminists, committed to a radical change in the ways people relate to one another.
2. There were no great inherent power differentials between us: Both researchers and collective members possessed areas of competence and power. Once the information-sharing issue was resolved, we could relate as equals.
3. The internal policies and structure of the collective militated against hoarding information and power. Group members quickly raised the researchers' consciousness so that distribution of information and power in professional as well as other spheres became the only moral choice.
4. Neither collective members nor researchers had anything to hide. Basically, we liked and respected one another. The researchers felt positive about the organization. The analyses, criticisms, and suggestions we had to offer were meant in good faith and were received as such.

The evolving relations between the researchers and the collective

Throughout the research, power relations continued to play an important, if subtle, role in the interaction between the collective and the researchers. When the research began we had a great deal of power, because we were necessary if the collective was to receive funding. We were also powerful by virtue of our experience, our higher salaries, and the fact that we could withhold information. Understandably, there was resentment against us. As the research approach changed, this power differential was neutralized to some extent. Differentials of salaries and education remained but became less important as the relationship between researchers and collective members developed. The researchers' areas of expertise and power were balanced by those of collective members. Mutual respect developed. Researchers and collective members became increasingly known to each other as women and as friends, rather than as components of a research process.

Although we never lost our sense of moral obligation to consult the collective, we soon came to value highly the collective members' contributions in their own right. So interactive did we become that our frequent consultations with the collective became a matter of some amusement. Toward the end of the report writing, enough trust and understanding had built up among us that such detailed consultation became unnecessary.

Although our roles as researchers, as women, and as feminists did not clash again as they had in the beginning of the research, the integration of these roles, inevitably, was not perfect. The following comments made by group members to the researchers illustrate both the meshing and the separation of these roles.

I was thinking about the research the other day, and realized that I have a hard time separating the effect of being researched from the effect of the researchers themselves on the collective. . . . There's human input from you two, as people, and as members of the collective, and then there's the research. . . . You've become such a part of the collective that it's a little hard to separate all that out, which is a real statement in itself.

I still have some sense of both of you holding back, so as not to influence the direction of a decision at the collective. . . . You both will go only to a point of giving us feedback about what you see happening, and then pull back any sentence which would direct where we were going to go. [fieldnotes]

One woman said, "I prefer it when you're not being researchers!"

Over the three-year period of the research, many collective members came and went. At the end of the research period, only two members had been active in the collective as long as the researchers had. The researchers had built up an immense body of knowledge about the Health Collective. We had thus assumed positions of relative power in much the same way that experienced members of the collective did. There was a difference between our original source of power and our later source of power. Originally, our power stemmed from our privileged positions as professionals and was resented. Later, we had power in the group as people who had been there for a long time and had therefore something unique to contribute.

Such power no longer seemed problematic to us as researchers. Any difficulties we had in that regard we could deal with as people in a complex personal situation, not as researchers in a professional context. As we completed our data collection, we spent less time at the collective's office and clinic. We experienced problems of withdrawal from our involvement with the collective, our own conflicts as well as the disappointments of collective members who had become used to our presence and our contributions to collective meetings. Because we had established a pattern of honesty and openness with collective members, however, we could be open about our own conflicts, the pressures on our time, and the necessity of withdrawing.

Applicability to other research settings

We are aware that our research setting was unique. Not every researcher has an opportunity to work out ethical problems in such a satisfying way. We know that in the broader context many questions remain. What happens if there is something to hide, on the part of either researchers or researched? What if researchers and group members don't like, respect, or trust one another? What if there are large built-in power differentials, such as status, education, or wealth? What if the researchers are so different from the group they are studying that satisfactory communication is impossible? What if the goals of the research are opposed or detrimental to the goals of the pepole being studied? Should we research only those people with whom we can establish a relationship of respect and trust based on honesty and not deceit? These are questions that we did not have to face in our work with the Health Collective but that emerged as we have compared our situation to that of colleagues in other projects.

We have no answers to these questions. We can only point out what we have learned from our own experience and plead for a serious consideration of these issues at every stage of every research undertaking. The issues involved are ones of the purpose of research, ownership of information, power, respect, and trust. Where each researcher draws her or his ethical and practical lines must be an individual decision and must depend on the specific situation.

In discussing some of these problem areas – the ethics of research, reciprocity between researchers and researched, and the maintenance of social distance between researchers and those we study – Hughes comments on the immense complexities of the issues:

I seem to be getting this somewhat confused, but the whole thing is confusing, and that is as it must be. We can stop now and again, draw up an elaborate questionnaire and put it through all the proper machines and find the paths from here to there. But that will always be nothing more than a stopping place. One must take off again, get new experiences, and make new discoveries enlarging and alternating what one knows already. [Hughes 1974:332]

At the very least, we must clearly specify the issues to ourselves and be aware of the choices we are making and our reasons for these choices. Such an examination of our choices may in itself result in dramatic changes in the way we do our research. In many cases, our choices are dictated not by research necessity but by tradition, habit, or personal fears of vulnerability.

We must be prepared to take some risks, both professionally and personally. We will probably be surprised to find how feasible it is to be open with people we study. The result, we suspect, will be more human, more moral, and more perceptive field research.

Part V Education systems

There is already a large literature on the anthropology of education, but little of it deals with the research process. The next two articles describe some of the problems and the social complexity encountered in doing research in the context of a school system.

Donald A. Messerschmidt takes us into a rural Wyoming school district in a study of educational administration under strained social, contractual, and professional circumstances (Chapter 13). The chapter reveals the serious problems that are sometimes encountered at the interface of federal-local research in America. This sort of experience heightens awareness of the researcher role and the expectations of one's subjects, the strategies researchers employ, the methods that require creativity and clarity, and the serious challenges of studying power in American society.

R. Timothy Sieber's chapter describes field research in a polyethnic and multi-social-class inner-city community (Chapter 14). The focus of his contribution is on the comparison of differential pupil role socialization at three schools and an investigation of their social-class and ethnic implications. Sieber gives special attention to comparing the situational constraints on participant observation in formal organizations and in the community. He concludes with an argument for the utility of participant observation as a core methodological technique in the study of culturally complex urban settings.

13 Constraints in government research: the anthropologist in a rural school district

DONALD A. MESSERSCHMIDT

Introduction

It is difficult and not entirely flattering to describe one's professional and personal fieldwork problems.[1] Trouble between anthropologist and subjects is rarely acknowledged and even more rarely described and analyzed in the literature.[2] Nevertheless, such analysis may serve as a catharsis for the researcher who searches the field experience for answers to the perplexing question of what went wrong, and it may serve as well to remind others that the anthropological enterprise is not as precise an art or science as we may wish it to be. Certainly graceful entrée, good rapport, grand results, and pleasant afterthoughts are not always the fare of anthropologists in the field.

This chapter is about a difficult field experience in rural America. It is a case study of research in the federally funded Experimental Schools Program for small rural school districts in the mid 1970s. It is the study of a bumpy and uncomfortable relationship among three partners to local educational development and research:

1. Officials of the National Institute of Education's Experimental Schools Program office in Washington, D.C.
2. Local rural school administrators in River District, Wyoming, who participated in the Experimental Schools Program
3. Researchers at Abt Associates, Inc., who were contracted to document and evaluate the rural Experimental Schools projects, including the author-anthropologist, who was Abt's on-site researcher in River District

I studied educational change in River District for three years, from 1973 to 1976, as a long-term resident-observer. The research went quite well at first, but during the second and third years both internal and external problems began to show their negative effects on rapport and results. What went wrong reflects a combination of (1) an initially naive approach to conducting research in my own society for the first time; (2) deeply felt suspicions, fears, and resentments held locally toward the federal government; and (3) the perplexing problems of a poorly designed and ineptly admini-

185

stered federal program. My account of the River District experimental schools research experience is thus a study of methods and roles and of some limitations to contract anthropology research in a school district at home in rural America.

Experimental schools

The developments that led to the planning and implementation of the Experimental Schools (hereafter ES) project in River District began in March 1972, when the U.S. Office of Education announced a nationwide competition for small rural school districts interested in participating in a program of planned educational change. Shortly after the announcement, the ES program was transferred to the newly created National Institute of Education (NIE), which was to be responsible for its implementation and evaluation.

The ES program was established by Congress in 1971. It embodied two experiments, one in funding and one in studying projects of locally inspired and directed educational change in American schools. Program planners chose to emphasize a holistic approach to problems of educational change. They encouraged community involvement in project planning and implementation and insisted that applied social scientists be hired to study the change activities and to evaluate project results. [3]

The ES program was designed to test the overall hypothesis that comprehensive educational change is more likely to lead to significant improvement in the quality of schooling than are piecemeal, categorical, or incremental (and primarily curriculum-centered) changes. [4] The program announcement instructed competing school district leaders to consider projects that addressed local needs and that would ensure simultaneous and holistic improvements in curriculum; in staff development; in community participation; in the use of time, space, and facilities; in administration, organization, and governance; and in evaluation. Rural school administrators who were willing to commit their districts to such a program of comprehensive change over a five-year period were invited to apply. Among the attractions were local planning to attend to locally recognized needs and the promise of high levels of funding with few strings attached. With a minimum of red tape, rural school systems were to be given a chance to catch up to their urban counterparts in terms of innovative educational programming. Crucial to the experiment was the requirement that local projects be subjected to an outside research and evaluation effort to be conducted on-site by a resident nonlocal researcher. Of approximately 320 responding rural school districts, 10 were selected for funding; among them was River District in southern Wyoming.

The school district

River District encompasses half of Spring County, Wyoming. The district is very large in area, approximately 4,300 square miles, (11,100 square km) (almost the size of the state of Connecticut), but small in population, approximately 1 square mile (2.6 square km) per person. This part of Wyoming is a high regional extension of the western Great Plains. Local elevations range from 6,000 to 12,000 feet (1800 to 3600 m). The district and the county are known for cattle and sheep ranching and for an important coal and uranium mining industry.

River District was created in 1972 out of the amalgamation of five previously autonomous rural districts. The impetus for local school consolidations goes back to the 1920s, when there were thirty-five separate districts in the county. By the mid 1960s, these had been gradually consolidated into eight districts. In December 1971, by order of the state Board of Education, these districts were further consolidated into two. This last consolidation was effected only after protracted and unsuccessful consolidation negotiations at the county level.[5]

The announcement of ES early in 1972 came at a time when the unified school district was in its infancy and when local administrators, educators, trustees, and townspeople were still uncomfortable working together in one large educational unit. When the announcement was received, some local people saw it as a chance to put together some of the organizational and educational reforms necessary for the unification to succeed. Application to ES was widely discussed in school offices and throughout the district's nine towns and villages. Support was guardedly enthusiastic.

In 1972 and 1973, local administrators, teachers, and townspeople throughout the district met and struggled to make a plan for comprehensive educational change and improvement. When I arrived in 1973, the ES planning phase was almost completed, but not without serious disputes betwen the local people and federal officials over how to begin implementation in the schools and classrooms. Some unity had been achieved in the new district through the community-oriented planning process. Nonetheless, some serious questions had been raised about the nature of federal involvement.

Abt Associates

In announcing the awards in 1972, federal officials emphasized that the ES program was designed to study the process of planned comprehensive change in these select sites so that other school districts might benefit from their experiences. To accomplish this goal, Abt Associates, an applied social science research firm in Cambridge, Massachusetts, was selected to conduct the outside evaluation of the program. In order to document the local projects, a number of independent on-site researchers were contracted by Abt Associates (see Fitzsimmons 1975, Herriott 1977, Wacaster and Firestone 1978). I applied to Abt Associates as a trained educator and anthropologist with experience in community studies (abroad) and an interest in the theory of social and cultural change. I was hired in July 1973 and sent immediately to Spring Creek, River District's administrative headquarters town. There my wife and I bought a house and I settled in as a resident on-site researcher and ethnographer.

Abt's overall research proposal was entitled a "Longitudinal Study of Educational Change in Rural America." The research plan had five separate but coordinated parts, of which two were site specific and three were based on cross-site data and analyses:

Site-specific studies
1. A series of site history and context studies
2. A series of ethnographic case studies
Cross-site studies
3. A community change study

4. An organizational change study

5. A pupil change study

The on-site researchers were most concerned with the two site-specific studies (see Fitzsimmons, Wolff and Freedman 1975; Messerschmidt and Richen 1975; Messerschmidt 1979a, 1979). But each of us had a hand in gathering and evaluating data utilized in the cross-site studies as well.[6]

The on-site researcher

When I entered River District in July 1973, I was new to anthropological research at home in my own society.[7] Never before had I studied people so like me. I was quite familiar with the western frontier life style and world view, which reminded me of the Alaskan frontier on which I had been raised. I could also identify with the educators, for I had once taught school.

As a researcher, however, I was something of an anomaly in Wyoming. I was at once a corporation researcher and an anthropologist, two professional roles not well understood or appreciated in River District. These roles were, in effect, just as experimental in the context of River District as was the new ES project.

During three years of active research there, I experienced both the promise and the problems of applied research in rural America. Promise was implied in the pioneering opportunity I had to apply the perspectives and insights of anthropolopgy to a contemporary social issue, the improvement of rural education. The problems lay hidden within the same opportunity, but particularly in the nature of the contract and in the context of working within, and studying, the cultures of power at both the local school and federal bureaucracy levels. This combination created a sensitive and potentially explosive situation. Unfortunately, the problems of research came to outweigh the promises, and it is those problems that are the main concern of this chapter.[8]

Scope of study

My job in River District was to document local efforts to plan, implement, and evaluate the ES project in comprehensive educational change and to examine ethnographically and holistically the place of schooling within the rural community context. In preparing to conduct the research, I could either select a few schools and classrooms in several towns to describe and analyze as more or less representative of the entire school district or I could examine school administration and governance as the locus of decision-making power and authority for the ES project and for the newly unified district at large.[9]

For a variety of reasons, the study of schools and classrooms was not feasible in River District. Size alone dictated caution – there were twelve separate schools in this large district, situated in seven of the nine towns and villages and on one isolated ranch. Getting between the two schools farthest apart was a 120-mile (193 km) drive on roads that in bad weather could remain impassable for days. The logistics of travel created serious problems in representative sampling and in timing that only a team of several researchers could have solved, but, except for a six-month period in 1974, I worked entirely alone. Consequently, I chose the second option, a study of school-system and ES project administration.

As the focus of my research effort, the administration was attractive for several reasons. First, it was the more manageable unit. There were fewer administrators than teachers and students and fewer offices than schools and classrooms with which to contend. But it was also intrinsically more interesting as a place to observe how traditionally conservative power brokers (school administrators) dealt with the mandate for radical change implied by ES. Furthermore, the shifts of power and authority that recent school consolidation had created and the conflicts deriving from change in leadership styles and personalities (and in educational objectives) created a potential conflict situation that I felt might show me as much or more about local school-district culture and political process than could anything else available. As a result of the recent consolidation, several previously powerful superintendencies had been reduced to administrative principalships under one superintendent and an assistant headquartered in Spring Creek. Consolidation had also given a new look to the composition of the school board and its approach to mediating district educational issues.

Rather early in the research it also become clear that much of the energy in planning and implementing the ES project was being expended in the district's central offices, not in the schools and classrooms for which the program was designed. This top-heavy appearance to the project reflected the situation of recent consolidation and centralization of authority as well as the personalities of those in authority.

As I delved deeper into the data on district and project administration, other explanations for the top heaviness emerged. One was the local administrators' inability fully to understand and implement the ES concept. This problem was not entirely their own fault, for the federal design of the program was confusingly vague. A second problem was the rapid emergence of philosophical differences between the local people and the federal agency officials. These difficulties are best understood as differences in perception about the meaning of experimental schools for River District. Differences in perception were in turn a function of the cultural gap that separated the two parties (Messerschmidt 1979a, 1979b). The culture of small rural communities and school systems is in many ways incompatible with that of a large Washington-based national educational establishment. If we define culture as "the acquired knowledge that people use to interpret experience and generate social behavior" (Spradley and McCurdy 1975:5), and if we have some understanding of the world view, cognitive orientations, and social expectations of people in both situations, then clearly the nature of the western rural experience is fundamentally different from that of the urban East.

A third problem was the disabling effects of great changes in the social economy and population of River District. School systems are typically among the first institutions to be affected by rapid changes in the larger social environment. Southern Wyoming was at this time undergoing a great energy resource development boom in coal and uranium mining. The resulting flurry of economic activity and rapid population growth created confusion in local institutions. Local school administrators as well as local town and county governments were inadequately prepared for change (see Nellis 1974, Messerschmidt and Richen 1975).

Given the chaotic atmosphere created by school consolidation and rapid economic development, school administrators in 1972 saw the announcement of the ES program as a potential catalyst for district unity and as a means of change that might help cope with growth. Here was a program around which all the various manifestations of local change might coalesce and become more manageable (Messerschmidt 1979a, 1979b).

Studying up

By choosing to focus my research at the top of the school and project hierarchy, I was really choosing to study the culture of power – the potential power either to promote or stifle educational change in River District. In so doing, I was taking a cue from Laura Nader and others who advocate studying the "cultures of power" in American society. Ethnographic research in one's own society provides anthropology with many prospects for what Nader has called "studying up" (1974). She characterizes studying up as a worthy endeavor for anthropologists "to contribute to our understanding of the processes whereby power and responsibility are exercised in the United States . . . The quality of life . . . may depend upon the extent to which citizens understand those who shape attitudes and actually control institutional structures" (1974:284).

Choosing the school-district administration as the unit of study entailed observation and documentation of institutional structures and of bureaucratic activities of school-district management. The managers, in this instance, included the two superintendents, four area administrative principals and their subordinates (principals and head teachers), a small ES project staff (director, evaluator, and coordinators), the leaders of local citizen committees, and a board of nine elected trustees. My strategy was to observe and record interaction not only between and among these people but also between them as insiders and the host of outsiders with whom they had to contend. In the group of outsiders, federal project officers from NIE, and I, the man from Abt, figured more or less prominently.

Relationships between insiders and outsiders are important, given that the administration of public agencies such as school districts is typically closed to persons outside of the bureaucracy and is often carefully guarded and kept secret by the insiders. Max Weber, one of the first students of the sociology of bureaucracy, has explained that the notion of bureaucracy and of bureaucratic authority and management is based on principles of official and hierarchical jurisdictional areas, of established roles and duties ordered by fixed rules and regulations, of management by written and often secret documents ("the files"), of regular activities and responsibilities assigned to qualified and certified officials who act in routine, controlled, and predictable ways (Gerth and Mills 1946:196 ff.). Whereas the officials, as insiders, are privy to the internal operations of the bureaucracy, outsiders are not (with rare exceptions).

When I began my research in River District I was made an exception by my generous hosts in the district's central administration. Early in the research both the superintendent and the president of the school board insisted that I be given access to whatever data I needed to complete the study. "We have nothing to hide," they assured me. By the end of my first year of study, however, their openness to the research had declined markedly. I was soon closed out of some of the more important sources of data, especially in the realms of administration and decision making at the top. I shall return to the reasons for this change, but first I need to say something about my methods and my roles.

Methods of inquiry

Because the educational administration, like any bureaucracy, is only one part of a larger sociocultural system, and because the context of the River District educational bureaucracy was important to study, I also chose to engage in a holistic study of the community. Given such a large and many-stranded research effort, I occasionally found myself in the awkward position of juggling various methods and of playing many roles at one time. I often found myself reacting to decisions and actions of others that I did not fully understand or appreciate at the time and that I had very little control of.

My methods of inquiry were drawn directly from traditional anthropology; they were neither complex nor esoteric. The sociologist George Homans has noted that "people who write about methodology often forget that it is a matter of strategy not of morals. There are neither good nor bad methods but only methods that are more or less effective under particular circumstances in reaching objectives on the way to a distant goal" (1949:330). My particular strategies included variations of participant observation, unstructured interviews, some reliance on secondary sources (file documents, scholarly studies, newspaper accounts), and comparison of the data and insights from River District with other community studies and studies of educational and social change cross-culturally. The approach was entirely inductive. Working hypotheses were generated as the data were collected. The analog to this method in sociology has been referred to as "grounded theory" (Glaser and Strauss 1967, Smith and Pohland 1976).

Participant observation has long been a standard tool in anthropology. It is a qualitative orientation and assumes that there is value in analyzing human behavior by active participation in the life of the observed and by subsequent introspection. It is the method of *verstehen* or understanding, which Max Weber espoused (Weber 1949, Truzzi 1974).

Ray Rist pinpoints the underlying assumptions of participant observation in these terms:

Emphasis is placed upon the ability of the researcher to "take the role of the other"; to grasp the basic underlying assumptions of behavior through understanding the "definition of the situation" from the view of the participants; and upon the need to understand the perceptions and values given to symbols as they are manipulated by man. Qualitative research is predicated upon the assumption that this method of "inner understanding" enables a comprehension of human behavior in greater depth than is possible from the study of surface behavior, the focus of quantitative methodologies. [Rist 1976:10]

Depending upon the situation, I participated and observed in various ways. Sometimes I played the role of a purely unobtrusive observer, sitting around, loitering and lurking in school offices, for example, much as anthropologists do as a matter of course.[10] Sometimes I observed events in the school district quite openly and somewhat more obtrusively.

For example, I sat in on administrative council meetings for as long as I was welcome (the first year). I attended school board meetings and ES committee meetings regularly. I was present for most of the meetings between local project and school staff and the officials from NIE. I participated in or observed various town and county meetings dealing with governance of the hospital, the fair, and other public institutions and agencies. I took an active role as a community member in the school district's cultural education committee. I was a member of a community chorus organized and directed by my wife. I was a visitor and speaker in local churches. I participated in the annual Ranchers' Family Camp Meeting at a nearby mountain retreat.

This combination of settings, memberships, and experiences provided me with good data on the community at large and on the specific cultures of power, schooling, hobbies, and religion in River District, as well as comparative data with which to analyze many other local cultural scenes (Spradley and McCurdy 1972) which go into making up the whole community. In these instances, I quietly but openly took notes and often followed up cogent points later by interviewing selected participants.

In structured interviews, I used an interview schedule and made appointments to meet with individuals whom I considered to be expert informants on a particular topic. Some of these interviews were tape recorded, and the transcripts were returned to the informants for correction, amendment, or deletions. (Not one person ever chose to make changes.)

More often, interviews were casual and unstructured. I would ask questions about a variety of topics – schooling in the past, community life, political issues, project goals and planning – sometimes taking my cues from the structured interview schedule. Unstructured interviews typically took place over coffee in the central school-district office, during breaks in formal meetings, in faculty lounges, at parties, and in the homes of local townspeople.

Finally, I spent many hours leafing through back issues of the local newspaper, school files, and records of the county historical society. I sometimes drove hundreds of miles to study archival collections at the state university or in the state capital.

There is nothing particularly novel about these methods; they are quite typical of the anthropological enterprise, especially as it was developed for work in nonwestern communities far from River District. In time, however, I began to realize that some methods did not seem to fit the unique situations that I was encountering here at home. Some of my seemingly innocuous requests, such as access to the files, took on the air of investigation and interference, particularly after local perceptions about the boundaries of privacy (and bureaucratic secrecy) were sharpened by national events in 1974.

Roles and rapport

My specific research techniques turned out not to be the only factor in my undoing in River District. The various roles I played and how I was thought to fit in locally – the meaning and deeper implications of my presence as the man from Abt or "the fed," as I was sometimes called – seemed to raise even more serious questions and anxieties among my hosts and informants.

When I first approached River District, I did so with great sensitivity, on the advice of Ron Estes and Robert Herriott of Abt Associates. They had warned that each field researcher on this project,

injected into an existing social system, will assume a role within that system, and will at the same time maintain a social role within a research organization, as well as a position within the community of scholars of his academic field. The complexity of this role set, as well as the great potential for role conflict implicit in its composition, dictate that the conduct of the role be approached rationally and with extreme care. [Estes and Herriott 1972:3]

During the first introductions with the school-district superintendent, my Alaskan upbringing was remarked upon as an asset for living in rural Wyoming. There was a clear implication of shared values and attitudes about politics, daily living, hunting, and the outdoors, and a connotation that easterners, in contrast to westerners, did not fit in and were somehow suspect.

When I said that I was an anthropologist, one administrator responded, "You're a *what?*" Then, after a pause, "Oh, you look for arrowheads and dead Indians." I explained that I was an ethnographer of contemporary society and living peoples. [11] Even that role carried with it a certain mystique of the adventurer, a traveler of the world, one who dabbles in the exotic, a teller of myths (Braroe and Hicks 1967, Richardson 1975).

I brought with me a style and a method of inquiry unheard of and unappreciated by those who administered River District: participation, observation, interviews, and the ever-present ear – a penchant for hanging around, talking, and listening in the hopes of discerning someone's real feelings about an issue, feelings that sometimes conflicted with the ideals written in reports for public consumption. [12] To some, my listening and loitering seemed to be loafing. Much later, near the low ebb in my relationships with the locals, the superintendent bluntly called this style "eavesdropping."

How many times was I called "the evaluator," during the first few months, because the contract dubbed all of the outside research effort "evaluation"? The educator subculture is one "obsessed with evaluation" (Wolcott 1975c), but evaluation is usually conducted by school administrators to assess programs and subordinate staff. When those same administrators begin to feel that they are themselves being judged, evaluation begins to take on negative connotations. From the start, I detected a fear on the part of educators in River District of being evaluated. I had to explain over and over again that any evaluation I might engage in as a researcher would only be a summative, occurring at the end of the project. I took great pains never to appear to be evaluating anyone's actions.

How many times was I called "the observer," with the unmistakable connotation of "spy"? It was a standing joke, of sorts, with one administrator that I was "federal agent Me-109," linking my patronym and role with the German Luftwaffe's Messerschmitt-109 aircraft of World War II fame.

Some concern over my role as observer became apparent at the time I attended a school administrators' conference in Cheyenne, Wyoming, in 1974. During a party one evening, River District's assistant superintendent began to introduce me to his colleagues from other districts in the state. He began with a story about a confidence man who arrived in town posing as a stucco repairman. As the story goes, the repairman eventually skipped out with down payments for no work, leaving behind the disgruntled victims, the so-called "stuckees." "Don's job here is something like that," he concluded, "he's our observer, and we are the observees!"

I was also called a "journalist" and my work was branded by one school district administrator as "sensationalism" and "melodrama" based on "distorted facts . . . taken out of context" or "conjured up" from a crystal ball. At one point, the administrators threatened to sue if I published certain notions about the local ES project and the school administration. Some of that same analysis was later published and also used in my final project report (Messerschmidt 1979a, 1979b), but the threats never got beyond pointed suggestion.

In another role, I was a family man, a property owner, a voter, and a taxpayer, but most of all a newcomer. Somehow, with this plethora of roles and statuses, I had to settle into the community and try gracefully to achieve acceptance in a small town and to exist comfortably with some of my key informants as neighbors. It seemed at first as though everybody knew all about us while we struggled valiantly to get to know each of them one by one.

At a holiday party for school administrators, to which my wife and I were invited, the topic of the town water supply came up. Our daughter had recently taken ill, and the doctor had suggested that we boil her drinking water as a precaution. When I suggested in conversation that the quality and safety of the town's water supply might be in doubt, I was abruptly interrupted and loudly admonished by one administrator: "If you talk about our 'bad' water system like that, Don, how do we know what you'll say bad about our school system. You're a 'scientist,' Don; where's your facts?"

Then, too, I had to maintain my standing as an anthropologist, to keep up with the professional literature, to write and publish, and to fly here and there to give symposium papers and defend my dissertation in order to ensure my employability after the years of rural isolation on this project were over. A rancher on the school board, one whom I saw only infrequently, once remarked: "How can you do your job *here*, Don, when you are away at meetings all the time?" It was a small community, and word got around quickly about my activities.

At first, people were just curious. They took their slow, measured time, as rural people tend to do, to check us out. For the townspeople it was not so much my credentials as a researcher as it was our looks as a family that interested them – whether or not I as an individual and we as a family unit were okay. Other researchers have reported similar experiences: that it is not what you do but whether or not you are okay as a person that counts. [13]

My amorphous role as "government researcher" caused the most misunderstanding and some mild contempt, especially among the hard-working ranchers of the region. I recall an especially outspoken rancher who remarked: "It must be nice, Don. Your job is like a paid vacation." My defense was less than convincing to men and women like him who were contemptuous of soft, white-collar, pencil-pushing jobs of contemplation, as mine appeared. Like bureaucrats and eastern politicians, researchers did not rank high in local esteem.

There was less concern in school circles with my researcher role (except when I was mistaken for an evaluator), given that research is a national educational priority, has credibility in education, and in this instance was a precondition for receiving federal funding for the local ES project. This particular precondition, however, gave my research role a certain subtle measure of clout over the renewal of funding of the local project in 1976. That clout emerged soon enough as an underlying theme in my eventual undoing.

The issues of my undoing

A year into the research, in the autumn of 1974, two outside factors disrupted the research effort and permanently affected my rapport in River District. During the year, there had been considerable local–federal strife and tension over the form that the local project should take and over the meaning and level of involvement on the part of federal monitors. [14] Eventually these problems were resolved, temporarily forgotten, or put aside, as local and federal officials alike tried to work out more stable relations and get on with the project.

This was also a time when I was increasing my research activity. With a year of attempted rapport building behind me and trust seemingly well established between me and the locals, a more intense effort at documentation was now beginning. Because of the complicated logistics of working in so diverse and large a school district, and because of an increased workload imposed by Abt Associates at this point, I obtained the help of another anthropologist as an associate researcher for six months, from July to December 1974. Marilyn C. Richen assisted me with the development of an extensive school-district history (Messerschmidt and Richen 1975) and with parts of the larger case study, as well as with the collection of students' academic records to be used in the comprehensive cross-site pupil change study (Abt, Cerva, and Marx 1978).

Unexpectedly, however, two exogenous factors upset our best intentions. The first was passage by Congress of the Family Educational Rights and Privacy Act, better known as the Buckley Amendment to the Omnibus Education Bill of 1974. This amendment challenged many traditional assumptions about school-system operations and increased local administrator anxieties in River District about federal involvement in local educational affairs. The second factor was a simultaneous and significant change by NIE officials in the ground rules governing the conduct and the products of our on-site research. NIE's change of rules, detailed below, undermined the good rapport, trust, and neutrality that I had been striving so long and hard to cultivate and maintain. The concurrent Watergate scandal, which was dominating national news throughout the latter part of 1974, only increased local suspicions about anything involving the government.

The Buckley Amendment

The Buckley Amendment became law, in its first form, in November 1974. Almost overnight, apprehensions and largely negative reactions to it were heard across the nation (see Worzbyt 1976).

Intended to protect the public's right to privacy and to prevent mishandling or misuse of all categories of individual school file materials (such as academic records, letters of reference, and other confidential statements), this law at the same time required major changes in school operating style, particularly a new openness in dealing with parents and the general public. Compliance was to be enforced by a clause that stated that federal funding would be withdrawn or withheld from educational agencies or institutions that had policies of denying or otherwise preventing parents, students over eighteen years of age, and school alumni access to their child's or to their own pupil records (Section 438).

At first, before certain qualifying amendments were passed, this was interpreted locally as an open invitation to litigation by parents seeking redress of presumed violations of privacy. The mere possibility of court action against the school district put members of the educational establishment at all levels on the defensive. Moreover, the law permitted teachers, as previous students and alumni, access to their own college and university job-placement files, files in which some of their employers may have placed damaging comments. This issue about what was in the files raised quesions of whether or not school files were accessible by researchers and other nonlocal third parties, such as the social scientists employed by Abt Associates. Although it was primarily this latter concern that affected my rapport and research directly, the overall negative climate created by the new law was immediately reflected in my work primarily by constraints the local people placed on my access to data.

While they sought clarification about outsider access to school files, the superintendents decided that I was to be barred from all documents and all administrative meetings in which management and personnel issues were being discussed. And even after my right of access to the files and other records and local data was firmly established by NIE officials, I was still barred from many files and politely but firmly disinvited to many meetings. Local concern had shifted, from the question of if the records and information should be made available to me as the outside researcher, to the question of how I might analyze and publish that information about the school district. Local administrators felt that it was safest to deny me access.

Changing ground rules

Concern and anger generated by the Buckley Amendment, however, were not the entire reason for local displeasure. NIE's sudden change of rules about the conduct of research and reporting procedures gave the locals further incentive to control my access to data.

Carol Colfer has described the problems created by changing our research ground rules in an article based on experiences at another rural ES project site (Colfer 1976). Her observations correspond closely to my own. The staff of Abt Associates (called "Crex" in her account), had, from the beginning, maintained a strict prohibition on the flow of information between the on-site researchers and ES government officials, in order to secure and ensure research credibility on site. This simply meant avoiding contact with NIE officials on or off the site. Any communications of a nonsubstantive or contractual nature were to be channeled through Abt Associates' headquarters staff in Cambridge, and from there to the relevant officials at NIE in Washington, D.C. Above all, no substantive reports about individual projects would go to NIE until after June 1978, when the whole ES program would be over.[15] By avoiding formative feedback, the researchers at each site assumed that concerns about evaluation and threat of reprisals to local projects would not arise.

It was with these understandings that I entered River District in 1973. Objectivity and detachment were essential to build a good image and rapport. The potential clout that I appeared to have (if my findings were communicated early to NIE) was understood but unspoken. Federal officials, for example, could have used the data I collected to make decisions about future funding of the site. Funding for the last phase of the project was scheduled to be considered in 1976, and as that date approached, local concern about the image of the project was heightened. Naturally, I was concerned, therefore, about what and to whom information from the site was reported.[16] Understanding and coping with these issues were part of the process of creating a working strategy for the study of power in River District. It was clear in my case, as in Colfer's, that spelling out the basic ground rules about the nonreportive nature of the research and about our strict avoidance of federal officials was "necessary in order to gain the confidence and trust of the local people" at the start (Colfer 1976:33).

A year into the research, officials at NIE changed the rules and suddenly demanded that on-site researchers report their findings regularly to the funding agency. The reasons and the timing of their demands were clearly related to NIE's own need to account to Congress about its activities (Sproull, Weiner, and Wolf 1978). When NIE faced a congressional threat to cut funding in 1974, officers within the institute responded by raising questions about the accountability of many of their programs, including experimental schools. Within ES it was thought necessary to require reports from all contracting organizations. That meant, in turn, that each on-site researcher with Abt Associates would have to submit reports for immediate evaluation, well before the end of the research period.

NIE's purpose was ostensibly to determine the relevance, utility, and competence of the research, but on-site researchers felt that the information in these reports could also be used to evaluate progress of local projects. What had begun as a form of summative research (to be reported only at the end of the project in 1978) would, by this change of rules, become formative research (available to be fed back immediately into the project), thus changing the nature of the experiment. When this was pointed out to federal officials through Abt Associates channels, they insisted that we submit our reports as working papers and that we not show them to our local informants – a what-they-don't-know-won't-hurt-them attitude. This seemed tantamount to secret research and made the researchers uncomfortable. If word got out in River District that I was sending secret working papers to the funding agency, it would not only breach confidences already secured and threaten my rapport but it would also certainly be interpreted as a gross violation of basic professional ethics.

The on-site researchers balked. As Colfer (1976) points out, we were forced to make a choice: to quit, to acquiesce and submit secret reports, or to prepare fully public reports and submit them simultaneously to our hosts and to NIE. Quitting was a very real possibility, and the fact that it was seriously discussed among some researchers led officials at Abt Associates to confront NIE officials with a formal request to back down from the new ruling.

Eventually, a compromise was reached that, we hoped, would allow on-site researchers to maintain their credibility and would eliminate concern about secrets, feedback, and reprisals. We still had to prepare the so-called "working papers," but after we submitted them to Abt Associates they were sent not to officials within the ES program but to an ethnographer working in another NIE program elsewhere in the institute. He agreed to read our reports privately and to take steps to assure their inaccessibility to ES program officers. It was his job to make independent judgments about the competence of each researcher and the relevance and utility of each report vis-à-vis the objectives of NIE. Then he was to make a verbal report, without reference to the substantive information in the reports, to the ES program officers. [17]

Hence, by a roundabout process, we researchers would avoid violating our on-site promises about reporting back to ES staff, while at the same time we would satisfy NIE's need to know and to appear accountable. No one quit, but some of us still considered the compromise a subtle form of secret reporting. In the end, most of us shared our reports with our local informants anyway.

The first annual working paper

Throughout the controversial negotiations about reporting, I was busy analyzing data and writing with the assistance of Marilyn Richen. Our working paper dealt with the planning year (1972–1973) and the first year of limited implementation (1973–1974) in the River District schools. We intended it briefly to describe school and project administration, the ethnographic context of change, and federal–local relations. We told the superintendents that we would share the first complete draft with them and with other persons they chose and would ask their opinions. All the while, we discussed the data with them openly and candidly. Our rapport was good and there seemed little problem with this open approach.

By November 1974 the first draft was ready. We felt that it was an essentially complimentary view of the site and the local project issues. We were confident that it breached no code of ethics and that no confidential information was revealed. All of the problems we described that had occurred during those first two years had been aired in public, or semipublicly, and at times even with NIE project officers present. Many of the data were corroborated through several sources, both inside and outside of the school administration. In the paper we raised serious questions only about NIE's operating strategies toward the school district (Messerschmidt and Richen 1974, Messerschmidt 1979a).

When other on-site researchers showed their reports to their hosts and informants they heard comments like "Oh, this is just anthropology," and little more. But when we finally shared our report with the superintendents in River District, all hell broke loose.

Our candid discussion of federal–local rapport during the first two years was interpreted as an attempt to open old wounds and to jeopardize future funding. In the context of the concern over privacy and secrecy brought on by the Buckley Amendment and the Watergate scandal, River district administrators saw our report as a document revealing the inner workings of the local educational bureaucracy. Regarding the compromise about reporting to NIE, the superintendents now informed us that they saw no compromise at all. To them, NIE was simply one part of a blurry and amorphous big bureaucracy in Washington, D.C., and no one associated with it could be trusted.

What rapport I had built and Marilyn Richen and I had enjoyed so far in River District was now rapidly dissipating. Our report was branded as sensationalism and called libelous. At this point the decision to close the files and keep me out of administrative meetigs was made. I was reassured that there was nothing personal in this action and that both Marilyn and I were well liked as individuals. It was just that the report – and the changes that its writing and submission to NIE implied – told them that I was no more than another powerless cog in the system, a system that they simply could not trust. I was, indeed, the fed they had suspected me to be all along.

In retrospect, it was indeed naive for me to have seen myself as anything other than a person contracted up through the research firm to a powerful federal agency. I had built my good rapport in River District on sand. The storms of the Buckley Amendment and the changing rules at NIE had suddenly washed it all away.

Summary and conclusions

Hindsight is an important product of experience; from past experiences come insight and wisdom. With insight also comes the stuff of more effective and more realistic strategies for future action.

When I entered River District in 1973 I knew, in a fuzzy way, that I was embarking on nontraditional anthropological research. But I was ill prepared for the new conditions I was about to encounter. I now know some of the feelings that Stanley Diamond describes looking back on a similarly difficult research journey "to an area that was ethnographically important, which I knew, and politically explosive, which I didn't know" (1964:123).

Some may argue that there are few if any differences between research methods appropriate in communities at home and away from home, that methods for studying the culture of power, for example, are fundamentally alike whether the research is conducted in Africa, Asia, or America. By this logic, I would expect researchers examining systems of power anywhere in the world to gather data in ways similar to mine and to encounter the same sorts of constraints on access, limitations on the scope and depth of inquiry, uncomfortable role relationships with the powerful, and the secrecy and privacy that pervade cultures of power everywhere. It has even been suggested that although bureaucracy (as a principal context of power in society) is not the same thing as community, the ethnographic study of bureaucracy is, in principle, no different from the study of community except in the nature of the data (Britan 1978; Britan and Cohen 1980).

I am uncomfortable with this point of view, particularly as it applies to the study of power in the contemporary United States. It glosses over at least three fundamental considerations: (1) differences in researcher role; in other words, in who the researcher appears to be to his or her informants; (2) differences in how anthropological method is best applied to fit the at-home bureaucratic situation; in other words, what the researcher appears to be doing; and (3) considerations of power itself; the nature of control and authority in relations between researcher and employer and between researcher and subjects. I will comment on each of these three considerations in turn.

On role

Differences in role relationships are rooted in the nature of the expectations that exist between researchers, their employers, and their subjects, and of the strategies necessary to establish an effective researcher–informant relationship in the bureaucratic setting. It is a commonplace assumption that the anthropologist in a foreign tribal or peasant society, perceived as a stranger, can be excused for all sorts of misunderstandings, improprieties, gaps of knowledge, and insensitivity to local codes of etiquette. But that sort of excuse is a luxury that the anthropologist at home is not allowed to enjoy. In doing fieldwork in our society we have little time to learn, no margin for blunders, and often little or no time to reconsider and reapproach the informant or the data. We can all too easily compromise ourselves and our data through inappropriate actions and insensitivities regarding how we are viewed and expected to act by our hosts. In situations where we are studying bureaucratic systems or are contracted to a powerful research firm or government agency, the problems are greatly exacerbated.

In River District I appeared, at first, to be little different from the local people. I was clearly a newcomer and an outsider, but essentially I was just another American, as much a member of the society as anyone else around me. To this degree I was, in effect, no stranger at all.

But in my formal pose as a professional anthropologist, responsible to a contract firm ultimately beholden to a federal agency, I was cast in role relationships quite unlike those of the typical friend or regular member of the community. Although I tried to avoid appearing too close to the federal agency and I worked to establish good rapport on an interpersonal basis, the differences inherent in my professional contractual responsibilities emerged as the central criteria for acceptance – or in my case, rejection – when the sensitive issues generated by the Buckley Amendment and reports to NIE were raised.

On methods

In terms of differences in method, perhaps Yehudi Cohen is partly correct when he implies that the traditional anthropological enterprise is not adequately prepared to accomplish the objectives of research in societies other than those of tribal or peasant peoples (1977:389). I am not altogether convinced, however, that we totally lack what he calls the requisite "concepts, paradigms, and methods" to study all or part of our own modern industrial society. Rather, the problem lies in the dearth of new and innovative strategies with which to employ our well-tested concepts, paradigms, and methods. There are many studies that employ good method and theory in the study of American society. Only a few, however, deal specifically with cultures of power, where innovative research strategies are most needed. One recent work that exemplifies a successful blend of the old methods and the new research at home is Wolcott's (1977) study of teachers and educational technocrats in an Oregon school district. In that work, Wolcott demonstrates the application of age-old participant observation and interview techniques and the concept of moiety organization (borrowed directly from study of tribal societies) to a modern, formal, dualistic bureaucratic organization.[18]

On power

Anthropologists at home present many faces, confront many challenges, and suffer many gains and setbacks in the course of their work. Applied anthropologists in particular, charged as they are with practicing what they know about social behavior and cultural

systems in the throes of change, frequently find themselves in situa-
tions in which the dictates of the powerful and the constraints of the contract severely limit
their ability to function well. Humanistic solutions to social problems get lost in the
shuffle to conform to rules and the typical rush to get a job done. Despite the best
intentions of the people involved, concerns for maintaining institutional agendas or for
defending the host organization or agency against threats – particularly by keeping the
processes of power and authority secret and unapproachable to outsiders – tend to
undermine individual human integrity and good purpose.

Anthropologists who presume to study the issues of bureaucracy, power, and authority
(and it seems unlikely that sensitive applied anthropologists can avoid such issues) should
beware. Until we are more experienced in "working for the man" (Chambers 1977b),
"bargaining with the devil" (Clinton 1976), or "managing and being managed" (Trend
1978), we must proceed with caution. More than a decade ago, Eric Wolf observed:

If I am correct in saying anthropology has reached its present impasse because it has so systematically
disregarded the problems of power, then we must find ways of eduating ourselves in the realities of
power . . . [and the] processes of power which created the present-day cultural systems and the
linkages between them. [Wolf 1969:10]

Wolf's admonition still holds today. As Walter Goldschmidt recently told us, "We fear
power, we avoid the center of power, we do not even see the uses of power within the tribes
we study" (1977:297).

In conclusion, we must squarely face and learn to cope with the close relationship
between the phenomenon of power that we study and the methods and roles that we, as
anthropologists, employ in that endeavor. Knowing this, we are sometimes constrained,
but more often challenged, to invent better tactics with which to proceed.

14 Many roles, many faces: researching school–community relations in a heterogeneous American urban community

R. TIMOTHY SIEBER

In 1972 I embarked on fifteen months of field research[1] in Chestnut Heights, a polyethnic and multi-social-class New York City community, and in its three elementary schools.[2] At the time, I was unaware that the complexities of this field situation would severely put to the test the traditional anthropological methods – participant observation and interviewing – with which I had chosen to approach the research. In this chapter I examine my fieldwork experiences in this heterogeneous community and its schools, emphasizing the implications that the cultural complexities of the field situation had for problems of entry, rapport building, data collection, and analysis. My account is intended as a case illustration of the variety of problems, particularly in rapport building, that are likely to fall to the lot of participant observers researching complex urban communities and their relations with the formal institutions that serve them. Despite the many field difficulties that will be enumerated, I contend that traditional anthropological field methods are adequate to the task of investigating complex urban situations.

The research problem

The aim of my research in Chestnut Heights was twofold: (1) to examine the elementary-school classroom as a setting for child socialization in bureaucratic behavior; and (2) to investigate the implications of such school-based socialization for the formation of social-class and ethnic subcultures in community life. My interest in the first of these problems was chiefly generated by the work of Leacock (1969) and Dreeben (1968), whose studies of school-based enculturation had emphasized children's role socializations in the domain of formal organizational behavior. My graduate training, strong in British social anthropology, predisposed me to focus investigation on classroom social organization as the basic situational milieu for the child's organizational role socialization. Previous research suggested the guiding hypothesis of my study: that the organizational role socialization of the school pupil constitutes early preparation for his or her future role behavior as employee, client, consumer, and citizen in large-scale formal organizations of the American polity and economy.

In addition to documenting the content of the norms, values, and general expectations maintained by the school staff for pupil conduct, I was interested in investigating the means by which such expectations are communicated to children in the school. Durkheim's pedagogical writings (1956, 1966), as well as my own previous exploratory field research, suggested the school disciplinary process as the central vehicle for the transmission to pupils of school expectations for their behavior. In my focus on classroom social organization, I therefore sought to give special attention to its disciplinary and social-control dimensions.

As regards the second of my research problems, Eddy (1965), Leacock (1969), Rist (1970), and Gintis and Bowles (1972–1973) had reported significant patterned variations in the nature of the pupil role socializations received by children of different class and ethnic groups in American society and had suggested that such variations contribute to the intergenerational reproduction of class and ethnic subcultures in American life. My desire to complete a comparative case study of the pupil role socializations experienced by a social-class and ethnically diverse sample of school pupils led to my choice of Chestnut Heights as a research site.

Chestnut Heights is a New York City community whose population exhibits great diversity both ethnically and in social class. As well as having a culturally heterogeneous population, the community is served by three quite different elementary schools – one public, one Catholic, and one Episcopal. The heterogeneity of the community and its schools permitted the comparative study of pupil role socializations I desired. Another contributing factor in my choice of Chestnut Heights as field site was my familiarity with it, acquired during two years of residence there while a graduate student and a previous brief period of field research in an adjacent neighborhood.

The research setting

The community

Chestnut Heights is a quiet, medium-density residential community of 9,000 people located in New York City. Its twenty-one square blocks of tree-lined streets and attached four-story townhouses are naturally bounded on three sides by an expressway and two wide commercial thoroughfares. It is outstanding for its cultural heterogeneity: Over forty ethnic groups are represented in a population that residents call "polyglot" or "Heinz variety." Marked differences in economic standing are also present among the residents; they range from the relief-receiving poor to the well-to-do upper middle class. In residents' cognitive maps of the community, in marriage and intermarriage patterns, in community political cleavages, and in social interaction, however, three broad categorical groupings subsume all other identities. These groupings are the Oldtimers, the Brownstoners, and the Spanish.

Oldtimers. This group includes the area's longest-term residents, the European-derived Catholic ethnic groups that comprise 70 percent of the local population. Dominant among them are the third-generation Italians[3] and smaller populations of third-generation Syrians and fifth-generation and longer resident Irish. Terming themselves "working people," Oldtimers characteristically engage in local small business; work as skilled or semi-skilled workers in maritime shipping, manufacturing, and construction; or hold lower-level civil service or other white-collar positions.

Brownstoners. These newcomers to the area since 1960 comprise 15 percent of the local population. They are predominantly Anglo-Saxon, Protestant, young, and cosmopolitan. As professional people, most have migrated to New York City for career reasons and work in the city's downtown business district in law, publishing, architecture, finance, advertising, public relations, or the arts. The term "Brownstoner" derives from "brownstone," the name given the community's modal dwelling type, the attached four-story nineteenth-century townhouse. These young professionals came to be closely identified with the low-cost townhouses they purchased and avidly rehabilitated. Not all Brownstoners are homeowners, however; many tenants have followed in the wake of the homeowners. My own residence in the neighborhood occurred as part of the continuing in-migration of this grouping.

Spanish (Hispanos). The third major group is the Hispanics, a diverse group of people who have migrated to the area since the 1950s. Whereas Oldtimers and Brownstoners live residentially interspersed throughout Chestnut Heights, the Hispanics are residentially segregated on its fringes. Puerto Ricans predominate, making up more than 80 percent of the Hispanics, although substantial minorities of Cubans, Dominicans, and Colombians are also present. Although approximately 40 percent receive public assistance, most Hispanics consider themselves to be working people. They are generally more marginally employed than Oldtimer working people, however. Many work as low-paid factory operatives in a variety of local seasonal industries, especially garment work, or as lower-echelon service workers in restaurants, health institutions, and janitorial services. The most well-to-do, largely Cubans and Colombians, own small businesses or work in lower-echelon white-collar employment as bank tellers, store clerks, or clerical workers. Occupational designations are not important in Hispanic references to themselves, however. The most important designation is that relating to language and culture – that they are Spanish, or *Hispanos.* They contrast their group with the "Americans," whom they see to include both Oldtimers and Brownstoners.

The community's three elementary schools

Chestnut Heights is served by three elementary schools located in the community: PS 4, a public school; the Wright School, a private Episcopal day school; and St. Michaels School, a Catholic parish school. In this heterogeneous community, where clear group boundaries are evident in most spheres of social life, children are recruited into the schools and their component classrooms in such a way that these group boundaries are preserved in the social organization of elementary education.

PS 4. The public school is the largest of the elementary schools, with 782 pupils. At 59 percent of the enrollment, Hispanic children predominate in the school. Ninety-seven percent of Hispanic children are Puerto Rican. The remaining 41 percent of the school enrollment is evenly split between children of Oldtimers and Brownstoners. Even though the school draws its enrollment from the immediate neighborhood, it lacks close integration with the local community. The school is an organ of city and state government, from which it receives its funding, and is subordinate to extensive, higher disttict- and system-wide levels of administration. Its staff members are recruited from outside the neighborhood as well. Fewer than a quarter (23 percent) of its teaching and administrative staff of forty-three persons are members of ethnic groups resident in Chestnut Heights, and only four (9 percent) of the staff reside locally. Informal, nonschool interaction between staff and community residents rarely occurs. The staff also maintain highly negative views of the neighborhood and its residents. The nonlocal control and staffing and the school's heterogeneous enrollment preclude its identification with any of the community's groups in the way that St. Michaels and the Wright School are thought of as belonging, respectively, to the Oldtimers and the Brownstoners.

The Wright School. This school, an Episcopal private day school, is the smallest of the three schools with an enrollment of seventy-two. The school is highly autonomous in its operations, as it has only nominal ties to a diocesan school system that provides few services and little supervision for the school. Its funding is purely local, through endowment income and tuition receipts. The school's operations reflect its progressive educational philosophy, termed by staff as "modified open classroom." The Wright School has close ties to the Brownstoner segment of the community. Forty-three percent of its pupils are from local Brownstoner families; most of the remaining enrollment is of West Indian children from other neighborhoods. All but one member of the adult staff of twelve are locally resident Brownstoners. The school and the attached church premises also serve as the prime location for Brownstoner civic association meetings and other social functions, such as the yearly arts-and-crafts sale and the annual spring house tour reception.

St. Michaels School. While St. Michaels is part of a large but loose diocesan school system, the school is largely locally controlled and autonomous in formulating educational policies. Moreover, its autonomy is enhanced because the school is financed entirely through local parish sources. The school has close ties to the Oldtimers, most of whom send their children there. A large minority of the enrollment (35 percent) is composed of Hispanic children, primarily from the more upwardly mobile and better-off national groups, such as the Cubans and Colombians. Ninety-four percent of St. Michaels' sixteen teaching staff members are members of Oldtimer ethnic groups, and 87 percent reside locally.

Most Oldtimer voluntary associational life in the community is done under the rubric of the local parish, and within the parish the school serves as the physical and symbolic focus of nearly all this associational life. The building and grounds are used for an extensive array of activities, numbering in the hundreds over a year's time, from the at least monthly dinners, dances, and gambling events sponsored by various associations to the regular monthly meetings of the nearly twenty parish organizations (such as the Mission Guild, the Home-School Association, the Parish Council, the Women's Society, and so forth). Two-thirds of the school's budget is financed through the proceeds generated by the many activities sponsored by these organizations.

Research methods and procedures

In studying Chestnut Heights and its schools I decided to rely primarily on participant observation, supplemented wherever possible with in-depth and other interviewing of informants. A major factor in my decision to use traditional methods was the desire to compensate for my choice of a nonconventional, familiar American site by using methods that maximized face-to-face encounters and social immersion in the study community. I had been taught that it was only through such immersion and deep personal encounter that one experienced the fieldwork rite of passage. A traditional methodological stance was also consistent with my training and, it seemed, with my aim to complete basic anthropological research on my chosen problem. I put participant observation and interviewing to different uses however, in my investigations of school life and of community affairs.

School research

My research in the three study schools was concentrated on a sample of eight classrooms chosen from the first and fifth grades in each school. My general procedures were the same in each of the classrooms. For the most part, I operated as a silent observer, usually sitting at the back of the classroom taking running notes on selected areas of classroom behavior. In each class I periodically sought and received teacher permission to sit more toward the middle of the room, amongst the children, so as to record closer observations of some forms of pupil behavior. In keeping with the expressed desires of school personnel, however, I attempted to keep a low profile in the classrooms. While being an adult gave me freedoms not permitted pupils – for example, I could leave the room or school for any purpose and at my own discretion – I tried to observe the general classroom standards of behavior established for pupils.

My attention in the classrooms focused on two main areas: (1) social organization – classroom roles, formal and informal subgroups, ritual and routine behavior, and the activity schedule; and (2) school discipline, including all teacher statements evaluating behavior and accompanying sanctions of behavior, sanction-eliciting forms of pupil behavior, and any noticeable results from teacher application of sanctions. My general practice was to stay with the class through the entire day, coming to the school in the morning, lining up with the children in the schoolyard, following them to the classroom and through the day's schedule, and so forth.

I also sought opportunities for informal interaction and conversation with the school staffs. Most days I took several short breaks from the classroom to visit the teachers' lounge or its equivalent in each school. I also ate lunch each day in the schools with the teachers in their staff dining areas. My conversations with teachers in these informal settings provided a rich source of information on their perceptions of a wide variety of school matters. These settings also gave me the opportunity of speaking with most of the teachers in each school and allowed me informally to interview the study teachers about events I had observed in their classrooms. These informal interviews supplemented more formal ones with the study teachers.

I also spent a considerable amount of time, largely after regular school hours, attending school-wide, as opposed to classroom, events and affairs – staff meetings, teacher union meetings, parent–teacher conferences, special assemblies, parent association meetings, school holiday pageants, fund-raising events, and so forth. These settings permitted gathering of information through observation and interview on school social organization, particularly intrastaff relations, school educational goals, policies, and philosophies, and school–community relations. Such contextual data were indispensable to proper analysis of classroom organization and behavior.

Research on community life

My research on community affairs centered on delineating significant group boundaries and patterns of intergroup relations in Chestnut Heights. I sought information on these topics as an aid to explaining differential patterns of pupil recruitment to the three local schools and the differing character of school–community relations in each case. Another purpose of the community research was to provide a context for interpreting the class and ethnic implications of observed variations in pupil role socialization in the schools.

Through my earlier research in the area, I had become aware of the considerable local political ferment in Chestnut Heights. This active political life was a reflection of the substantial population changes in the area resulting from the in-migrations of Brownstoners and Hispanics. It seemed that many expressions of group identities, boundaries, and alignments would be evident through study of community political activity.

Each of the community's three major groupings has its own maze of voluntary associations, whose activities give expression to the groupings' respective public concerns, cultural outlooks, and visions for the community's future. Most of these associations take an active role in community politics by attempting to advance their grouping's usually conflicting interests in a wide variety of local political struggles, including but not limited to contests for local elective offices. When I began my research, the balance of power in community politics had been moving for several years toward increasing Brownstoner ascendancy. On many issues of concern to the community, such as the desirability of preservation over new housing development, each of the groupings had its own position, responding to its own values and perceived needs.

Quasi-governmental and governmental boards and commissions – including the 97th Police Precinct Community Council, the District 41 Community School Board, and the District 33 Planning Board – also held regular public meetings and a number of special open hearings on issues of local concern, such as the proposal for modernizing and expanding the local waterfront containerport, and the proposal for constructing a new high school, in which site location was the issue. Such hearings and meetings were often raucous affairs, with speakers and segments of the audience from the range of community groupings articulating and debating differing viewpoints. Similar articulation of local issues and expressions of group alignments and cleavages were also evident in the more than a dozen local candidates' nights held in connection with local electoral political contests.

Throughout the fifteen months of my research, the majority of evenings each week was spent in attending meetings and other functions of the community's various voluntary associations, ranging from the Brownstoner-controlled Chestnut Heights Association and the Burkham Court Improvement Association, to Oldtimer groups such as the St. Michaels Golden Age Society and the LaBella Democratic Club, to Hispanic associations such as the Anti-Poverty Program-linked LaLucha League and the St. Michaels Cursillo devotional association. Excluding the governmental boards, over the course of my research I attended at least one meeting or other function of over 110 different voluntary associations.

Little of this associational activity had direct bearing on the community's schools. I did, however, give special attention to the somewhat separate sphere of education-related associational and political activity that flourished within the arena of the public-school system's community school district, an administrative unit encompassing twenty-four elementary and junior high schools in a geographical area much larger than Chestnut Heights. It was fortunate also that the biannual Community School Board election took place during my research. The three-month election campaign spawned dozens of special meetings, candidates' nights, and debates on local educational issues; it reactivated a series of local parent, community, and teacher interest groups and drew many other local associations into supporting candidates for election and articulating their perceptions of the schools and educational issues.

Generally, before first attending some function of any local association, I would approach its formal leader for an interview focusing on Chestnut Heights intergroup relations and during the interview seek permission to attend a meeting. I was never denied such permission. The meetings and other functions of these associations represented important phenomena for study in themselves, but they also afforded opportunities for informal interaction with and interviewing of participants, for renewing previous acquaintances, and for making new ones. Contacts made with participants during these affairs often led to arrangements for interviewing them at a future date in their homes.

My focus on intergroup relations led beyond investigating the political and associational to the employment of other research methods. I completed a great deal of observation and interviewing of a more general nature – in the shops and on the stoops and streets of the area – on such matters as shopping patterns, neighboring interactions, children's play patterns, interethnic face-to-face relations, and the history and character of the community. Largely through contacts made in voluntary associational meetings, I also conducted a series of more formal interviews, at their homes, with an ethnically and class stratified sample of thirty residents on the subjects of ethnic classifications and education. I also conducted some archival research at the local historical society on the history of population shifts in the area and in two of the local churches on interethnic marriage patterns as reflected in their marriage records. Although I did not employ any formal survey methods, for some purposes I found more impersonal approaches to residents both possible and effective in this urban community.

To engage quick, unself-conscious answers on the location of community boundaries, for example, I posed as a lost stranger and systematically stopped strangers on the street with inquiries on this subject.

Gaining entry and building rapport: a multifaceted process

In seeking to undertake research in Chestnut Heights and its schools, I discovered that each segment of the diverse study population required a somewhat different avenue of approach. The quality of the rapport I was able to achieve and maintain with each segment was variable as well. The teaching staffs of the schools perceived my activities differently, in keeping with the constraints afforded by school social structural characteristics and the varying quality of school–community relations in each setting. Perceptions of me by community residents were similarly variable.

In taking into account my complement of statuses as young, male, single, middle-class, student, WASP, community resident, and, last but not least, researcher, each segment of the research community tended to interpret my status and activities in terms that were familiar to them. On the basis of these interpretations, each group made its assessment of the potential benefits and dangers that my activities implied for them and cooperated with me in a fashion consistent with this assessment. As a consequence, the community presented a quite variable profile of situations calling for differing strategies of entry, rapport building, and even data collection. My concurrent study of the different groupings and institutions, as well, precipitated boundary and loyalty conflicts whose management required some special adaptations on my part. I begin discussion of these matters with treatment of my experiences in the schools, reserving until later the consideration of my experiences in researching community life outside the schools.

Research at PS 4: the stranger within

Gaining entry to PS 4 was a bureaucratically cumbersome process that consumed a full year. Fortunately, I had anticipated the delays and had begun the process a year before I planned to start my observations there. The Bureau of Educational Research of the Board of Education of the City of New York has ultimate authority over all research, external and in-house, that takes place in the city school system. Following standard procedure, I submitted a proposal, personal information, and letters of university sponsorship to them for their preliminary screening and approval. This preliminary approval was to take six months, and occurred only after my initial materials had been lost in their office and then resubmitted.

It was then necessary for me to approach PS 4's principal to gain her written approval of my project. This approval was easily granted, although I later learned that the teaching staff had not been informed of my impending presence until some months later when I first began to appear at their classroom doors with the principal. With the principal's authorization in hand, I then was required to secure the approval of the community district superintendent, to whom more materials were submitted. It was a quirk of fate that led to a relatively painless securing of his permission. The community superintendent was at that point in time in a lame duck position; because he had been terminated in favor of his deputy he was due to leave office in a matter of weeks. In a conference I had with him him and his designated successor, the latter pressed him to have my request presented to the community school board for public discussion and debate. This would have no doubt led to considerable delay, if not to other difficulties. The deputy's request provoked the superintendent, in dramatic display of his flagging authority, to sign my authorization without further word and summarily to dismiss me. A final submission of the principal's and the superintendent's authorizations to the Bureau of Educational Research yielded, some months later and after telephone promptings, my final approval from them.

Once inside PS 4 I entered into successive study of four of its classrooms over a ten-week period. The resulting extended observations of the study classrooms permitted me to gain a relatively intimate knowledge with their day-to-day operations. Because of my classroom and other school activities, the staff became habituated to my presence in the school. Although I did come to enjoy cordial relations with most of the staff, particularly with the study teachers, my growing familiarity with classroom life did not result in an increasing acceptance by the staff. Instead, the amount and natural quality of the information I was gathering on their classrooms rendered me a dangerous threat to the boundaries of their authority. This is because my other research activities placed me in frequent association with people who are normally excluded from the knowledge I came to possess.

Warren (1973, 1975), Dreeben (1973), and others have written of the closed, sanctuary-like character of classroom life for most teachers, who work largely in isolation from and out of view of other adults, ideally guided in their actions by internalized professional norms of conduct. Indeed, I was not in the school long before I realized that my role as classroom observer afforded me more detailed information of life in the study classrooms than was available to any other outside category of person, whether administrator or parent or teacher or pupil from another class.

As an observer I was also able to witness the ways in which these other categories of people are restricted in their access to information on normal behavior in the classroom. Except for custodians and older pupils,[4] classes observe special patterns of behavior when visitors make their infrequent appearances in the room. Teachers and pupils alike exhibit tension, and pupils exhibit a learned set of responses in the form of increased behavioral caution, restraint, and formality that contrasts with their usual style of action. Teachers normally prod pupils into this style of behavior with such comments as, "Children, we have a visitor in the room!" or, "Boys and girls, while Miss Fox is visiting show her how nice you can be!" Such caution was especially observed during visits from school administrators, either during their usual momentary visits at the doorway or during more extended observations. These more formal observations of teachers' classroom performances are conducted annually by school administrators for purposes of personnel evaluation. The annual fifteen- to thirty-minute observations provide the occasion for the most sustained administrative presence in any given classroom.

Contending with staff fears of evaluation

Several factors led teachers to view me as an evaluator potentially serving the interests of local and even higher-level school-system administrators. I was conducting lengthy, silent observations, and, like the administrators during their evaluations, from the rear of the room. Also, the teaching staff had not been consulted by the principal when she granted me permission to study their classrooms. Relations in general between PS 4's teaching staff and its triple-tiered administrative hierarchy were also, I learned at the school, characteristically strained and impersonal. The teachers' propensity to view me as an evaluator was also compounded by my contacts with supraschool levels of administration. I had received research permission from the district and central offices and, as part of my information-gathering activities, regularly visited the district office, where I had encountered the principal and some of the staff. For this reason, to my chagrin, in my first week at the school I was introduced several times as "the man from the district office."

Finally, my educational status as doctoral candidate led many teachers to assume that, like most doctoral candidates in education, I was completing an evaluation of their classroom or their teaching, in spite of the different descriptions I gave them of my research interests. The field services division of the school of education at my university had, in fact, conducted several official evaluations of school programs in the local district. Most teachers knew little of the nature of anthropological research and its potential contributions to education, and there seemed never to be adequate time for full explanations. Also, in the highly bureaucratic public-school system, the importance of all higher educational advancement is generally reckoned in terms of the attendant increased salary increments and promotional opportunities that accrue. I discovered that the teachers, not unexpectedly, were highly conscious of educational credentials and tended to equate doctoral study with aspirations for promotion to the supervisory ranks.

For these reasons, regardless of the number and extent of my explanations that I was interested in the basic features of schoolroom life, there was the continual desire of staff to believe that I aimed to judge their classroom behavior and teaching performance on the basis of their traditional professional norms. Throughout the period of my research in the school, there existed a residual staff suspicion of me because of this perceived vulnerability to my supposed professional judgments. Teachers, for example, regularly apologized to me for the academic performance deficiencies of their pupils – that they were not yet doing complex sentences or long division, and so forth. Similarly, when I arrived at their classes to begin observations, several teachers unfavorably compared their teaching to idealized and unrealistic conceptions they maintained of the performance of colleagues I had previously visited.

Other remarks of teachers acknowledged their awareness of my unusual access to information on the intimacies of life in some classes. Their perceived vulnerability, for example, was often expressed in joking. In my presence one teacher quipped to another who was about to receive my visit that "You haven't got a thing to worry about – only three people have lost their jobs so far!" Knowing of my interest in pupil peer relations, teachers frequently drew laughter in the lunchroom by warning their colleagues to watch their behavior, since I might be studying their peer groups too. Also, as compared with the staffs of the two non-public schools, the staff at PS 4 showed resistance to granting me anything resembling fictive teacher status. My general curiosity about the school and my resulting attendance at all types of school functions, including staff meetings, were not rebuffed, but they were not positively welcomed. Staff members indicated in nervous remarks that it would be more appropriate were I to restrict my study to children's activities. I was also never invited to informal staff gatherings away from the school, as I was in the private schools.

I attempted to allay the teachers' fears first by unobtrusively noting that my observational data were confidential and second by demonstrating this fact in my behavior, by disclosing as few of my impressions as possible when queried by other staff. I believe neither response did much to reduce the teachers' suspicions. To some extent I was able more successfully to mitigate these suspicions of me as a dangerous evaluator by taking on classroom duties that are usually associated with the more subordinate student role.

Such duties entailed helping to carry and lift heavy objects, assisting in the various forms of classroom clean-ups, making minor repairs to equipment such as phonographs, and so forth. At teachers' requests, I also frequently assisted children with various kinds of schoolwork, for example, going around the room to check answers or to help on certain simple cognitive operations. On many occasions I was asked to spend time assisting individual children by reading with them. At other times I was commissioned to lead small groups in recitation (reading out loud) or in math and spelling exercises with the use of flash cards.

This avenue of response was not without its problems, however. Although I did not feel I could refuse occasional requests to watch over the class when the teacher momentarily left the room, some teachers were less than pleased that for ethical reasons I eschewed any disciplinary role toward the children. Performance of other classroom duties, nevertheless, aided in the establishment of rapport with the study teachers by allowing me to reciprocate their cooperation with my research and by permitting expressions of deference that countered their fear of me as a dangerous evaluator.

Adapting to school organizational boundaries

In spite of, or perhaps because of, their fears of professional evaluations I might make of their performance, and the vague sanction given my efforts by higher administrative authorities, the PS 4 staff accepted my presence in their school as legitimate. In their assessment of this legitimacy, it was clear that my residence and research in the neighborhood were, at best, irrelevant factors. While all the teachers knew that my research carried beyond the school, my neighborhood activities appeared to be of little interest to them. Never, for example, did they ask what I had learned of the neighborhood.

I quickly learned that the teachers' lack of interest masked their fear of the threat to the boundaries of their authority that my simultaneous school and community activities posed for them. Again, their suspicion was that my outside contacts would lead me to divulge normally secret, damaging information to people who could then use it against them; in this case, the outsiders were parents and community activists. The few times that I mentioned in the school any item of information, however innocuous, showing personal familiarity with parents or community leaders resulted in looks of apprehension, raised eyebrows, noticeable tension, and momentary cooling of relations. For a few teachers, the mere fact of my residence in the community represented grounds for suspicion. My obvious membership in the Brownstoner category must also have been a factor in generating this suspicion.

It was necessary, in consequence, for me to be discreet while in the school about the existence of my contacts per se with parents as individuals and with community groups aligned with parents' interests. While I thus resolved not to discuss my neighborhood activities inside the school, I should add that there was no necessity for these activities to be conducted under stealth in order to be concealed from the teachers. The school staff, who resided elsewhere, were never present in the community when I worked there. This made it quite possible for me to adapt to the situation by keeping my outside life separate from my school life, much as the teachers themselves did.

The private schools: St. Michaels and the Wright School

Gaining entry to the private schools, St. Michaels and the Wright School, was a direct and uncomplicated matter. At St. Michaels, with an introduction from a community leader, I met with the principal to explain my research. After two days, during which time she checked that teachers in the requested grades were willing to entertain my presence, she granted oral approval. At the Wright School, the principal's permission was forthcoming within an hour of my meeting her. After we discussed my research plans, she had me wait in her office while she consulted with the first- and fifth-grade teachers whose classes I wished to study, and then she granted permission.

Both St. Michaels and the Wright School are neighborhood schools in the way that no big-city public school can ever be: They are both locally controlled and financed, and they have next to no administrative subordinance to higher-level structures. Additionally, the schools' respective teaching staffs reside in the community, for the most part, and share common ethnic and social-class orientations with the families they serve. School personnel and pupil families view each other in a much more positive and less suspicious way than is the case in the public school. Parents at both private schools are more knowledgeable and supportive of existing school practices as well. The cultural discontinuities between school and community, in sum, are not so great as in the public-school situation.

Both schools, being less bureaucratized, exhibit more collegiality in staff relations, show less concern with protecting their boundaries from outside interference, and are more permeable to community influences. The fluidity of school boundaries is evident in the many important supportive roles that parents, particularly at St. Michaels, play in the day-to-day operations of the schools – staffing the library, assisting in the school office, patrolling the halls, and substituting for absent teachers in emergencies. More than a few of the teachers, in turn, are parents or former parents of children in the schools. At St. Michaels, some are former pupils as well, and as community residents most teachers participate in the Brownstoner or Oldtimer associational activity that is centered around the schools.

In contrast with the situation at PS 4, where my simultaneous involvement in school and community affairs caused boundary conflicts and necessitated special adaptations on both fronts, at the private schools my simultaneous school and community activities positively reinforced one another in enhancing the rapport I was able to develop with informants in both settings. My entry into the private schools was eased by the fact of my previous ongoing participation in Brownstoner and Oldtimer community activities, where I had demonstrated my interest in and concern for the community and had become known to teachers in both schools. Even before I approached the schools for research permission, their staffs had had opportunities to observe and judge me.

Inside the private schools, my research procedures were the same as in the public school, yet the relative informality and flexibility of the institutions and their greater permeability to outsiders led the teaching staffs to define my activities in a more accommodating and favorable fashion. Where in the public school I was considered as a stranger, in both private schools I was quickly assimilated into the schools as an honorary member of their faculties. I was careful to keep my observations and interviews confidential, of course, but the staffs expressed no anxiety over school or classroom secrets that I could disclose to outsiders or administrators.

Treated and referred to by staff and parents alike as "Tim, the teacher," I was routinely invited to official and unofficial staff functions and honored with the staffs at their respective school testimonial dinners held for them by parents at the end of the school year. In addition, two months after completing my research at St. Michaels, the school lived up to the role assignment it had given me and asked if I might substitute teach for a week in one of my previous study classrooms.

Situational constraints, rapport, and research methodology:
a comparison of classroom and community

In all the schools I was restricted to a considerable degree to the role of silent, relatively passive observer. This was especially true of my activities in the classroom. There are many reasons that contributed to this restriction. As formal organizations, schools represent tightly bounded and articulated social systems. Institutional status roles are few in number, and in the interests of rational attainment of formal goals, they are carefully circumscribed by rules. Maintenance of procedure, order, and schedule are the predominant concerns of those in authority.

For the researcher the consequence is little maneuverability for role negotiation or action. The press of classroom and school routine allows researchers little latitude for accommodating their own agendas, which are fundamentally extraneous to institutional operations. In the classroom, for example, spontaneous interaction with participants is next to impossible. It is rarely possible to interview teacher or pupil participants to an event, such as a violent dispute, either during or immediately after it, when actors' accounts would be most fresh and accessible. Instead, hours can intervene before the schedule permits a few brief questions of actors, if it does so at all. Additionally, because participants' behavior is largely of a ritual or routine nature, there are few occasions for nondisruptive informal interaction with them. I found that variations in the degree of my acceptance by the school staffs did not alter these situational constraints peculiar to the classroom. Whether in PS 4 or private-school classrooms, my status as an outsider was always evident.

Because of the constraints against participation, my ethnographic accounts of class-room life are from an observer's viewpoint far more than from the viewpoint of a participant. The restrictions I encountered appear to be fairly typical in anthropological investigations of school life (Khleif 1974; Wolcott 1975d). Khleif has pointed out that as compared with the normal anthropological field situation the school setting "lacks . . . avenues for participation" by the fieldworker, that studying schools is an "essentially observer's, not a participant's function," and that the anthropologist finally "remains more of a stranger than a friend" (Khleif 1974:391).

As compared with my school activities, the greater diversity of research methods used in the community reflects the greater scale, complexity, and social heterogeneity of the community as a domain of inquiry requiring more diverse methods of approach. Also true, however, is that the more loosely structured domain of Chestnut Heights community life permitted such methodological flexibility on my part. Community life offers many opportunities for striking more of a balance between observation and participation and consequently presents greater possibilities for conversations and interviews with actors.

My residence in the community, in particular, was indispensable in granting legit-imacy to my presence there and in opening up many avenues for participation in its life. With considerable naturalness, for example, my residence there allowed me to shop for all my personal goods and services locally, seek my medical and dental care there, participate in the activities of my own block association, register to vote, be canvassed by political workers, be invited to political meetings of various kinds, take two adult-education courses at local churches, and utilize other community facilities such as the bank, post office, and bars. After my research had gotten under way and my local relationships broadened because of it, I engaged in mutual visiting and entertaining with neighbors and other informants, attended their weddings and other special occasions, celebrated religious and secular holidays with them, and exchanged cards, food, and other gifts at Christmas.

My local residence also legitimated my presence at the many community functions I attended. Residents, who knew I was conducting a study of the neighborhood, neverthe-less complimented me for my regular attendance at these affairs. None of the community functions, except block parties, were attended by more than a small minority of residents. My presence at them was seen by many as indicating my active involvement and my concern and interest in the community. In more than one organization, because of my dedicated record of attending meetings, and in spite of the fact that I had played no active roles in them, I was even offered positions of leadership.

A great many of the association affairs I attended were benefits and fund raisers of various kinds. These included boxing matches sponsored by the local Longshoremen's Union Scholarship Fund, bake and plant sales held by the PS 4 Parents Association, the Chestnut Heights Association's annual art show and sale, and its community house tour, the testimonial dinner sponsored by the LaBella Democratic Club for its leader, LaLucha's Puerto Rican Discovery Day Street Fair, and the St. Michaels Parish Council's special Hawaiian night and "St. Paddy's" dinner dances. My attendance at these affairs demonstrated my moral and material support for the sponsoring organizations and their constituencies.

The participation roles that were possible permitted my engagement in many forms of reciprocity with local residents. These ranged from those intrinsic to unfettered informal conversation and face-to-face interaction to those with a more material basis, such as the dispensing of Halloween candy, patronage of local businesses, or financial contributions to community organizations and causes. All contributed to sustaining interaction with residents, allowing for mutual demonstrations of good will, and defusing suspicions on both sides. In consequence, I was permitted great flexibility and latitude in actively negotiating my role with different individuals and organizations and was able to gain greater access to actors' perspectives than I was in the school setting. These aspects of my community relationships, as I have noted, increased my acceptance by the private-school staffs, facilitated easier access to information on schoolwide affairs, and made my private-school research less tension ridden, although they did not influence the quality of the classroom data I was able to obtain.

Problems in managing diversity: loyalty conflicts and the maintenance of confidence

To some extent my ability to maintain rapport with so many separate groups was enhanced by the structural boundaries and political cleavages dividing them. I learned to adapt my speech usages, language choice (English or, occasionally, Spanish), topics of conversation, and interaction style to the group I was currently dealing with. Because the different groups so rarely came into personal contact with one another, I was largely able to keep my relationships with them distinct from one another. In attending events in the Hispanic blocks, for example, I hardly ever encountered anyone from among the Brownstoners or the Oldtimers. Similarly, Oldtimer and Brownstoner gatherings, whether formal or informal, were typically group homogeneous. Although each group maintained extensive stereotypes of the others, each was fundamentally ignorant of the others' ways and lived its own life largely in isolation from the others. Similar boundary maintenance, as I have noted, insulated public-school staff from community residents. My research in this heterogeneous community and its schools constituted, in some respects, several separate but concurrent fieldwork experiences.

Many boundary and loyalty conflicts were, nonetheless, unavoidable. Demands, some more subtle than others, were made for me to demonstrate loyalty by performing services to show gratitude for aid and confidences extended me. Had I been studying a single group or institution I would have been more easily able, ethically and politically, to respond to these demands. Because many of the requests would have entailed public actions implicitly or explicitly counter to the interests of other groups in the community, I had to decline or otherwise evade most of them. Some of these loyalty and boundary problems arose from role conflicts generated by simultaneous school and community research, and others arose from simultaneous research on different community social groupings.

Not surprisingly, most of the difficult requests came from the Brownstoners. Because of my cultural similarities to them, Brownstoners tended to assume, inaccurately, that I shared their judgments and general outlook on the community and its groups. They expected that I would not hesitate to lend whatever skills or information I possessed to serve their interests in community affairs. For example, with the explicitly stated aim of improving the Wright School's image and enrollments, I was asked by the local Brownstoner-controlled weekly newspaper to write articles favorably comparing the school to the others in the community. In another case, the primary Brownstoner civic association, the Chestnut Heights Association, which had few if any ties to the local Catholic parish of St. Michaels, wished its cooperation in their efforts to "improve the neighborhood." Aware of my acquaintance with parish figures, the association's leadership pressed me to serve as their St. Michaels liaison.

The PS 4 teachers were realistic in their fears that my outside contacts with parents would subject me to pressures to divulge confidential information of their classroom performance. The staff saw the middle-class Brownstoner parents as pushy, interfering, and condescending. Brownstoner parents, who enjoyed a measure of influence over school affairs through their control of the Parents Association, did in fact attempt to extract information from me on teachers' classroom performances. They hoped to use this information in their political efforts, as individuals and through the Parents Association, to change school practices and, in some cases, personnel. My own ties to the school were not threatening to the Brownstoners, who assumed that I shared their own negative stereotypes regarding the teachers, who they thought of as provincial in outlook and manners, lacking in social sophistication, and lower in social standing than themselves. With the Brownstoners it became necessary for me to protect the confidentiality of my classroom observations by scrupulously refraining from reporting them, even though this did dampen rapport with some parents who resented my terse, vague responses to their questions. As one parent remarked to me, "You sure don't let out much, do you?"

Whereas Brownstoner parents sought to use me in their efforts to intervene in PS 4 affairs, and my school research enhanced my status with them, my school connections were a hindrance to the development of rapport with Puerto Rican parents. The Puerto Rican parents view themselves and are viewed by the school as socially subordinate to the teachers and as linguistically inept in dealing with the school authorities. Each party considers the other to be culturally inept in their dealings together. The Puerto Rican parents had little familiarity with the nature of graduate research and interpreted my presence at the school to mean that I was a functionary of the school system, despite my many attempts to explain otherwise. As an "American" who was not too dissimilar in appearance and manner from the school staff, and as one who had access to their children's classrooms, most Puerto Rican parents assumed I was in a position to judge their children's school performance and to influence their fortunes there. I found interviews with the parents, in their homes or elsewhere, to be punctuated by displays of deference and by their insistent seeking of my reassurance that their children were well behaved in school. No substantive information on school practices was forthcoming from them. I learned to approach Hispanics whenever I could by referring not to my PS 4 connections but rather to my status as a university student. This was not entirely successful, however. My strategy of approaching the group through its voluntary associations, most of which had dealings with the school, made it difficult for me to shed the label of "the man from the school."

I learned a great deal from the more politically active Puerto Rican parents, such as those associated with the local antipoverty organization's Education Action agency. Their comments in interviews invariably centered, perhaps again in response to my imputed school status, on their extensive criticisms of the school's methods of handling and categorizing their children and on the Brownstoner parents' insensitivities to them in Parents Association activities. Interviews and other interaction with Hispanics unconnected to the school similarly gravitated to the unjust treatment they believed they were accorded by Brownstoner civic and political organizations. Never, however, did the Hispanics – whether parents, community leaders, or other residents – ask more than sympathy of me.

Oldtimers did not fully assimilate my explanations of my research and were wont to categorize me in more familiar ways, as "that college boy" or as an aspiring schoolteacher "working on his master's." Many of the St. Michaels parents, of course, knew me as Tim the teacher. In retrospect, I can only conclude that they saw my specific research activities as rather benign in nature and as having little to offer them one way or another. In any case, any advantages that they could gain from my research data were overshadowed by my more immediately useful moral support of and involvement in their financially beleaguered parish school. Being vaguely associated with the school staff enhanced their acceptance of me, as teachers are viewed as dedicated and underpaid professionals whose work constitutes a sacrifice for the good of the community and its children. The only problem requests from Oldtimers were for my labor in Democratic Party political work in support of candidates for elective office opposing Brownstoner-supported candidates.

In such a heterogeneous research site, with so many different and competing interests, it was clear from the outset that no single group's perspective could offer a complete, unbiased account of the community. Questions of objectivity aside, it is clear that the plurality of viewpoints in the community provided a constant check against any one of them gaining ascendancy in my analysis. Curiously, this was particularly true in the case of the Brownstoners, the grouping whose cultural outlook I shared more than any other in my private life. My relationships with Oldtimers, Hispanics, and school personnel assisted in giving me a more detached and comparative perspective on the Brownstoners' roles in the community and toward me as a researcher. Perhaps not unexpectedly, I found it necessary to develop an especially critical and questioning frame of mind in my dealings with the group I most resembled.

Conclusions: Is participant observation viable as a core methodological technique?

Because participant observation is tailored to the study of informal, face-to-face behavior, many anthropologists have questioned the technique's utility to research in complex urban settings. Some have pointed out the limitations of participant observation's characteristic ground-level underview for an understanding of urban form and organization (Fox 1977:19–20, 157ff.) The greater degrees of scale and complexity and the higher levels of sociocultural integration demonstrated in urban settings can severely tax the utility of a methodological technique refined in the study of clearly bounded, small-scale cultural units (Weaver and White 1972). Similar objections have been made regarding the technique's weakness in producing significant insights into formal organizations and the cultural roles they play in complex societies. Steward noted that ethnographic research "could deal only with . . . culturally-prescribed *institutional behavior*" and believed that in factories and other national institutions such as schools, "this behavior would represent only a very incomplete portion . . . of the larger cultural functions of the institution itself" (1955:63, his emphasis).

It would appear, however, that so long as thoughtful adaptations are made to the exigencies of the newer urban research settings, participant observation can continue to serve as the core methodological technique in anthropological research. Wolf (1966) and Weaver and White (1972), among others, have contended that the task of contemporary urban anthropology is to elucidate the often neglected linkages between face-to-face behavior and "large-scale sociopolitical phenomena and issues" (Weaver and White 1972:117). This end does not require the abandonment of traditional ethnographic methods, Weaver and White suggest, but rather their continued employment, in a "strategy of working from the bottom up, drawing on intensive analysis to find the threads by which the sociocultural determinants of action within situational constraints influence these larger phenomena" (Weaver and White 1972:117).

My own research has led me to argue elsewhere (Sieber 1978) that such analytic linkages as these observers call for are facilitated when research focuses on informal face-to-face behavior occurring in schools and similar public institutions. This is because schools and kindred ideological institutions serve their "larger cultural functions," in Steward's terms, by carrying out "people work" (Goffman 1961) – by inculcating new forms of social relations, values, and skills in their clients (Sieber 1979). The primary vehicle for such "people work" is the naturally occurring, face-to-face informal interaction among teachers and pupils in the classroom, a phenomenon highly amenable to study by participant observation.

In Chestnut Heights, through supplementary participant observation research on community social differentiation, it was possible to suggest linkages between these observable school processes, the New York City occupational structure, and local patterns of class and ethnic differentiation. Such analytic linkages were possible because, in facilitating pupils' socialization in modes of behavior appropriate to formally organized work settings, the schools' social processes contribute to the orderly future recruitment of the community's young people into adult occupational roles. Comparative school analysis, as well, indicated that the differing pupil role socializations afforded by the schools consolidate local group identities and boundaries by offering children the socialization variant fitting them to assume the characteristic adult work roles of their particular group (Sieber 1978).

My Chestnut Heights research leads me to believe that, in participant observation in complex urban settings, problems of rapport and situation management more than equal any analytic problems that may arise from deficits in collectable field data. In the case of my own research, data generated through participant observation have lent themselves to forms of computer-assisted quantitative analysis, as well as more conventional qualitative forms of analysis. In any case, other methods (such as interviewing and archival research) are available as complements to participant observation to ensure that the collected data are adequate for analytic purposes.

The sheer complexity of many urban communities, however, with their cultural heterogeneity and conflict and their welter of structural boundaries, can approach practical unmanageability for the solitary participant observer. The necessity of regularly crossing social boundaries untraversed by locals can bring social and psychological tensions to the research process. Such tensions, moreover, are especially likely to fall to the lot of participant observers heeding Nader's (1974) advice to "study up," particularly if study focuses on the relations of large-scale organizations with their publics, as my own experience with public education indicates. The researcher must adapt to different settings that require differing balances of participation and observation. He or she must learn to play many roles and to present many faces.

Yet it is precisely these features of cultural heterogeneity, social complexity, role differentiation, and multiple levels of integration that, anthropological theory has long noted, characterize the urban scene in complex societies. My own research experience suggests that there are benefits to be gained from encountering these features directly in the research process, rather than attempting to circumvent them, if indeed it is possible to do so. Participant observation in complex urban settings affords the researcher personal social experience and thereby enhances analytical appreciation of cultural complexity. The regularly occurring discontinuities in one's own research behavior can serve to alert the researcher to the patterning of such complexity. The encountered structural discontinuities, cleavages, and boundaries also provide a necessary temper to the tendency of participant observation research to overemphasize cultural uniformity and consensus in study populations.

The practical problems and social tensions that participant observation generates for the researcher are not, in any case, new or unusual in anthropological research. Similar experiences have been reported by others, as in Henry's study of political attitudes among Trinidadian workers and management in a political situation that had become highly polarized during her research (F. Henry 1966, 1969). Powdermaker (1966) acknowledged similar problems in describing her 1930s research on race relations in a southern American town. Such problems as I experienced in using participant observation in Chestnut Heights do not appear to be different in kind from those encountered by other researchers in complex settings, whether the settings are modernizing or industrial, rural or urban, here or abroad.

The traditional anthropological search for homogeneous groups and communities, for which the method of participant observation was developed and is still most applicable, will no doubt continue to lead many researchers to a more manageable focus on well-bounded cultural isolates or on organizations and higher-status groups as if they were self-enclosed entities. Dividing responsibility for different sociocultural groups and institutions among different fieldworkers in "team research" (e.g. Price 1972) is another promising option in the handling of culturally diverse situations, one that allows the individual researcher to avoid boundary and loyalty conflicts. To achieve closer analytic linkages between informal face-to-face behavior and higher-level structures and cultural processes, however, most researchers will have to confront the kinds of social tensions I experienced in Chestnut Heights. My own experience indicates, in balance, that accommodation to the tensions is both possible and profitable for the participant observer.

PART VI Contract anthropology

The contract has become a symbol of those who have made their mark as applied anthropologists. The sorts of expectations and issues that contracts pose, however, require the anthropologist to be very sensitive, very creative, and very wary.

Kerry D. Feldman takes us through two difficult cases of contract research in Alaska, one for the federal government and one for the state (Chapter 15). He describes and analyzes problems of ethics, time constraints, and incompatible expectations, and he discusses the ways he approached them and ways in which they might have been avoided. Often, he notes, the hiring agency is itself at or near the center of the problem under investigation. This is a conclusion (and a barrier to good research) that is familiar to many who have shared the contract experience.

Ruth M. Houghton identifies anew one of the oldest and most serious problems of doing anthropological research anywhere, the communications gap (Chapter 16). In her case, there is a three-way gap between the hiring agency, the researcher, and the subjects of study. Her research was conducted in rural Nevada for a federal agency. Her methods of working with the local people and the problems of communicating her findings to the agency in particular were complicated by the history and goals of the agency and its past relations with local citizens. Her advice is relevant to all who deal with relatively inflexible bureaucrats and a suspicious public.

15 Anthropology under contract: two examples from Alaska

KERRY D. FELDMAN

Almy (1977) has discussed the problems involved in engaging in anthroplogical research as a member of, and on behalf of, an operational decision-making agency. Her comments were primarily directed toward contractual arrangements between an anthropologist and international-assistance nature rural-development agencies. The problems noted, however, are relevant to a consideration of contractual work within one's own society:

1. Many academics have minimal contact with non-academic society, except in their roles as researchers of exotic cultures. They thus find it easier to subscribe to the major current in American ideology which equates power with abuse, and bureaucracy with corruption by the rich and exploitation of the poor...Anthropologists beginning agency work with this negative attitude, however unconscious, guarantee both themselves and their agencies a bad time. For this and other reasons it is probable that the majority of anthropologists today are unfit to function adequately in an agency setting. (p. 281)
2. Anthropologists have seldom been in a position to comprehend the resource constraints under which agencies in their research area work...This is a joint failure of the agencies...and of the discipline, which trains its members to research and write without regard for the needs expressed outside the ivory towers. (p. 282)
3. Agency work usually involves teamwork, whereas the academically trained anthropologist is familiar only with isolated projects for which he or she is solely responsible for design, execution, and report writing. (p. 283)
4. Most agencies still think of anthropologists as generalists, like Malinowski or Mead, not realizing that various specialties identify most sociocultural anthropologists graduating from universities today. (p. 285)
5. The contracted work is usually something to be performed on some group other than the contracting agency, whereas the holistically oriented anthropologist usually views the job as involving an understanding of the contracting agency as well. (p. 286)
6. The research project itself may reflect the agency's goals, assumptions, and hidden orders from higher up, which may, in the anthropologist's opinion adversely affect the subject population. The ethical position of the anthropologist (Society for Applied Anthropology 1974) will not allow him or her to engage in projects that will adversely affect the lives of those studied. (cf. Almy

223

1977:286–288). The anthropologist then must either quit, render himself or herself ineffective, or ignore personal ethics and go along with the agency.

7. In general, bureaucratic constraints in a variety of areas are unfamiliar ground rules for the anthropologist (for example, inadequate time frames, format and jargon needed for reports).

These problems and others will be explored in light of two contrasting contract efforts I engaged in among Alaskan-based agencies, one of which, in 1975, was with a federal agency, the other of which, in 1976, was with a state agency. The involvement with the federal agency resulted in my becoming part of a legal action against the U.S. Department of the Interior by the State of Alaska Department of Law. The sequence of events in this situation is instructive not only for the anthropologist who might be considering non-academic contract work (or a career with a public agency) but also for agencies considering employing anthropologists on a contract basis for a specific task.

Contract anthropology: federal agency

In the spring of 1975, I received a phone call from the Anchorage-based Outer Continental Shelf (OCS) Office of the U.S. Department of the Interior. A social scientist was needed to write the draft environmental impact statement (EIS) for the proposed leasing of tracts in the Gulf of Alaska for oil exploration. The social scientist was to evaluate possible impacts on human social and cultural groups in the area and elsewhere in the state of Alaska if oil exploration was engaged in there and extraction of the oil was to commence. A complete description of the initial discussion period with the OCS office elucidates the subsequent legal action.

My name had been suggested to the OCS office by a faculty member of a local community college, who had received a similar call. Because his primary graduate training had been in the field of archeology, he felt unprepared to write an EIS on contemporary human social systems. His split assignment at the college had required him to teach an introductory sociology class, which seems to have been the reason why the OCS office called him about the request. It was explained to me by the OCS office that if I was unavailable for the task, the archeologist or perhaps even a sociology student would be contracted to do the work. This apparently cavalier attitude on the part of the OCS office toward locating a qualified social scientist to begin preparation of a document supposedly important in the decision-making process of the Secretary of the Interior to lease or not lease outer continental shelf tracts for oil exploration in an environmentally rich area disturbed me. In addition, the small, predominately native (Tlingit) village of Yakutat was very likely to be used as a staging ground for operations.

My initial reaction was to refuse to accept the contract work, because (1) I had no prior fieldwork experience in the state of Alaska (having arrived from the University of Colorado two years earlier after completing a dissertation on urban squatters in the Philippine Islands, I then became absorbed in administrative work at a fledgling university); (2) the OCS office refused my request for travel funds to visit the area in question for personal research among the inhabitants; (3) the report was to be completed in two weeks, then later extended to four weeks, which was in my opinion still too brief a time period; (4) only already published materials could be used, which were almost nonexistent for Yakutat and other communities. Nevertheless, I consented to write the EIS, provided that the OCS office would give me a written statement to the effect that my report would not be changed by them except for minor editing on format, style, and grammar to keep it consistent with other sections of their report. My motivation in accepting the task does not, in retrospect, appear to me sufficient justification for taking part in an obviously pro forma exercise that had little chance of being a valid impact statement. My justification was this: If I did not do the work, there seemed little likelihood of a trained professional social scientist being utilized for the draft document.

Different expectations of the contract situation between the organization and myself characterized the entire relationship. Foster (1969:157) summarizes well the differing expectations between representatives of disciplines and those of professions. First, the report was to me a document for which I would have to accept personal responsibility. OCS insisted that this was not the case, because I would not be cited as an author. Not being listed as an author of my report did not alter in any way my feelings about responsibility.

Second, the OCS office assumed that much consistency should characterize the entire EIS, especially as regards the projected population figures for the area resulting from high and low development scenarios. They opted for a method of projecting population inducements to various communities that was arbitrary, resulting in an unrealistically low figure for increased population in the largely native village. I was not an expert in demographic projections related to large-scale technological projects, so I wished to utilize figures prepared by a presidential commission on the same project during the preceding year. Whereas the OCS increased-population projections for Yakutat were fewer than 200 people even under high impact conditions, the presidential commission (also perhaps in a somewhat arbitrary manner) projected figures in the thousands. Since I had to limit my database to existing sources of information, I wished to include the commission's figures. OCS compromised by allowing references to both estimates. In editing my report, however, they always added words that indicated that the commission's estimates were unrealistic in comparison with their own. The need for internal EIS consistency meant accepting the OCS office's game plan for playing down possible major impacts in all ways in the reports, I subsequently discovered.

Third, although the contract required me to examine social and cultural impacts, the OCS office expected me to focus exclusively on social impacts (jobs, schools, sewage, electricity available, roads) rather than cultural ones. They really did not know what a cultural impact on a generally native village might be. Most of the communities to be affected were nonnative, and culture change was not a item of major concern. I felt that the task required attention to the implications of culture change in the largely native village and attempted to explain to the project director the basic rudiments of Northwest Coast culture. (I had done fieldwork among a British Columbia coastal native group and was familiar with the literature on this ethnographic area.) To most of the OCS person-nel, a native was a native, and no understanding of cultural differences between the Indian, Aleut, and Eskimo populations of Alaska was evidenced by office staff, with one exception. To most of the OCS staff, it seemed to me, it was only a short time until these anachronistic cultures would be absorbed into the dominant culture. The project director was personally convinced that the native peoples of Alaska had already been given too much special consideration and social and economic assistance.

What was expected of me, it seemed, was to be a company man. Foster (1969:156) refers to this as the assumption that "achievement of organizational goals represents the highest value." This form of behavior was the basis for the promotions individuals received within the agency and it was implicitly held up to me as a behavioral norm worthy of acceptance. In this case, being a company man meant accepting the agency's nonpublicized goal of moving as quickly as possible to open up oil exploration and development staging areas, regardless of social or cultural impacts. By engaging in general discussions with various persons in the office, this attitude became quite apparent to me. I felt trapped by the situation. The part-time nature of my involvement with the agency, plus my training and experience as a social scientist in an atmosphere of academic freedom, precluded my becoming a company man and thereby relinquishing personal responsibility for my report and accepting a constraining value decision – development of potential oil production sites regardless of the negative social and cultural consequences to the inhabitants of the area – that had nothing to do with social science.

Cordial interpersonal relations characterized my relationship with the entire OCS office staff until I discovered that my hand-written reports about the village of Yakutat were being significantly changed in the typed version. The OCS officer in charge of the EIS made no attempt to conceal his so-called editorial alterations. He was somewhat surprised when I confronted him with the situation. The final version of the EIS was his responsibility, he explained, not mine, so I did not have to worry about the changes. It was at this point, about midway through the six-week interaction period, that our perceptions of each other began to change. I began to keep copies of everything I wrote, and he must have made some sort of decision to wait until I had completed my report and ended the contract period before he again made major editorial changes. It was at this point that an anthropologist more experienced in contract work would, in my opinion, have terminated the contractual agreement unless stronger safeguards were taken to ensure the validity of the report. Because these safeguards were impossible to obtain from the OCS office, given its understanding of its task, we should have terminated the contract agreement.

As I completed my report, the OCS office hired a full-time sociologist (a former college instructor of sociology whose doctoral studies were in the field of education), a conscientious person, but one who had never seen Alaska, an Alaskan native village, or a major oil development operation offshore. He completed the EIS section on social and cultural impacts and the director submitted a final edited version. It was not until several months later that I found a copy of the final EIS, discovering also many major changes in my report. Major impacts were altered to read as minor ones, in accord with the seemingly a priori conclusion reached by the OCS office that only minor impacts to social systems would result, no matter what the magnitude of the discovery of oil might be. The leases were taken, a half million dollars was bid on the various tracts, but to date no major discovery has resulted.

The Department of Law of the State of Alaska asked near the end of 1975 if I would submit an affidavit concerning the alteration of my report by the OCS officer as part of a legal action the state was taking to halt or slow down the proposed leasing action.[1] I filed the affidavit with the state, which presented its case to a court in Washington, D.C. Subsequently a front-page story in a local newspaper disclosed my charges in bold headlines, creating somewhat of a furor at the OCS office. Their reply to the press was that only politically motivated aspects of my report were changed. They did not understand, the project director explained to the press, how I could be upset, as we had ceased the contract work under cordial circumstances and I was paid around $700 for my work. This was true; we had parted cordially, because I was unaware of the final alterations to be made. Although I did not return to confront the project director directly upon discovering the alterations, I did invite representatives from his OCS office to participate in a panel discussion with me at a conference during which the question of ethics and social science in regard to preparing EIS documents were discussed. Lawyers for the state requested that I not confer about the dispute with local OCS people named in my affidavit. This has prevented, even to the present, a personal discussion of our varying expectations. I was told by a member of the local OCS office, however, that an investigator from the Department of the Interior visited Anchorage to find out who I was and what I might be up to. It was inconceivable to them, it seemed, that a social scientist would attempt to protect his discipline from misuse without other motives being involved. For nearly a year I remained concerned that my phone was being tapped and my personal life being scrutinized in preparation for a character attack at a court hearing, because, in my opinion, the substance of my charges could not be challenged. No court hearing was requested, however; the state lost its appeal, leasing action was held, and a new administration took over in Washington. With the Carter administration and a new Secretary of the Department of the Interior, a new attitude characterized the local OCS office, one that allowed for a slower-paced leasing schedule, and more complete EIS attempts.

In doing contract work for any local branch of a federal agency, the anthropologist is inevitably affected in this work by decisions, modus operandi, and pressures present but not always seen from the national headquarters of that agency. It is difficult to separate the limiting political aspects of such contract tasks from the social science. Although the university-based and trained anthropologist is familiar with the political parameters of university decisions in regard to new positions, funding for new programs and such, he or she is likely to be rigid in dealing with non-university bureaucracies, expecting at times the ideals of a nonpoliticized university quest for learning and new knowledge to be real, operative qualities outside the university. This is a chimera, an immature expectation perhaps resulting from reading classic ethnographies without finding therein a personal account of the numerous political or local bureaucratic constraints imposed on most, if not all, data gathering and reporting.

Graduate training and contract work

More than a recounting of the Camelot episode (Horowitz 1974) is required in graduate coursework to avoid the culture shock sometimes entailed in doing research within one's own society under contract for one of our own bureaucracies. A more productive working relationship is evidenced in Clinton's (1975) experience, with the other end of the spectrum found in D. Jones's (1971) work. As courses in fieldwork are now part of graduate training programs (rather than expecting students to absorb reliable field method strategies by osmosis from reading ethnographies), the growing literature on anthropologists in agency settings could be included in such courses, or perhaps more appropriately in applied anthropology courses (Barnett 1956, Erasmus 1961, Foster 1969, Beals 1969, Mair 1969, Cochrane 1971, Belshaw 1976).

What should be clearly recognized is the possibility that any contracting agency may already have goals in mind for the work requested and want documentation for an already held position. As Trend (1977:212) has noted, experienced applied social-science research organizations are "willing to work on problems that have been partially defined beforehand by a government agency." The individual anthropologist must decide whether such limitations are unacceptable and avoid attempting midstream to redirect the goals of an entire multi-faceted bureaucracy that possibly is scattered all over the country. Part of the problem may also reside with the agency, in that a strictly policy implementation matter (for example, opening up areas for oil exploration as rapidly as possible) might involve something requiring what the agency calls research but that in actuality is documented propaganda. Although anthropologists are familiar with hypothesis-testing research that delimits the range of data sought, they are not familiar with or trained in attempting to squeeze data into a policy-defined research effort. In this regard, Chambers (1977a:419) notes: "The academic orientation is usually toward testing and elaborating methodological assumptions. Non-academics tend to relate method and strategy to client needs and to the exigencies of a particular research situation." He refers later to the "culture of policy," which, besides being a clever pun, draws attention to the problems noted in the case study above. At this point, however, I am still uncertain of whether I was calculatedly deceived or whether I did not appreciate the "culture of policy" of the Anchorage OCS office. Fairness to the agency requires this more favorable interpretation of the contract's fulfillment on its part.

Contract work: state agency

The OCS project was undertaken at the end of a semester during a time when I served as head of the division of social sciences. Administrative duties made such nonacademic projects too time consuming. To gain more time for research work, I resigned from the administrative position. A phone call from the Alaska State Human Rights Commission almost immediately thereafter brought me into a six-month, part-time contract arrangement to work on a project I thought would be challenging and interesting. Having felt burned by the OCS experience, I explained at the outset the parameters of agency control over my work that I would accept. The response to this statement, and subsequent agency interaction, were completely different from the OCS experience. I would be free to utilize whatever methodology seemed appropriate to me to accomplish the project's task, within budgetary limits, and no alteration, not even editing, of my final report would be made. Why the difference in treatment?

The structure of the Human Rights Commission partly accounts for the difference. There are two major components of the commission: (1) a governor-appointed board of commissioners composed of unsalaried citizens from around the state; and (2) an office staff of salaried employees who report to an executive secretary who in turn is accountable to the commissioners. The legal and investigative expertise of the office was part of a bureaucratic operation, with various levels of decision making, daily duties to attend to, and performance evaluations of the staff made annually. The policy-making power of the commission resided with the commissioners, however, and new citizen appointments were regularly made. The commissioners also judged whether allegations made and investigated were valid and ordered appropriate penalties or alterations in behavior. They were citizens, primarily from minority groups, whose actions were measured not in terms of whether they reached some bureaucratic measure of performance but in terms of adequacy in equitably combating various forms of discrimination. They did employ measures of the office staff's organizational efficiency by analyzing a number of cases received and closed annually. As minority citizens, they had nothing to gain from bureaucratic doubletalk, vest-pocket agendas, or alterations of research reports. Actually, they were themselves impatient at times with the extensive rules by which they had to govern themselves and with any indication of organizational self-serving or issue obfuscating by the staff. When I informed the chairwoman of the commission that I could undertake the project only with the understanding that I would also be observing and reporting on the commission, she welcomed the suggestion. It was a matter of common sense to her that any research attempt to assist the commission in its work would have to consider the functioning of the commission itself. The commission might have been part of the problem they were hiring me to work on, and, if so, she wanted this reported.

The project was complex, centering on discovering the need for and interest in establishing local human rights commissions in nine Alaskan communities. In addition, where feasible, attempts were to be made to assist local groups in establishing local human rights commissions by city ordinance, however titled and empowered. The communities (Fairbanks, Juneau, Ketchikan, Dillingham, Bethel, Barrow, Nome, Kodiak, Sitka) were over 1,000 miles apart (1600 km), ranging in size from over 45,000 people to less than 3,000, with ethnic composition ranging from predominately nonnative Caucasian to primarily native (Eskimo, Aleut, Indian) centers. I was to be paid a substantial salary (approximately $7000) for the six months of part-time work (full-time during the summer months), derived from grant funds provided by the Alaska Humanities Forum, which had funded the commission's grant request proposal.

In distinction to the OCS contract situation, my tasks were much less specified than researchers are accustomed to. This end of the research freedom–control pendulum presents as many, if not more, problems than the other end. Again, there was the initial feeling on my part that my time had been bought by the organization, and that they were more knowledgable than I about how it should be spent. It was their project, after all. Whereas the OCS organization knew how to control the individual social scientist (the entire machinery of the Department of the Interior was behind them) and how to place in a proper perspective the academic credentials and titles an individual paraded around, the commissioners were in a different situation. None had the degree or education I had; this was for most their first experience with holding a position of substantial public power and they expected (most of them, at least) that a social scientist would have special, unique methods for obtaining information that lay people would not be familiar with. I was referred to as "Dr." at initial meetings, and I reciprocated in the first few weeks of interaction by playing the role of a completely self-sufficient and competent social scientist from the university. (At the OCS office I was addressed and referred to by my first name from the beginning of the interaction.)

My tasks were identified as follows:

1. "Map" the operating structure of the commission, including the goals and principles by which it attempted to be guided.
2. Devise a data-gathering strategy for the nine communities, including ways of quickly identifying key individuals and validating informant observation.
3. Discover a report-writing style that would best convey to the commission the results of my research (professional-journal style or popular-media style; amount of detail, proportion of generalization statements to concrete detail, and other style and format questions needed to be resolved).
4. Establish a mechanism by which local action groups could be effectively formed in the communities, bringing the knowledge and expertise of the state-level commission to bear when needed.
5. Formulate a strategy for ensuring continued local human-rights group action after I ended the project.

I did not grasp the full complexity of these five tasks until about one-quarter of the way through the project. I did point out to the commission at our first formal meeting prior to fieldwork that nine communities was probably too large an undertaking for a six-month project. It was never clear to me upon what basis these nine were selected. If this project had resulted from a proposal that I had written, there would have been two phases to it: (1) a trial case of one or two communities, which would have required six months to complete, and (2) an expansion of the project to another community for another six months to control experimentally more of the variables involved in changing local government based on knowledge gained in Phase 1. The researcher should have been able to live for three to six months in the communities to gain at least a working knowledge of their stresses, areas of political power, communication links, economic situations, and personalities of members of the city councils and the mayors. With nine communities involved, however, the above information had to come from the perceptions of key informants in the project, as there would be no time available for me to live in any of them for longer than a few days. In Alaska, we have come to call this form of community research hit-and-run anthropology. The negative effect of this mode of data gathering is that small communities become entrenched in their suspicions of outsiders who drift in, drift out, and file reports that possibly no one reads.

The anthropologist as quick change artist

Establishing a workable role in a research setting is among the first tasks facing the anthropologist. The role must be flexible enough to allow a wide range of data-gathering activities, honest enough so as not to deceive the people as to why the researcher is there, and somehow acceptable to the people studied. For the traditional ethnographer there is usually ample time in which to work out an acceptable role definition with the group. I had engaged in to fieldwork projects prior to the State Human Rights Commission project which prepared me, I thought, for this task. Among Kwakiutl-speaking Indians of British Columbia I had spent one summer engaged in ethnohistoric research and eventually was accepted as a person attempting to learn about their remembered history. I spent the daytime hours with the village elders and other time with younger people joining them in whatever they were doing (subsistence fishing, partying, playing cards, working on equipment). It took only about three weeks to change some of the initial roles assigned to me by various subunits in this village of around 1,100 people. These initial roles were: a new minister (we occupied the former minister's home, as he was literally thrown out of town the day we arrived); a new doctor (our house was across the boardwalk from the missionary hospital, and several of my informants resided there); a drug pusher (some young people back from college assumed that young Caucasians would be selling drugs). Establishing a workable role in an environment that remains unchanging while the researcher is there is not usually an insurmountable task. Time and patience, careful and clear repetition of one's purpose, and much visibility among the group will solve many of the problems of adequate role definition. The only problems encountered in this regard after several weeks were with the young people who returned home late from school in Vancouver. These had to be assured and convinced I was not intent on digging up graveyards.

In an urban environment, satisfactory role definition is more complicated (Chambers 1977b:262). The study population of my Philippine urban work was scattered along a north-south route some 20 miles (32 km) in length, and even at the end of the ten-month project I was still explaining my purpose to people. The experience I had gained on role definition in the traditional ethnographic experience among the British Columbia natives only minimally transferred to this Philippine urban setting of over four hundred thousand people, most of whom were recent migrants from other islands following World War II. I found that intensive interviewing and participant observation required more formal procedures for gaining entrée. Through my work with local medical professionals in establishing a paramedic training program for the urban squatters I hoped to study, formal meetings with barrio leaders were arranged. In this manner I was passed on from house to house in a barrio. But each time I went to a new location for work, I had to have a formal introduction arranged by a locally known and respected person. This was essential in some areas for guaranteeing my personal safety. The local person who would take me around the barrio established my role for me by what he or she said in introducing me. This third-party introduction was needed also when I worked through governmental institutions of the city. There was no homogeneous group, geographically or socially, with which I could establish an identity once and for all and then proceed with research.

These two experiences in role identification were not inadequate preparations for the contract work research with the Alaska Human Rights Commission. The ingredients were all scrambled: time, social context, geographical context, mission, product expected. I went through three phases, it seems, in my anticipation of encountering the nine communities. At first I was excited to be out again doing research. I climbed aboard the plane to visit a southeast Alaskan Caucasian community wearing a sports jacket, briefcase in hand, per diem in my pocket, and a sense of being part of the Alaska State

Human Rights Commission. They were the good guys, were they not, battering down the walls of injustice. When I discovered that my task required sitting in a motel room for several hours initially making phone calls to set up meetings, often with people who didn't want to see me, flagging taxis to move me around quickly (it rains in southeast Alaska more often than not at the time of year I was there), and listening to pieces of community life without knowing how they fit toegther and with very little time to sort them out, I began to lose my enthusiasm for the task. The second phase found me putting off boarding another plane for other communities on any pretext. As I visited the rural communities (referred to as bush communities in Alaska) I discovered that the Alaska State Human Rights Commission was not viewed in as favorable a light as I had anticipated. Now my entrée was somewhat destroyed. I shifted from explaining that I was with the commission to saying that I was working on a project for the commission. This allowed me personal space, more independence. Both the with and for statements were true, but I emphasized each in different contexts. This changed my attitude toward myself also. I was an anthropologist, not simply a commission employee and I had the holistic approach of anthropology's ancestral spirits to carry forward. Some of the pieces began to fit together, because community problems tended to be structurally similar. This led me to my third phase, a renewed enthusiasm for the project, for its challenges, and for dreary hotel rooms. By midsummer I was in a fishing community on the coast and my report to the commission from that city was a radical change from earlier reports. I attempted to synthesize the numerous interviews into a readable, comprehensive document that would educate the commissioners by placing human rights concerns in their broader sociocultural setting. When, because of some of their culturally patterned behaviors, Filipinos were resentfully discussed in the coastal community, I drew upon knowledge of Philippine culture gained from my earlier fieldwork. When employers referred derogatorily to native Alaskan work habits, I added in my reports what I knew about the subsistence life style the native people were supplementing by wage labor. I began linking economic variables with cultural ones, educational problems with bureaucratic pressures, history with legal questions, social arrangements with cultural norms. I learned to apply the holistic view of anthropology to understanding small towns' discrimination problems.

The major limitation on my work was time, and this forced me to utilize the key-informant method. I have usually found that this method limits the range of variability discovered in societies and leads to unimodal descriptions of multimodal phenomena. It was a limitation I could not escape given the contract I had accepted. The more rigorous methods of social science are sometimes unfeasible. When in doubt about a respondent's assertion, because an adequate test of it by other means was not possible due to time constraints, I would note the assertion in the report to the commission but include a caveat about the degree of confidence I could place in it. The commission wanted more of this ethnographic reporting. I came to see that any social-service institution operating in a multicultural setting of any size needs the anthropological approach for adequate functioning.

My role definition varied somewhat from community to community, ranging from Human Rights Commission investigator to social scientist, management consultant, and social-change activist. Several role changes might occur during a single day. All roles were accurate, in a sense, but each was somewhat determined for me by the perceptions of the person I was interviewing.

The contracting agency as part of the problem it investigates

The State Human Rights Commission recognized that few of its cases came from rural areas in the state. Yet, the cases that were brought before it from rural areas indicated that severe human rights problems existed there. The project I headed was an attempt to alleviate this situation by attempting to work with local people in outlying areas to establish local human rights commissions. A local commission would need to be established through an ordinance passed by the local city council.

A rural community in Alaska generally is a predominately native settlement, of which there are around 200. During the previous year, in 1975, 16 percent ($n = 100$) of the cases brought to the commission were by Alaska natives, but the majority of these were by residents of urban centers. Females charging sex discrimination accounted for 40 percent of the 618 cases that year. Black citizens filed 22 percent of the charges, which is a much higher proportion than their total population proportion in the state.

An examination of the characteristics of the personnel of the commission's regional offices revealed a partial explanation of these results. Most staff workers were female or black, with a few Caucasian males employed as well. There were no field investigators or regional directors who were native Alaskans (Eskimo, Indian, or Aleut). It would sometimes happen in the northern region that a black male investigator from an urban center would visit a small community to investigate charges filed by a native person. I discovered negative (discriminatory) feelings on the part of many native people towards black people, and they preferred not to discuss their complaints with a black investigator. In southeast Alaska, the office director was a Caucasian female, and a different problem was discovered. Native males did not wish to utilize her services, and native females were somewhat reluctant to confer with a Caucasian, regardless of sex. The personnel infrastructure of the commission was interfering with its operation in outlying areas. Rather than becoming defensive when confronted with my observations, the commission responded immediately by putting a native male in the southeast office and by setting up a regional office with a native male as director in the northern Eskimo area. (The latter effort was already in progress prior to my work in the north.) In a way, these decisions were compromises with the ideals of the commission itself, because they accommodated native prejudices toward blacks on the one hand (racism) and traditional native attitudes toward males as rightful holders of positions of power (sexism). Nevertheless, the commission had been remiss in its failure to employ native people in nonclerical staff positions (although native males and females were members of the Board of Commissioners at the time) and acknowledged this omission by hiring the native males for the positions created.

Anthropologists in contract situations for agencies are likely to be aware of the inter- and intrasystemic nature of any research problem. "Studying up" organizations (Nader 1974) is one means that allows the social scientist to understand a formerly overlooked area of the social system in our own society: the decision makers and power brokers of the system.

There is the danger, however, that in doing contract work the anthropologist will be so intent on satisfying the agency who has purchased his or her services that this aspect of social-science research will be overlooked. When this occurs, the holism of anthropology is not brought to bear on the tasks.

In traditional fieldwork projects in other cultures, the researcher is generally aware of the potential impact that agencies have on the population and even on the data-gathering process itself. Schwab (1970:104) reports that during his Rhodesian urban study, "my field assistants reported that African policemen were interrogating our African informants after they had completed their interviews with them . . . It was quite obvious to us that if the police continued to interrogate our informants, the study would abruptly end." Usually the public agency involvement in any research effort is more unobtrusive and remote, and requires careful tracking to discover the linkages. Some researchers, however, claim that if contract work is undertaken the researcher must avoid bringing to the public view the agency-related material that will bring an unfavorable response from the public.

The researcher, working for a commercial firm, or even for a governmental agency, must develop an ethic of responsibility. He defines the problem on which he will work in a way which will be useful to his sponsors. He deals only with material which is salient to their defined needs and interests. He writes, edits, and censors his own material so that it will appear in a way which enhances the interests of his employers. There is no implication here of outright dishonesty. The researcher who did other than this would be violating his contractual obligation to his employers if he exposed them to an unfavorable limelight or to public attention which might cause embarrassment. This is only to be expected. [Vidich and Bensman 1968:408–409]

This expectation in my opinion limits the role of the social scientist to such an extent that doing social science is not really possible. The researcher has another option: to point out to the agency that a problem can only be fully explored if the agency itself is allowed to be part of the research problem investigated. It is in my opinion outright dishonesty to claim that a piece of research represents objective social-science findings when in fact it does not and it intentionally omits relevant data. Such research is part of an epistemological imperialism, not social science per se. It removes from the researcher part of the responsibility of defining his or her role vis-à-vis any contracting unit.

The end of the affair

When is contract work ended and how does this end differ from the conclusions of self-generated research?

In self-generated research, I am aware of the intellectual tradition which preceded my own research on a topic. Conceptually, I fit my research into a stream of work made real by its summation in written reports, monographs, or conference papers. I can continue to be a part of this stream by further research and publication, or I can simply read about its continuation. The work then belongs to the world of scholarship. The act of writing can ritualistically (or psychologically) mark the conclusion of such a research effort for the individual. Whether or not the task was worth the effort, pain, and expense is often measured by terms of the document (written, film presentation, etc.) that summarizes the effort and that can be evaluated by professional peers. There continues to be a sense, however, of the document's partial definition of my identity. I conceived the project, nurtured it, gave it birth, and know it came from me (even if others contributed much to its production).

In contract work, a different set of personal reactions to the end of the work are likely. The product is not as much mine as it is the agency's. I may not be aware of the agency's traditions in regard to the contracted work and cannot fully appreciate where it fits into its stream of work. Libraries and colleagues are not likely to see the material products (report, etc.), so that the act of writing will not have its usual cathartic effect on me. For all I know, the report might eventually be lost by the agency. I end up with memories, filed reports, and a paycheck. When contract work ends, the termination of the personal concern and effort is abrupt and seemingly conclusive. The perhaps enjoyable involvement with nonacademics terminates and the academic subculture again encapsulates me. The contract period may seem not so much a part of my continued personal and professional functioning and identity but a chunk of time and energy wrenched out of my personal context. It began in medias res and ends the same way, because the agency's life quickly moves on to new problems and I may have no time to reenter its work stream.

In terminating my contract work with the Human Rights Commission I felt that the work was incomplete, even though I had met the conditions of our agreement. Of the nine communities, only three seemed interested in and capable of organizing a drive to establish local commissions. Eventually, some positive results were achieved in those communities that are only now being realized. Only one community went through all the stages of setting up a local commission. The other two communities would have been further along, I believe, if the contract period had not ended, because one community already had a human rights commission established by a city ordinance but the mayor had withheld suitable funding for anyone to head it, and the other had an active citizens' group (before I arrived) that urged the city council to adopt such an ordinance. Even though I had to return to university tasks at the beginning of the academic year, I flew to the former community to meet with a local newspaper editor who supported the establishment of a local Human Rights Commission and arranged for the director of the Anchorage Human Rights Commission (where I lived) to travel to the city and meet with the local city council. He provided data that demonstrated that the presence of the state's Human Rights Commission office in Anchorage did not reduce the local commission's workload significantly (an argument that the mayor had raised, as a branch of the state office was in the city). It was this kind of continued contact with each community that was needed, I think, to bring to fruition the efforts of local groups who wanted a viable Human Rights Commission but lacked the knowledge needed to counteract the efforts of other groups and individuals who rejected the proposal.

The completed reports on each community for the commission contained information for future action. Part of my noncontinuance of active involvement with the project on a volunteer basis was a professional decision: I did not wish to become known as the human rights anthropologist. I do not wish presently to be primarily an advocate of any ideological position, but rather a student of society, although advocacy work is not opposed in my opinion to the gathering of objective social-science data (see Jacobs 1974, Peterson 1974 for a more complete discussion of advocacy work in anthropology).

Because social agencies are praxis oriented, the end of the research effort with them occurs when the researcher is no longer a part of this praxis. In theoretical research, one can continually be involved (or feel involved) in the work by further reading on the subject, even when active research on one's own on the subject has terminated.

Anthropology in one's own society

As Hughes (1974:332) observed, "We may one day be studying no one but our peers, people who might just as well be studying us." The challenges facing a Yoruba anthropologist studying the Yoruba are probably no different than those facing American anthropologists studying American urban society. Effective application of the methods of participant observation and holistic research (Basham 1978:300) to work among "co-culture bearers" is made difficult by an overfamiliarity, in some cases, with the subject matter. Whereas anthropologists in other countries have accused Western anthropologists of never understanding fully their societies or cultures because of the unavoidable strangeness of the researcher to the society studied, this very strangeness, we often claim, allows a more objective and perceptually innovative response on the trained observer's part. Anthropology performs the dual function of making what is strange (to a nonparticipant) at least understandable from some theoretical premise and, conversely, making what may appear to be understood (to the insider) into something strange, not immediately apparent, or at least problematical. The initial impetus for this dual functioning is, however, not the answer but the type of question one brings to a subject. Question types flow from disciplinary paradigms (Kuhn 1967), and the anthropological paradigm has been said to consist of the comparative method, the holistic approach, an emic/etic analytical dichotomy, case-study emphasis, and a systems/processes approach (Hunter and Whitten 1977). To what extent is the anthropologist at home able to provide an etic analysis of his or her own society? To what extent is an emic analysis objective in such a situation? One assumes that one does not have to track down conceptual, structural–functional linkage in one's own society to the extent that this is required when one is a total stranger. Perhaps underlying the traditional anthropological paradigm was an unstated assumption: The observer is a total stranger. By being a stranger, unique question types could be generated, at least more easily: *"Nemo judex in causa sua"* (no one should be a judge in his own case) the old Roman proverb states, but if pushed too far this maxim would preclude Homo sapiens from studying Homo sapiens, wherever found.

I think that some degree of strangeness to a situation is required to understand it adequately or ask adequate questions about it. In studying aspects of one's own society, it is extremely difficult to assume the various poses Hatfield (1973) satirically ascribes to the anthropologist in another society: the incompetent dope, the incompetent child, the incompetent pawn, the anthropologist as Fort Knox, the anthropologist as sahib, and so forth. It seems essential, however, that in the anthropologist's own head he or she feels like a stranger to some degree to the subject matter of the investigation. Too easily one assumes that one knows relationships, latent functions, and symbolic meanings, simply because the research is done in one's own society. The task is to make the familiar seem strange to oneself.

Attempting anthropology under contract is doubly difficult in this regard, because one might need to become a stranger to both the contracting agency and the project's subjects. The anthropological paradigm can be made operational, without a doubt, in research on one's own society, under the contract relationship. If the pitfalls described above in contract work are avoided through open discussion of expectations at the outset of the venture, the unique approach of anthropology to understanding social processes could become more accepted and more often requested by contracting agencies. The anthropologist will be in a position, as Evans-Pritchard suggested, to "see problems in their full administrative context as well as their full anthropological context" (Evans-Pritchard 1946:97). Problems in our society generally could profit from both perspectives.

16 Talking to an agency: communicating the research findings

RUTH M. HOUGHTON

Lounging there at ease against the wall was a slim young giant, more beautiful than pictures. His broad soft hat was pushed back; a loose-knotted dull-scarlet handkerchief sagged from this throat; and one casual thumb was hooked in the cartridge belt that slanted across his hips. He had plainly come many miles from somewhere across the vast horizon as the dust upon him showed. [Wister 1902:6–7]

This is the American culture hero, the cowboy. Considered "spectacular and romantic" by scholars (Webb 1931) and other Americans, the cowboy life style was an integral feature of nineteenth-century western North America. Today cowboys at home on the range have become another endangered species. Cattle live in feedlots rather than on the open range, and cowboys drive trucks instead of horses across the vast horizon. Reflections and remnants of this cowboy life style are to be found in some communities of the American West, however, including rural Nevada, where I conducted research in 1976 for a United States government agency. The nineteenth-century patterns of open-range land use and social isolation persist here and are justified locally by community values of independence and pioneer self-sufficiency. Modern economic demands and changing priorities in American land use suggest that the open-range cattle ranch is an anachronism.

The agency for which I worked (the Bureau of Land Management, U.S. Department of the Interior) is required to carry this message of changing conditions to the ranchers and other residents of rural Nevada. Thus in my work I was confronted with a major quandary. My task was to describe for the agency the regional life style and its social components and values, values that include an attitude of autochthonous rights and privileges in land use. The agency attitude, however, is governed by national American goals for land-use policy and the modern demands of urban recreationists for access to rural lands. Agency staff and their national goals were viewed by local community residents as uncaring and ignorant of local conditions, whereas local residents were considered hostile and obstructionist by agency personnel. The romantic haze of cattle ranching added to this charged atmosphere and obscured views from both sides. The agency was accused locally of trying to put ranchers out of business and destroying the

238

fabric of local communities. Where did my work fit in and how was I to proceed in this setting? As a result of this project and several years of reflection since then, I realize that a critical aspect of my work was to be able to communicate to the agency staff the knowledge I had of the local communities and life style. I had to learn how to talk to the agency.

To talk to the agency I had to recognize the culture of the agency itself and present my research results in such a form that they could be integrated into agency activities and given priorities by staff.[1] I also had to be cognizant of my own research goals, however, and to utilize my anthropological perspective to develop and present my data. I learned that there are two major dimensions of the culture of an agency that an anthropologist must consider: (1) the agency's activities and goals and the contribution an anthropologist can make to these must be recognized by the research as she or he proceeds; and (2) the researcher must learn the communication patterns of the agency to be able to transmit research results to agency staff members.

The first dimension, the agency activities and goals, requires a knowledge of the agency history as well as present operations. In some respects the Bureau of Land Management (BLM) is similar to other federal and state government agencies, in that its activities are directed toward the so-called public good, that amorphous quality that is transmitted and interpreted at various administrative levels and originates, theoretically, with elected officials and their constitutents. As one reads the literature of public administration, however (an area of political science that an anthropologist must consider when venturing into the agency domain), it becomes clear that many variations of policy interpretation and administration exist for any agency.

In certain features, though, the agency I worked for is unique. It has the largest land base of any federal agency, and it is being required to shift rapidly from its traditional stance as a western agricultural agent to a new orientation that includes many diverse clients. These clients are gaining expertise in lobbying and judicial tactics that result at times in great pressure on the agency, yet the agency lacks the public interest and lobbying support that other agencies may draw upon in times of crisis. The broad range of issues the agency must consider is bewildering to me and must certainly be taxing to staff members or citizens who knew it in its earlier and simpler days.

The second aspect of talking to an agency requires that the researcher understand how to communicate with staff members. Communication with staff members is complicated by (1) the fact that anthropologists and their work are frequently unfamiliar to the personnel of agencies for which research might be conducted; (2) the highly academic rather than applied orientation of anthropology; and (3) a staff that in many agencies is oriented more to natural science and quantified analysis than to social science and its qualitative approach.

To consider the first complication, it must be noted that sociocultural anthropology is unknown in many government departments, including the BLM. This and most federal agencies know only of archeology and found it hard to apply this knowledge to sociocultural analysis. Agency-oriented archeology has been widely established for a decade or more, particularly for salvage work in which an area is surveyed before dams or roads are constructed. Some salvage ethnology is being done today, especially in California, but most sociocultural anthropology remains foreign to American agencies, as indicated by the fact that although the federal government has an employment register through which hiring is administered, the category of sociocultural anthropologist did not even exist on this register in 1976, when I was employed. The closest job category was sociologist, something I am not.

Another feature of the communication realm that must be recognized is that anthropology is an academic discipline in which a theoretical self-consciousness prevails. Most government agency staff, as well as people in business and others in the nonacademic world, do not admire academic and theoretical concerns. These people want "real-world" knowledge and definitive action with applications of knowledge. They consider academicians such as anthropologists to be unrealistic and of little immediate value. An anthropologist, however, is trained (particularly at the graduate level) to respect academic standards and there is a feeling in the discipline, though it is seldom expressed, that people holding doctorates and working at nonuniversity jobs must be only temporarily employed outside a university. The serious anthropologist who works full-time in a nonacademic position must justify this strange behavior. Applied anthropology is good in textbooks, but full-time employment in this sphere is considered suspect.[2]

Additional problems of agency communication come with the third complication – the fact that staff in many agencies, and certainly in the BLM, are oriented to natural science rather than to social science in their training and work. Staff knowledge is geared to quantitative rather than qualitative analysis. Also, staff members may have selected jobs in natural-resource management rather than in the people-oriented fields of social science because of greater interest in resources than in people. Anthropologists, with their primary orientation toward social sciences and only occasional brushes with the natural sciences, are not always well prepared for quantitative analysis.

The agency

The Bureau of Land Management, United States Department of the Interior is a major agency in the western states because of its role in regulating use of federally owned public lands. These lands were once administered by the U.S. Land Office, created in 1812 to regulate disposal of land. The 1872 Homestead Act and the 1877 Desert Land Entry Act were administered by this office. In 1934 Congress passed legislation to regulate grazing of the public lands and created the Grazing Service, which was merged with the Land Office in 1946, creating the BLM. Today the BLM also administers recreation, mineral exploration and leasing, wildlife habitat, and other public land uses. Sixty-eight percent of Nevada's land area is administered by the BLM, and a total of 86 percent of the state is controlled by various federal government agencies rather than state and local authorities or private owners (only Alaska has more federal land within its borders).

The former western frontier of open lands and free-riding cowboys was effectively closed in 1934 by the creation of the Grazing Service and subsequent increased regulation by the BLM (see Webb 1931, Peffer 1951). As early as the turn of the century, grazing on upland and mountain areas came under regulation by the U.S. Forest Service, but vast plains and valley lowlands remained open in the West until 1934. Many residents in western communities vividly remember the impact of this final closing of the open range.

The final loss of open range was signaled by the 1934 Taylor Grazing Act, which created the Grazing Service and established regulations for use of the American grazing lands that many ranching families had used freely for fifty to seventy years. A few large operators like John Taylor (unrelated to the Taylor of the Grazing Act) and the Miller and Lux outfit had used vast areas of Nevada for cattle and sheep ranching. Small operators, sometimes lacking a permanent base or home ranch, also had used the open range. Now all users were to be restricted. They were required to prove their claims of use and establish that they could also provide winter feed from their own private lands, so that grasslands could be left to rest and be protected while new growth came in the spring. Payment for range use and limits on numbers of animals also were requirements of the Taylor Act, and Grazing Service staff rather than ranchers were to decide how many animals grazed and when, where, and for how long grazing was allowed. One provision of the act that did gain public support, however, was the requirement that a range user be a United States citizen. This article of the act was directed against the Basque sheepherders, many of whom gradually built up their own blocks and used public rangeland in competition with other users. Many Basque herders intended to return home to Spain or France with their profits rather than remain in America, so they seldom became U.S. citizens. (Basques in the American West are described by Douglass and Bilbao, 1976.)

Since 1934, many other changes have come to the BLM that affect ranchers in Nevada and other western states. A multiple-use policy is in effect on the range and on other American lands such as the areas regulated by the United States Forest Service. This multiple-use philosophy for BLM lands was established by the BLM Organic Act of 1976. It allows diverse users access to the land so that off-road vehicle drivers, bird watchers, and other recreational users all are welcome. This act also specifies more rigid guidelines for protection of animal species and habitats. The policy further restricts the traditional land-use patterns of ranchers and other residents of rural western communities.

An example of the impacts of multiple use and its impingement on ranchers involves the disposition and handling of wild horses and burros.[3] Both species are legacies of Spanish contact in the New World and are not indigenous to America. Protected now by 1959 and 1971 acts of Congress, wild horses were previously hunted for dog food (A. J. Liebling, "The Mustang Buzzers," *The New Yorker*, April 3 and 10, 1954). Today horses (as well as burros) are increasing rapidly in number, and 35,000 of them, or more than half the United States population of wild horses, are in Nevada. Wild horses, or mustangs, compete with domestic stock for water and forage and utilize resources allocated to domestic stock and paid for by ranchers. Urban residents across America, however, believe mustangs are an important symbol of the west that should continue to be protected and even be allowed to increase in number. The promustang people are well organized as a lobby force for congressional action. Ranchers and range-management experts often regard mustangs as "old plugs" that are worthless, although some range and ranch people privately admit that they too like to see a few wild horses because this sight represents freedom.

The problem of multiple use for the range users is compounded by the legal structure of American government. The BLM is the agency required to implement congressional acts and national decisions about BLM lands because it is an arm of the federal government.

But this situation places the agency at odds with rural residents, especially ranchers. The government operates under the congressional mandate that publicly owned lands such as BLM's millions of acres are collectively owned by all United States citizens. People like the rural Nevadans who live adjacent to the lands and may depend on the lands for economic survival do not have a legal priority over other Americans in resource use. Local ranchers, however, argue that they must have some say in the control of these lands, and in 1979 the Nevada state legislature initiated legal action against the BLM so that Nevada could gain more local control of these lands. The outcome of this move is uncertain.[4]

BLM administration in Nevada is directed from the state office (Reno), with six district offices to handle local matters. The state office staff coordinates agency planning for all six districts, and as individuals the BLM people in Reno have infrequent contact with rural residents. The outlying district-office people have the responsibility of day-to-day communication with rural residents. Many rural people resent most BLM activities and all federal government intervention. Tensions run high at times and provide a difficult setting for district employees who must confront irate citizens and implement agency programs. The agency is locally perceived an a vague and impersonal force that becomes focused when a BLM employee appears. Thus accumulated anger and frustrations are sometimes expressed to hapless staff members who may have had nothing to do wih the events causing the local concern.

Within the agency a policy of frequent staff transfers prevails, so that many BLM employees remain for only two or three years in one district. Hence they fail to become integrated into local social networks. However, the transfer policy does serve to protect agency staff. In some small towns of the state, some businessmen might occasionally refuse to serve a BLM staff member as a means of expressing local resentment against the agency's activities. Some employees and their spouses have received counseling to enable them to cope with such overt negative public opinion.

Some local sentiments are expressed in these comments:

We should have BLM get out of here; that is not personal as there are some nice guys there, but we need local control.

The BLM is out to put ranchers out of business.

For most ranchers this BLM situation is the toughest thing we have had to face for years.

We have great ore and water in this area that we could use if the government were less restrictive. [field interviews]

Some resentment is caused by frustration at the impersonal character of the agency. A newspaper editor emphatically asked during an interview: "How can you talk to a bureau?"

Thus I was confronted by this complex setting in which an agency and the local population were adversaries. I was unaware of the complex history of the agency when I started my research in 1976, nor did I realize at the time that knowledge of BLM would be essential to the research task.

The research task

I started doing fieldwork in Nevada in 1965 with the traditional other-culture experience, in this case analysis of a Nevada American Indian reservation community (Houghton 1968,

1973a, 1973b). My work in Nevada continued, and by 1976 I had expanded it to include the economy and culture of the entire northwestern region of the state. In 1976 I met BLM state office personnel while I was organizing a statewide conference on public land use (Houghton and Nappe, 1977). I was organizing the conference with funds granted me by the Nevada Humanities Committee, a nonprofit organization that has a counterpart in each state. These state humanities committees receive funding from the National Endowment for the Humanities to further understanding of community issues by bringing together laypeople and university-based specialists in various kinds of information programs.

I learned that the BLM had a need in its planning activities for a description of the population of one district, the district that includes an Indian community that I had studied. (The research that I conducted for the BLM has been reported in an agency publication, Houghton 1976, and in Houghton 1978a, 1979b). This research was to be a description only, and no hypothesis was to be tested. In May 1976 I signed a contract with the BLM to complete a report that would "describe extant cultural groups and their relationships to, and dependence upon, attributes and management of national resource lands in Humboldt and Pershing County areas of Nevada." These relationships were to be "affective and emotional rather than instrumental and economic."

The information was to be used as background preparation for agency activities and future policy decisions. The report was part of a socioeconomic profile of the Winnemucca district, and the objective of a socioeconomic profile for this or other districts was

to assure that the BLM has available, at the state and district level, information pertaining to:
1. socio-economic factors that affect, or are affected by, management of national resource lands;
2. infrastructures relating to national resource lands;
3. Bureau relationships and coordination with governmental entities (federal, state, and local), action, study and interest groups, and key institutions and individuals. [BLM Planning System Manual #1601]

Research results

In my final report, local values that characterized the district were emphasized. These included a regard for individuality and self-reliance as paramount qualities. Personal interaction and the identification of unique features of people and of local places were also important. Three major principles of social organization emerged as the bases for the local analysis of the resident population of the district. People were organized into groups by three major criteria, and these groups may cross-cut each other in actual practice. The three principles of social organization were: (1) length of residence of local people; (2) ethnic ties, which may be used to identify individuals: and (3) the specific geographic locale in the district that may be associated with a person to describe him or her.

The first of these, long-term residence, dominated many other criteria used by local residents to describe an individual. Long-term residence was valued highly, because it signified that a person was committed to living in the district and thus was considered to care about the local people and the local landscape. This principle accounted for much of the strong influence that ranchers have maintained here and in other rural areas of the state. Long-established residents such as ranchers represent continuity in Nevada, where history has involved rapidly fluctuating population growth and membership because of the mining booms and later tourism and gaming developments.

The second of these principles of social organization was ethnic ties, including racial identification. Major ethnic groups that have remained viable cultural entities included Basques and Paiute Indians. Basques started arriving in the late nineteenth century as sheepherders. Some became respected citizens and ranchers while others lost their economic holdings under the 1934 Grazing Act. Today Basque is a generally respected identification. Indians were the original residence group, but they do not enjoy high status because they do not share Euro-American attitudes towards work, productive land use, or the value of the English language. Other groups, such as the Chinese, once lived in the area, brought in for construction of the transcontinental railroad in the 1860s. But the Chinese disappeared from the region early in this century. A more newly arrived ethnic group, the Mexicans, was identified. There are Mexican farm and ranch laborers in the area, but their purported illegal entry gives this group a low local status. It should be noted that many individuals found here were not classifiable as members of a particular ethnic group, and in general a nonethnic identification was of higher status than an ethnic identity.

The third principle of social grouping was to identify people with a specific locale. Each town or valley in the district was considered unique, and a person's birthplace or present location was used to identify her or him with local referents. By contrast, temporary residents or newcomers lacked a clear identification with locations in the district. It should be noted that district residents had little interest in classifying people with reference to employment. This approach contrasted with urban practice in large-scale society in which persons are known more by what they do than who they are. This attitude toward length of residence creates a major barrier for BLM employees who come to the district as temporary residents lacking any permanent or long-term identification. They are conspicuously identified by themselves and others in terms of job activity rather than as unique personalities or individuals. In addition to overcoming the barriers created by BLM association, these employees also lack local ties that can positively integrate them into the community. They must strive to become personally known and individually identified by the local residents. Despite the barriers, however, some BLM employees in this and other Nevada districts have succeeded in becoming established in local communities.

Religious identification can also be important in some rural Nevada districts because of the state's history as part of Deseret, the Mormon state. Few Mormons, however, are found in the district I studied.

Research methods

Culture and community

The definition of culture has long been argued about by anthropologists, but training in anthropology does not prepare anthropologists for the problem of explaining culture to nonanthropologists. One approach that I found useful for discussion with both agency personnel and others is to use the words "life style" instead of culture and to talk about what anthropology can learn. My own understanding of culture was best expressed by Marvin Harris (1971:136) as the "total socially acquired life-way or life-style" of a group of people. This assumes that a culture is a sociocultural system. Therefore:

We may thus speak of the functional unity of socio-cultural systems as a basic postulate underlying much of socio-cultural analysis. It remains, however, a matter of empirical research to identify the fuctions of a given [cultural] trait, that is, its precise contribution to the maintenance of the system, including always, first and foremost, the survival and reproduction of the group itself. [Harris 1971:141]

Harris goes on to explain that a culture has technology, social organization, and ideology as major components.

There are three adaptive aspects of the total social system: 1) ecology, or the way the system is adapted to the physical environment, 2) the social structure, or the arrangements by which an orderly social life is maintained, and 3) the mental characteristics that fit people to their social structure and their ecology. [Harris 1971:144]

The use of these statements for reasonable explanation requires that one provide everyday examples, if possible, and they can be used as the basis for an explanation of the researcher's own project. In any event, the researcher must explain what she or he is doing and why. In my case, I spoke of the lack of information about how ordinary people lived and the life style to be found in the district. I explained that there was a current need for information to be used in the decision-making process by the agency and that this information would affect local people. My work would be used by the agency; thus the research project was not an academic exercise that would end up in an archive as just another report. It was of immediate value.

I explained that information I acquired was to be confidential and that I would be visiting with people in the district to learn of their opinions and lives. I was defined and accepted by subjects as a communicator between them and the agency. Many people felt distant from the impersonal agency, so, as one person said, "I am glad to be asked what I think so that BLM can hear me." I described my project more often than I defined culture, but I implied that the ordinary life style of the district was as worthy of analysis as was some distant exotic culture.

The notion of culture must be considered with the concept of community as a basic framework for analysis. Anthropology interprets materials by means of the intensive, small-scale approach of participant observation and assumes that the community is a basic social unit of any culture. The large scale of complex societies has deterred some anthropologists from studying their own cultures and has raised doubts in other disciplines about the efficacy of anthropological analysis in large societies. Weaver and White, however, have responded to this criticism in their discussion of urban anthropology:

In sum, as regards to notion of scale, we find that the immediate contribution of anthropologists is not an attack upon large-scale sociopolitical structure and issues, where sociology, economics, political science, history, and applied disciplines are particularly strong, but a strategy of working from the bottom up, drawing upon intensive analysis to find the threads by which the sociocultural determinants of action within situational constraints influence these larger phenomena. Informal social processes, nonformal types of action decision making, and the study of fundamental modes of human transaction and communication – with the anthropological analysis of the symbolic and material components of action – figure as principal contributions, drawing from what we have learned in the study of nonurban societies and studies of the community and total society. [Weaver and White 1972:117]

In studying rural American society the notion of community is a basic framework for analysis. A community is a social network with historical continuity and spatial boundaries. Residents may be dispersed over a large area, over many square miles, but if they regularly interact and can identify individuals at the distant boundary, a unity can be established. In Nevada there are natural, physiographic barriers and transportation links that help identify social boundaries as well. A town in itself can be seen as community, but a dispersed rural population may also have this same kind of unity. Often schools and their participating families are good indicators of social-intercourse networks and parameters (see Burch 1969).

As fieldwork proceeds, the researcher can often identify community boundaries through mutual expectations, such as in dress or greetings, that prevail. In Nevada today, cowboy hats and boots are not a good index of life style, because many nonranch people affect this style of dress. A rancher is also just as likely to wear a baseball cap and rubber boots for protection from sun and wet fields. By comparison, on the west coast of rural New Zealand where I have also conducted research (Houghton 1978b), regional boundaries are visible because within this area people will wave or signal from their cars to other passing vehicles, even if they are unacquainted with the passengers. Outside of the coast this is an infrequent practice. I recall one man, serving as temporary relief driver for a gasoline distributor, who was reprimanded for failing to wave back at strangers. He soon acquired the habit. Coast New Zealanders value personal acknowledgment, just as Nevada ranchers value their style of dress, as a community boundary marker.

Interviews

In the Nevada research I interviewed fifty people, each for an hour or more and always in their own homes or offices. I encountered only one refusal. People were selected on the basis of personal acquaintance or introductions by others, never at random. They represented the major communities and a variety of economic sectors and ages as well as both sexes. It took about two weeks to complete the interviews, as each hour of interviewing required some additional time for preparation and transcribing and analyzing notes.

Logistic considerations must figure in planning research because of travel time and cost. The study region of 10,000 square miles (26,000 square km) has slightly fewer than 10,000 people. Many parts are sparsely populated and it took several hours on dusty secondary roads to reach a family home. Sometimes a specialized vehicle was required. There was no public transportation in much of this region. Other researchers concurrently studying another Nevada Great Basin ranching community solved the travel problems by means of horses or even private planes. One such researcher relied extensively on a rough-country motorcycle for local transport.

My interviews were arranged by appointment, and at the first meeting the purpose of the research was explained. I always emphasized that I was not a regular employee of the

BLM. Being an independent researcher was an advantage in this region. Each interview started with some personal conversation, so that I was identifiable as an individual with a personal history and a family. This introduction style established the type of familiar ties that characterized local relationships.

Interviews did not have a schedule of topics, because of federal government restrictions from the Office of Management and Budget requiring approval of formal interview schedules to be used by a minimum number of subjects. Also, I wanted to cover a variety of topics as they might be introduced by the interviewee. I did expect people to talk about their own family circumstances and opinions, and I was striving for an interviewee-centered interview rather than one that was researcher oriented.

People freely expressed their opinions about the BLM, but they did not dwell on this issue. They spoke of their lives and hopes. The western ideal of individualism prevailed in comments like this: "We will fight to survive. We like this life. People are now gone who can't stay here and take it." On the other hand, ranchers also recognized that circumstances were changing:

There are so few of us now compared to townspeople. Ranchers used to pay their bills once a year and the town waited for us to come. Now they have income from tourists and the farmers and they do not depend on us anymore. [field interview]

In agency research the interview is a major source of general information, but it must eventually be supplemented with systematic and detailed data collection. In the kind of short-term, intensive interviewing that I conducted, the anthropologist is more of an observer than a participant. The intensive effort requires that rapport must be established quickly for effective communication. There is seldom a second chance to correct a disastrous move or misunderstood motives. The researcher must convey personal honesty and openness.

Simultaneously, there must be an accurate representation of the purpose of the study, the agency, and the researcher. I found that the successful researcher must have certain personality features with which to handle the brief but intensive contact with people. The interviewer cannot be overbearing, yet he or she must be confident and calm and able to accept what comes, whether it is verbal abuse or distasteful food. Nor is it easy to receive a strong rebuke from an angry man who is a local leader. In New Zealand I encountered a man who disliked the idea of any government agency hiring a consultant. He objected to my intruding on his family privacy. We met several times, and finally, to my surprise and pleasure, he publicly apologized to me, and, as an indication of his respect for me, called me a "lady."

An identity as an academic is a liability in a rural community. Any unknown person is an intruder, a new face, in the face-to-face society of Nevada. The elite-and-aloof perception of academics creates barriers that must be anticipated and overcome. On occasion, however, one has to assert academic qualifications and identity to be heard with respect by agency staff and other specialists. It takes some practice and a few mistakes to decide when to be introduced as "Dr." and when to get down to informal, first-name presentation. As a female I also had to deal with the barriers that introductions create, because few women are expected to be highly qualified academically. I have now acquired business cards for meeting agency people, and some other people, because these cards are references that many professionals understand and respect. In the meantime, it took some practice and a few mistakes to decide when to be introduced as "Dr." and when to use informal "Ruth." One informant solved the academic status problem by calling me "Dr. Ruth" to reconcile the distance of academic respect with a more personal identity.

The intensive listening required by interviewing is exhausting. In one instance, two months and hundreds of interviews left me unable to relax and listen casually even in groups of people I already knew. The bulk of my Nevada work, however, was briefer and I was never isolated from family concerns as I was in New Zealand. I suggest that for a project of less than six months, in which interviewing is basic to the data gathering, it is best to work alone and intently. This very deep immersion in the new setting allows some fresh insight that the researcher soon loses if distracted by family issues or a more casual pace of entry and work. This is especially important for married women who have many demands and expectations placed on them by others.

The kind of short-term project described here is likely to become more important in the future for agencies that require or allow some social anthropological analysis but are unwilling or uninterested in funding the in-depth study that is traditional and preferable in anthropology. An intensive but short research effort is better than no anthropology at all. It is important to consider this kind of research when a compromise between expediency and scholarship arises; some knowledge of social anthropology can be directed toward agency policy and activities in a short-term project.

Working for an agency

The methods of research are important, but the information obtained does not serve its major purpose if the officers of the agency or organization involved cannot interpret and utilize what an anthropologist offers. The anthropologist offers a philosophy and specific information.

To one who wishes to study farming [or ranching] societies as wholes because he believes that farming problems go beyond such matters as markets, credits, and the techniques of production, cultural anthropology offers useful procedures and experiences. [Redfield and Warner 1940:993]

Our specific findings arise from the research itself, but agency staff must have confidence in the researcher, the anthropologist. In turn, the anthropologist must make a special effort to be aware of agency goals and problems if the research is to be successfully integrated into agency activities. In short, the anthropologist must understand the full context of both agency and research problems in order to communicate the results adequately. The holistic nature of anthropology allows a researcher to consider and adapt to unanticipated problems or new areas of information that arise. Both the researcher and agency officials should be willing to adapt to these new concerns, and it is useful if one representative of the agency can be a contact to whom the anthropologist can go when new issues appear.

I found this adaptability important in my experience in Nevada because even before the contract was signed a problem arose in terminology. BLM uses the word "cultural" to mean the cultural resources of archeology, so it was confusing for them if I was designated a cultural anthropologist. I had to establish my identity as a "sociocultural" anthropologist in order to communicate more clearly in agency jargon.

An unanticipated area of research with the BLM involved the problems of staff communication with local residents. The faceless impersonality of the agency is offensive in a society in which personal and individual identity are paramount. The local population was one described by a new BLM staff member: "I have never seen so many independent, strong-willed people in my life as there are around here. They all say: 'Don't interfere with me!' "

Local problems of BLM staff crystallized for me when I was having a meal with a ranch family at their home, which was several hours' drive from town. The only access road ran near the house and was little used. As we ate, a truck came by, but the two men in it looked the other way as they passed by. It was a BLM truck and the men's failure even to slow down and acknowledge the local residents was commented on in a negative way by the ranch family and their employees. I later talked with the two BLM men, and they and other staff members volunteered that they simply did not know how to meet local people either in business or casual encounters. They solved this by ignoring some local people. Later a professional psychologist conducted some training sessions in this and other BLM offices to deal with these problems.

Despite employee concern, the agency still gives greatest priority to resource management rather than people management. I think what is needed here is Goffman's perspective:

When an individual enters the presence of others, they commonly seek to acquire information about him or to bring into play information about him already possessed . . . Information about the individual helps to define the situation, enabling others to know in advance what he will expect of them and what they may expect of him. [1959:1]

Such information can be used to control the impression an individual presents. BLM personnel, as individuals, were often well liked, and specific personal characteristics, some insignificant as a fondness for watermelon were cited with approval by district residents. But when they are known only as faceless representatives of an impersonal entity, BLM staff are not warmly regarded.

The research I conducted in Nevada and New Zealand brought me into close contact with land-use planners, urban planners, and resource planners. Few planners have training in anthropology, although some have studied sociology as part of urban planning. Lynch (1976) notes that interaction between people and place is a basic consideration in planning decisions. He emphasizes that planners must consider "human feelings set in a whole context, physical and social" (personal communication, 1979) and in his work Lynch outlines many of the practical issues that planners must face. These include many questions that anthropologists can help answer, including describing the interaction between space and place as set within the dynamics of a cultural system. How does a farmer regard the land? How does it support the farmer's perception of his or her life style? How does it contribute to his or her income?

In addition to providing information, the anthropologist can assist in interpreting available quantitative data. In this contribution the anthropologist might perhaps offer alternative explanations of findings. Some data may have a different meaning when examined qualitatively, because numerical analysis may limit the suggested interpretations. Agency personnel and other outsiders often interpret the statistics without knowing about the local satisfaction and stable communities. Agency staff may view the region as a backwater. This perception, if held by agencies' staff members making decisions and planning for the region, hinders growth potential for the region.

Another area of concern for the researcher is the fact that training and orientation of the agency staff are in physical sciences where quantification of data is paramount. Qualitative data are unfamiliar and hence suspect. Many short-term social-science research projects, however, do not lend themselves to quantification. It becomes all the more imperative that the anthropologist's reports be written in clear, everyday language. Information that could be developed and presented statistically, if time and resources allowed, must be considered qualitatively. And reports must be as concise as possible. It is also valuable to add a summary so that readers can use that if they lack time for the entire report.

Conclusion

The purpose of this chapter has been "to try to instill an approach, a sensitivity, an inventiveness and a set of principles for the cultural solution of . . . problems" (Arensberg and Niehoff 1964:9). As anthropology moves further into the world of applied research, as it moves closer to the researcher's own society, there will be a great need to modify traditional research methods. Working at home requires more awareness of everyday events, simply because much that appears to be familiar and known actually is not. A major aspect of my research was the problem of trying to talk to the agency for which I worked; communicating research findings is an important but often neglected aspect of method.

In preparation for learning how to talk to an agency, the researcher must learn something of the history of the agency and its present activities. In addition, he or she must know the priorities and framework of administration so that she or he can assess where and what kinds of statements of the research are of value to the agency goals. Along with this, the researcher must recognize that training and interests of staff members are significant, because research information offered to the agency must be intelligible to staff if the research is to be used by the agency. If, for example, the researcher learns that the agency resists the knowledge being offered, the researcher may find a new field of inquiry to consider – the reasons that an agency refuses to accept what the researcher has presented.

A separate but of course related problem is the actual fieldwork for the research. Rural communities, especially dispersed ranching communities, can be effectively studied by means of modified ideas about community. Great distances may be involved in which community members live and interact, and many boundaries that may not be visible do exist and define the social units and community lines.

A final problem of my work that may arise for other research projects with agencies is the complex and sometimes hostile environment that prevailed between some local residents and the agency. In my research it was assumed by some people that the agency was not genuinely interested in local people and local ideas. The agency was considered big and impersonal, unreachable for ordinary communication. "This report will be just a smokescreen for the bureaucracy," was one comment I heard. Another person suggested that although it appeared that my research was to be useful, "BLM must have a hidden purpose for this study." Agency staff members were also skeptical of local residents. And the views of both sides were further complicated by the legacy of romantic ranch and cowboy life styles.

Nonetheless, I recommend that more anthropologists become involved in research at home. The work has the potential for enhancing anthropological knowledge and contributes to policy and programs of agencies involved. In times of increasing travel costs it also serves to offer a very productive alternative to the traditional faraway field sites. In my work I have come to know a great deal about the dust and the many miles of the vast horizon of Nevada, and all of it lies less than 300 miles (480 km) from home.

Part VII Reflections
on anthropology at home

The observations and reflections of a seasoned anthropological researcher, one with experience both at home and away, cross-culturally, conclude our trek through the work of contemporary anthropologists at home in North America. Harry F. Wolcott (Chapter 17) compares and contrasts how the places and the topics of his research have affected data-gathering style, how fieldwork time is structured, the level and intensity of participation and impression management, empathy, and other concerns through the final analysis and writeup of the results. His statements that individual anthropologists need cross-cultural research experience whereas the discipline itself needs to practice anthropology at home are both cogent and controversial.

17 Home and away: personal contrasts in ethnographic style

HARRY F. WOLCOTT

It has taken me a long time – literally years – to realize that I follow somewhat different styles in ethnographic research depending upon whether I am at home in a familiar setting in my own society or away in some unfamiliar place.[1] Now that I recognize these differences and have begun to ponder their impact on my research, I wonder if others are similarly influenced by circumstances at home and away. A review of the differences that I have been able to discern provides the basis for the premise of this chapter, that although cross-cultural fieldwork has been (and, I am quite certain, will continue to be) the sine qua non for the individual ethnographer, the most important consequence of the cumulative ethnographic endeavor is not an accumulation of hard-won insights into the lives of members of remote societies but the cross-cultural perspective it provides for examining our own lives.

In several paired sets of observations that follow, I have noted contrasts in research styles in settings that I refer to simply as Here and There. "Here," in my case, refers to ethnographic research conducted in the milieu of the American public school, its local community, and the community of educators (1973, 1974b, 1975a, 1975c, 1975d, 1977, 1978, 1981). Other than a contextual analysis of apple pie, what could be more down-home than that? "There" refers to my fieldwork in seemingly more exotic settings, specifically in a Northwest Coast (Kwakiutl) village, an urban African township, and – to a modest extent – a Malay village (1967, 1974a, 1974b, 1980).

Contrasts in fieldwork: here and there

Serendipity

I begin with a discussion of serendipity because it allows me to note a certain element in my own career that is markedly different from that of most anthropologists. My primary professional concern is with the anthropology of education. A colleague in anthropology once remarked, "You're lucky. You always know what you should be studying and writing

255

about." In fact, however, the preoccupation with education-related research that he noted in my career has often seemed less enviable to m ? than it does to him. I envy the freedom and catholic interests of a cultural anthropologist. My research Here has always had to exhibit a primary concern for education, the subject of my major training and commitment. In research Here, however, time, place, and focus have always been relatively subject to my control.

Subsequent to my dissertation research among the Kwakiutl – an interdisciplinary study in anthropology and education – I have taken the opportunity afforded by two full-year sabbatical leaves to broaden my own perspective, on those occasions traveling far outside my customary bailiwick and concerning myself less with the educational process and with schools hardly at all. There serendipity played a bigger role – I have set out for places at periods of time largely determined by others (personal contacts influenced the choice of region, institutional calendars determined when I should depart and return) and with my research purposes defined in the broadest of terms. That flexibility was epitomized in research in Zimbabwe (or Rhodesia, as it was then called), where I assumed that I would devote my time to studying the education of African students but instead spent a year examining African urbanization, with a focus on the institution of the municipally operated beer gardens that make and sell traditional beer for urban Africans (Wolcott 1974a). Among friends unfamiliar at the time with the realities of social life in southern Africa I was chided for having "spent a year off drinking with the natives."

I recognize that most anthropologists do not set out for exotic climes with such loosely structured research objectives. Few, however, live with such constraints on what they otherwise attend to, unless, like me, they have permanent assignments to one of the discipline's subfields, such as educational, legal, or medical anthropology.

Type of note taking

Many anthropologists make a distinction between two types of field account: the journal and the fieldnotes. A journal may contain diarylike notes about everything and anything. Some anthropologists continue their daily journal writing even when they are not in the field. Fieldnotes are quite different from journal notes. Fieldnotes are systematic and specific, compiled on an ad hoc basis as the fieldworker's store of information on particularly important topics (local child-rearing practices, community social structure) accumulates.

Regardless of the setting, note taking is always an onerous task. Here I find myself taking extensive notes of the running account or journal type, and Here the note-taking chore threatens to become overwhelming, as I continue to identify elements in the social setting that have not yet received adequate attention. If I do not record everything, I at least try consciously to review everything I might record. The note-taking chore suffers from such compulsiveness, but in the end the notes are relatively complete and useful, a valuable asset for further analysis. The shelves of my study groan under dozens of notebooks from each local research effort, and when my graduate students express interest in seeing how I handle the problem of note taking and subsequent cataloging, these are the notes I show them.

In contrast, there, from the very first, it is the magnitude of all that is unfamiliar that overwhelms me. I rationalize that trying to obtain complete journal notes of everything would preclude adequate opportunities of participating and gaining perspective. With no hope of ever keeping notes on everything, I find myself relying almost exclusively on sets of fieldnotes: information on topics of selected focus. These notes have proved rich resources in preparing accounts about the specialized subjects which they deal with, but their utility is limited almost exclusively to the single topic they address. Here, in trying to look at everything, I inevitably attempt too much; There I look at fewer things and hope they will prove to be the right ones.

Time available for fieldwork

Here the total time available for fieldwork has been generous. In two local studies I had access to my research sites until I was personally satisfied that the account was complete. In one case (Wolcott 1973) this was achieved through the luxury of extending the field observations over two full years. The fieldwork was less intense in the second year than in the first, but it was adequate for maintaining a presence in the field and especially helpful for discerning patterns of behavior and for attempting to view them in broad context. In the other case the gradual but nonetheless complete phaseout of an educational research-and-development project provided a natural finale for the period of observation as well.

There, by contrast, time has always been constrained by external circumstances known prior to my arrival but totally incidental to the research focus. Or, put another way, time constraints played a critical role in determining what I could select for my research focus in the first place. Here my experience has been that I could continue my field observations as long as necessary, although opportunities for fieldwork at any particular moment have been subject to the interruptions of obligations at home and office. There I have always felt that my days were numbered, although the sense of urgency about getting on with it has also been accompanied by the luxury of a short period of almost uninterrupted fieldwork.

I do not mean to suggest that time Here can always be extended at the fieldworker's discretion or that research There is always less bothered by interruption – although that has proven to be the case for me. I certainly am not arguing that fieldwork should be entirely free of time constraints. In reading accounts of fieldwork one often gets the impression that the ethnographer laments not having been able to stay longer. My experience as consultant to a long-range and generously funded national study in which field researchers stayed on site for as long as three years has led me to realize that ethnographers can spend too much as well as too little time in the field (Wolcott 1978:160). What I want to emphasize is that time is almost always scarce in a distant setting. That constraint exerts a force that would be better off not exerted, creating pressure on the overseas researcher of the sort that can lead to hasty work, unchecked observations, and so forth. My preference is to avoid what researchers of other persuasions refer to as quick-and-dirty studies. Though I am distracted by all the forces competing for my attention in locally conducted research, I have been satisfied knowing that I could monitor the research setting as long as needed and would have time to mull over my observations while I still had access to the site.

Type of participation

In familiar settings Here I find myself spending more time as observer, less time trying to be an active participant. I feel no need to demonstrate to the locals that I am virtually one of them. There, I am of necessity more actively involved, because I must gain some competence in doing all sorts of things in the new setting, although many of those activities are but tangentially related to fieldwork itself (for example, learning how to buy and use local products, pay bills, find my way around geographically and socially).

As for participating so wholeheartedly that I live my way into another culture, I guess I have become more skeptical of others' ability to accomplish such a feat as I have sensed the difficulty of doing it convincingly myself. I harbor the suspicion that the natives have been humoring us all these years in their reassurances that we have become just like them. During my fieldwork among the Kwakiutl, a villager once remarked (after a few beers) that I was a "real Indian." My reaction at the time was that the comment was well meant, but I have not tried to be real Indian again. Though I am willing to participate as circumstances allow and am fully committed to the anthropological tenet of experiencing another culture firsthand in order to learn about it, I also realize that personally I feel most comfortable and most productive in the role of an obviously present but relatively uninvolved and unobtrusive observer. I feel particularly fortunate when I am treated as a privileged observer, allowed to witness more of the total scene and entrusted with more personal opinions than are shared with the casual visitor because my purposes for inquiring are regarded as legitimate and sincere.

Impression management

Turning now to the professional stance one assumes in fieldwork, I use anthropologist Gerald Berreman's notion of "impression management" (Berreman 1962). On this point, even more than on others, the reader must realize that I am describing fieldwork settings as I perceive them. Images that I may wish to convey are of course not necessarily those I do convey. Like most fieldworkers, I have been accused of being a spy, of being perfunctory, of failing to attend or to attend equally to every possible perspective. On the other hand, I have been amazed at people's willingness to confide in me. Some informants seem particularly anxious for the opportunity to help others understand their ways or their point of view. Often, however, I feel that people confide in order to share with a sympathetic stranger the quiet desperation of their lives.

Here, working among people who are somewhat familiar with research procedures – even if, as is the case with many educators, they set little store by them – I portray myself as a social scientist who needs to know. (At times, in the public arena of the schools, I have to rescue myself from a self-righteousness that would insist that I have a right to know.) I am inclined to be impatient with facades and to push my way through to meet key people. At home I do not hesitate to confront sensitive issues directly. Admittedly, whether at home or away I find myself gravitating toward sensitive issues as a means of focusing my research. For example, the manner in which school principals handle the touchy business of teacher evaluation helped me to sharpen the perspective of my inquiry into the principalship. The ambiguity of funding certain welfare services directed toward problems created by heavy urban beer drinking from moneys earned by selling the beer to urban dwellers brought a sharper perspective to that inquiry.

But in the overseas setting I strive to act the part of the appreciative guest. I bend over backwards to show my gratitude for attention and cooperation. I patiently wait and hope that things will work out, that opportunities will arise, that someone will think to invite me into settings where I am hesitant to intrude. I respect the very privacies and sensitive issues There that I try to invade Here. "After all, it's their life, and they can live it as they please," I remind myself.

Empathy

Following closely on the last point, I find a marked difference in my ability to empathize in strange and in familiar settings. Here I am often angry, impatient, and frustrated by the settings I observe, and I hope as I prepare the accounts based upon these observations that I may incite others to examine and possibly alter the circumstances. In something of the style that characterized Jules Henry's (1963) writings about American society, my anger is a source of personal energy, for it is borne of frustration with what is, coupled with hopes for what might be. Like most ethnographers I strive for objectivity (and find it useful to distinguish between objectivity and neutrality), but, lest there be any confusion in my reader's mind, I endeavor to state clearly my personal feelings toward the subjects of my studies. In one study (Wolcott 1977) wherein my personal dismay was at once a useful source of energy and a potential threat to a hope of adequate objectivity, the completed monograph begins with a chapter titled "Bias at Work: Proceed with Caution."

My involvement There is less, my detachment greater. I tend to be sympathetic and patient, striving to understand what concerns others, not what concerns me, and to portray it accurately. My accounts reveal a functional bias, not with a seal-of-approval functionalism but with a conscious effort to provide a basic description of how things are. Any suggestion I offer about how things might be different There I have invariably directed toward those like me (other members of white, middle-class society) rather than to the indigenous population. Teachers, educational innovators, missionaries, community developers, even Zimbabwe's "European" beer garden officials may find implicit (and sometimes explicit) recommendations in my writings, but neither Kwakiutl nor Malay villagers nor urban Africans will find similar guidelines.

How I proceed with writing

It was in reflecting on how I proceed with the inevitable task of preparing a written account that I first realized differences between my fieldwork styles at home and away. It is not surpising that I discovered the differences in this facet of my work, for I am very (perhaps excessively) writing oriented. I am in favor of joining the writing task with fieldwork rather than making it subsequent to it. I think about writing from the first days in the field as I begin to contemplate possible audiences, type and length of possible manuscripts, subtopics to include, possible analytical frameworks, and potential titles. If this appears to be working backward, it is probably due to my preoccupation with ethnographic description rather than with major theoretical issues. Perhaps one should be more concerned with the research *problem* than with the ethnographic *product*, but for me, writing *is* the problem.

My writing Here begins as a response to the realization that I must get on with the task of organizing data already accumulated. Difficult as fieldwork is, once the writing task looms there is a great temptation to occupy yourself solely with fieldwork by convincing yourself that you do not yet know enough about the people being studied to write about them. Until that critical juncture is passed, there is always the risk that the fieldwork will become an end in itself; data gathering is nicely accommodating, in that it is an endless assignment. Formidable as are the combined tasks of maintaining one's presence in the field and keeping up with the note taking that must accompany it, the moment for facing the task of writing is by far the most formidable to me. Until that step is taken, however, there is no possibility for ethnography. I begin writing to bring order to what I have done and efficiency to the fieldwork that will continue. My writing Here might be described as variety-reducing behavior – it helps me get at the basic issue of deciding what to say about what I have learned.

By marked contrast, writing There, at least in two major opportunities for cross-cultural work (Wolcott 1974a; 1980), has begun much earlier in the fieldwork. In each case I completed a first draft of what became a final (though vastly revised) manuscript within six months of my arrival. My reason for such an early start was that I realized that I had too little rather than too much to say. Writing There is a variety-generating exercise to force me to organize what little I know and to identify gaps that must be filled in, facts that must be checked, descriptions that must be added, if there is to be any account at all. Writing There is intentionally premature, an attempt to commit myself to a modest statement rather than an effort to cull the best from rich resources. From the time of that first draft the focus of my attention shifts, if ever so slightly, from the field setting to the written material itself, and all subsequent reading, watching, and listening become a sieve for checking accuracy, providing fuller context, and, of course, examining meanings within that context.

Further, while it has always been my practice to enlist friends and colleagues as reader-critics of early drafts, in the cross-cultural setting I have used the procedure of circulating preliminary manuscripts among a select group of readers familiar with the field setting as an explicit fieldwork technique designed (and virtually guaranteed) to elicit feedback and reaction (Wolcott 1975b:116). I think the procedure has much to recommend it.

Relating to and drawing upon the work of others

There is no doubt that the special anthropology-and-education focus of my work Here, versus the opportunity I have to indulge broader anthropological interests in other settings, greatly influences many or most of these contrasts in research style. In perhaps no category is the difference more clearly related to those different purposes than in the way I find myself drawing upon existing anthropological literature to identify concepts or models useful for organizing, analyzing, and writing up a new study. Here, working in the familiar setting of the American public school, I rely on anthropology to bring the familiar and ordinary into new and, I hope, clearer perspective. In earlier works I have employed widely used concepts such as annual cycle and life cycle, enculturation and socialization, real and ideal world, rites of passage, social control and social structure, theme, world view, and, of course, the master concept that underlies anthropology, culture itself.

For one study of the American educational scene (Wolcott 1977), I took a further step by making early and explicit use of a concept derived from the study of comparative social structure, the concept of moiety. A society with a moiety form of social organization is divided into two and only two major divisions, each of which is called a moiety.

One reason for employing a descriptive and neutral concept like moiety was related to certain misgivings I felt in my assignment to and involvement with that particular project, one of a series of assignments during some eleven years spent in an educational research-and-development center. I was not in sympathy with the aim of the project – the development of a planning–programming–budgeting system for schools – and I was distressed by the heavy-handed manner in which a pilot test of the new system had been implemented in a nearby school district. Because of those negative feelings, I recognized the need for keeping my bias manageable.

In addition, I wanted to see the anthropology of education more firmly rooted in anthropology. Rather than bemoan the slight anthropological underpinnings at times evident in some of our work, I thought I would make a self-conscious effort to strengthen those underpinnings in a study of my own. I reviewed notes made during the meetings of project staff and meetings of teachers in the school district in hopes of finding an appropriate model that would invite comparison between the behaviors I had observed and behaviors that ethnographers have described in other settings.

The moiety concept seemed to provide a model with that potential. I was particularly interested in parallels between the literature concerning dual division and a division I identified between groups tentatively labeled as classroom-oriented and system-oriented educators. The moiety literature provided the kind of perspective and analogy I had been seeking. The observations of others who reported on moiety systems in preliterate societies gave me a comparative basis for examining a case of well-intentioned but unsuccessful contemporary educational innovation in terms of a moietylike division in the educator subculture. I subsequently called the two groups "teachers" and "technocrats." The terms *conceptual antithesis, rivalry, reciprocity,* and *complementarity,* employed by others for describing traditional moiety interaction (see Lowie 1948), served initially as a basis for helping me organize my observations and eventually became chapter headings in the analytical section of the monograph.

"Moiety" is a relatively straightforward term, although admittedly it is not as straightforward as I thought when I first decided to use it. In any case, it is not a concept resulting from the efforts of a particular group of researchers to identify a neat set of interrelated variables to explain phenomena observed across cultures. In fact, the concept of moiety is so seemingly straightforward that, to the best of my knowledge, no one has ever made a systematic review of it in the literature. Efforts to summarize that literature resulted in a chapter describing moieties in traditional society (Wolcott 1977:129–144).

Most important, I was drawing upon a social-structural concept from the study of preliterate societies for an examination of a professional and cultural subgroup, educators, in contemporary society. In this regard it may be of interest to note that although no one took issue with my earlier effort to show how contemporary African drinking is linked to traditional beliefs and practice, my attempt to examine educator subculture in a moiety perspective precipitated some critical reactions. Colleagues raised such issues as whether my teachers and technocrats were part of the same cultural group (I had argued that they are all educators at heart, in basic agreement about education's broadest goals but differing on how best to achieve them) or whether they represented two distinct groups with quite different ideologies. One colleague expressed concern about the extent to which I had made too great an effort to "achieve a 'moiety-like' fit with the data." This is a perennial and legitimate concern in the anthropological penchant for comparison, although I do not recall reviewers raising a similar question when I tucked data into someone else's categories in my earlier studies. (In my writing I try to neutralize the ever-present problems of intrusive analysis by providing sufficient descriptive data so that others may make independent analyses.) My colleague also reminded me of the likelihood that my introduction of moiety terminology would foster the "glib acquisition of yet another new term" in educational jargon. That risk I took knowingly.

In contrast to my somewhat independent style Here in linking my work with the work of others, I would characterize my use of the existing literature There as dependent. It is always comforting to drop a name or two (in parentheses) to show how others have identified similar issues or made similar observations to one's own. In the unfamiliar setting There, however, I find myself drawing upon the work of others not for perspective but for support. I do this not because others have reached similar conclusions independently but because my opportunities for firsthand observation are limited. My practice of writing an early field draft There helps me recognize gaps and areas of thin description that can be strengthened by a careful combing of the existing literature. Similarly, the work of others can be used to raise questions, although in the less familiar setting I think I use those questions more to guide the fieldwork and to achieve closure in the manuscript than to probe unresolved issues.

For example, in my fieldwork in southern Africa I subtitled my monograph "Integrated Drinking in a Segregated Society" (1974a), using "integrated drinking" in the sense proposed by Child et al. (1965) in their cross-cultural examination of alcohol use and its consequences. But I neither extended nor critiqued their work; I simply fit my data into their schema so that I could turn my focus to other areas more central to an examination of the urban African setting.

Generalization

In work Here I confidently portray the cases I observe as natural histories characteristic of classes of events rather than limited to the instance at hand. If I have been academically circumspect in written claims that the study of one village school or one elementary-school principal provides valuable insight into all intercultural classrooms or all principalships, I have been less circumspect in my spoken claims on behalf of the generalizability of each study. To those studies I brought years of experience in a variety of roles in the formal educational establishment. As I wrote I consciously tried to explicate the myriad ways that the single cases were similar to others and to make my statements relevant to the American educator subculture in general. In Wolcott 1977 I was careful to note my personal enthusiasm for viewing educator subculture as a moiety system. My seeming effort to sell the universality of my analysis produced some unexpected resistance. Observers point out that Americans in general tend to resist high-pressure sales tactics. I wonder if that also applies in the social sciences, where vested interests in explanations are often regarded with a degree of suspicion related more closely to the extent of personal enthusiasm than to the potential of the idea.

There my work reveals a subtle distinction between concern for detail regarding the unknown and generalization about the known. The Kwakiutl village setting is described with specific detail, although, as I have noted, the processes involved in its classroom are broached more widely as I venture in my concluding remarks to go beyond the particulars of the case to discuss the generalizability of the message (see Wolcott 1967 and, especially, 1974b). My descriptions of urban Africans and rural Malays are presented with conservative specificity, but programs designed and administered by westerners to provide them with amenities or community revitalization are treated in a natural-history style that emphasizes their universal features.

The cross-cultural perspective in perspective

The point of these personal reflections on differences in ethnographic style at home and away is neither to reveal secrets about my own research nor to indict other ethnographers because of problems that may be unique to my commitments, training, and fieldwork opportunities. The point is that quite without realizing it I have developed somewhat different patterns for doing ethnographic work at home and away, patterns that reveal my own style for coping with the obvious difficulties of cross-cultural settings and the less obvious but comparable difficulties associated with doing research in my own society.

Having discovered these differences in my work, I have begun to wonder if similar patterns can be discerned in the work of others. I rather imagine they can, although I expect many anthropologists who have lived and worked among strangers long enough to know not only their customs and language but the intricacies of their typical ways of thinking or their humor would want to argue that they feel perfectly at home among them. Indeed, some anthropologists insist that they are marginal in their own society and only at home among "their" people somewhere else.

I share with many others the opinion that cross-cultural fieldwork, preferably at the time of one's first sustained research experience, should continue to be the sine qua non for the individual ethnographer. Without that cross-cultural and comparative basis, we might lose track of how even our own behavior as fieldworkers reflects cultural influences. The importance that I have assigned to time in these reflections about fieldwork serves as a case in point. A concern about *time* frames comparable to our own is hardly a universal human trait.

Today one hears a lament among anthropologists that the opportunities for cross-cultural fieldwork are limited. I am not convinced this is so, in spite of obvious restrictions on social research in many areas of the world. I think graduate students and their advisers ought to make every effort to locate cross-cultural sites for doctoral studies, and preference should continue to be given to work in other countries. I know from personal experience that my introduction to field research – the year in the Kwakiutl village – was one of the most important (as well as one of the most difficult) years of my life both professionally and personally. I notice that graduate students who do not conduct their formal dissertation research in a cross-cultural setting are inclined to make careful note of their foreign travel and experience, and I concur with what I take to be their implicit acknowledgment of the value – necessity, really – of some kind of firsthand confrontation with appreciably different cultural systems.

In my special-interest area of anthropology and education, most individuals intending to conduct future research in the school are not only products of those schools but have served in the teaching ranks as well. In this field the need for a cross-cultural perspective is perhaps more critical than for those who will work in settings less familiar. I noted earlier my concern about the absence of a solid anthropological base in some of the work turned out as educational ethnography. One possible explanation is that in the past decade numerous educational researchers have tended to confuse an important fieldwork technique – firsthand observation – with ethnography itself. Consequently there has been a tendency in education to label any sort of descriptive study as ethnography (Wolcott 1975a, 1981).

It is impossible to mandate that cross-cultural fieldwork be required as a formal prerequisite for conducting educational ethnography. Nor would I want to propose anything that might discourage the wider use of natural observation in education. Educational research needs intuitive and sensitive observers to contribute to a descriptive literature about classrooms and schools that will complement the educator's preoccupation with experimental method. Still, a sustained effort to persuade those interested in doing classroom ethnography to engage first in cross-cultural fieldwork can help underscore the critical point that it is the cultural perspective, not the research technique, that distinguishes the work of the ethnographer from the work of other describers.

Self-conscious concern among anthropologists about method has probably contributed to a confused feeling among anthropology's patron audiences, including professionals in fields such as educational research, that to the ethnographer method is everything. Anthropological writings occasionally add to the confusion by seeming to equate the difficulties encountered in fieldwork with the worth of the completed study, a confusion nicely illustrated by the question of whether one has to eat "soup with a chicken head floating in it, instead of steak" in order to get a family system correctly recorded on paper (Slater 1976:130). Certainly anthropology does have something to offer educational researchers in the way of method, particularly with its emphasis on the fieldworker as the research instrument. However, it also has important lessons to offer all educators in terms of such traditional ethnographic interests as the concern for cultural context, the search for organizing and unifying themes among different groups of people, the relationship between world view and child-rearing practices, or the importance of the total social milieu in the process of enculturation. It is a matter of perspective, not method, to get busy educators to look beyond the urgencies of class size, contract negotiations, or declining test scores and to see themselves as products as well as transmitters of culture.

The "compleat" ethnographer

Having paid homage to the cross-cultural endeavor as the sine qua non for the individual anthropologist, let me close by repeating my not-so-traditional suggestion that ethnographic research carried out in one's own society may be the sine qua non for anthropology itself. While I have gained essential and invaluable insight into cultural processes in fieldwork There, I have also come to appreciate how much more fully I am able to observe and to understand what goes on in the society (or more precisely, in those microcultural systems) in which I am a genuine rather than a would-be participant. Only Here, I feel, do I observe, participate, and write under conditions in which I am most likely to understand most of what is going on, with humor, nuance, double entendre, conflicting explanations, and so forth all apt to go noticed rather than unnoticed. Only Here is it likely that the subjects of my studies will not only see the published results but also will know how to raise academic issue with them and thus be able to subject me to possible talk among my colleagues, just as I may, however inadvertently, create risks for them among theirs.

I would like to suggest that just as we have in the past held firmly to the belief that the compleat ethnographer ought to do fieldwork in a quite different society from his or her own, we now begin to think of conducting ethnographic research at home as an equally important part of a well-rounded career. That practice need not deter anyone from pursuing topics of only esoteric interest, but it might provide occasion and impetus for more ethnographers to take a hand in addressing patron audiences of nonanthropologists as well as audiences composed only of professional peers. We can hardly claim that we lack role models; this is the kind of thing that Margaret Mead did and urged others to do throughout her distinguished career. Her earliest work, *Coming of Age in Samoa* (1928), in print now for more than half a century, bears the subtitle "A Psychological Study of Primitive Youth for Western Civilisation." That subtitle served notice about what were to become Mead's preoccupations: looking at American life anthropologically and probing anthropological studies for their insight in understanding how and why we ourselves behave as we do. I think anthropologists would be the beneficiaries if more people understood the message that Mead and many others tried to convey about the overriding anthropological concern for culture and for the relevance of that concern in helping us understand not only the lives of others but our own lives as well.

I also think it would be salutary for anthropologists to conduct their research and write their ethnographies based upon fieldwork completed at least occasionally under the best rather than the worst of conditions – for example, in situations where language is not a barrier or where personal disorientation is a matter of indulgence rather than necessity. Think of the impact it would have on every anthropologist – and on such popular disciplinary concerns as ethics, objectivity, world view, and the nexus between personality and culture – if the first assignment we gave to all new appointees in academic or applied settings was to prepare an ethnography of their own new organization or department.

Contributors

Agnes Aamodt is an associate professor in the College of Nursing, University of Arizona at Tucson. She has degrees in nursing, child development, and anthropology. She received her Ph.D. in anthropology from the University of Washington in 1971. Her dissertation was entitled "Enculturation Process and the Papago Child: An Inquiry into the Acquisition of Perspectives on Health and Healing." She has published on health and healing from the perspectives of children and adolescents and in relation to health-care systems, including "The Care Component in Health and Healing Systems," in *Anthropology and Health*, edited by Eleanor Bauwens (St. Louis: Mosby, 1978).

John L. Aguilar is an assistant professor of anthropology at Arizona State University. He received his B.A. in sociology from UCLA in 1967 and his M.A. and Ph.D. in anthropology from, respectively California State University, Los Angeles, in 1970, and the University of California, San Diego, in 1977. His doctoral studies were sponsored by the National Institute of Mental Health and the Ford Foundation. In addition to anthropology, he has taught the sociology and history of Mexican-Americans (Chicano studies) at California State University, Los Angeles, and at Occidental College, Los Angeles. He has conducted fieldwork in the United States and Mexico and is currently writing a book on the social and psychological consequences of deprivation among Indians of a biethnic community in southern Mexico.

John W. Bennett is a professor of anthropology at Washington University, Saint Louis, Missouri. He is also affiliated with the university's East Asia Studies Center and the Department of Technology and Human Affairs. He is a program associate of the Land Tenure Center, University of Wisconsin, and a visiting professor at the Office of Arid Land Studies, University of Arizona, Tuscon. His chapter in this book is based on extensive research in a semiarid region of the northern Great Plains from ecological and economic developmental viewpoints. He is currently engaged in a research program on

268   *Contributors*

pastoral livestock development in several African countries. In a more general vein, he is concerned with developing theoretical models for handling behavioral components of agrarian and rural development programs, with particular emphasis on environmental research and cooperative and collective resource management systems. He has published many articles and several books. Among the latter are *Northern Plainmen: Adaptive Strategy and Agrarian Life* (Chicago: Aldine and AHM, 1969–1976) and *The Ecological Transition: Cultural Anthropology and Human Adaptation* (New York: Pergamon Press, 1976).

Paul Bohannan is professor of anthropology at the University of California, Santa Barbara. He was educated at the University of Arizona, Oxford University, and the Chicago Institute for Psychoanalysis. His first fieldwork was in Africa (Nigeria and Kenya), but since the early 1960s he has been working in the United States with divorcees, stepfathers, ethnic groups, and the old men in center-city hotels who are the subjects of his article in this book. He has published widely in the major journals of anthropology and has written a number of books. He recently served as the president of the American Anthropological Association.

Elizabeth L. Byerly has a BSN degree in nursing (1955) from the University of Iowa and advanced degrees in both nursing (M.N., 1958) and anthropology (Ph.D., 1970) from the University of Washington. She is an associate professor at the Intercollegiate Center for Nursing Education at Spokane, Washington and was principal investigator (1977–1980) in the NIH project, Health Care Alternatives of Multiethnic Migrants, in Washington state.

Kerry D. Feldman is professor and chairman, Department of Anthropology, University of Alaska, Anchorage. He moved to Alaska shortly after taking his Ph.D. degree in Anthropology (1973) at the University of Colorado, Boulder. His research interests and activities include fieldwork in Alaskan communities and fieldwork among the squatter barrios of Davao City, Philippines. His publications include articles in *Urban Anthropology*, *Human Organization*, and the *Journal of Anthropological Research*.

Susan Brandt Graham is assistant professor of anthropology at the University of Missouri, Kansas City. She holds a B.A. (1967) in anthropology from the University of Oklahoma and an M.A. (1970) and Ph.D. (1975) in anthropology from the University of Arizona. She has also pursued graduate studies at the University of Chicago on a Woodrow Wilson Fellowship (1967–1968). Her primary research interests are the contemporary United States, social-network analysis, and communities in complex societies. She continues to generate material from her dissertation research on the social networks of a company town in southern Arizona, on which her chapter in this volume is based. Related articles appear in *The Social Science Journal* (1978) and *Urban Anthropology* (1981).

John L. Gwaltney is professor of anthropology in the Maxwell Graduate School of Citizenship and Public Affairs at Syracuse University. He received his Ph.D. in anthropology from Columbia University in 1967 and holds an honorary D.Sc. from Bucknell

University. Blind since birth, Dr. Gwaltney's study of the Chinantec of San Pedro Yolox, Oaxaca, Mexico, published as *The Thrice Shy: Cultural Accommodation to Blindness and Other Disasters in a Mexican Community* (New York: Columbia University Press, 1970) was awarded the Ansley Dissertation Award for 1967. He is the author of numerous articles and essays on race relations and authors a column on native anthropology for the newsletter of the Association of Black Anthropologists. His latest book, *Drylongso: A Self-Portrait of Black America* (New York: Random House, 1980), is a product of the field research discussed in his chapter for this volume.

Lawrence Hennigh is an adjunct professor of anthropology at SUNY College, Potsdam, New York, and formerly an on-site researcher and consultant for Abt Associates, Inc., of Cambridge, Massachusetts. He took his B.A. (1955) and M.A. (1965) at the University of Washington and his Ph.D. in anthropology at Washington State University (1978). His research includes fieldwork in arctic Alaska and in Oregon. He has published articles on traditional and modern Eskimo culture, educational anthropology, and modern community study.

Ruth M. Houghton is a researcher with Otago University, Dunedin, New Zealand. She has been adjunct research professor, Desert Research Institute, Reno, Nevada, and a parttime lecturer (1968–1979) in the University of Nevada system at Reno and at Western Nevada Community College. She has also taught in universities in Ireland and New Zealand. She holds a B.A. honors degree (1963) from the University of Utah and an M.A. (1968) and Ph.D. (1973) in anthropology from the University of Oregon. She has edited *Nevada Lifestyles and Lands* (1977) and *Native American Politics in the Western Great Basin Today* (1973), both published in Reno at the Bureau of Governmental Research, University of Nevada.

Nancy Kleiber holds a Ph.D. degree (1972) in anthropology from the University of California at Davis. In 1974 she was appointed a research associate at the University of British Columbia, first at the Resource Science Center and later in the School of Nursing. In 1977 she was appointed visiting assistant professor of anthropology and lecturer in the Department of Health Care and Epidemiology. She is currently living in Noumea, New Caledonia. She is the author, with Linda Light, of a number of papers and publications on the topic of feminism and health care, including *Caring for Ourselves: An Alternative Structure for Health Care* (1978) and "Interactive research in a health care setting," in *Social Science and Medicine* (1978).

Seena B. Kohl is professor of anthropology/sociology and coordinator of women's studies at Webster College, Saint Louis, Missouri, where she has initiated and developed a student research program for the study of local communities and their organizations. She has been associated with the Saskatchewan Cultural Ecology Research Project since its inception in 1963, specializing in social organization, family life and the role of women in the economic enterprise. She is presently engaged in examining the relationship between the individual life cycle, the family developmental cycle, and the structure of work as these factors relate to women's lives. Among her publications based on the Saskatchewan research is *Working Together: Women and Family in Southwestern Saskatchewan* (1976).

Linda Light is a graduate student in sociology at the University of British Columbia, Vancouver, Canada. Since the late 1960s she has worked on various research projects in London, England, and in British Columbia, including a London School of Economics–based study of Scotland Yard and a University of British Columbia–based study of the Vancouver Women's Health Collective, on which her chapter in this volume is based (1974–1977). She is currently doing work on the relationship between feminism and collectivity. She is the author, with Nancy Kleiber, of several papers and publications on feminism and health care, including *Caring for Ourselves: An Alternative Structure for Health Care* (1978) and "Interactive research in a health care setting," *Social Science and Medicine* 12:193–98 (1978).

Donald A. Messerschmidt is associate professor of anthropology at Washington State University in Pullman, Washington. He has conducted research at home in rural Wyoming and eastern Washington state as well as with Tibetan refugee-immigrants in Maine and with ethnic and caste groups in the Nepal Himalayas. He has been an on-site researcher and consultant for Abt Associates, Inc., of Cambridge, Massachusetts and a consultant to various state, national, and international agencies. He has degrees in both education and anthropology and took his Ph.D. in anthropology at the University of Orgeon in 1974. He has published numerous articles in journals, including *Human Organization* and *Human Ecology* and a monograph on his research in Nepal (1976a).

Craig A. Molgaard received his Ph.D. in anthropology in 1979 from the University of California at Berkeley. His doctoral dissertation was based on a study of alternative health-care beliefs and practices among New Age agricultural workers in central Washington state. He was a research associate (1977–1980) at the Intercollegiate Center for Nursing Education at Spokane, Washington and is currently a research associate in the Department of Medical Statistics and Epidemiology, Mayo Clinic, Rochester, Minnesota.

David Serber received his Ph.D. in anthropology from the University of California at Berkeley in 1976. He has taught there and at Carnegie Mellon University, the College of Marin, and San Quentin Prison. He has received a number of research fellowships and grants from the National Science Foundation, the National Institute of Mental Health, and the Wenner-Gren Foundation for Anthropological Research, and he has participated in a National Academy of Sciences panel on government regulation. Serber has conducted research on insurance regulation, the politics of national health insurance, price competition in the real-estate industry, and has worked as a consultant to the Federal Trade Commission. He has published a number of articles on organizations, government regulation, and law and power, and he was recently an invited participant in the Wenner-Gren Foundation's Burg Wartenstein Conference on the Exercise of Power in Complex Organizations. Dr. Serber has worked as a senior analyst with Berkeley

Planning Associates and now has his own firm, David Serber and Associates, in Berkeley, California.

R. Timothy Sieber is associate professor of anthropology at the University of Massachusetts, Boston. He received his B.A. from Haverford College (1968) and his M.A. (1971) and Ph.D. (1976) from New York University. He is coeditor of *Children and Their Organization* (Sieber and Gordon 1981) and has contributed articles to *Urban Anthropology, Human Organization, Anthropology and Education Quarterly,* and other journals. He is currently completing a book on pupil-role socialization in American elementary schools.

Harry F. Wolcott is professor of education and anthropology at the University of Oregon. He joined anthropology to his career in education during his doctoral studies at Stanford and in his dissertation research in a village school among the Kwakiutl Indians of British Columbia. His subsequent studies, both at home and away, have been conducted under the auspices of the University of Oregon during his continuing assignment in the university's educational research-and-development center and two periods of sabbatical leave spent overseas. He is a fellow of the American Anthropological Association and the Society for Applied Anthropology and past president of the Council on Anthropology and Education.

Richard Zimmer teaches at Hutchins School, Sonoma State University at Rohnert Park, California. He holds a Ph.D. in anthropology from the University of California at Los Angeles (1976). He is interested in a variety of questions surrounding the role of voluntary associations as agents of economic development, support and crisis intervention, and socialization. His current research involves child-care and social-service provision as well as the effects of automation in modern offices. His publications include "The state of studies in political anthropology on Latinos in the U.S." (1975), and "Necessary directions in child care research" (1979).

Notes

Chapter 1 On anthropology at home

1 Some social research firms hiring anthropologists to study American society these days still feel that research in another society is an important precondition to successful research in one's own. See, for example, the criteria for the selection and employment of anthropologists in one project at Abt Associates, Inc. (Fitzsimmons 1975, Herriott 1977). Paul Bohannan, paraphrasing other past presidents of the American Anthropological Association, wondered recently how we can reduce the prejudice against hiring people who study their own society "especially if they have not proved their intrepidity by 'traditional' field research" (1980:509).

2 To Lévi-Strauss, "primitive" societies are not backward or retarded, but "possess, in one realm or another, a genius for invention or action that leaves the achievements of civilized peoples far behind" (1963:102).

3 See Warner (1959), Hsu (1963), Powdermaker (1966; 1939), Schneider (1968), Spradley (1970), Pilcher (1972), and Wolcott (1977).

4 None of the more than forty other individuals who originally submitted outlines and manuscripts for this volume did either.

5 The Bibliography is not meant to be complete or exhaustive. See also the bibliographies in Gillin (1957), Ryan (1957), Streib (1957), Sirjamaki (1971), and Eddy and Partridge (1978).

Chapter 3 Unseen Community: the natural history of a research project

1 The Unseen Community project was supported by the Center for Studies of Metropolitan Problems, National Institute of Mental Health Grant No. 5-RO1-MH-25996, Paul Bohannan, principal investigator. We wish to thank Elliott Liebow and Richard Wakefield for special interest and help.

2 The Western Behavioral Sciences Institute (WBSI) is a not-for-profit research institute with headquarters at 1150 Silverado Street, La Jolla, California 92037, Dr. Wayman J. Crow, director. It maintains a staff of interviewers, coders, and secretaries under the direction of Rosemary J. Erickson, coordinator of research. I want to thank Crow, Erickson, Peter Shoup, Patricia Falck, Chester Niebrugge, and the entire staff for trust and help provided.

3 Other publications about this research include Bohannan and Eckert (1976), D'Arcy (1976), Bauer (1977), Eckert (1980), and Bohannan (1981).
4 Some of the major pieces in this literature are: Bogue (1963), Shapiro (1971), Siegal (1977), Spradley (1970), and Stephens (1976).
5 California's Proposition 13 may mean that subsequent renewal plans may also not materialize.

Chapter 4 Common sense and science: urban core black observations

1 The field project, "The Life History as a Key to Afro-American Communal Character," was sponsored by a National Endowment for the Humanities Senior Fellowship and by grants-in-aid from the American Philosophical Society and from the Social Science Research Council, 1973–74.
2 The real names of informants quoted in these pages have not been employed.
3 In the black English especially of their generation, the word "quartet" has the additional meaning of a small vocal ensemble.

Chapter 5 Observer participation and consulting: research in urban food cooperatives

1 For a review of these arguments see Zimmer (1976).
2 See Malinowski's classic statement (1961). For a review of ethical conflicts in traditional fieldwork see Jarvie (1969), Kloos (1969), and Wax (1971).
3 See Leavitt (1964) for a general discussion of the problems of management-consultant studies.

Chapter 6 The masking of social reality: ethnographic fieldwork in the bureaucracy

1 This work was supported by the Wenner-Gren Foundation for Anthropological Research, the National Science Foundation, and the Merriam Davis Fund. I acknowledge with thanks the assistance of Kathleen Ealing, Lynn B. Cooper, and Professor Laura Nader.
2 Unlike most national industries, there is little federal regulation of the insurance industry; rather, each state regulates independently of every other state. The U. S. Supreme Court in *United States* vs. *South-Eastern Underwriters* (1944) held that insurance companies conducting their activities across state lines are subject to federal antimonopoly legislation within the regulatory power of Congress under the Commerce Clause. Soon thereafter, Congress passed the McCarren-Ferguson Act, declaring that in "the continued regulation and taxation of insurance by the several states. . . . No act of Congress shall be construed to invalidate, impair, or supersede any law enacted by any state for the purpose of regulating the business of insurance. . . . Provided, that after Jan. 1, 1948, . . . the Sherman Act . . . the Clayton Act . . . and the Federal Trade Commission Act . . . shall be applicable to the business if not regulated by the state." This returned the taxation and regulatory powers to the individual states, where they remain today. [*United States* vs. *South-Eastern Underwriters Association* (Ga. 1944) 64 S. Ct. 1162, 332 U.S. 533, 88 L.Ed. 1440, rehearing denied 65 S.Ct. 20, 323 U.S. 811 L.Ed. 646; McCarren-Ferguson Act 2, ch. 20, 59 stat. 34 (1945), as amended 15 U.S.C. 1012(b) (1964). For legislative history, see congressional debate, 91 *Cong. Rec.* 499–509, 1112–22, 1470–73, 1548–59 (1945). As introduced, the bill was based on a draft by the legislative committee of the National Association of Insurance Commissioners. See 91 *Cong. Rec.* 504 (1945).]
3 It should be noted that those workers who consented to outside interviews felt that if departmental supervisors discovered that they had agreed to this, reprisals would be forthcoming. Therefore, all such interviews were held secretly, and the identity of all informants was and remains confidential.

Chapter 7 Longitudinal research in rural North America: the Saskatchewan Cultural Ecology Research Program, 1960–1973

1 A more detailed history of SCERP, including specific data on time spent in the field, nature of interview protocols, comprehensive bibliography, and other information, is found in Bennett and Kohl (1980).

2 For appraisals of cultural ecology as a field of study see Bennett (1976a), Netting (1977), Moran (1979). The initial classic theoretical statement is Steward (1955).

3 For a description of the Jasper region, see Bennett (1969 or 1976b). (Bennett 1976b is a revised and supplemented version of Bennett 1969.) For various appreciations of the Saskatchewan and Canadian Plains context, see Mackintosh (1934), Alty (1939), Hedges (1939), Lipset (1950), C. Schwartz (1959), Stegner (1962), and Richards and Pratt (1979).

4 See Foster et al. (1979) for a survey of longitudinal fieldwork research in anthropology.

5 See Bennett (1967, 1969, and 1976b) and Braroe (1975) for studies of the Hutterites and Amerind people.

6 The following persons were involved in research in Jasper over the years: J. W. Bennett, Neils Braroe, Ivan Clark, Lyle Dunwald, Mary C. Hanson, S. B. Kohl, Leslie Potter, Peter Rompler, Charles Thomas, and Suzanne Findlay.

7 For more details about fieldwork roles in the study of family life and sex roles, see Kohl (1976).

8 During the period of the research, this generalized local anxiety about the project lessened, although it never completely disappeared. Over time, friendship and familiarity allowed for open discussions of the use and object of such research. Such discussions forced the researchers to make explicit their value system and ideas about what was good; likewise, the critics had to make their values, doubts, and fears explicit. For the ranchers, the practical and the tangible, not ideas or theoretical knowledge, were good, this fact reinforced data collected in other ways that dealt with these persons' attitudes toward education.

9 See Kohl and Bennett (1965 and 1976) and Kohl (1976). (Kohl and Bennett 1977 is a revised and enlarged version of the 1965 work.)

10 Bennett's previous fieldwork research in rural America began in the 1940s; see Bennett (1943) and Bennett et al. (1942). An early article prefiguring some of the basic cultural-ecological issues developed in SCERP is Bennett (1944).

11 Although official records, land tenure maps, historical documents of early settlement, and interviews with early settlers were used, the primary data in the reconstruction of the development of Jasper as a social and economic system came from the development of the fieldwork enterprise. These data were obtained through the method of constructing the family's genealogy, which mapped their kinship and marriage connections within the region. For the most part, these genealogies begin with the family's entrance into the region, not because this is the point at which the informant's lineage began but because of the objectives of the study. The genealogies were collected not for a formal kinship study aimed at delineating the total universe of kin but to obtain data on the instrumental and integrative functions of kinship within a particular habitat.

12 A foretaste of the management-style analysis can be found in Bennett (1980a).

Chapter 8 Social networks and community administration: a comparative study of two mining towns

1 The names used in this chapter for the mining company and the two towns are pseudonyms.

2 The research upon which this chapter is based was conducted in partial fulfillment of the requirements for the doctoral degree in the Department of Anthropology at the University of

Arizona. Dr. Edward H. Spicer, committee chairman, and Drs. Theodore E. Downing and the late Thomas B. Hinton, committee members, are thanked for their guidance and advice. Gordon and Brandt Graham, Lena Romero, and Lois and Clinton Brandt all provided special forms of assistance without which the study could not have been completed. Perhaps the greatest thanks of all should go to the people of the two towns for allowing me to share their lives. I hope they will feel this reporting of their lives is honest, accurate, and, above all, fair. Tables 8.1, 8.2, and 8.3 appeared initially in Graham (1981).

Chapter 10 Neighboring: discovering support systems among Norwegian-American women

1 All translations are according to *The Norwegian English Dictionary* by Einar Haugen (Madison: University of Wisconsin Press, 1965).
2 Many thanks to I. and I. Danielson, L. Gustafson, E. and E. Hansen, V. Lubnow, D. McCurdy, A. Neiderhauser, H. Nelson, J. Spradley, and M. Stalland.

Chapter 11 Applied ethnoscience in rural America: New Age health and healing

1 The research project on which this paper is based was funded by a three-year grant, #NU00592, from the Department of Health, Education, and Welfare, Public Health Service, Division of Nursing. We would like to thank Charles T. Snow for comments and suggestions on an earlier draft of this manuscript. A special note of appreciation is in order to Roberta Flemens, who cheerfully typed and proofread this chapter.
2 The theory behind the methodology of ethnoscience can be traced to the German historicism of Dilthey, Scheler, and Mannheim and the notions of von Humboldt, Brinton, and Powell on types of cognitive styles and folk psychology (Berger and Luckman 1966; Merton 1968). More recent antecedents involve the work Goodenough (1956), Lounsbury (1956), Frake (1961), and Conklin (1962) in attempting to minimize ethnographer bias, discover what phenomena are of significance to the people of any given culture or subculture, and gain access to the underlying principles of organization for such semantically encoded information (Tyler 1969). The methodology per se involves an integration of Morris's (1938) concepts for the structural treatment of meaning and basic strategies from structural phonetics for the isolation of distinctive features and for descriptions based on combinations of such features.
3 The traditional ethnoscience approach to semantic theory can be viewed as an extension of Bloomfieldian structural linguistics and a parallel to the use of semantic features in generative linguistics as exemplified by Katz and Fodor (1963). The most general notion associated with discrete-feature or combinatorial semantics is that the semantic features that constitute a word's meaning are interpretable as the necessary and sufficient conditions for its application (Kay 1975). A number of problems associated with discrete-feature ethnoscience have been pointed out by Burling (1964), Weinreich (1966), Gladwin (1971), Lakoff (1972), Fillmore (1974, 1975), and Kay (1975). These include the notions that discrete-feature analysis permits multiple solutions to the analysis of lexical sets, that lexical sets vary as to their amenability to discrete-feature analysis, that formal elegance of analysis does not ensure cognitive validity, and that as a semantic theory the discrete-feature model is removed from concern with how individuals interpret texts in their own language.

Nondiscrete or frame semantics has been proposed as an alternative by Fillmore (1974, 1975) and Kay (1975). As a semantic theory it has three main advantages over the discrete-feature model. The first advantage is that it offers an integrated view of a number of linguistic issues, including the nature of meaning, the acquisition of meaning, the comprehension of texts, and historical semantic change. The second advantage is that it offers clearer analogs to current research findings in the general field of cognition. This includes the research of Rosch (1973, 1975, 1976) on graded vs. discrete category boundaries, the research of Kempton (1978) on graded vs. discrete class inclusion relations, that of Berlin and Kay (1969) on category foci, Bruner (1964) on enactive and iconic memory, and Lindsay (1963), Dreyfus (1972), and Minsky (1974) on mental pictures and frames in the field of artificial intelligence. The third advantage is that nondiscrete semantics allows for consideration of extralinguistic contextual factors such as status of speaker and hearer, type of scene or speech situation, type of speech event or speech act, real world beliefs of the speakers, and the previous history of discourse between speakers in the analysis of the distribution of both precise and vague linguistic categorizations (Zadeh 1965, 1976; G. Lakoff 1972; Labov 1973).

Chapter 12 Interactive research in a feminist setting: the Vancouver Women's Health Collective

1 The research that led to this paper was supported by a Demonstration Grant #610-1020-20A from the Research Programs Directorate of the Department of National Health and Welfare of the Canadian federal government. The paper has benefitted from the comments and criticisms of the members of the Vancouver Women's Health Collective, to whom the authors are most grateful. The authors wish to thank the Department of Anthropology and Sociology, University of British Columbia, for providing the secretarial assistance for the preparation of this paper.
2 In 1979, the collective underwent some major changes. Although its collective structure remains essentially the same, there is a greater emphasis on criticism and self-criticism sessions as a technique of self-evaluation and change. The group has also become less service oriented and more concerned with developing and using a radical political analysis of the existing health-care system and the society in which it functions.

Chapter 13 Constraints in government research: the anthropologist in a rural school district

1 I am indebted to a large number of people who assisted me in the preparation of this study. They include the project staff at Abt Associates, Inc., directed by Robert E. Herriott; several anthropology colleagues and associates; outside consultants engaged by NIE and Abt Associates; and, not the least, my hosts and informants in River District, Wyoming. I cannot name everybody, but I do want to acknowledge a few people who have been particularly helpful. They include my associate researcher in 1974, Marilyn C. Richen, and my two most recent critical reviewers, Jacquetta Hill and Harry Wolcott. Homer G. Barnett was quite helpful in the early stages of data analysis and his teachings are a continual inspiration. Kareen, my wife, was a constant companion throughout the research experience and subsequent work on project papers, reports, and articles.
  Much of this paper has been drawn from Messerschmidt (1975 and 1979). The observations and opinions expressed in this study are entirely my own and do not necessarily reflect those of the officers or staff of Abt Associates, the National Institute of Education, or River District schools. "River District" and all other local place names used here are pseudonyms.
2 There is little doubt that the ethnographer's presence can affect the data. Acknowledging this is particularly important in applied research, particularly when the researcher is somehow the focus of controversy. Ignoring it implies that we somehow have no effect on our data and is a less than truthful condition. Karl Heider, in a neat turn of the phrase "ethnographic present," has called this condition of neglect an example of "ethnographic absence" (1976:51).
3 As elsewhere in the research on the rural Experimental Schools Program, a distinction is made between the projects, the activities of ten local school district communities, and the program, or the

Experimental Schools Program as a nationally conceived endeavor that includes all of the involved rural communities and local projects (as well as eight other urban experimental school projects). See Corwin (1977) and Herriott and Gross (1979).

4 One contemporaneous and one recent study of educational change in America have upheld the rationality of this assumption. See Ford Foundation (1972) and Pincus and Pascal (1977).

5 For a discussion see Messerschmidt and Richen (1975:1043–1098).

6 The substantive results and analyses of the ES projects in ten rural school districts may be found in a number of published and forthcoming works prepared by the staff of Abt Associates, Inc. They include Fitzsimmons and Lavey (1975, 1977), Fitzsimmons, Wolff, and Freedman (1975), Fitzsimmons and Ferb (1977), Herriott (1977, 1980), Abt, Cerva, and Marx (1978), Rosenblum and Louis (1978), a special issue of *Rural Sociology* edited by Wolcott (1978), and Herriott and Gross (1979).

7 My previous fieldwork experience fit the more traditional, exotic image of anthropology. It was conducted among Nepalese villagers (Messerschmidt 1976a) and Tibetan refugees (Messerschmidt 1976b).

8 For a much more complete account of the River District ES project and its substantive outcomes, see Messerschmidt (1979).

9 There are excellent examples of similar kinds of research in the ethnographic literature on schooling. Studies by Henry (1963), Warren (1967), Rosenfeld (1971), Hill-Burnett (1973), Khleif (1974), and Singleton (1976), are representative of research in schools and classrooms. Although studies by anthropologists of educational leadership, administration, and bureaucracy are fewer, the works of Spindler (1963), Vidich and McReynolds (1971), Gallaher (1973), Wolcott (1973, 1977) and Warren (1976) are relevant. Few studies in either category, however, deal with rural school situations and none (with the possible exception of Wolcott 1977) approach an educational situation as complex as Experimental Schools.

10 Lurking has been described by Stricklund and Schlesinger (1969) as a subtle form of information gathering that implies being in the right place or the right company or conversation at the right time to hear conversations and at times to participate in conversation about topics of interest. The data gathered in such a setting may or may not be jotted down, but it is usually held until a convenient time for recording it. Informants know all the while, of course, that the researcher's purpose in being present is research related, so there is nothing secret or unethical about the activity.

11 I referred to the study of "living peoples" and consciously avoided the more usual anthropological term "informant" because of the latter term's spy-like connotation as someone who "informs" to the authorities. "Living people," "interviewees," or "subjects" are more neutral terms. The term "informant" is quite common, however, in the literature on anthropological research and is used frequently throughout this account of the River District ES research.

12 Much of the data acquired from bureaucrats, especially in the form of plans and progress reports, is what is supposed to be happening, what should happen (ideally), and what is expected to happen, but not always on what *is* happening or has really happened. Often the data on what really happens are found only in the candid and somewhat offhand or private remarks of the system managers and the bystanders. (Some indications of the reality of a situation may come from disgruntled or marginal members of the group under study, but great caution is warranted in using this information, for it may be distorted.) The distinction here is between the ideal, which is most often expressed verbally and on paper for outside observers, and the real, which is often expressed privately, if at all. Gerald Britan has noted the same problem in his research within a federal agency (Britan 1978; Britan and Cohen 1980). The ideal/real distinction is one that anthropologists have long noted in their research.

13 For a similar account, see Elliott Liebow's reflections on "A Field Experience in Retrospect" in *Tally's Corner* (1967:232–256).

14 This tension is described in detail in Messerschmidt (1979).

15 Of course, local school officials were free to communicate with any party to the research at any time and in any manner they might choose.

16 I was also aware that as a social scientist I had no natural place in the rational scheme of the school bureaucracy. The anthropologist in this situation is typically seen as "at best extraneous; at worst... an active interferer" (Britan 1978:5). I was both – extraneous at first, but an interference and a threat in the long run. "To study a bureaucracy, an anthropologist must find his place in a sharply delimited environment. He must cope with the paramount relationships of power and authority, with overt manipulations of political power, and with the conscious biasing of data to meet personal and professional goals" (Britan 1978:5).

17 This compromise system of indirect reporting through Abt Associates in Cambridge to the uninvolved ethnographer at NIE in Washington, D.C., worked without internal incident. But it was not entirely satisfactory from the point of view of the people in River District. There was also provision for other social scientists to read and consult with the on-site researchers, Abt staff, and NIE officials about the nature and quality of the research effort. The history of the development of a panel of consultants is partly described in Fitzsimmons (1975); see also Herriott (1977).

18 Wolcott's study (1977) is only one of several successful adaptations of traditional anthropological methods and theory to studies of modern American society. See also the works of Hsu (1963), Henry (1963), Powdermaker (1939, 1966), Spradley (1970), Spradley and McCurdy (1972), Pilcher (1972), Wolcott (1973), and Goldschmidt (1978). See also the essays in Jorgenson and Truzzi (1974), and in Hymes (1974), for examples.

Chapter 14 Many roles, many faces: researching school–community relations in a heterogeneous American urban community

1 I thank Nicholas S. Hopkins and Susan Reverby for their valuable comments on earlier versions of this paper. The reported research was carried out under support of P. H. S. Grant No. 17216 from the Center for Urban Ethnography.

2 "Chestnut Heights" is a pseudonym, as are all other proper names in the chapter, except for the designation of New York City.

3 As a shorthand, and in keeping with local usage, I eliminate hyphenated forms (e.g., Irish-American) in discussing the community's groups.

4 "Extra-good behavior" was expected to be demonstrated toward visiting pupils from lower grades, so as to set a good example for them.

Chapter 15 Anthropology under contract: two examples from Alaska

1 Hanrahan and Gruenstein recount my OCS experience. They conclude by noting; "the reality of Yakutat's situation is clearly closer to Feldman's portrayal than the environmental impact statement's. Yakutat residents found that the oil companies had almost overwhelmed their simple fishing village way of life through plans that were set in motion long before the OCS lease sale for the gulf was even held" (1977:287). The authors interviewed a former employee of the Anchorage OCS office, who stated that the EIS being prepared (October 1976) for the Kodiak area of the Gulf of Alaska was being written by "half of the Los Angeles" OCS office staff, assigned to temporary duty in Alaska (p. 285).

Chapter 16 Talking to an agency: communicating the research findings

1 McDowell (1978) notes a hazard of agency work: that the subject of her research, race relations, had a very low priority to the agency requesting her work. This aspect of an agency culture may be beyond the control of a researcher.

2 This was reaffirmed for me at the 1978 annual meeting of the American Anthropological Association in Los Angeles, where there was a heated discussion of nonacademic employment for anthropologists.

3 The multiple-use policy regulates and balances the use of all BLM resources: lands, minerals, forest, range, watershed, wildlife, and recreation. Wild horses and burros are regulated by the multiple-use act as well as wild horse and burro acts, some aspects of endangered species legislation, and the Environmental Protection Act.

4 Another case with some similar issues involves the disposition of Alaskan lands. Most of Alaska's land area was federally rather than state owned until Alaska Native Claims Settlement Act was passed by Congress in 1971. That act granted Alaskan Indian and Eskimo groups rights to land, but the balance of the unallocated land remained in dispute until late 1980 when Congress acted to resolve the remaining issues.

Chapter 17 Home and away: personal contrasts in ethnographic style

1 The author gratefully acknowledges the help of the late Shirley M. Kennedy in providing inspiration and editorial review during the preparation of early drafts of this chapter.

Bibliography

Aamodt, A. M. (1976) "Observations of a health and healing system of a Papago community." In M. Leininger (ed.). *Transcultural Health Care Issues and Conditions*. Philadelphia: Davis, pp. 23–26.
  (1978) "The care component in a health and healing system." In E. Bauwens (ed.). *Anthropology and Health*. St. Louis: Mosby, pp. 37–45.
Abdellah, Faye G., and Eugene Levine (1965) *Better Patient Care Through Nursing Research*. New York: Macmillan.
Abrahamsen, Martin A. (1976) *Cooperative Business Enterprise*. New York: McGraw-Hill.
Abt, Wendy Peter, Thomas Cerva, and Thomas Jakob Marx (1978) "Why So Little Change? The Effects on Pupils of the Rural Experimental Schools Program." Cambridge, Mass.: Abt Associates, for the National Institute of Education.
Aceves, Joseph B. (1978) "Competence by blood: Ethnological fieldwork in the ancestral village." Presented at symposium, "Anthropologists and Origin Cultures," at the 77th annual meeting, American Anthropological Association, Los Angeles.
Aldrich, Howard E., and Jeffrey Pfeffer (1976) "Environments of organizations." *Annual Review of Sociology* 2:79–105.
Allen, James B. (1966) *The Company Town in the American West*. Norman: University of Oklahoma Press.
Allport, Gordon W. (1942) *The Use of Personal Documents in Psychological Science*. New York: Social Science Research Council.
Almy, Susan W. (1977) "Anthropologists and development agencies." *American Anthropologist* 79:280–292.
Alty, S.W. (1939) "The influence of climate and other geographical factors in the growth and distribution of population in Saskatchewan." *Geography* 24:10–33.
Amador, Donald H. G. (1973) "Homosexual research methods as seen by a homosexual." Anthropology Department, California State University, Los Angeles. Unpublished paper.
Andreski, Iris (1970) *Old Wives' Tales: Life Stories from Ibibioland*. New York: Schocken Books.
Angrosino, Michael V. (1976) "The evolution of a new applied anthropology." In Michael V. Angrosino (ed.). *Do Applied Anthropologists Apply Anthropology?* Southern Anthropological Society Proceedings No. 10. Athens, Ga.: The Society for Applied Anthropology, pp. 1–9.

Angrosino, Michael, et al. (1977) " 'Myth of nonacademic anthropology' criticized." *Anthropology Newsletter* (correspondence) 18 (10):18.

Arensberg, Conrad, and Arthur Niehoff (1964) *Introducing Social Change: A Manual for Americans Overseas.* Chicago: Aldine.

Ashenbrenner, Joyce (1975) *Lifelines: Black Families in Chicago.* New York: Holt.

Bachrach, Peter, and Morton Baratz (1963) "Two faces of power." *American Political Science Review* 56:947–952.

Bailey, F. G. (1977) *Morality and Expediency: The Folklore of Academic Politics.* Chicago: Aldine.

Barnes, J. A. (1969) "Networks and political process." In J. Clyde Mitchell (ed.). *Social Networks in Urban Situations.* Manchester, Eng.: University of Manchester Press, pp. 51–76.

Barnett, H. G. (1953) *Innovation: The Basis of Cultural Change.* New York: McGraw-Hill.

(1956) *Anthropology in Administration.* Evanston, Ill.: Row, Peterson.

Basham, Richard (1978) *Urban Anthropology.* Palo Alto, Cal.: Mayfield.

Bastide, Roger (1973) *Applied Anthropology.* Trans. Alice L. Morton. New York: Harper & Row.

Batalla, Guillermo Bonfin (1966) "Conservative thought in applied anthropology: A critique." *Human Organization* 25:89–92.

Bauer, Marilyn S. (1977) *Downtown Redevelopment in San Diego: A Case History.* LaJolla, California: Western Behavioral Science Institute.

Bax, Mart (1977) "Network structuralists and network actionists: An old dichotomy under new cover." Presented at the annual meeting, American Anthropological Association, Houston.

Beale, L. J. (1975) *The Revival of Population Growth in Nonmetropolitan America.* Economic Development Division, Economic Research Service, U.S. Department of Agriculture, ERS–605.

Beals, Ralph L. (1962) "Acculturation." In Sol Tax (ed.). *Anthropology Today.* Chicago: University of Chicago Press.

(1969) *Politics of Social Research: An Inquiry into the Ethics and Responsibilities of Social Scientists.* Chicago: Aldine.

(1976) "Anthropology and government: Unwilling bridegroom and reluctant bride." In James P. Loucky and Jeffrey R. Jones (eds.). *Paths to the Symbolic Self: Essays in Honor of Walter Goldschmidt.* Los Angeles: Anthropology UCLA, Vol. 8, pp. 159–173.

Beattie, J. (1964) *Other Cultures: Aims, Methods, and Achievements in Social Anthropology.* New York: Free Press.

Beckhard, Richard (1971) "Helping a group with planned change: A case study." In Harvey A. Hornstein, Barbara Benedict Bunker, W. Warner Burke, Marion Gindes, and Roy J. Lewicki (eds.). *Social Intervention: A Behavioral Science Approach.* New York: Free Press, pp. 286–293.

Belshaw, Cyril S. (1976) *The Sorcerer's Apprentice: An Anthropology of Public Policy.* New York: Pergamon.

Bennett, John W. (1943) "Food and social status in a rural society." *American Sociological Review* 8:561–569.

(1944) "The interaction of culture and environment in the smaller societies." *American Anthropologist* 46:461–478.

(1967) *Hutterian Brethren: The Agricultural Economy of a Communal People.* Stanford, Cal.: Stanford University Press.

(1969) *Northern Plainsmen: Adaptive Strategy and Agrarian Life.* Chicago: Aldine.

(1976a) *The Ecological Transition.* New York: Pergamon.

(1976b) *Northern Plainsmen: Adaptive Strategy and Agrarian Life.* Rev. and enl. ed. Arlington Heights, Ill.: AHM.

(1980a) "Management style: A concept and method for the analysis of family-operated agricultural enterprise." In Peggy Barlett (ed.), *Agricultural Decision Making: Anthropological Contributions to Rural Development*. New York: Academic Press, pp. 203–237.

(1980b) *Of Time and the Enterprise: North American Family Farm Management in a Context of Resource Marginality*. Minneapolis: University of Minnesota Press.

Bennett, John W., and Seena Kohl (1980) "Longitudinal research in cultural ecology: A history of the Saskatchewan Cultural Ecology Research Program 1960–77." *Prairie Forum* 4:197–219.

Bennett, John W., Harvey L. Smith, and Herbert Passin (1942) "Food and culture in Southern Illinois–a preliminary report." *American Sociological Review* 7:645–660.

Berger, Bennett M. (1971) *Working Class Suburb: A Study of Auto Workers in Suburbia*. Berkeley: University of California Press.

Berger, Peter, and Thomas Luckman (1966) *The Social Construction of Reality*. New York: Doubleday.

Berlin, Brent, and Paul Kay (1969) *Basic Color Terms: Their Universality and Evolution*. Berkeley: University of California Press.

Bernstein, Marver (1955) *Regulating Business by Independent Commission*. Princeton, N.J.: Princeton University Press.

(1972) "Independent regulatory agencies: A perspective on their reform." *The Annals of the American Academy of Political and Social Science* 400:14–26.

Berreman, Gerald D. (1962) *Behind Many Masks*. Society for Applied Anthropology Monograph No. 4. Lexington, Ken.: The Society for Applied Anthropology.

(1968) "Is anthropology alive? Social responsibility in social anthropology." *Current Anthropology* 9:391–396.

Billingsley, Andrew (1971) "The treatment of Negro families in American scholarship." In Robert Staples (ed.). *The Black Family*. Belmont, Cal.: Wadsworth, pp. 28–34.

Black, Mary (1969) "Eliciting folk taxonomy in Ojibwa." In Stephen A. Tyler (ed.). *Cognitive Anthropology*. New York: Holt.

Blau, Peter M. (1963) *The Dynamics of Bureaucracy*. Chicago: University of Chicago Press.

Blauner, Robert (1970) "Black culture: Myth or reality." in Norman E. Whitten, Jr., and John F. Szwed (eds.). *Afro-American Anthropology*. New York: Free Press, pp. 347–366.

Blok, Anton (1973) "Coalitions in Sicilian peasant society." In Jeremy Boissevain and J. Clyde Mitchel (eds.). *Network Analysis: Studies in Human Interaction*. The Hague: Mouton, pp. 151–166.

Blom, J. P., and John Gumperz (1972) "Social meaning in linguistic structures." In J. Gumperz and D. Hymes (eds.). *Directions in Sociolinguistics*. New York: Holt, 407–34.

Bogue, D. J. (1963) *Skid Row in American Cities*. Chicago: University of Chicago Press.

Bohannan, Laura (1973) "Shakespeare in the bush." In Alan Dundes (ed.). *Even Man His Own Way*. Englewood Cliffs, N.J.: Prentice-Hall, pp. 477–486.

Bohannan, Paul (1981) "Eating habits of elderly residents of center-city hotels." In Christine Fry (ed.). *Dimensions of an Anthropology of Aging*. Brooklyn, N.Y.: Bergin Press, in press.

(1980) "You can't do nothing: Presidential address for 1979." *American Anthropologist* 82:508–524.

Bohannan, Paul, and Kevin J. Eckert (1976) "A community of loners." *Proceedings of the Second SRO Conference*. St. Louis, Mo.: St Louis University, n.p.

Boissevain, Jeremy (1973) "An exploration of two first-order zones." In Jeremy Boissevain and J. Clyde Mitchell (eds.). *Network Analysis: Studies in Human Interaction*. The Hague: Mouton, pp. 125–148.

Boswell, D. M. (1969) "Personal crises and the mobilization of the social network." In J. Clyde Mitchell (ed.). *Social Networks in Urban Situations.* Manchester, Eng.: Manchester University Press, pp. 245–296.

Bott, Elizabeth (1957) *Family and Social Network.* London: Tavistock Publications.

Bowen, Elizabeth S. (1954) *Return to Laughter.* New York: Harper.

Bradwin, Edmund W. (1968) *The Bunkhouse Man: A Study of Work and Pay in the Camps of Canada, 1903–1914.* New York: AMS Press.

Braroe, Niels (1975) *Indian and White: Self-Image and Interaction in a Canadian Plains Community.* Stanford, Cal.: Stanford University Press.

Braroe, Niels W., and George L. Hicks (1967) "Observations on the mystique of anthropology." *Sociological Quarterly* 8: 173–186.

Britan, Gerald M. (1978) "Some problems of fieldwork in a federal bureaucracy." Presented at the annual meeting of the American Anthropological Association, Los Angeles. Nov.

Britan, Gerald M., and Ronald Cohen (eds.) (1980) *Hierarchy and Society: Anthropological Perspectives on Bureaucracy.* Philadelphia, Pa.: ISHI Publications.

Bruner, Jerome (1964) "The course of cognitive growth." *American Psychologist* 19:1–15.

Buder, Stanley (1967) *Pullman: An Experiment in Industrial order and Community Planning.* New York: Oxford University Press.

Burch, W. R. (1969) "The nature of community." In John Forster (ed.). *Social Process in New Zealand.* Auckland: Longman, Paul, pp. 79–101.

Burling, Robbins (1964) "Cognition and componential analysis: God's truth or hocus pocus?" *American Anthropologist* 66:20–28.

Byerly, Elizabeth, and Craig A. Molgaard (1982) "Social institutions and disease transmission." In Thomas Maretski and Noel Chrisman (eds.), *Clinical Anthropology.* Doordorf, The Netherlands: Reidel, in press.

Byerly, Elizabeth L., Craig A. Molgaard, and Amanda L. Golbeck (1979a) "Dissonance in the desert: What to do with the goldenseal?" In M. Leininger (ed.). *Transcultural Nursing.* New York: Masson International Nursing Publications.

(1979b) "Internal category structures: Fuzzy sets in nursing research." Presented at symposium "Ethnography in Nursing Research," at the annual Communicating Nursing Research Conference, Western Interstate Commission for Higher Education, Denver.

Byerly, Elizabeth L., Craig A. Molgaard, and Charles Snow (1978) "The fruit flies: Alternative healing systems of migrant agricultural workers as strategies for coping with stigma." Presented at the annual meeting of the American Anthropological Association, Los Angeles.

Capener, H. R. (1975) "On a discipline in search of application." *Rural Sociology* 40:398–410.

Cassell, Joan (1977) "The relationship of observer to observed in peer group research." *Human Organization* 36:412–416.

Chambers, Erve (1977a) "Policy research at the local level." *Human Organization* 36:418–421.

(1977b) "Working for The Man: The Anthropologist in policy relevant research." *Human Organization* 36:259–267.

(1979) "The burden of profession: Applied anthropology at the crossroads." *Reviews in Anthropology* 6:523–540.

Child, Irving, M. K. Bacon, H. Barry III, C. Buchwald, and C. R. Snyder (1965) "A cross-cultural study of drinking." *Quarterly Journal of the Study of Alcohol,* Supplement No. 3.

Cicourel, A. V. (1964) *Method and Measurement in Sociology.* New York: Free Press.

Clark, Margaret (1970) *Health in the Mexican American Culture.* Berkeley: University of California Press.

Cleland, Robert Glass (1952) *A History of Phelps Dodge, 1834–1950.* New York: Knopf.

Clinton, Charles A. (1975) "Anthropologist as a hired hand." *Human Organization* 34:197–204.

(1976) "On bargaining with the devil: Contract ethnography and accountability in fieldwork." *Council on Anthropology and Education Quarterly* 8:25–28.

Cochrane, Glynn (1971) *Development Anthropology*. New York: Oxford University Press.

Cohen, Yehudi (1977) "The anthropological enterprise." *American Anthropologist* 79:388–396.

Colfer, Carol J. Pierce (1976) "Rights, responsibilities and reports: An ethical dilemma in contract research." In M. A. Rynkiewich and James P. Spradley (eds.). *Ethics and Anthropology: Dilemmas in Fieldwork*. New York: Wiley, pp. 32 – 46.

Collingwood, R. G. (1946) *The Idea of History*. Oxford: Clarendon Press.

Committee on Minorities in Anthropology (1973) *Report of the Committee on Minorities in Anthropology*. Washington, D.C.: American Anthropological Association.

Conklin, Harold C. (1962) "Lexicographic treatment of folk taxonomies." In E. W. Householder and Sol Saporta (eds.). *Problems in Lexicography*. Bloomington: University of Indiana Press.

(1964) "Ethnogenealogical Method." In Ward Goodenough (ed.). *Explorations in Cultural Anthropology*. New York: McGraw-Hill, pp. 25–55.

Cook-Gumperz, Jenny, and John Gumperz (eds.) (1976) *Papers in Language and Context*. Berkeley: University of California, Language Behavior Research Laboratory, Working Paper No. 46.

Corwin, Ronald G. (1977) *Patterns of Federal–Local Relationships in Education: A Case Study of the Rural Experimental Schools Program*. Cambridge, Mass.: Abt Associates.

Cushing, Frank H. (1970) *My Adventures in Zuni*. Palo Alto, Cal.: American Way.

D'Addario, Omega (1978) "Marginality in the field," Presented at symposium. "Anthropologists and Origin Cultures," at the 77th annual meeting of the American Anthropological Association, Los Angeles, November 18, 1978.

D'Arcy, Adelyse Marie (1976) "Elderly Hotel Residents and Their Social Networks in Downtown San Diego." M.A. thesis, San Diego State University.

Dalton, M. (1959) *Men Who Manage: Fusions of Feeling and Theory in Administration*. New York: Wiley.

D'Andrade, Roy G. (1976) "A propositional analysis of U.S. American beliefs." In K. H. Basso and H. A. Selby (eds.). *Meaning in Anthropology*. Albuquerque: University of New Mexico Press, pp. 155–180.

Despres, L. A. (1968) "Anthropological theory, cultural pluralism, and the study of complex societies." *Current Anthropology* 9:3–26.

Devereaux, G. (1967) *From Anxiety to Method in the Behavioral Sciences*. New York: Humanities Press.

Diamond, Stanley (1964) "A revolutionary discipline." *Current Anthropology* 5:432–437.

(1974) *In Search of the Primitive*. New Brunswick, N.J.: Transaction Books, E. P. Dutton.

Douglass, W. A., and Jon Bilbao (1975) *Amerikanauk: Basques in the American West*. Reno: University of Nevada Press.

Dreeben, Robert (1968) *On What Is Learned in School*. Reading, Mass.: Addison-Wesley.

(1973) "The school as a workplace." In Robert M. W. Travers (ed.). *Second Handbook of Research on Teaching*. Chicago: Rand-McNally, pp. 450–473.

Dreyfus, Hubert L. (1972) *What Computers Can't Do*. New York: Harper & Row.

Durkheim, Emile (1956) *Education and Sociology*. Trans. and ed. S. D. Fox. New York: Free Press.

(1966) *Moral Education*. E. K. Wilson and H. Shnurer (ed.). New York: Free Press.

Eckert, J. Kevin (1977) "Older Persons Living in Single Room Occupancy Hotels." Ph.D. dissertation, Northwestern University.

(1980) *The Unseen Elderly*. San Diego: The Campanile Press.

(1981) "Health status, adjustment, and social supports of older people in hotels." In Christine Fry (ed.). *Dimensions of an Anthropology of Aging*. Brooklyn, N.Y.: Bergin Press, in press.

Eddy, Elizabeth M. (1965) *Walk the White Line: A Profile of Urban Education*. New York: Anchor.

Eddy, Elizabeth M., and W. L. Partridge (eds.) (1978) *Applied Anthropology in America*. New York: Columbia University Press.

Edelman, Murray (1964) *The Symbolic Uses of Politics*. Urbana, Ill. University of Illinois Press.

Epstein, A. L. (1958) *Politics in an Urban African Community*. Manchester, Eng.: University of Manchester Press for the Rhodes-Livingston Institute.

Erasmus, Charles J. (1961) *Man Takes Control*. Indianapolis: Bobbs-Merrill.

Erickson, Rosemary, and Kevin Eckert (1977) "The elderly poor in downtown San Diego hotels." *The Gerontologist* 17:440–446.

Estes, Ron, and Robert E. Herriott (1972) "The role of the on-site researcher in Project RURAL." Cambridge, Mass.: Abt Associates. Unpublished working paper.

Evans-Pritchard, E. E. (1946) "Applied anthropology." *Africa* 16:92–98.

    (1970) *The Nuer*. New York: Oxford University Press.

Everhart, Robert, B. (1977) "Between stranger and friend: Some consequences of 'long-term' fieldwork in schools." *American Educational Research Journal* 14:1–15.

Fahim, Hussein M. (1977) "Foreign and indigenous anthropology: The perspective of an Egyptian anthropologist." *Human Organization* 36:80–86.

Fahim, Hussein, Katherine Helmer, Elizabeth Colson, T. N. Madan, Herbert C. Kelman, and Tabal Asad (1980) "Indigenous anthropology in non-Western countries: A further elaboration." *Current Anthropology* 21:644–663.

Fanon, Franz (1968) *The Wretched of the Earth*. New York: Grove.

Fillmore, Charles J. (1974) "The future of semantics." In C. Fillmore, G. Lakoff, and R. Lakoff (eds.). *Berkeley Studies in Syntax and Semantics*. Berkeley: University of California, Department of Linguistics and Institute of Human Learning, pp. 4–18.

    (1975) "An alternative to checklist theories of meaning." In Cathy Cogen, Henry Thompson, Graham Thurgood, Kenneth Whistler, and James Wright (eds.). *Papers Presented to the First Annual Meeting of the Berkeley Linguistics Society*. Berkeley: Berkeley Linguistics Society, pp. 123–31.

Firestone, William (1975) "Educational field research in a 'contract shop' " *The Generator of Division G., American Educational Research Association* 3:3–11, 15.

Fischer, Ann (1970) "Fieldwork in five cultures." In Peggy Golde (ed.). *Women in the Field*. Chicago: Aldine, pp. 267–289.

Fischer, Claude S., Robert M. Jackson, C. Ann Steuve, Kathleen Gerson, and Lynne McCallister Jones, with Mark Baldassare (1977) *Networks and Places: Social Relations in the Urban Setting*. New York: Free Press.

Fitzsimmons, Stephen J. (1975) "The anthropologist in a strange land." *Human Organization* 34:183–196.

Fitzsimmons, Stephen J., and Thomas Ferb (1977) "Towards the development of a community attitudes assessment scale." *Public Opinion Quarterly* 41:356–373.

Fitzsimmons, Stephen J., and Warren G. Lavey (1975) "Social Economic Accounts System (SEAS): Toward a comprehensive community-level assessment procedure." *Social Indicators Research* 2:389–452.

    (1977) "Community: Towards an integration of research, theory, evaluation and public policy." *Social Indicators Research* 4:25–66.

Fitzsimmons, Stephen J., Peter C. Wolff, and Abby J. Freedman (eds.) (1975) *Rural America: A Social and Educational History of Ten Communities* (Vols. 1 and 2). Cambridge, Mass.: Abt Associates, for the National Institute of Education.

Ford Foundation (1972) *A Foundation Goes to School*. New York: The Ford Foundation.

Foster, George M. (1969) *Applied Anthropology*. Boston: Little Brown.

    (1972) "A second look at limited good." *Anthropological Quarterly* 45:57–64.

Foster, George M., Thayer Scudder, Elizabeth Colson, and Robert V. Kemper (eds.) (1979) *Long-Term Field Research in Social Anthropology*. New York: Academic Press.

Fox, Richard A. (1977) *Urban Anthropology: Cities in Their Cultural Settings*. Englewood Cliffs, N.J.: Prentice-Hall.

Frake, Charles O. (1961) "The diagnosis of disease among the Subanun of Mindanao." *American Anthropologist* 63:113–132.

Freilich, Morris (1970) "Fieldwork: An introduction." In Morris Freilich (ed.). *Marginal Natives: Anthropologists at Work*. New York: Harper & Row, pp. 1–37.

Galarza, Ernesto (1971) *Barrio Boy*. Notre Dame, Ind.: University of Notre Dame Press.

Gallaher, Art Jr. (1973) "Directed change in formal organizations: The school system." In F. A. J. Ianni and E. Storey (eds.). *Cultural Relevance and Educational Issues: Readings in Anthropology and Education*. Boston: Little Brown, pp. 323–338.

Gans, Herbert J. (1965) *The Urban Villagers: Groups and Class in the Life of Italian-Americans*. New York: Free Press.

Gerth, H. H., and C. Wright Mills (eds. and trans.) (1946) *From Max Weber: Essays in Sociology*. New York: Oxford University Press.

Gillin, John (1949) "Methodological problems in the anthropological study of modern cultures." *American Anthropologist* 51:392–399.

   (1957) "The application of anthropological knowledge to modern mass society: An anthropologist's view." *Human Organization* 15:24–29.

Gintis, Herbert, and Samuel Bowles (1972–1973) "IQ in the United States class structure." Parts 1 and 2. *Social Policy* 3:65–97.

Gladwin, Hugh (1971) "Semantics, schemata and kinship." Presented at the annual meeting of the American Anthropological Association, New York.

Glaser, Barney G., and Anselm Strauss (1967) *The Discovery of Grounded Theory: Strategies for Qualitative Research*. Chicago: Aldine.

Glazer, Nathan, and Daniel P. Moynihan (1963) *Beyond the Melting Pot: The Negroes, Puerto Ricans, Jews, Italians, and Irish of New York City*. Cambridge, Mass.: MIT Press.

Gluckman, Max (1969) "Introduction." In A. L. Epstein (ed.). *The Craft of Social Anthropology*. London: Tavistock, pp. xi–xx.

Goffman, Erving (1959) *The Presentation of Self in Everyday Life*. Garden City, N.Y.: Doubleday.

   (1961) *Asylums: Essays on the Social Situations of Mental Patients and Other Inmates*. New York: Anchor.

Golde, Peggy (1970) "Odyssey of encounter." In Peggy Golde (ed.). *Women in the Field: Anthropology Experiences*. Chicago: Aldine, pp. 67–93.

Goldschmidt, Walter (1977) "Anthropology and the coming crisis: An autoethnographic appraisal." *American Anthropologist* 79:293–308.

   (1978) *As You Sow: Three Studies in the Social Consequences of Agribusiness*. Montclair, N.J.: Allanhead, Osmun.

Goodenough, Ward H. (1956) "Componential analysis and the study of meaning." *Language* 32:195–216.

   (1963) *Cooperation in Change*. New York: Russell Sage Foundation.

Graham, Susan Brandt (1975) *A Comparison of Social Networks in a Company-Owned Town and an Incorporated Town in Southern Arizona*. Ph.D. dissertation, University of Arizona. Ann Arbor: University Microfilms.

   (1978) "A comparison of social networks in two Arizona mining towns." *The Social Science Journal* 15:113–122.

288   Bibliography

(1981) "Community, conformity and career: Patterns of social interaction in two Arizona mining towns." *Urban Anthropology* 9:in press.

Guemple, Lee (1972) "Introduction." In Lee Guemple (ed.). *Alliance in Eskimo Society, Proceedings of the American Ethnological Society 1971, Supplement*. Seattle: University of Washington Press for the American Ethnological Society, p. 7.

Gwaltney, John L. (1970) *The Thrice Shy: Cultural Accommodation to Blindness and Other Disasters in a Mexican Community*. New York: Columbia University Press.

(1973) "Myth charter in the minority–majority context." In Morton H. Fried (ed.). *Explorations in Anthropology*. New York: Crowell, pp. 421–429.

X — (1976) "On going home again–some reflections of a native anthropologist." *Phylon* 30:236–242.

(1980) *Drylongso: A Self-Portrait of Black America*. New York: Random House.

Hanrahan, John, and Peter Gruenstein (1977) *Lost Frontier: The Marketing of Alaska*. New York: Norton.

Harriman, Dorothy, Jenna Jordison, Diana Lion, and Helena Summers (1977) "Professional research in an aprofessional setting: On being researched." Presented to the annual meeting of the Society for Applied Anthropology, San Diego, and the Annual Canadian Sociology and Anthropology Association meeting, Fredericton, New Brunswick.

Harris, Marvin (1971) *Culture, Man and Nature*. New York: Random House.

(1977) "Potlatch." In *Readings in Anthropology Annual Editions*. Guilford, Conn.: Dushkin Publishing, pp. 223–228.

Hatfield, Colby R., Jr. (1973) "Fieldwork: Toward a model of mutual exploitation." *Anthropological Quarterly* 46:15–29.

Hayano, David M. (1979) "Auto-ethnography: Paradigms, problems, and prospects." *Human Organization* 38:99–104.

Hayes-Bautista, David E. (1976) "Deviant delivery systems." Presented at the Western Health Consortium, San Francisco.

Hedges, James B. (1939) *Building the Canadian West*. New York: Macmillan.

Heider, Karl G. (1976) *Ethnographic Film*. Austin: University of Texas Press.

Hennigh, Lawrence (1970) "Functions and limitations of north Alaskan Eskimo wife trading." *Arctic: Journal of the Arctic Institute of North America* 23:24–34.

(1972) "You have to be a good lawyer to be an Eskimo." In Lee D. Guemple (ed.). *Alliance in Eskimo Society, Proceedings of the American Ethnological Society 1971, Supplement*. Seattle: University of Washington Press, pp. 89–109.

(1978) "The good life and the taxpayers' revolt." *Rural Sociology* 43:178–190.

Henry, Frances (1966) "The role of the fieldworker in an explosive political situation." *Current Anthropology* 7:552–559.

(1969) "Stress and strategy in three field situations." In F. Henry and S. Saberwal (eds.). *Stress and Strategy in Fieldwork*. New York: Holt, pp. 35–46.

Henry, Jules (1963) *Culture Against Man*. New York: Random House.

Herriott, Robert E. (1977) "Ethnographic case studies in federally funded multi-disciplinary policy research: Some design and implementation issues." *Anthropology and Education Quarterly* 8:106–115.

(1980) *Federal Initiatives and Rural School Improvement: Findings from the Experimental Schools Program*. Cambridge, Mass. Abt Associates.

Herriott, Robert E., and Neal Gross (eds.) (1979) *The Dynamics of Planned Educational Change: Case Studies and Analyses*. Berkeley: McCutchan.

Hessler, Richard M., and Peter Kong-Ming New (1972) "Toward a research commune." *Human Organization* 31:449–450.

Heydebrand, Wolf (1977) "Organizational contradictions in public bureaucracies: Toward a Marxian theory of organizations." *Sociological Quarterly* 18:83–107.

Hicks, Ronald (1978) "Jobs be damned." *Anthropology Newsletter* (correspondence) 19 (November):2, 21.

Hill-Burnett, Jacquetta (1973) "Event description and analysis in the microethnography of urban classrooms." In F. A. J. Ianni and E. Storey (eds.). *Cultural Relevance and Educational Issues: Readings in Anthropology and Education*. Boston: Little Brown, pp. 287–303.

Homans, George C. (1949) "The strategy of industrial sociology." *American Journal of Sociology* 54:330–337.

Honigmann, John J. (1976) *The Development of Anthropological Ideas*. Homewood, Ill.: Dorsey Press.

Honigmann, John J., and I. Honigmann (1978) "Responsibility and nurturance: An Austrian example." *Journal of Psychological Anthropology* 1:81–100.

Horn, Beverly M. (1975) *An Ethnoscientific Study to Determine Social and Cultural Factors Affecting Native American Women During Pregnancy*. Ph.D. dissertation, University of Washington.

Horowitz, Irving L. (1974) *The Rise and Fall of Project Camelot: Studies in the Relationship between Social Science and Politics*. Cambridge, Mass. MIT Press.

Houghton, Ruth M. (1968) *The Fort McDermitt Indian Reservation: Social Structure and the Distribution of Political and Economic Power*. M. A. thesis, University of Oregon; Ann Arbor, Mich.: University Microfilms.

(1973a) "Reservation politics and OEO community development, 1965–1971." In R. M. Houghton (ed.). *Native American Politics: Power Relationships in the Western Great Basin Today*. Reno, Nev.: University of Nevada, Bureau of Government Research, pp. 38–45.

(1973b) *Adaptive Strategies in an American Indian Reservation Community: The War on Poverty, 1965–1971*. Ph.D. dissertation, University of Oregon; Ann Arbor, Mich.: University Microfilms.

(1976) "Sociocultural values and groups." *Socio-Economic Profile, Winnemucca District, Nevada*. Reno, Nev.: U.S. Department of the Interior, Bureau of Land Management, Nevada State Office.

(1978a) "Sociocultural research and planning and management of a Nevada Bureau of Land Management Grazing District." *Proceedings, First International Rangeland Congress*. Denver: Society for Range Management, pp. 87–9.

(1978b) *The West Coast: Regional Lifestyles and Regional Planning*. A report submitted to the Ministry of Works and Development, New Zealand.

(1979a) "Anthropology and regional planning in New Zealand: The West Coast." Presented at annual meeting of the Southwestern Anthropological Association, Santa Barbara, Cal.

(1979b) "The people of a Nevada grazing district." *Rangelands* 1:47–9.

Houghton, Ruth M., and Leontine Nappe (eds.) (1977) *Nevada Lifestyles and Lands*. Reno, Nevada: University of Nevada, Bureau of Government Research.

Hsu, Francis L. K. (1963) *Clan, Caste and Club*. New York: Van Nostrand Reinhold.

(1973) "Prejudice and its intellectual effect in American anthropology: An ethnographic report." *American Anthropologist* 75:1–19.

Hughes, Everett C. (1974) "Who studies whom?" *Human Organization* 33:327–334.

Hunter, David E., and Phillip Whitten (1977) *The Study of Cultural Anthropology*. New York: Harper & Row.

Hurston, Zora Neale (1970) *Mules and Men*. New York: Harper & Row.

Hymes, Dell (ed.) (1974) *Reinventing Anthropology*. New York: Random House, Vintage Books.

Jacobs, Sue Ellen (1974) "Action and advocacy anthropology." *Human Organization* 33:209–215.

Jaffe, Louis (1954) "The effective limits of the administrative process: A re-evaluation," *Harvard Law Review* 67:1105–35.

Jarvie, I. C. (1969) "The problem of ethical integrity in participant observation." *Current Anthropology* 10:505-508.

Jones, Delmos J. (1970) "Towards a native anthropology." *Human Organization* 29:251–259.

   (1971) "Addendum: Social responsibility and the belief in basic research, an example from Thailand." *Current Anthropology* 12:347–350.

Jones, LeRoi (1967) *Tales.* New York: Grove.

Jongmans, D. G. (1973) "Politics on the village level." in Jeremy Boissevain and J. Clyde Mitchell (eds.). *Network Analysis: Studies in Human Interaction.* The Hague: Mouton, pp. 167–218.

Jongmans, D. G., and P. C. W. Gutkind (eds.) (1967) *Anthropologists in the Field.* Assen, The Netherlands: Van Gorcum.

Jorgenson, Joseph G., and Marcello Truzzi (eds.) (1974) *Anthropology and American Life.* Englewood Cliffs, N.J.: Prentice-Hall.

Kapferer, Bruce (1973) "Social network and conjugal role in urban Zambia: Towards a reformation of the Bott hypothesis." In Jeremy Boissevain and J. Clyde Mitchell (eds.). *Network Analysis: Studies in Human Interaction.* The Hague: Mouton, pp. 83–110.

Katz, Jerrold J., and Jerry A. Fodor (1963) "The structure of a semantic theory." *Language* 39:170–210.

Kay, Paul (1966) "Comments on Colby." From "Comment on ethnographic semantics: A preliminary survey, by B.N. Colby." *Current Anthropology* 7:20–23.

   (1975) "Tahitian words for race and class." *Journal de la Societe des Oceanistes.* Special Issue:1–34.

   (1977) "The myth of nonacademic employment: Observations on the growth of an ideology." *Anthropology Newsletter* (commentary) 18 (October):11–12.

Keiser, R. Lincoln (1970) "Fieldwork among the vice lords of Chicago." In George D. Spindler (ed.). *Being an Anthropologist.* New York: Holt, pp. 220–237.

Kempton, Willett (1978) "Category grading and taxonomic relations: A mug is a sort of cup." *American Ethnologist* 5:44–65.

Khleif, Bud B. (1974) "Issues in anthropological fieldwork in schools." In George D. Spindler (ed.). *Education and Cultural Process: Toward an Anthropology of Education.* New York: Holt, pp. 389–398.

Kinn, Jan Otto (1978) "The lure of the mountains." *The Norseman* 6:144–147.

Kleiber, Nancy, and Linda Light (1978) *Caring for Ourselves: An Alternative Structure for Health Care.* Vancouver, B.C.: The School of Nursing, University of British Columbia.

   (1977) "Interactive Research in Health Care." *Social Science and Medicine* 12:4A (July).

Kloos, Peter (1969) "Role conflicts in social fieldwork." *Current Anthropology* 10:509–511.

Kluckhohn, Clyde (1949) *Mirror for Man: The Relation of Anthropology to Modern Life.* New York: McGraw-Hill.

Knapp, Joseph G. (1959) *The Rise of American Cooperative Enterprise: 1620–1920.* Danville, Ill.: Interstate Printers and Publishers.

Kohl, Seena B. (1976) *Working Together: Women and Family in Southwestern Saskatchewan.* Toronto: Holt, Rinehart and Winston of Canada.

Kohl, Seena, and John W. Bennett (1965) "Kinship, succession, and the migration of young people in a Canadian agricultural community." *International Journal of Comparative Sociology* 6:96–115.

   "Succession to Family Enterprises and the Migration of Young People in a Canadian Agricultural Community." In K. Ishwaran, ed. *The Canadian Family,* rev., Toronto: Holt, 1976.

Komarovsky, Mirra (1967) *Blue-Collar Marriage.* New York: Random House.

Kuhn, Thomas (1967) *The Structure of Scientific Revolutions*. Chicago: University of Chicago Press.

Kushner, Gilbert (1969) "The anthropology of complex societies." In B. J. Siegel (ed.). *Biennial Review of Anthropology*. Stanford: Stanford University Press, pp. 80–131.

(1973) *Immigrants from India in Israel: Planned Change in an Administered Community*. Tucson, Ariz.: University of Arizona Press.

Labov, William (1973) "The boundaries of words and their meanings." In C. J. N. Bailey and Roger Shuy (eds.). *New Ways of Analyzing Variation in English*. Washington, D.C.: Georgetown University Press, pp 340–373.

Lakoff, George (1972) "Hedges: a study of meaning criteria and the logic of fuzzy concepts." *Papers from the Eighth Regional Meeting, Chicago Linguistics Society*. Chicago: Chicago Linguistics Society, pp. 183–228.

Leacock, Eleanor B. (1969) *Teaching and Learning in City Schools*. New York: Basic Books.

Leavitt, Harold J. (1964) "Applied organizational change in industry: Structural, technical, and human approaches." In W. W. Cooper, H. J. Leavitt, and M. W. Shelly (eds.). *New Perspectives in Organizational Research*. New York: Wiley, pp. 55–71.

Lévi-Strauss, Claude (1963) *Structural Anthropology*. Trans. Claire Jacobson and Brooke Grundfest Schoepf. New York: Basic Books.

Liebow, Elliott (1967) *Tally's Corner: A Study of Negro Streetcorner Men*. Boston: Little, Brown.

Lindsay, Robert (1963) "Inferential memory as the basis of machines which understand natural thoughts." In E. A. Fergenbaum and J. Feldman (eds.). *Computers and Thought*. New York: McGraw-Hill, pp. 217–233.

Lipset, Seymour M. (1950) *Agrarian Socialism*. New York: Doubleday Anchor.

Litwak, Eugene and Ivan Szelenyi (1969) "Primary group structures and their functions: Kin, neighbors and friends." *American Sociological Review* 34:465–481.

Lounsbury, Floyd (1956) "Semantic analysis of Pawnee kinship usage." *Language* 32:158–194.

Lowie, Robert H. (1948) *Social Organization*. New York: Rinehart.

Lucas, Rex (1971) *Minetown, Milltown, Railtown: Life in Canadian Communities of Single Industry*. Toronto: University of Toronto Press.

Lynch, Kevin (1976) *Managing the Sense of a Region*. Cambridge, Mass.: MIT Press.

McDowell, Sophia F. (1978) "Fieldwork in an army milieu." *Human Organization* 37:196–201.

McGrath, Joseph E. (1964) "Toward a 'theory of method' for research organizations." In W. W. Cooper, H. J. Leavitt, and M. W. Shelly (eds.). *New Perspectives In Organizational Research*. New York: Wiley, pp. 533–568.

Mackintosh, W. A. (1934) *Canadian Frontier of Settlement, Volume I: Prairie Settlement – The Geographical Background*. Toronto: Macmillan.

McLaurin, Melton Alonza (1971) *Paternalism and Protest: Southern Cotton Mill Workers and Organized Labor, 1875–1905*. Westport, Conn.: Greenwood.

Maday, Bela (ed.) (1975) *Anthropology and Society*. Washington, D.C.: The Anthropological Society of Washington.

Mair, Lucy (1969) *Anthropology and Social Change*. New York: Humanities Press.

Malinowski, Bronislaw (1929) "Practical anthropology." *Africa* 2:23–38.

(1961) *Argonauts of the Western Pacific*. New York: Dutton.

(1967) *A Diary in the Strict Sense of the Term*. New York: Harcourt Brace & World.

Mann, Floyd D. (1971) "Studying and creating change." In Harvey A. Hornstein, Barbara Benedict Bunker, W. Warner Burke, Marion Gindes, and Roy J. Lewicki (eds.). *Social Intervention: A Behaviorial Science Approach*. New York: Basic Books, pp. 294–309.

Maquet, Jacques (1964) "Objectivity in anthropology." *Current Anthropology* 5:47–55.

Maruyama, Magorah (1969) "Epistemology of social science research: Exploration in inculture researchers," *Dialectica* 23:229–280.

(1974) "Endogenous research vs. delusions of relevance and expertise among exogenous academics." *Human Organization* 33:318–322

Matthiasson, John S. (1974) "Commentary." *Human Organization* 30:323–324.

Mayer, Adrian (1966) "Quasi-groups in the study of complex societies." In Michael Banton (ed.). *The Social Anthropology of Complex Societies.* London: Tavistock, pp. 97–123.

Mead, Margaret (1928) *Coming of Age in Samoa.* New York: William Morrow.

Merton, Robert (1968) *Social Theory and Social Structure.* New York: Free Press.

(1972) "Insiders and outsiders: a chapter in the sociology of knowledge." *American Journal of Sociology* 78:9–47.

Messerschmidt, Donald A. (1975) "Problems of role and method on-site: A case study." Presented at symposium, "The Translation of Anthropological Skills to Substantive Research in Experimental Schools," Council on Anthropology and Education, at the annual meeting of the American Anthropological Association, San Francisco.

(1976a) *The Gurungs of Nepal: Conflict and Change in a Village Society.* Warminster, Eng.: Aris and Phillips.

(1976b) "Innovation and adaptation: Tibetan immigrants in the United States." *The Tibet Society Bulletin* 10:48–70.

(1979) "River District: A search for unity amidst diversity." In Robert E. Herriott and Neal Gross (eds.). *The Dynamics of Planned Educational Change: Case Studies and Analyses.* Berkeley, Cal.: McCutchan, pp. 74–111.

(1981) "Indigenous anthropology: Some observations." *Current Anthropology* 22: 197–98.

Messerschmidt, Donald A., with Marilyn C. Richen (1974) *On Face and Interface: Dynamics of Educational Change, A Case Study of Experimental Relations between a Federal Agency and a Rural School District.* Cambridge, Mass.: Abt Associates, for the National Institute of Education, working paper no. 1.

(1975) "A social and educational history of Carbon County School District No. 2, Carbon County, Wyoming." In Stephen J. Fitzsimmons, Peter C. Wolff, and Abby J. Freedman (eds.). *Rural America: A Social and Educational History of Ten Communities, Vol. 2.* Cambridge, Mass.: Abt Associates, for the National Institute of Education, pp. 921–1104.

Minsky, Marvin (1974) *A Framework for Representing Knowledge.* Cambridge, Mass.:MIT Artificial Intelligence Laboratory, memo no. 306.

Mitchell, J. Clyde (1969) "The concept and use of social networks." In J. Clyde Mitchell (ed.). *Social Networks in Urban Situations.* Manchester, Eng.: University of Manchester Press, pp. 1–50.

Molgaard, Craig A. (1979) *New Age Hunters and Gatherers.* Ph.D. dissertation, University of California at Berkeley.

(1982) "American fairies: An aspect of counter-culture healing beliefs." In *Proceedings of the International Conference on Creatures of Legendry.* Omaha: University of Nebraska Press, in press.

Molgaard, Craig A., Elizabeth L. Byerly, and Charles T. Snow (1979) "Bach's flower remedies: A New Age therapy," *Human Organization* 38:71–74.

Moran, Emilio (1979) *Human Adaptability: An Introduction to Ecological Anthropology.* North Scituate, Mass.: Duxbury.

Morris, Charles W. (1938) "Foundations of the theory of signs." *International Encyclopedia of Unified Science* 1:2.

Murray, Albert (1970) *The Omni-Americans.* New York: Avon.

Myrdal, Gunnar (1962) *An American Dilemma, Twentieth Anniversary Edition.* New York: Harper & Row.

Nader, Laura (1974) "Up the anthropologist – perspectives gained from studying up." In Dell Hymes (ed.). *Reinventing Anthropology.* New York: Random House, Vintage Books, pp. 284–311.

Nash, Dennison (1963) "The ethnologist as stranger: An essay in the sociology of knowledge." *Southwestern Journal of Anthropology* 19:149–167.

Nash, Dennison, and Ronald Wintrob (1972) "The emergence of self-consciousness in ethnography." *Current Anthropology* 13:527–533.

Needleman, Jacob (1970) *The New Religions.* Garden City, N.Y.: Doubleday.

Neimeyer, Rudo (1973) "Some applications of the notion of density." In Jeremy Boissevain and J. Clyde Mitchell (eds.). *Network Analysis: Studies in Human Interaction.* The Hague: Mouton, pp. 45–64.

Nellis, Lee (1974) "What does energy development mean for Wyoming?" *Human Organization* 33:229–238.

Nelson, Hal (1977) "Epistle to the anthropologists." *Anthropology Newsletter* (commentary) 18 (April):10–12.

Netting, Robert McC. (1977) *Cultural Ecology.* Menlo Park, Cal.: Cummings.

Nukunya, G. K. (1969) *Kinship and Marriage among the Anlo Ewe.* New York: Humanities Press.

O'Connor, James (1973) *The Fiscal Crisis of the State.* New York: St. Martin's Press.

Offe, Claus (1973a) "The abolition of market control and the problem of legitimacy." *Kapitalistate,* nos. 1 and 2.

(1973b) "Class rule and the political system: On the selectiveness of political institutions." Unpublished paper.

Olson, Mancur (1965) *The Logic of Collective Action.* Cambridge, Mass.: Harvard University Press.

Ortego, Philip D. (1973) "The Chicano renaissance." In Livie Isauro Duran and H. Russell Bernard (eds.). *Introduction to Chicano Studies.* New York: Macmillan, pp. 331–350.

Owen, Bruce M., and Ronald Brautigan (1979) *The Regulation Game: Strategic Use of the Administrative Process.* Cambridge, Mass.: Ballinger.

Partridge, William L. (1973) *The Hippie Ghetto: The Natural History of a Subculture.* New York: Holt.

Paul, Benjamin D. (1953) "Interview techniques and field relationships." In A. L. Kroeber (ed.). *Anthropology Today.* Chicago: University of Chicago Press, pp. 430–451.

Paz, Octavio (1961) *The Labyrinth of Solitude.* New York: Grove Press.

Peffer, Louise (1951) *The Closing of the Public Domain.* Stanford: Stanford University Press.

Pelto, Pertti J. (1970) *Anthropological Research: The Structure of Inquiry.* New York: Harper & Row.

Pelto, P. J., and G. H. Pelto (1975) "Intra-Cultural Diversity: Some Theoretical Issues." *American Ethnologist* 2(1):1–19.

Peterson, John H., Jr. (1974) "The anthropologist as advocate." *Human Organization* 33:311–318.

Pilcher, William W. (1972) *The Portland Longshoremen: A Dispersed Urban Community.* New York: Holt.

Pincus, John, and Anthony H. Pascal (1977) *Education and Human Resources Research at Rand.* Santa Monica: The Rand Corporation.

Posner, Richard A. (1974) "Theories of economic regulation." *Bell Journal of Economics* 5:335–358.

Powdermaker, Hortense (1939) *After Freedom: A Cultural Study of the Deep South.* New York: Viking.

(1966) *Stranger and Friend: The Way of an Anthropologist.* New York: Norton.

Price, John A. (1972) "Reno, Nevada: The city as a unit of study." *Urban Anthropology* 1:14–28.

Redfield, Robert, and W. Lloyd Warner (1940) "Cultural Anthropology and modern agriculture." In *Yearbook of Agriculture: Farmers in a Changing World*. Washington, D.C.: U.S. Department of Agriculture, pp. 983–993.

Reiter, Rayne (ed.) (1975) *Toward an Anthropology of Women*. New York and London: Monthly Review Press.

Richards, John, and L. Pratt (1979) *Prairie Capitalism: Power and Influence in the New West*. Toronto: McClelland and Stewart.

Richardson, Miles (1975) "Anthropologist – the myth teller." *American Ethnologist* 2:517–533.

Rist, Ray C. (1970) "Student social class and teacher expectations: The self-fulfilling prophecy in ghetto education." *Harvard Educational Review* 40:411–451.

(1976) "On the relations among educational research paradigms: From disdain to detente." Presented at workshop, "Exploring Qualitative/Quantitative Research Methodologies in Education," Far West Laboratory for Educational Research and Development, in cooperation with the National Institute of Education and the Council on Anthropology and Education. San Francisco.

Roethlisberger, I. J., and W. J. Dickson (1939) *Management and the Workers*. Cambridge, Mass.: Harvard University Press.

Romano, Octavio I. (1968) "The anthropology and sociology of the Mexican American." *El Grito* 2:13–26.

Rosaldo, Michelle Zimbalist, and Louise Lamphere (eds.) (1974) *Woman, Culture, and Society*. Stanford: Stanford University Press.

Rosch, Eleanor H. (1973) "On the internal structure of perceptual and semantic categories." In T. Moore (ed.). *Cognitive Development and the Acquisition of Language*. New York: Academic Press, pp. 111–144.

(1975) "Human categories." In N. Warren (ed.). *Advances in Cross-Cultural Psychology*. London: Academic Press, pp. 000–000.

(1976) "Basic objects in natural categories." *Cognitive Psychology* 8:382–439.

Rosenblum, Sheila, and Karen Seashore Louis, with Nancy Brigham and Robert E. Herriot (1978) *A Measure of Change: The Process and Outcomes of Planned Change in Ten Rural School Districts*. Cambridge, Mass.: Abt Associates, for the National Institute of Education.

Rosenfeld, Gerry (1971) *"Shut Those Thick Lips!": A Study of Slum School Failure*. New York: Holt.

Rosengarten, Theodore (1974) *All God's Dangers: The Life of Nate Shaw*. New York: Avon.

Rosenthal, Robert (1966) *Experimenter Effects in Behavioral Research*. New York: Appleton-Century-Crofts.

Ross, J. K., and M. H. Ross (1974) "Participant observation in political research." *Political Methodology* 1:63–88.

Rothschild-Whitt, Joyce (1976) "Conditions facilitating participatory-democratic organizations." *Social Inquiry* 46:75–86.

Ryan, Bryce (1957) "A sociologist's view." *Human Organization* (commentary) 15:32–37.

Sanjek, Roger (1976) "Who are the folk in folk taxonomies: Cognitive diversity and the state." Presented at symposium, "Theoretical Implications of Cognitive Diversity – Some Whys and Therefores," University of Alabama, Birmingham.

Sayles, Myrna (1978) "Behind locked doors." In Elizabeth Eddy and W. L. Partridge (eds.). *Applied Anthropology in America*. New York: Columbia University Press, pp. 201–228.

Schensul, Stephen L. (1974) "Skills needed in action: Lessons from El Centro de la Causa." *Human Organization* 33:203–209.

Schneider, David M. (1965) "American kin terms and terms for kinsmen: A critique of Goodenough's componential analysis of Yankee kinship terminology." *American Anthropologist* 67:288–308.

(1968) *American Kinship: A Cultural Account.* Englewood Cliffs, N.J.: Prentice-Hall.

Schwab, William B. (1970) "Comparative field techniques in urban Africa." In Morris Freilich (ed.). *Marginal Natives: Anthropologists at Work.* New York: Harper & Row, pp. 73–121.

Schwartz, Charles (1959) *The Search for Stability: Contemporary Saskatchewan.* Toronto: McClelland and Stewart.

Schwartz, T. (1968) "Beyond cybernetics: Constructs, expectations and goals in human adaptation," Presented at symposium no. 40, "The Effects of Conscious Purpose on Human Adaptation," Wenner Gren Foundation of Anthropological Research. Burgwarstein, Austria.

(1978) "Where is the culture? Personality as the distributive locus of culture." In *The Making of Psychological Anthropology.* Berkeley and Los Angeles: University of California Press, pp. 419–441.

Serber, David (1975) "Regulating reform: The social organization of insurance regulation." *Insurgent Sociologist* 3:83–105.

(1976) *Politics of insurance regulation.* Ph.D. dissertation, University of California at Berkeley.

Shapiro, Joan Hatch (1971) *Communities of the Alone.* New York: Association Press.

Sieber, R. Timothy (1978) "Schooling, socialization and group boundaries: A study of informal social relations in the public domain." *Urban Anthropology* 7:67–98.

(1979) "Schoolroom, pupils and rules: The role of informality in bureaucratic socialization." *Human Organization* 39:273–282.

Sieber, R. Timothy, and Andrew J. Gordon (eds.) (1981) *Children and Their Organizations: Investigations in American Culture.* Boston, Mass.: G. K. Hall.

Siegal, Harvey A. (1978) *Outposts of the Forgotten: Socially Terminal People in Slum Hotels and Single Room Occupancy Tenements.* New Brunswick, N.J.: Transaction Books.

Simmel, Georg (1950) *The Sociology of Georg Simmel.* Trans. and ed. Kurt H. Wolff. Glencoe, Ill.: University of Illinois Press.

Singh, R. L. Janmeja (1971) *Community Mental Helath Consultation and Crisis Intervention.* Berkeley, Cal.: Book People.

Singleton, John (1976) "The ethnography of a Japanese school: Anthropological field techniques and models in the study of a complex organization." In Joan I. Roberts and S. K. Akinsanya (eds.). *Educational Patterns and Cultural Configurations: The Anthropology of Education.* New York: David McKay, pp. 279–288.

Sirjamaki, John (1971) "A footnote to the anthropological approach to the study of American culture." *Social Forces* 24:253–263.

Slater, Mariam K. (1976) *African Odyssey.* Garden City, N.Y.: Anchor Books.

Smith, Dorothy E. (1975) "An analysis of ideological structures and how women are excluded: Considerations for academic women." Unpublished paper.

Smith, Louis M., and Paul A. Pohland (1976) "Grounded Theory and Educational ethnography: A methodological analysis and critique." In Joan I. Roberts and S. K. Akinsanya (eds.). *Educational Patterns and Cultural Configurations: The Anthropology of Education.* New York: David McKay, pp. 264–279.

Society for Applied Anthropology (1974) "Statement on professional and ethical responsibilities." *Human Organization* 33:facing p. 219.

Sordinas, Augustus (1978) "Ethnography in need of native ethnographers." Presented at symposium, "Anthropologists and Origin Cultures," at the 77th annual meeting of the American Anthropological Association, Los Angeles, November 18, 1978.

Spicer, Edward H. (1974) "The problem and meaning of structural change in the AAA." *Newsletter of the American Anthropological Association* 15:1, 10–13.

Spicer, Edward H., Asael T. Hansen, Katherine Luomala, and Marvin K. Opler (1969) *Impounded People: Japanese-Americans in the Relocation Centers.* Tucson, Ariz.: University of Arizona Press.

Spindler, George D. (1973) "An anthropology of education." *Council on Anthropology and Education Newsletter* 4:14–16.

Spindler, George D. (ed.). (1963) *Education and Culture: Anthropological Approaches.* New York: Holt.

(1970) *Being An Anthropologist: Fieldwork in Eleven Cultures.* New York: Holt.

Spradley, James P. (1970) *You Owe Yourself a Drunk: An Ethnography of Urban Nomads.* Boston: Little Brown.

Spradley, James P., and Brenda Mann (1975) *The Cocktail Waitress.* New York: Wiley.

Spradley, James P. and David W. McCurdy (1972) *The Cultural Experience: Ethnography in Complex Society.* Chicago: Science Research Associates.

(1975) *Anthropology: The Cultural Perspective.* New York: Wiley.

Sproull, Lee, Stephen Weiner, and David Wolf (1978) *Organizing an Anarchy: Belief, Bureaucracy and Politics in the National Institute of Education.* Chicago: University of Chicago Press.

Srinivas, M. N. (1966) *Social Change in Modern India.* Berkeley and Los Angeles: University of California Press.

Stegner, Wallace (1962) *Wolf Willow: A History, Story and Memory of the Last Plains Frontier.* New York: Viking.

Steiner, Stan (1972) "Commentary." *Human Organization* 31:101–102.

Stephens, Joyce (1976) *Loners, Losers, and Lovers.* Seattle: University of Washington Press.

Steward, Julian H. (1955) "The Concept and Method of Cultural Ecology." In Julian H. Steward (ed.). *The Theory of Culture Change.* Urbana: University of Illinois Press.

Stigler, George J. (1975) *The Citizen and the State: Essays on Regulation.* Chicago: University of Chicago Press.

Streib, Gordon (1957) "Commentary." *Human Organization* 15:30–31.

Stricklund, Donald A., and Lester E. Schlesinger (1969) " 'Lurking' as a research method." *Human Organization* 23:248–250.

Sturtevant, William (1964) "Studies in ethnoscience." In K. Romney and R. d'Andrade (eds.). *American Anthropologist* 66 (special issue):99–131.

Taylor, Carl C. (1945) "Techniques of community study and analysis as applied to modern civilized societies." In Ralph Linton (ed.). *The Science of Man in the World Crisis.* New York: Columbia University Press, pp. 416–441.

Thomas, Elizabeth (1965) *The Harmless People.* New York: Vintage.

Thompson, Laura (1977) " 'Myth of nonacademic anthropology' criticized." *Anthropology Newsletter* (correspondence) 18 (December):17.

Toynbee, Arnold (1934) *A Study of History, Vol. 3.* London: Oxford University Press.

Trend, M. G. (1977) "Government and industry." *Human Organization* 36:211–213.

(1978) "Anthropology and contract research: Managing and being managed." *Practicing Anthropology* 1:13–17.

Truzzi, Marcello (ed.) (1974) *Verstehen: Subjective Understanding in the Social Sciences.* Reading, Mass.: Addison-Wesley.

Turnbull, Colin (1962) *The Forest People.* New York: Simon & Schuster.

(1972) *The Mountain People.* New York: Simon & Schuster.

Tyler, Stephen A. (ed.) (1969) *Cognitive Anthropology.* New York: Holt.

Uchendu, V.C. (1965) *The Igbo of Southeast Nigeria.* New York: Holt.

Umpqua Regional Council of Governments (1976) "South Umpqua school district, 1976 Douglas County housing survey." Unpublished paper, Roseburg, Oregon.

Undset, Sigrid (1942) *Kristin Lavransdatter*. New York: Knopf.

U.S. Department of Agriculture (1977) *Draft Environmental Statement for the Row, South Umpqua and North Umpqua Planning Units of the Umpqua National Forest*. Umpqua National Forest, Roseburg, Ore.: The Department of Agriculture.

Vidich, Arthur J., and Joseph Bensman (1968) *Small Town in Mass Society: Class, Power and Religion in a Rural Community*. 2nd ed. Princeton: Princeton University Press.

Vidich, Arthur J., and Charles McReynolds (1971) "Rhetoric versus reality: A study of New York high school principals." In Murray L. Wax, Stanley Diamond, and Fred O. Gearing (eds.). *Anthropological Perspectives on Education*. New York: Basic Books, pp. 195–297.

Wacaster, C. Thompson, and William A. Firestone (1978) "The promise and problems of long-term, continuous fieldwork." *Human Organization* 37:269–275.

Waddington, C. H. (1977) *Tools for Thought*. New York: Basic Books.

Wallace, A. F. C. (1969) "Review of American kinship: A cultural account." *American Anthropologist* 71:100–106.

Wamsley, Gary L., and Mayer Zald (1973) *The Political Economy of Public Organizations*. Lexington, Mass.: Lexington Books.

Warner, W. Lloyd (1959) *The Living and the Dead: A Study of the Symbolic Life of Americans*. New Haven, Conn.: Yale University Press.

Warren, Richard L. (1967) *Education in Rebhausen: A German Village*. New York: Holt.

⎯⎯ (1973) "The classroom as a sanctuary for teachers: Discontinuities in social control." *American Anthropologist* 75:280–291.

⎯⎯ (1975) "Context and isolation: The teaching experience in an elementary school." *Human Organization* 34:139–148.

⎯⎯ (1976) "The school: Authority, its sources and uses." In Joan I. Roberts and S. K. Akinsanya (eds.). *Schooling in the Cultural Context: Anthropological Studies of Education*. New York: David McKay, pp. 104–114.

Wax, Rosalie H. (1971) *Doing Fieldwork: Warning and Advice*. Chicago: University of Chicago Press.

⎯⎯ (1978) "Notes from a pioneer." *Natural History* 87:90–94, 98.

Weaver, Thomas, and D. White (1972) "Anthropological approaches to urban and complex society." In Thomas Weaver and D. White (eds.). *The Anthropology of Urban Environments*. Washington, D.C.: Society for Applied Anthropology, monograph no. 11, pp. 109–125.

Webb, Walter Prescott (1931) *The Great Plains*. New York: Ginn.

Weber, Max (1949) *The Methodology of the Social Sciences*. Ed. trans. Edward A. Shils and Henry A. Finch. New York: Free Press.

Weidman, Hazel Hitson (1970) "On ambivalence in the field." In Peggy Golde (ed.). *Women in the Field*. Chicago: Aldine, pp. 239–263.

Weingrod, Alex (1962) "Administered communities: Some characteristics of new immigrant villages in Israel." *Economic Development and Cultural Change* 11:69–84.

Weinreich, Uriel (1966) "Explorations in semantic theory." In Thomas Sebeok (ed.). *Current Trends in Linguistics, vol. 3*. The Hague: Mouton, pp. 395–477.

Werner, Oswald, and Joann Fenton (1973) "Method and theory in ethnoscience, or ethnoepistemology." In R. Naroll and R. Cohen (eds.). *Handbook of Method in Cultural Anthropology*. New York: Columbia University Press, pp. 537–578.

Wertz, Richard W. (ed.) (1973) *Ethical and Social Issues in Biomedicine*. Englewood Cliffs, N.J.: Prentice-Hall.

Whitten, Norman (1970) "Network analysis in Ecuador and Nova Scotia: Some critical remarks." *Canadian Review of Sociology and Anthropology* 7:269–280.

Whyte, W. F. (1943) *Street Corner Society*. Chicago: University of Chicago Press.

Wigginton, Eliot (ed.) (1972) *The Foxfire Book*. Garden City, N.Y.: Doubleday Anchor.

Willis, William S., Jr. (1973) "Skeletons in the anthropological closet." In Morton H. Fried (ed.). *Explorations in Anthropology*. New York: Thomas Y. Crowell, pp. 459-475.

Wilson, James (1974) "The politics of regulation." in James W. McKie (ed.). *Social Responsibility and the Business Predicament*. Washington, D.C.: The Brookings Institution, pp. 000–000.

Wister, Owen (1902) *The Virginian*. New York: Macmillan.

Wolcott, Harry F. (1967) *A Kwakiutl Village and School*. New York: Holt, Rinehart & Winston.

(1973) *The Man in the Principal's Office: An Ethnography*. New York: Holt, Rinehart & Winston.

(1974a) *The African Beer Gardens of Bulawayo: Integrated Drinking in a Segregated Society*. New Brunswick, N.J.: Rutgers Center of Alcohol Studies.

(1974b) "The teacher as an enemy." In George D. Spindler (ed.). *Education and Cultural Process: Toward an Anthropology of Education*. New York: Holt, Rinehart & Winston, pp. 411–425.

(1975a) "Criteria for an ethnographic approach to research in schools." *Human Organization* 34:111–127.

(1975b) "Feedback influences on fieldwork, or: A funny thing happened on the way to the beer garden." In Clive Kileff and Wade Pendleton (eds.). *Urban Man in Southern Africa*. Gwelo, Rhodesia: Mambo Press, pp. 99–125.

(1975c) "Fieldwork in schools: Where the tradition of deferred judgement meets a subculture obsessed with evaluation." *Council on Anthropology and Education Quarterly* 6:17–20.

(1975d) "Introduction." In Harry F. Wolcott (ed.). *Ethnographic Approaches to Research in Education: A Bibliography on Method*. Athens, Ga.: University of Georgia, Anthropology Curriculum Project.

(1977) *Teachers Versus Technocrats: An Educational Innovation in Anthropological Perspective*. Eugene, Ore.: University of Oregon, Center for Educational Policy and Management.

(1978) "Small town America in ethnographic perspective: An introduction." *Rural Sociology* 43: 159–163.

(1980) "A Malay village that progress chose: Sungai Lui and the Institute of Cultural Affairs." Unpublished manuscript.

(1981) "Mirrors, models and monitors; educator adaptations of the ethnographic innovation." In George D. Spindler (ed.). *Doing the Ethnography of Schooling*. New York: Holt, in press.

Wolf, Eric R. (1966) "Kinship, friendship and patron–client relations in complex societies." In Michael Banton (ed.). *The Social Anthropology of Complex Societies*. London: Tavistock, pp. 1–22.

(1969) "American anthropologists and American society." In Stephen A. Tyler (ed.). *Concepts and Assumptions in Contemporary Anthropology*. Athens, Ga.: Southern Anthropological Society Proceedings, pp. 3–11.

Wolfe, A. (1970) "On structural comparisons of networks." *Canadian Review of Sociology and Anthropology* 7:226–244.

Wolfe, Tom (1969) *Radical Chic and Mau-Mauing the Flak Catchers*. New York: Bantam.

Worzbyt, John C. (1976) "Pupil records: A crisis in perspective." *The School Counselor* 23:358–361.

Yablonsky, Lewis (1968) *The Hippie Trip*. New York: Pegasus.

Yanagisako, S. F. (1978) "Variations in American kinship: Implications for cultural analysis." *American Ethnologist* 5:15-29.

Young, Michael, and Peter Willmott (1957) *Family and Kinship in East London*. Baltimore: Penguin.

Zadeh, Lotfi A. (1965) "Fuzzy sets." *Information and Control* 8:338-353.

(1976) "A fuzzy algorithmic approach to the definition of complex or imprecise concepts." *International Journal of Man–Machine Studies* 8:249–291.

Zimmer, Richard (1975) "The state of studies in political anthropology on Latinos in the U.S." *Occasional Papers*, Latin American Studies Center, Bowling Green State University, Bowling Green, Ohio.

(1976) "Small-scale retail food cooperatives: Fragile mutual associations exploiting marginal economic niches." Ph.D. dissertation, University of California at Los Angeles. Ann Arbor: University Microfilms.

(1979) "Necessary directions in child care research." *Anthropology and Education Quarterly* 10:139–165.

Index

counterculture, 153
cowboys, 238
see also agriculture, farming and ranching
cross-cultural perspective, 255
cultural ecology, 6, 91–105, 275
see also adaptation
cultural resources, 248
see also archeology; ethnology, salvage
cultural scene, 133–149
culture
change, 225; *see also* social change
cocktail waitress, 65
core black, 46–61
see also ethnic groups, black American
definition of, 56, 104, 133–134, 244–246
of policy, 228
of power, 190, 192
shock, 16, 17, 109, 227
system, 54
see also subculture, shock
Cushing, F. H., 65

D'Andrade, R. G., 132
D'Arcy, L., 31, 36
Dalton, M., 24
Days Creek dam (Oregon), 128–129
debriefing sessions, 36–39
decision making, 223
see also bureaucracy and bureaucrats; government; management style analysis; policy
demonstration grant, 169
Denenberg, H. S., 83–87
dependency, fear of, 32
Despres, L., 6
Diamond, S., 3, 199
diaries, 42
see also autobiography; case history; family, history; life history
Dickson, W. J., 66
Douglas County (Oregon), 125, 129
Historical Society, 122
Dreeben, R., 202, 210
Dreyfus, H., 277
Durkheim, E., 203
dyad, as unit of social structure, 33

Eckert, K., 31–45
ecology, *see* cultural ecology
Eddy, E., 203

education
and anthropology 7, 122, 185–201, 202–220, 255–256, 259, 261, 278
ethnic, 202–220
health, 154
see also ethnic studies; evaluation, educational
efficacy, as rationale for research at home, 9, 12–13
Ellsworth, Wisconsin, 135
emic/etic analyis, 16, 23–24, 236
employment of anthropologists, 9–13, 15
enculturation, 46, 202
entrée into fieldwork, 7, 35–36, 52, 68, 79–80, 107–110, 155–158, 185
environmental impact statement (EIS), 224–227
Environmental Protection Act, 280
epigenesis, 12
Erasmus, C. J., 228
Erickson, R., 41
Estes, R., 192–193
ethical debt to minorities, 57
ethics, *see* anthropology, ethics of
ethnic groups, 64, 202–220
American Indian, 4, 93, 97, 110, 137, 153, 156, 242; Alaska natives, 224–233; Kwakiutl, 231, 255–264; Papago, 133, 138, 139, 140, 143
Basque, 241, 244
black American, 21, 46–61, 159
Bushman, !Kung, 60, 64, 69, 70, 74
Chicano, *see* Latino; Mexican; Mexican-American; Spanish-American
Hutterites, 93
Latino, 17, 63–76
Mexican and Mexican-American, 21, 155, 156, 244
Norwegian-American, 133–149
Puerto Rican, 159, 204, 217
Pygmy, 64, 69, 70, 74
Spanish-American, 203, 204, 205
Trukese, 23, 85
see also Anglo, Anglo-Saxon; Brownstoner; Caucasian; Euro-American; homosexual; longshoreman; Oldtimers; subculture, ethnic; urban research, among blacks; women, Italian-American, Norwegian-American
ethnic scholars, 15–26
see also anthropologists; ethnic studies
ethnic studies, 10, 15–26
ethnicity as a class variable, 106–107, 118
ethnographer, "Compleat," The, 265